British Prime Ministers
and Other Essays

A J P TAYLOR

British Prime Ministers and Other Essays

EDITED BY
PROFESSOR CHRIS WRIGLEY

ALLEN LANE
THE PENGUIN PRESS

ALLEN LANE
THE PENGUIN PRESS

Published by the Penguin Group
Penguin Books Ltd, 27 Wrights Lane, London w8 5TZ, England
Penguin Putnam Inc., 375 Hudson Street, New York, New York 10014, USA
Penguin Books Australia Ltd, Ringwood, Victoria, Australia
Penguin Books Canada Ltd, 10 Alcorn Avenue, Toronto, Ontario, Canada M4V 3B2
Penguin Books (NZ) Ltd, Private Bag 102902, NSMC, Auckland, New Zealand

Penguin Books Ltd, Registered Offices: Harmondsworth, Middlesex, England

This collection first published by Allen Lane The Penguin Press 1999
1 3 5 7 9 10 8 6 4 2

Set in 11/14 pt PostScript Adobe Sabon
Typeset by Rowland Phototypesetting Ltd, Bury St Edmunds, Suffolk
Printed in Great Britain by Clays Ltd, St Ives plc

A CIP catalogue record for this book is available from the British Library

ISBN 0-713-99260-3

Acknowledgements

I am grateful for the enthusiasm and encouragement of Dr Éva Haraszti Taylor. I am also grateful to Margaret Ainscough for help and to Margaret Walsh for so much continuing support. In memory of Arthur Wrigley (21 November 1912–26 May 1999).

Contents

CONTENTS

CONTENTS

Introduction

Alan John Percivale Taylor was born on 25 March 1906 at 29 Barrett Road, Birkdale, Southport, Lancashire. He died on 7 September 1990 in London. His parents, Percy Lees and Constance Sumner Taylor, were of the prosperous upper-middle class. Their main wealth came from the cotton textile trade.

Percy Taylor was the eldest brother of the second generation of the family firm, James Taylor and Sons, established in the early 1870s. James Taylor had prospered quickly as a trader on the Manchester Cotton Exchange. He had diversified into the ownership of mills at Preston and Blackburn, but this side of the business had been less profitable. He retired, a very wealthy man, at the age of fifty in 1889. Percy Taylor, who had joined the firm at the age of sixteen, was in effect the senior partner from 1898 until he sold his share of the business for £100,000 in early 1920 at the height of the post-First World War boom. From his early twenties Percy Taylor had earned £5,000 or more each year, then a very handsome income. Alan Taylor grew up in very comfortable circumstances.

He was a much-looked-after only child. An older sister, Miriam, died in infancy. After Alan's birth, Connie Taylor suffered a miscarriage, which adversely affected her health. Not surprisingly, both parents paid considerable attention to the delicate health of their surviving child. His mother, greatly anxious about his health, on the advice of a friend took him to a practitioner in homoeopathic medicine, with apparently beneficial results.

From 1906 until 1913, Alan Taylor grew up in a large house at 18 Crosby Road, Birkdale, which his mother ran with the assistance of several employees, including two live-in maids, one of whom was assigned to look after him. In his autobiography, *A Personal History* (Hamish Hamilton, 1983), he recalled of this young woman, Annie Clark, 'She adored me, hugged me, gave me whatever I wanted.' This was true also of his father. A family friend later recalled of father and son, 'They were so happy together.' Percy often took Alan to enjoy the delights of Southport pier, which included watching a stunt-man, 'Professor' Powsey, who cycled off a plank into the sea from the end of the pier. Like other children, he enjoyed games of 'Cowboys and Indians', in his case on the nearby sandhills.

He received less adulation than he wished from his mother; his autobiography and his other reminiscences make clear that he resented this and eagerly sought her attention. He also depicted her as rather a cold person, a view confirmed later by some others who had known her. Yet this seems unfair to her, as various accounts highlight how very anxious she was about his health and welfare. Whatever the truth of this may be, there can be no doubt that she was a major intellectual influence on her son until he was at least in his mid-twenties. During the First World War – with her brother, Harry Thompson, a conscientious objector – she and Percy moved from their pre-war Liberal politics to socialism. In her case, this soon developed into support of the Communist party.

Another important aspect of his upbringing was a Nonconformist background. His mother had been raised in a strict Methodist household, while his father had attended a Baptist chapel. In Southport the Taylors attended the Hawkshead Street Congregational chapel. Percy Taylor was generous with funds for the chapel's treats for poor children, and the Taylors were close friends of the Sunday School secretary, Joshua Blackwell, and his wife; but they were not notably devout. When Alan Taylor lost his faith in his teens at Bootham School, it was not a matter which would bring him trouble at home.

However, throughout his life and in his writings various Nonconformist attitudes were present. From early and repeated reading of John Bunyan's *Pilgrim's Progress* he later became prone in book reviews and other writing to personify people or groups in a similar way. Notable instances of this occur among his book reviews. He headed one review on Edwardian Radicalism 'Mr High Mind's Party' (in the *New Statesman*, 29 November 1974) and another, on Kingsley Martin, the former editor of the *New Statesman*, 'Recalling Mr Fearful-for-truth' (in the *Times Literary Supplement*, 13 April 1973). Though from wealthy – even privileged – circumstances, the Nonconformist as well as the northern background enabled him, while often an 'insider' (as an Oxford don or as a television regular), to feel himself to be an outsider. He also frequently declared that his background had taught him, 'I am no better than anyone else, but no one is better than me.'

As an only child he played mainly by himself and he learnt to read early. When he went to a nursery school he was already reading *Pilgrim's Progress* and other books, so he did not need to be taught to read. He kept apart from most other children, preferring the company of his books or his toy soldiers.

After his mother's miscarriage in 1913, she, Alan and Annie Clark spent the winter of 1913–14 in Italy, at first at Alassio, then in Milan. This stay in northern Italy may well have contributed to his eventual choice of a research topic in 1928–30. On their return, the family lived in Buxton until 1919, a town he much enjoyed.

The other major early influence on Alan Taylor was Bootham School, York. Had the First World War and conscription (in 1916) not intervened, he would have gone instead to Rugby, his name having been put down for that public school years earlier. Connie Taylor's brother, Harry Thompson, the conscientious objector, was gaoled for his beliefs. His sister supported him vigorously, Alan later commenting that the issue was as powerful in changing her views as a religious conversion. On realizing that Rugby had an Officer Training Corps (OTC), the Taylors withdrew his name and instead placed him, at the age of thirteen, at Bootham, a Quaker public school.

Alan Taylor wrote in his autobiography, 'The five years between 1919 and 1924 when I was at Bootham created me as an individual.' There he had to mix with others of his own age. He came to love studying churches and he read more widely. He liked Bootham's

Quaker ethos. He was very pleased that the masters treated him as an intellectual equal. From Bootham he won an exhibition to Oriel College, Oxford, shining in his knowledge of Gothic architecture.

Most of Alan Taylor's career as a historian was linked to Oxford University. He was an undergraduate student there in 1924–7. He tried to return there within a year of taking up a lecturing post at Manchester University in 1930, and he succeeded in 1938. Thereafter he remained at Oxford, lecturing until 1963 and remaining, first as a Fellow then as an Honorary Fellow of Magdalen College, until his death. He declined opportunities of professorial posts elsewhere.

In later life he played down almost any influences on him as a historian. He projected himself, in his autobiography and elsewhere, as a self-taught original. Perhaps in this he was asserting that he was more a gentleman amateur than a professional. There is something in his self-taught claims, in that he arrived at Oxford very well read in history. At Bootham he had read not only many works of such past great historians as Acton, Gibbon, Grote, Macaulay and Seeley but also more recent books by G. M. Trevelyan, J. and B. Hammond, R. W. Postgate, R. H. Tawney, Sir J. Marriott, C. Grant Robertson, H. A. L. Fisher, A. F. Pollard and C. R. Fay. The characteristic attitudes of Oxford of his time would have reinforced his taste for suggesting that he possessed effortless intellectual superiority. In reality he often worked very hard and from an early age was intensely competitive. That he secured the glittering prize of First Class Honours when he graduated was most probably less of a surprise than he later liked to make out.

At Oxford as an undergraduate and afterwards, his natural bias was towards his family. Before going to Oxford he had toured Germany and France with his mother. At the end of his first year there he accompanied her again, this time round Soviet Russia. The following May he returned home and assisted the Preston strike committee during the General Strike of 1926, but he spent much of the summer with his friends. From early on at Oxford he had assumed he would join his uncle Harry Thompson's solicitor's practice in London, which specialized in trade-union work.

As usual, he was very well provided for. In his second year at Oxford his father had given him a fish-tailed Rover sports car, one of the very few cars owned by Oriel College's undergraduates at the time. Indeed, as he records in his essay 'Class War: 1926', it was also one of the few cars available to the Preston strike committee during the General Strike. When he began to work for his uncle, his parents provided him with a costly six-room flat beside Hampstead Heath, plus a housekeeper. When he tired of working as an articled clerk, his parents funded his return to Oxford, where he worked on prize essays – without success, however.

His parents' support enabled him to go to Vienna in the early summer of 1928 to see whether the eminent Austrian historian, A. F. Pribram, would supervise his research. Red Vienna appealed to him, but perhaps he also realized that research using German-language documents would equip him well to compete for jobs in the academic labour-market. Once based in Vienna, he lived the life of the gentleman scholar. Not only did he learn German, he also learnt to skate and to ride and went regularly to the opera and in his second year bought a season ticket for the Vienna Philharmonic. Nevertheless, he did work hard to perfect his German and he did spend much time in the archives. His second year of research was funded, at least in large part, by a Rockefeller research fellowship.

Alan Taylor's research area was an aspect of diplomatic history. He analysed a potential European crisis concerning northern Italy in 1848, studying the attitudes and actions of the Austrian, French and British governments. This later became his first book, *The Italian Problem in European Diplomacy, 1847–1849* (Manchester University Press, 1934).

In the 1920s there was substantial public as well as academic interest in diplomatic history, much of it linked to the contentious matter of the origins of the Great War. Alan Taylor wrote in the *Times Literary Supplement* in January 1956 of the interest in diplomatic history that existed in the period between the two World Wars: 'It would be foolish to pretend that their sudden interest in contemporary history was detached and "scientific". It was a political interest, forced upon them by the event of the First World

War. The twentieth century would have shown less concern with diplomatic history if the Bismarckian peace had endured. The diplomatic history of our time has always been a study of war origins, by no means to its advantage.'

Nevertheless, the study of war was central to a large proportion of his work. This is well illustrated in this collection by his television lectures, 'How Wars Begin' and 'How Wars End'. War was a central theme in his major diplomatic history, *The Struggle for Mastery in Europe* (Oxford University Press, 1954) as well as in what is probably his best-known book, *The Origins of the Second World War* (Hamish Hamilton, 1961), and in his illustrated histories, *The First World War* (Hamish Hamilton, 1963) and *The Second World War* (1975). At the end of his career, in a diary column in the *London Review of Books* in March 1982, he commented on the study of war, 'For fifty years I had been teaching history and writing books about it. All my books and all my lectures had been implicitly about war, from the Napoleonic Wars to the shadow of the final war under which we now live.'

The focus of much of his writing was often on emperors, kings, prime ministers and other leading politicians, not on broad social movements. Those who attracted his special interest were often major figures involved in great wars: Bismarck, Lloyd George, Churchill and even Beaverbrook. These were men of war, women rarely attracting his attention. In writing of such figures he provided colourful portraits, sometimes approaching caricatures. In so doing there was a radical Taylorian touch, a populist strand. If his subjects were traditional, his approach was irreverent. He was on the side of the good soldier Svejk, Old Bill (Bruce Bairnsfather's cartoon creation of the First World War survivalist) or, more generally, 'the British people'.

Alan Taylor's time in Vienna (1928–30) and his work on Austria-Hungary's history ensured that the history of the Habsburg monarchy was a major interest of his for the next two decades. One of his best and most enduring books, *The Habsburg Monarchy*, was published first as *The Habsburg Monarchy 1815–1918* (Macmillan, 1941), then substantially rewritten and published as *The Habsburg Monarchy 1809–1918* (Hamish Hamilton, 1948). He long remained interested in writing and lecturing about Metternich, the Emperor Francis Joseph, and Austria-Hungary. This is well illustrated by his early lectures to Historical Association branches. In December 1930, soon after taking up his first university post at Manchester, he spoke on 'Metternich as an Austrian and European Statesman' at the Lancashire (Central and North) branch. In early 1938 he talked on the subject, 'The Conflict of Nationalities in the Austrian Empire', at the Bolton branch.

As an assistant lecturer in History at Manchester University, he lectured on European history, 1494–1914. He later recalled that he then 'read a good deal about the French Revolution and Napoleon'. In his introduction to *Revolutions and Revolutionaries* (Hamish Hamilton, 1980), he commented that he was returning to his first love – the French Revolution of 1789 and the Central European revolutions of 1848 – and that it was 'only now that I have got as far as writing a book about them'.

It is a pity that he did not write more substantially on the French Revolution and the Napoleonic period much earlier. There had been an opportunity after the publication of his impressive volume in the Oxford History of Modern Europe, *The Struggle for Mastery in Europe 1848–1918* (Oxford, Clarendon Press, 1954). There was then some talk of his being invited to write a predecessor volume on European diplomacy 1789–1848. Neither he – nor any other potential author (including the later US Secretary of State, Henry Kissinger) – took it on. However, he did begin his second series of television lectures, 'When Europe Was the Centre of the World', in autumn 1957 with 'The Fall of the Bastille' and 'Napoleon'.

The biggest influence on Alan Taylor during his eight years at Manchester University (1930–38) was Lewis Namier, the eminent historian of eighteenth-century Britain and modern Europe, who arrived one year after him. Namier provided him with the stimulus of both a first-rate modern historian and one whose experience and knowledge of continental Europe fascinated him. When Namier arrived to take the chair of Modern History, he was forty-three and Alan Taylor was twenty-five. Taylor's first wife, Margaret, later recalled that the younger generation of Namier's friends 'looked up to him as a father-figure and a *grand seigneur*'. Namier encouraged Alan Taylor's interest in Central European history, and it was through him, either as editor of a series of books or as a contact with publishers, that Alan Taylor came to publish his first books: *The Italian Problem in European Diplomacy 1847–1849* (Manchester University Press, 1934), *Germany's First Bid For Colonies 1884–1885* (Macmillan, 1938), *The Habsburg Monarchy 1815–1918* (Macmillan, 1941), as well as his and W. McElwee's abridged translation of Heinrich Friedjung's *The Struggle for Supremacy in Germany 1859–1866* (Macmillan, 1935).

In 1938, after several attempts to secure a post in his old university, Alan Taylor returned to Oxford, having been elected a Fellow of Magdalen College. He arrived with an established reputation as a diplomatic historian. He had bought a set of the 54 volumes of published German diplomatic documents on the period 1871–1914 from a Jewish refugee from Nazi Germany in 1933. After reading these, he had worked through the published British and French documents before teaching from 1935 a Special Subject, 'England and the Making of the *Ententes, 1898–1907*'. At Oxford he wrote the first version of *The Habsburg Monarchy* and *The Course of German History* (Hamish Hamilton, 1945) during the Second World War. After the end of the war he began writing a book on European diplomatic history 1878–1919, intended for Hamish Hamilton. This became his major work, *The Struggle for Mastery in Europe 1848–1918*, a volume in the Oxford History of Modern Europe. He wrote much of it in 1950–51.

He continued to work on Central European and diplomatic history until his university lectureship expired in 1963. In 1952 and 1953 he wrote his brief biography, *Bismarck* (Hamish Hamilton, 1955). Invited to give the very prestigious Ford Lectures for 1956 at Oxford, he gave an original and irreverent survey of those who vigorously dissented from official British foreign policy from the time of the French Wars to the Second World War. These lectures were published as *The Trouble Makers: Dissent over Foreign Policy 1792–1939* (Hamish Hamilton, 1957). He also worked steadily over several years on a successor volume to *The Struggle for Mastery in Europe 1848–1918*. This was to be his best-known and most controversial book, *The Origins of the Second World War* (Hamish Hamilton, 1961).

Alan Taylor's book on the origins of the Second World War caused uproar – more so than he had anticipated. Shortly before delivering the typescript, he had written to Hamish Hamilton, 'I'm pleased with it. But I think it will annoy the old boys who thought they had settled everything about the Second World War years ago.' What shocked critics was the suggestion that Hitler had not planned the war and that he was not solely guilty of the war in Europe occurring when it did.

With the book Alan Taylor was deliberately opening up a subject that had hitherto (since the end of the Second World War) been closed and that had been held near sacrosanct. In so writing on the subject, he followed an old pedagogic approach that is often present in his essays. This is to take an unusual approach and argue it through, exercising his wit and his debating skills to see what new light such argument threw on an old question. He even made an occasional aside to his readers to alert them to what he was doing. For instance, when arguing that Hitler did not have deep-laid plans but proceeded one step at a time, he observed, 'Human blunders ... usually do more to shape history than human wickedness. At any rate this is a rival dogma which is worth developing, if only as an academic exercise.'

His book did set off one of the longer and more fruitful academic debates in modern European history. Yet, in spite of its superb style and its many revisionist merits, Taylor's book was one of the last of its kind. It highlighted vividly the dangers of heavy reliance on published diplomatic documents as a source, not least in this case as it encouraged him to separate the foreign from the domestic policy of the Nazi state. He also overstated the importance of Europe – and of Britain and France in particular – in the diplomatic events of the period. This in turn contributed to the book's dealing only with the origins of the war in Europe (which began in 1939) rather than with the wider world war (starting in 1941).

Above all, Alan Taylor failed to realize just how offensive many would find his revisionism, just sixteen years after the end of the Second World War. Given that he had been an active opponent of appeasement in the late 1930s and that his work (including *The Course of German History*) was often strongly anti-German, he was surprised to find himself condemned as an apologist for Hitler. In his autobiography Alan Taylor recorded the following story which underlined this point. On a trip to Munich, his taxi-driver, on finding out who his passenger was, shook his hand, saying, 'You are the man who proved that Hitler did not cause the war. I know you are right. I was in the SS and one of his bodyguard.' One of Hugh Trevor-Roper's more telling criticisms of the time was the question, 'Was Hitler really just a more violent Mr Micawber sitting in Berlin . . . ?'

After the often bitter controversies over *The Origins of the Second World War*, Alan Taylor's lectureship at Oxford University was terminated. He released to the press a statement of the bare facts which implied that he had lost his main job because of the book. In fact the situation was more complex. The special lectureship that he held was tenable for five years and renewable once; it involved less teaching and more time for research. By 1963 he had held the post for the full ten years, with his college funding the resulting loss of part of his teaching during that time. Another university might have promoted him to a Readership or a Personal Chair, or have made some special arrangement, given the distinction of his published work. At Oxford, nothing was done. Alan Taylor, who had been earning more money from the media and his books than from his university work since about 1951, declined to return to the teaching commitments of an ordinary lectureship. So in 1963 his regular lecturing in Oxford University ended, though he remained a Fellow of Magdalen College.

By the second half of the twentieth century Alan Taylor typified a fast-fading kind of historian: the gentleman scholar. He saw himself as being from the same mould as Edward Gibbon and Thomas Babington Macaulay. He felt he could be semi-detached from the restrictions of university teaching because of private income. Early on, he benefited from his parents' largesse; later on, from his own earnings from television appearances, newspaper articles, books and investments. He was cautious with money, very aware of how many of his relatives had lived to see their wealth severely dwindle. Not long after he began lecturing, his father gave him what was then a huge insurance policy, £2,000. By 1940 Alan Taylor had accumulated over £8,000, much of it from speculating on the Stock Exchange. While a lecturer at Manchester University, he lived in style on the edge of the Peak District. At Oxford he lived in the large and impressive Holywell Ford, owned by Magdalen College.

In his autobiography, commenting on his 1938 move from Manchester to Oxford, he remarked, 'if I had stayed at Manchester I should never have achieved anything except a few academic books. Without the contacts I made in London, which was easily reached from Oxford, I should never have become either a journalist or a television star. As I had never wanted to be a full-time academic, I suppose my move to Oxford was the best thing for me.' One can be sceptical about this claim to be less than fervent to return to Oxford. One can also suppose he would have been more eager to be a full-time academic had he gained the Regius Chair. Nevertheless, within this lies the truth of his driving desire to gain national recognition through the press and television.

He had begun by writing book reviews for the *Manchester Guardian*, initially books that Lewis Namier could not be bothered to review. He had learnt much about style from Namier. He also learnt much about writing 'taut journalistic prose' from A. P. Wadsworth, deputy editor of the *Manchester Guardian* and a good economic historian.

The Second World War gave Alan Taylor major openings in the press and on the radio. He was available to offer informed and often controversial views on Europe, while others were away on war service. From the autumn of 1943, when W. P. Crozier, the editor of the *Manchester Guardian*, was ailing, Alan Taylor wrote editorials on Hungary. After his friend A. P. Wadsworth succeeded Crozier, he eagerly took on writing many editorials on Europe, which he telephoned through from Oxford. This ended in early 1946 when Wadsworth would no longer tolerate his espousal of the Soviet Union. In 1946 Alan Taylor went to Czechoslovakia for three weeks, writing three articles on the political situation there for the *Manchester Guardian* in late July. Wadsworth thereafter employed him in writing centenary and other occasional history articles as well as book reviews, rather than on current international affairs.

Alan Taylor had not been called up for the armed forces but was at first allowed to continue to teach European History at Oxford University. He volunteered for the Home Guard and later was enrolled in Air Raid Precautions duties. Otherwise, he spent much time lecturing on Europe past and present (especially recent developments in the war) to service personnel through Oxford University's Adult Education Department and to the general public across southern England on behalf of the Ministry of Information. From May 1943, for four months full-time and thereafter for a few months part-time, he wrote on the history of Hungary and Germany for the Political Warfare Executive. When his account of German history proved too controversial, he revised it and published it as *The Course of German History* in 1945.

These wartime activities helped him to enter educational radio work for the Forces Network of the BBC. Between March and June 1942 he appeared on a weekly series entitled 'Your Questions Answered'. By the end of the war he had established himself as one of a roster of figures, including Harold Laski, to whom the BBC's radio producers would turn for debate on controversial topics.

When BBC television needed good arguers for a current affairs programme entitled 'In The News', it turned to Alan Taylor. He appeared on the programme forty-two times between August 1950 and December 1952 as one of four regular participants, the other three being Michael Foot, Bob Boothby and W. J. Brown. After the leaders of the political parties successfully demanded that orthodox Labour and Conservative figures should participate, he and the others appeared less frequently. In his case, he appeared on a further five occasions in 1953 and 1954. With the coming of commercial television in September 1955, Alan Taylor and the other three resumed their current affairs discussions for several more years under the programme title, 'Free Speech'.

The 'In The News' and 'Free Speech' programmes made Alan Taylor a national 'name', an early television personality. This gave him an entry into lucrative journalism. He wrote a weekly column throughout 1951 for the *Sunday Pictorial* which initially had the caption 'A million people see and hear this man on Friday night'. From January 1953 to June 1954 he wrote a weekly column for the *Daily Herald*. From the autumn of 1957 until 1978 he wrote frequently for the *Sunday Express*. His celebrity also gave him the opportunity to give lectures on history on television.

Alan Taylor's prominence as a television personality led John Irwin, the producer of 'In The News' and 'Free Speech', to go to Oxford University to hear the last of Alan Taylor's Ford Lectures in early 1956. Irwin went again to Oxford for one of Alan Taylor's regular lectures. He wrote in the *TV Times* in August 1957, 'I've seen nothing like it. That audience was hypnotized by Taylor's dynamic personality, his passionate sincerity, his wit, his command of words, his brilliant sense of timing, and his complete mastery of the subject – without a single note.'

Alan Taylor had broadcast history on the radio from 1947. Two of his first lectures were on British Prime Ministers – Lord John Russell (reprinted in the collection, *From Napoleon to the Second International*, Hamish Hamilton, 1993; Penguin, 1995) and Lord Salisbury (in this volume). Before embarking on the first series of televised lectures he commented, 'It's not only me on trial but the whole idea of lecturing on TV.' He was optimistic, observing, 'I do believe that the British public has an appetite for things which are intellectually interesting and stimulating to the mind.' He also rightly predicted, 'I expect we shall have a tremendous university of the air in no time.'

His career as a history lecturer on television began with a series of three half-hour lectures on the Russian Revolution. These were given at 6 p.m. on Monday evenings, 12–26 August 1957. They were followed by a further thirteen lectures on the theme 'When Europe Was the Centre of the World', broadcast usually at 6.30 p.m. on Monday evenings between 23 September 1957 and 10 March 1958. Associated Television Ltd (ATV) gave estimated audience figures of 750,000 for the 'When Europe Was the Centre of the World' series – not a bad figure, given that at the start of 1957 only 2,656,000 homes were able to receive Independent Television's transmissions. Bernard Sendall, Deputy Director of the Independent Television Authority, deemed Alan Taylor, with Dr Jacob Bronowski on science and Sir Kenneth Clark on art, to be one of its 'three main master-craftsmen in the art of lecturing'.

Alan Taylor followed these series of lectures with four further series of lectures for Independent Television. These were 'Prime Ministers' (six lectures, 1960), 'The Big Rows' (six lectures, 1964), 'World War' (ten lectures, 1966) and 'Revolution 1917' (five lectures, 1967). The first of these series is published for the first time in this book, though they were released on gramophone records by University Educational Records, London. These half-hour lectures on Prime Ministers were broadcast at 10.35 p.m. on Monday nights over a period of several months from July 1960. In an introduction to the series in the *TV Times*, 22 July 1960, Alan Taylor observed, 'All six dominated the political scene when they were in power . . . They would stand up on their feet and talk compellingly to an audience.' Alan Taylor returned to four of the subjects in the mid-1970s when he was the general editor of a series of short pictorial biographies of Prime Ministers published by Weidenfeld & Nicolson. At that time he wrote short introductions to *Sir Robert Walpole* (1976) by Betty Kemp, *Pitt The Younger* (1974) by Derek Jarrett, *Lloyd George* (1974) by Kenneth O. Morgan and *Stanley Baldwin* (1976) by Kenneth Young.

Alan Taylor also lectured on history on BBC Television from 1962. His BBC series, all of six lectures, were 'The Twenties' (1962), 'Men of 1862' (1963), 'The War Lords' (1976), 'How Wars Begin' (1977) and 'Revolution' (1978). The first of these stemmed from his work on his volume in the Oxford History of England, *English History 1914–1945* (Oxford, Clarendon Press, 1965). In introducing the lectures in the *Radio Times* (1 February 1962) he commented, 'These lectures are intended as serious history, or as serious as I can make it. They are exactly like lectures which I give at Oxford University except they are shorter and faster . . . The lectures are taken out of books and records as they would be on any earlier period. They are not presented as anecdotes or personal recollections.'

After eight series of television lectures between 1957 and 1967, there was a nine-year lull before he gave three more series. The second and third of these are reprinted in this volume. Before the first lecture of 'How Wars Begin' was broadcast, the *Observer*'s television critic, Stephen Gilbert, observed that it was twenty years since Alan Taylor's first series. 'You did it live in those days and though Eddie Mirzoeff has recorded this series of six, they are in effect live because they are all in one take and Taylor speaks without notes or autocue, developing his thesis on his feet. He cleaves to the spontaneity and he is right – the results are as fresh as a daisy' (*Observer*, 10 July 1977).

With a few exceptions, Alan Taylor's 1977 and 1978 series were well received, even though the approach of a 'straight lecture' may well have seemed a little dated by this time and his sense of timing was not quite as sharp as in the 1960s. Nevertheless, James Meade in the *Observer* commented of the second lecture in the 'Revolution' series, 'Here, in a format which fools will demean as "illustrated radio", he [Eddie Mirzoeff] points a camera at A. J. P. Taylor who, unrehearsed and seeking inspiration from near his left foot, delivers a tidy, sometimes funny lecture on Chartism, the movement's pre-cursors and most excitingly – he transmits his enthusiasm with goodwill – the extant land colonies' (*Observer*, 9 July 1978). Rosalie Horner, who went to the recording of the final episode, was told by Alan Taylor, 'I am never nervous before a programme, but there is a difference between being nervous and tense, which I am.' Eddie Mirzoeff, the producer, told her, 'We never know what he is going to say' (*Daily Express*, 8 July 1978).

By the time Alan Taylor came to record a final lecture series for Channel 4 – 'How Wars End' – Parkinson's Disease was prob-ably affecting his timing and his memory more than before. The series was much admired, but his timing was not as acute in giving each sentence as it had been for the series of the 1950s and 1960s.

Overall, Alan Taylor set a bench-mark for presenting history on television. Few tried to emulate his unscripted approach. He succeeded because of charisma, because of his own fascination with the subjects about which he was speaking and because of his own skilful artistry as a lecturer. The *Daily Telegraph*'s critic, Sean Day

Lewis, commented, after the second in the 'Revolution' series, 'The background is black, the clothes are neutral, the body is still, the visual display consists only of his attention – demanding right eye balanced by his gesticulating left hand, sometimes signalling the shovelling of parentheses and sometimes pointing the pedagogical finger.' He added the observation that 'Taylor is the historian of the illuminating detail' (*Daily Telegraph*, 14 July 1978).

Alan Taylor's subjects for the lectures were mainly wars, revolutions, statesmen and High Politics. Very little social history, even less about women. In introducing 'The Twenties' series, Alan Taylor wrote, 'My lectures are about public affairs: mainly about politics, often about economic development, sometimes about foreign affairs. These things are rather disapproved of nowadays. It is a grave charge to make against anyone that he is an old-fashioned political historian. However, like an ageing music-hall artist, I can't perform new tricks' (*Radio Times*, 1 February, 1962).

As well as being prominent on television, on the radio and in the popular press in the 1950s, Alan Taylor was an early leading figure in CND, the Campaign for Nuclear Disarmament. This was a cause in which he believed deeply. It was also one in which he could take an individualist, moral lead – a role much to his taste.

Alan Taylor saw himself as a modern Richard Cobden, in his case trying to argue nuclear weapons, not the Corn Laws, out of existence. Between 1958 and 1960 he stumped the country, speaking at large numbers of meetings. In his autobiography he observed, 'We were an odd collection, appointed by nobody and convinced that we could change the world by our unaided efforts.' In recollections that he wrote for Peggy Duff, CND's first Secretary, and which are reprinted in this book, he went further: 'We imagined that unilateral disarmament by Great Britain would set an example to other countries, perhaps to all. This was the last flash of British Imperialism, redolent of earlier times when perhaps our country really set an example to others, as over the slave trade.'

He had his moment as a latter-day Cobden or Bright. He even suggested that membership, like that of the Anti-Corn Law League of 1839–46, should be restricted to the few who could pay a very large subscription. When the organization of CND was placed on a democratic basis, he retired.

The later 1950s saw him move from writing for Left or Left-inclined newspapers (*Sunday Pictorial, Reynold's News* and the *Daily Herald*) to the robustly Conservative Express group of newspapers. This surprised many who knew him.

While his family circle (his father, mother and Henry Sara) and then Lewis Namier had been a powerful influence on him before his return to Oxford in 1938, the final major influence on him was Max Aitken, Lord Beaverbrook. Alan Taylor believed that he owed his appointment as a *Sunday Express* columnist from October 1957 to John Junor, the editor. It was more likely to have been due to Beaverbrook.

In 1955 Beaverbrook had written to Alan Taylor praising *The Struggle for Mastery in Europe* and asking for his sources on two points. In replying, Alan Taylor observed, 'It is agreeable to please historians; but even nicer to satisfy those who have made history.' The following year, Taylor wrote a favourable review of Beaverbrook's *Men and Power* (Hutchinson, 1956) which appeared in the *Observer*, 28 October 1956. In the review Alan Taylor observed, 'The present book is equally as exciting and equally entertaining' as Beaverbrook's earlier book, *Politicians and the War* (2 vols: Thornton Butterworth, 1928; the Lane Press, 1932). He went on to deliver the verdict, 'He may sometimes exaggerate the part that he has played in events. No one could exaggerate his gifts in chronicling them.' This almost certainly led to him writing for the Express Group newspapers. In 1964 Beaverbrook said that reading this review was the recollection that gave him most pleasure. (Alan Taylor's later review of Beaverbrook's book on the fall of Lloyd George is included in this volume.)

By the second half of the 1950s Alan Taylor was turning increasingly to twentieth-century British political history, in which Beaverbrook had been a major player. Hence Beaverbrook's knowledge and stock of anecdotes were even more fascinating to him than had been those of Lewis Namier. While many had found Namier a bore, very few – if any – whom Beaverbrook wished to charm would say that of the press baron. Indeed, like so many other younger men of ability, Taylor was captivated by Beaverbrook's sense of fun, his wit and his fund of good stories of the past. Taylor commented in his autobiography, 'He had a gift for making you feel when you were with him that you were the most important person in the world.'

Alan Taylor's friendship with Beaverbrook encouraged him in his efforts to complete his volume in the Oxford History of England. He completed the text of *English History 1914–1945* in July 1964, a month after Beaverbrook's death. Alan Taylor readily took on the task of writing the biography of his friend. The resulting book, *Beaverbrook* (Hamish Hamilton, 1972), was Alan Taylor's last large book. This received a mixed reception. Few shared Alan Taylor's enthusiasm for the book's subject. There was criticism of his avoidance of Beaverbrook's love life and his failure to explain fully the sources of Beaverbrook's wealth. More damaging still were later examinations of Beaverbrook's dubious use of evidence in his writing about the First World War and Alan Taylor's undue reliance on Beaverbrook's testimony. Yet the book was based on substantial use of Beaverbrook's Papers; it is enjoyable to read and benefits both from Taylor's very real interest in his subject and from his mature style.

Alan Taylor's last phase began as the Honorary Director of the Beaverbrook Library, 33 St Bride Street (in Express Buildings, just off Fleet Street) from 1967 to 1975. Sir Max Aitken had set it up as a memorial to his father. It housed Lord Beaverbrook's own Papers, as well as those he had bought over the years, notably the Lloyd George and the Bonar Law Papers. It provided Alan Taylor with an agreeable academic base; it brought him into contact with British and American scholars working on twentieth-century British history; it offered secretarial facilities and a location at the hub of British journalism. He encouraged researchers not only by his interest in their work but also by running an excellent research seminar in the Beaverbrook Library during university vacations. He edited a book of the earlier Papers given at the seminar, *Lloyd George: Twelve Essays* (Hamish Hamilton, 1971).

Alan Taylor drew on the archival resources of the Beaverbrook

Library not only for *Beaverbrook* but for several edited books, not least the letters and diaries of Frances Stevenson (who eventually became Lloyd George's second wife). He also wrote *The Second World War: An Illustrated History* (Hamish Hamilton, 1975), which complemented his earlier, much-admired *The First World War: An Illustrated History* (Hamish Hamilton, 1963).

By the time of his period in the Beaverbrook Library, Alan Taylor had mellowed and become something of the Grand Old Man of British historians. He was revered by many of the younger generation of historians of modern Britain. He himself was less competitive than before and willing to spare more time for young scholars.

After the closure of the Beaverbrook Library in 1975 he continued to promote history until the onset of Parkinson's Disease made much activity very difficult. He generously gave his time to lecture to Historical Association branches. His lecture which marked the Historical Association's seventy-fifth anniversary in 1971 is included in this book. He continued to give occasional lectures and research seminar papers at Oxford University. In March 1982 he delivered the Romanes Lecture, taking as his subject 'War In Our Time', which he ended with his favourite theme: the follies of keeping nuclear weapons. In 1983 he published his autobiography, *A Personal History*. He wrote his last book reviews for the national press in 1984 (the final review, on Eric Hobsbawm's *Worlds of Labour*, is included in this collection). He was able to attend his eightieth birthday celebrations in March 1986 and to write about reaching eighty (an essay also included in this volume). He died on 7 September 1990.

Since his death Alan Taylor's reputation as a major historian has not faded. His major works remain in print and continue to be discussed. His style, with its short, sharp sentences, its love of paradox and epigrammatic wit, has been very influential with many British and American historians. His impatience with received opinions about the past and his wide-ranging revisionism have been emulated by historians of the Right as well as of the Left. As time goes by, he seems to be among those historians – like Gibbon, Macaulay and G. M. Trevelyan – who are read long after their death.

BRITISH PRIME MINISTERS

Prime Ministers

First given as a series of television lectures in 1960. Forty years on, many historians believe party politics to have been stronger than Namier (and Taylor here) suggested. Also Ireland's problems seemed less resolved by Lloyd George from a perspective of 1968 and after.

Prime Ministers are a British invention and a fairly recent one. They are about two hundred years old, like steam engines. Literally the phrase means only First or Chief Minister. Such have always existed in this and other countries. Many Kings and Emperors have been glad to push the hard work on to some efficient agent. In this sense, Richelieu was the prime minister of Louis XIII. Metternich was the prime minister of the Austrian Emperor, Francis I, or so he imagined. Cardinal Wolsey and Thomas Cromwell were the prime ministers of Henry VIII. These men were the personal choice of their royal masters. They owed their position solely to royal favour and fell when that was withdrawn. The British Prime Minister, in modern times, has a different source of power. He has the support of the majority in the House of Commons, and the Monarch has to put up with him regardless of personal feelings. We assume that the leader of the majority party will be appointed Prime Minister automatically. The King or Queen has to exercise a real choice only if the party leadership is unclear or if the parties fall into confusion, as may happen in wartime or during a financial crisis. This system grew up gradually and by accident. In the eighteenth century it was assumed just as firmly that the King chose the man whom he personally favoured and that the majority in the Commons then accepted the King's choice.

One theme in the story of Prime Ministers is therefore this transformation in the source of the Prime Minister's power. Dr Johnson said that Walpole was a minister chosen by the King for the People, while the younger Pitt was a minister chosen by the People for the King. The remark was somewhat exaggerated. Nowadays we incline to think that the younger Pitt, too, was chosen by the King, though one factor in this choice was the calculation that the People favoured him. The change becomes a good deal clearer in the nineteenth century. Queen Victoria, we know, liked Disraeli and disliked Gladstone. Yet for much of her reign she had to accept Gladstone as Prime Minister and to leave Disraeli in opposition. By the twentieth century the Crown's task seems to have become a formal one. Even now there are exceptions. Lloyd George was not the leader of a party when he became Prime Minister, and Baldwin became leader of the Conservative party only after the King had chosen him as Prime Minister.

It is not only the Prime Ministers who changed their character. The parties, too, have changed their names and their characters over the centuries. In the eighteenth century they were called Whigs and Tories. In the nineteenth they became Liberals and Conservatives. In the twentieth Labour took the Liberals' place as the second party in the state. They changed in more than name. The eighteenth-century labels expressed only vague differences in outlook, and often not even that. The decisive factors in political manoeuvre were groups of families or of interest with constantly shifting allegiance. The nineteenth-century parties had real divisions of principle, though not as much as they imagined, and men were loyal to a government only as long as they wanted to be. Nearly every government between 1832 and 1874, for instance, fell because they were deserted by their own supporters, not because the opposing party grew stronger. Disraeli's government was the first to go to the polls in 1880, still undefeated in the House of Commons. By the twentieth century, parties have become, in the contemporary phrase, 'monolithic'. Members of Parliament are lobby fodder, and it is assumed, though not altogether correctly, that the voters also are fodder in the polling booths.

There is another element in politics which King and Prime Minister have to consider. This is the Cabinet. It, too, has known its ups and downs. In the eighteenth century, it hesitated to assert its unity against the King. The ministers were still the King's servants, and combination against their master was almost as shocking for them as for a trade union. Later the Cabinet grew more courageous. It imposed its will on the Crown and even on the Prime Minister, who in the nineteenth century was often overruled by his colleagues. This power did not last. The Prime Minister, secure in his leadership of the party, came to rank above the other ministers. Nowadays the Cabinet is less a meeting of equals than a board which receives instructions from the managing director. At least, this is what political scientists surmise.

Sir Robert Walpole

Sir Robert Walpole (1676–1745). Son of a small Norfolk land-owner, he became a magnate from the profits of office. He built a great mansion at Houghton and accumulated a collection of pictures, which was later bought by Catherine II of Russia and placed in the Hermitage gallery. Educated at Eton and King's College, Cambridge. Member of Parliament from 1701 to 1742. He was Whig secretary at war from 1708 to 1710 and was sent to the Tower by the Tories in 1712. George I chose him as Prime Minister in 1721, and George II, after some doubts, continued him in that office until 1742. He is commonly regarded as the first Prime Minister in the modern sense and certainly held office the longest. He was driven to war against his will in 1739 and fell in 1742, when he lost control of the House of Commons. He was created Earl of Orford, and, before he died in 1745, had the satisfaction of seeing his younger associates back in power.

Two hundred years does not seem a very long time. It hardly seems as though it would take us back to the dark ages. Yet Sir Robert Walpole, who flourished only just over two hundred years ago, is a figure of legend. According to popular opinion, so far as it thinks about Walpole at all, he was the founder of the modern British constitution. He was the first Prime Minister in the modern sense of the term. The first to preside over a united Cabinet. He was the first man to control a majority in the House of Commons and to owe his position as Prime Minister to the fact that he led a formed party in the House of Commons which sustained him in office. It is supposed, too, that he was the first minister who excluded (one might say) the king from political affairs and transformed the monarchy into the constitutional superior organization which we know today.

I propose first to examine some of these legends and to consider how far modern scholarship, which has worked a great deal on Walpole and on his time, confirms or denies them. One thing of course is quite beyond dispute: that from 1721 to 1742 Walpole was First Lord of the Treasury, the office which the Prime Minister nearly always holds. A longer run than any other man has had. Without doubt, therefore, he was a figure of great importance. Beyond that doubts begin. First of all, we no longer believe that Walpole was at the head of a formed or organized party in the House of Commons. It is quite true that after the Glorious Revolution and after the accession of the Hanoverians – particularly in 1714 when George I came to the throne – nearly everybody in political life, most Members of Parliament, most of those who were active in the country, were Whigs. But while this was a common outlook, while they all shared the same social background, there was no organized Whig party. There was virtually no organization of any kind in the House of Commons, at most an accumulation of personal groups and followings, half a dozen here, half a dozen there. Walpole himself had only a very small following of adherents, really not much more than members of his own family, his brother, his nephew, one or two he won over by marriage. In our sense of the term, therefore, party did not exist in the early eighteenth century.

More than this, Walpole is often alleged to have found a substitute for party in influence, at least that was the eighteenth-century term; to put it more crudely, by bribery and corruption. It has been said that he won men over either by straight cash payments or by offering them rewards. Now here again there is a certain element of truth in it. In the eighteenth century government could only maintain itself, could only keep things on an even keel at all, by distributing rewards; or, to put it another way, the only method by which government employment was distributed was by personal influence. When I say that government won men over by giving them rewards

I do not mean by that that it gave rewards to undeserving people, and I think this is very often the cause of misunderstanding. If you have to appoint somebody to work in a government office or you have to put somebody in command of the fleet, or whatever it may be, this is bound to be done on a basis of personal judgement, and in a small, closed society these judgements will be influenced by knowledge of personalities. After all we still choose our prime ministers to some extent in this way; it is not done altogether by formal election, the weight of personality still counts. And in exactly the same way in the eighteenth century when Walpole distributed the various offices and duties on the basis of his personal knowledge; of course he was hoping to gain political advantage from it but he was also hoping to secure, what seemed to him, the best man for the job.

Cash payments were a much smaller matter than has usually been alleged. This has been investigated in detail. We know approximately what Walpole spent on making his political position a bit easier. And it is now quite clear from an examination of these accounts that the sums involved were far too small to have made any significant difference. Indeed, most of the apparent corruption that went on was not much more than a form of a pension. Seeing at this time there was no system of pensions at all when a man of worthiness served the state or, to put it in more cynical terms, had been loyal to his political leader for twenty or thirty years, it was obvious that he should receive something at the end when he came to retire. But the idea that you could get men of one political point of view and, by giving them £100 or £1,000, change them over to quite a different point of view would have been a mistake in the eighteenth century as it would be at any other time. At worst Walpole bribed men, I might say, to support the cause which they would have supported in any case, though of course with less loyalty or with less regularity. Thus Walpole's standing in parliament, and it was considerable, rested exclusively neither on party nor on influence, but it rested also on his personal reputation. In this way Walpole perhaps deserves to be regarded as more significant than many prime ministers that came after. In later times, prime ministers have sometimes, perhaps often, maintained themselves by what is called the machine. Walpole had no machine, or had a smaller machine, and for that very reason had to exert his own personal influence over the House of Commons the more strongly. And this leads me to another point.

Walpole was not raised to power by the support of a majority. He was certainly not elected to the office of Prime Minister, he was chosen as his predecessors had been chosen in the sixteenth and seventeenth centuries by the King because George I believed, and as it turned out rightly, that he was the best man for the job. Walpole depended – if not solely at any rate predominantly – on the King's favour. If that favour was withdrawn then Walpole's position as Prime Minister was at an end. In 1727 King George I died. George II, like most members of the House of Hanover, had often quarrelled most bitterly with his father, and disliked all his father's advisers. George II came to the throne absolutely resolute that he would get rid of Sir Robert Walpole at once. And indeed, at their first meeting, he informed Walpole that he was about to lose office. But George II was already a middle-aged man, and within a week or two of becoming King he appreciated that, however tiresome Walpole might have been when serving George I from his point of view, he would be a valuable servant now that George II was King. It was solely because George II changed his mind that Walpole remained Prime Minister throughout much of George II's reign. Some ten years later, when the wife of George II died, Walpole's position became weaker. She had understood Walpole, she had sympathized with him, she had appreciated his services, and it was largely because of her that George II kept Walpole, regarding him with favour. Once the Queen was dead, Walpole's position became shakier. A few years later, George II decided that Walpole was not performing his duties adequately, that is not satisfactorily from the Crown's point of view; he turned Walpole out and that was an end of it. The support of the Crown, the favour of the Crown, the approval of the Crown, was the decisive factor which kept Walpole in power. In this way he was far from being a modern Prime Minister.

On the other hand he was not of course simply a court favourite. He was chosen by George I and sustained by George II because both kings believed that Walpole could do the job well. Well, what was his job – well, series of jobs – that Walpole was expected to do? He was First Lord of the Treasury. In later times, in the nineteenth and still more in the twentieth century, this has simply become a decorative title, a disguise one might say, for the Prime Minister who was expected to run the government generally. In the eighteenth century it still meant that he ran the finances. And one reason for Walpole's high position was simply that he was regarded as a good financier, that he conducted the financial affairs of the country satisfactorily. This belief that the Prime Minister had a special responsibility for finance ran on well into the nineteenth century. But more than this, Walpole undertook a new task that prime ministers, leading ministers of the Crown, had usually not performed before.

He was the first Prime Minister who did indeed seek to manage the House of Commons. Now I have already suggested to you that he didn't do this by means of a party machine but by means of his personal attendance at the House of Commons, by the way in which he won over Members of Parliament, listened to their grievances, sympathized with them, made them feel that his conduct of affairs and his personal approach were sympathetic. Our leading authority, Romney Sedgwick, says of Walpole that he was the Minister of the Crown in the House of Commons and the representative of the House of Commons in the closet. Throughout the seventeenth century politicians had pondered on this link, they had recognized that there must be a connection between the House of Commons and the Crown, which still did the governing. On the other hand they had not appreciated that this was a vital task. It was only youngsters who did the job, and as soon as they became any good they went to the House of Lords. Whether Walpole appreciated the significance of what he was doing we cannot say. Maybe he stayed in the House of Commons because he liked the atmosphere, because he was easy-going. Each year he used to say 'Well, I think I'll take a peerage soon,' and would thus have cut himself off from the very basis of his support. Nor did people learn this lesson for a long time. There were plenty of members in the House of Lords who were prime ministers in the eighteenth and for that matter in the nineteenth century, but Walpole in this way contributed a new thing. He made the minister in the House of Commons a much more significant figure than he had ever been before. Alas, we don't know very much about how he did it. None of his speeches have survived, we don't even know whether he was a great orator. We know that he could win people over – usually, he said, by talking bawdy because that was the only universal interest. Beyond this we have very little idea.

Does this mean the fact that he had more control over the House of Commons than previous leading ministers, does this mean that he ran the country? Not in the modern sense. The Crown, the King, was still the active head of government. The King still presided over the meetings with ministers and other dignitaries, known as Cabinet meetings. It sometimes was suggested that George I could speak no English and therefore did not attend Cabinet meetings. Untrue. We have plenty of records of George I at Cabinet meetings. George II attended them regularly. Another legend is that George I, unable to speak English, conversed with Walpole and others in dog Latin. This is a story which was invented fifty years later, invented I think as a joke. George I spoke good French, all his ministers spoke French; the papers, the official papers, were written in French and submitted to him; and the Cabinet, when they met with the King present, conducted their affairs in French. There was no problem here. George I was an active ruler of the country so far as there was anything to rule. There may have been – this is one of the dark corners of our history – there may have been a tiny inner group which often settled affairs before they met with the King. This tiny inner group, in so far as it existed, was the beginning, the first sketch for our modern Cabinet, where the few important ministers meet entirely alone without the King to conduct affairs. But even if this tiny inner group existed, and it certainly did sometimes, during Walpole's tenure of power, it was not yet a recognized body, nor was it, and this is very important, a united body. The ministers still took their own line. Walpole is supposed to have enforced Cabinet unity, but there is very little evidence for it. What Walpole did, and even this was new, was to insist that while his colleagues could take their own line in their own affairs, the Minister responsible for Foreign Affairs could have his own foreign policy, the man responsible for the navy could run the navy as he liked, they must not, while ministers, actively oppose his financial policy. And when he managed to throw out certain of his colleagues it was because they had broken this rule. When Walpole had actually advocated a particular financial line they had spoken against it in the House of Lords. Even this was a startling advance that ministers should not be free to attack each other. But beyond this in Walpole's time Cabinet unity did not go.

Walpole therefore now seems significant to us, not as the founder of the new form of constitutional government, but simply as an important individual, a man who for twenty years provided a measure of stability and quiet. As a young man he had experienced the turmoil of the Revolution and the bitter disputes between Whigs and Tories which had gone on in the reign of Queen Anne. He himself, when a Member of Parliament, had been sent to the Tower because of the savage way in which he had attacked the Tory government in 1711. His main interest in politics now was to quieten things down and, as this coincided with what most English people – at any rate in the governing classes – wanted, he remained in power. He remained in power not because he did things but because he didn't do things. On the few occasions when he attempted to do things he did not succeed. In 1733 when he tried to reform the entire system of taxation, to introduce a universal system of excise, there were disturbances and protests all over the country and Walpole, though supposed to be all-powerful, ran away. The excise scheme was never introduced. He learnt from this not to do things. Nor was he unwilling to be overruled. In 1739 many of his colleagues wished to go to war with Spain. This was the War of Jenkins' Ear. Captain Jenkins was supposed to have had his ear cut off by the Spaniards because he had refused to become a Roman Catholic. He put the ear in a bottle and displayed it before a committee of inquiry at the House of Commons. The nation was swept with enthusiasm into war. Walpole was against the war. He believed that it could produce no satisfactory result, and in any case it would upset the financial balance which he had created. Nevertheless he remained First Lord of the Treasury, he allowed his colleagues to conduct the war and himself tried to contribute to it, though badly.

When in 1742 he was finally turned out, this was not on any issue or principle, it was not because he was opposed to the war while other people wanted to carry it on. It simply was because he seemed to be failing in his powers, because, now that he was an old man, Members of Parliament were more and more restless under his guidance. He was certainly not turned out by any kind of party revolt. There were still in the House of Commons only some forty or fifty Tories. Yet when the attacks on Sir Robert Walpole began, these Tories took no part in them. In fact, broadly speaking, you could say that the Tories probably preferred Sir Robert Walpole to any other Whig and, when the House of Commons actually demonstrated its lack of confidence in Walpole in voting over a trivial matter, the Tory Members of Parliament had already left the House. It was dissident Whigs who showed that they no longer wanted Walpole. And these protests in the House of Commons would have not had the slightest effect had it not been for the fact that George II was also by now doubtful. He thought it might be nice to have a change. In any case, once upon a time Walpole provided a quiet life for the King, and now the King thought he could have a quieter life if he got rid of Walpole. And that is all there is to it.

Walpole's departure from office produced one striking evidence that our politics have changed or at any rate they have become civilized. Previously, the only justification, in theory at any rate, in turning a man out of office was that he had been a traitor or that he had failed in some way to perform his duties. Every leading minister who left office – unless of course he died – but every leading minister who was turned out was afterwards impeached or threatened with prosecution in some other way. There was vague talk of prosecuting Walpole. An inquiry was made into his finances, but it blew over. No prosecution was undertaken. This was startling. Walpole was the first great minister who left office without being prosecuted or punished afterwards. And yet the inquiry would not have been altogether unjustified. Walpole entered office, entered politics as a very humble country gentleman. When he left office he was one of the greatest magnates in the country. He had built himself a palace, he had accumulated a collection of pictures so great that when his son, fifty years later, sold it to Catherine the Great of Russia, it became the foundation of the Hermitage Gallery, where Walpole's pictures can still be seen. Indeed Walpole is the last Prime Minister, with one exception, who left office markedly wealthier than he had entered it. So that we can arrive at this paradoxical conclusion: Walpole was the first Prime Minister who was not prosecuted when he left office; he was perhaps the last Prime Minister who deserved to be prosecuted when he left office.

William Pitt the Younger

William Pitt the Younger (1759–1806). Younger son of the great Earl of Chatham and, in modern British history, the only son of a great man to rise as high as his father. (The first Earl of Salisbury, son of Lord Burleigh, accomplished the same feat at an earlier period.) Educated privately and at Pembroke Hall, Cambridge. MP, 1781–1806. Chancellor of the Exchequer, 1782–3. Prime Minister, 1783–1801 and 1804–6. The younger Pitt was the most competent peace minister of the eighteenth century and the first to present a Budget to the House of Commons. He led Great Britain in the war against revolutionary France, a war which he conducted badly. The income tax is his enduring memorial. Pitt left debts of £37,000, which Parliament paid.

When talking about the younger Pitt, a line of poetry comes into my head:

> The thing to make surrounding nations stare,
> Three kingdoms trusted to a schoolboy's care.

Suddenly this is the most immediately striking thing about William Pitt the Younger. He was far younger as Prime Minister than any other Prime Minister had ever been. He entered office as Chancellor of the Exchequer at twenty-three, became Prime Minister at twenty-four, held office as Prime Minister practically all his life, and died in office as Prime Minister in 1806, when he was only forty-six. You might say that for the whole of his adult life, with one tiny interruption from 1801 to 1804, he was Prime Minister. No one else has managed anything like this.

How did it happen? Here one can give almost a cynical answer: he was the son of his father. William Pitt the Elder, Earl of Chatham, was regarded – perhaps rightly – as the greatest British statesman of the eighteenth century. He had conducted the Seven Years War, the most victorious war in our history, he had added great new territories to the British Empire, he had built up a fame as the only man who could conduct the affairs of the country. In peacetime when he became Prime Minister again in 1766, his achievement had been little. He had broken down and withdrawn from politics and then contributed stirring, wise speeches but little activity. Nevertheless he left a name behind him of unique quality. Indeed, I think you can say he was the greatest British statesman between Oliver Cromwell and Winston Churchill, something of that kind. Whatever his achievements may have been, his reputation certainly was without doubt paramount, and this was the younger Pitt's first and no doubt most important asset. There is no other case in our history where father and son have both been men of superlative achievement and importance.

Of course the younger Pitt was not merely William Pitt the Younger; it was not only the name which brought him to supreme power in 1784. He had been trained by his father from the very beginning for this great position. When young William Pitt was a boy of nearly seven or eight he used to be taken in to his father at dinner and stood on the table in order to make a speech. You might say that he sucked oratory in with his mother's milk. More than this, he staked out his own claim from the very beginning. When he entered the House of Commons, and he did so at the very earliest moment he could, as soon as he was of age, he asserted himself as an individual. He did not belong to a group other than the group of the Pittites, those who had once supported and admired his father and who now transferred their support to him. He claimed to represent an individual patriotism, an individual distinction. He did not co-operate with the other great aristocrats of his time, he did not co-operate with any of the party associations; he always claimed to be, as his father had been before him, the one man who put country before party or before the advantage of any faction.

From the point of view of coming into office, he had one other great advantage, that the political system at the time was in great turmoil. George III had been King ever since 1760 and sought a Prime Minister who, rather in the way that Sir Robert Walpole had done long before, would conduct affairs in a quiet, smooth fashion, keeping people in a good temper, making things easy for the King. There had been, partly because of George's fault, partly because of the fault of others, great disasters. There had been the War of American Independence, the American colonies had been lost. Then there was more restlessness, discontent in the country over political matters than there had been for a century. The King's favourite, if you would like to call him that, the Walpole of the day, Lord North, had given up. He said he really could not go on any longer, he could not conduct affairs, there was too much hostility against him. The hostile politicians, those who had criticized not only Lord North but George III, called themselves Whigs in a different and narrower sense. They claimed to be an actual, specific party, they were out to force themselves on the King as a group. They claimed to dictate to the King who should be ministers and George III, in the disarray which followed the War of American Independence, was compelled to accept them. A whole group of political leaders, distasteful to the King, took over as ministers. They claimed that the King's independent position was at an end, that in future it would be a group, a cabal one might say, of politicians, not the King, who determined who was going to rule the country. The outstanding figure among these men who grasped at power for selfish – and sometimes unselfish – reasons was Charles James Fox. King George hated his position, felt that he was a prisoner; and moreover, once the war was over and peace had been signed, the indignation and restlessness in the country died down. Many people, many Members of Parliament, became uneasy and embarrassed that the King had thus been taken prisoner and had wished to see him liberated. William Pitt took office as Prime Minister in 1783 to liberate the King.

Historians have debated which of the two, the younger Pitt or George III, really kept the control. Whether, as was sometimes said, the younger Pitt came in as a real popular leader in the modern sense, supported in the parliament, supported in the constituencies, supported perhaps even by the party, and therefore George III had really now become simply a constitutional figurehead; or whether, on the other hand, it was George III who had really put William Pitt in and, once things had quietened down, George III reasserted his position which he held before the catastrophe of the American war. The truth seems to lie a bit in between. William Pitt was a new type of Prime Minister. He was stronger, more independent in his position. I do not think this is much to do with organization. Party was still rudimentary. The Pittites, those who consciously supported William Pitt, were still only a small group, thirty or forty of them at most. Even the wider Tory party, which is supposed to have come into existence during the time that Pitt was Prime Minister, was probably not much more than 100 or 150 strong. In any case their Toryism consisted mainly in the desire to hold office, and they would readily follow anyone else who gave them office just as much as the younger Pitt. He was strong because he was more independent in himself. As son of the great Earl of Chatham he had this supreme confidence that he could do things. The Earl of Chatham had once said, 'I know that I can save this country and no one else can.' He was probably justified in this claim. The younger Pitt said exactly the same; whether it was justified or not (I think it was less justified), it gave him a readiness to undertake things, to speak with a voice of authority that few of his predecessors ever had.

On the other hand, George III still counted for a great deal. In the year 1801 there was a dispute between Pitt and George. Pitt had just carried the union of Ireland. He was afraid that the French Revolution, which had taken place some years before, would spread to Ireland also and that it would be difficult for Great Britain, with the war against France on her hands, to keep Ireland down. He believed therefore that there should be a union of the two parliaments and that in exchange for this the Roman Catholics should be, in the phrase of the time, emancipated, that is to say that they should be allowed to take part in politics, that they should not only vote but that they should be allowed to sit in the House of Commons and in the House of Lords. George III was convinced that he was pledged by his coronation oath not to allow any change in the constitution and therefore to oppose Catholic emancipation. And when it came to a dispute between them, George won. George said, 'No, we cannot have Catholic emancipation,' and William Pitt resigned, with the assurance that he would never raise the question again. When he came back as Prime Minister in 1804, he came back recognizing that Catholic emancipation was not an issue which he could ever raise.

George III had powers all right. Of course he too had particular personal assets. Where William Pitt had the asset of his self-confidence, George III had a very peculiar asset, that he was mentally unstable and he could always threaten that if he was badgered by his leading minister he would go out of his mind. This is the threat which he used with regard to Catholic emancipation, that any further argument about Catholic emancipation would send him right out of his mind, he would be put in a strait-jacket and that this would be very inconvenient for the country. (He used this weapon, incidentally, in private also and prevented the marriage of most of his daughters, because he said if any of them got married this would send him out of his mind. At least one of them had her life ruined by it and had to drag on as an old maid.) This was not an abstract threat. It had happened in 1788 and it explains what a hold George III had over Pitt and how he counted. In 1788 George III went out of his mind. It was believed, though wrongly, that he would not recover. His son, George, Prince of Wales, later George IV, was slated to become Regent. And of course, if George, Prince of Wales, became Regent, ruler of the country, he would be able to decide who was Prime Minister. The Prince of Wales was a friend of the Whigs, he was a close friend of Charles James Fox. It was his intention, if he came in, to make Fox Prime Minister. And there was no dispute that he could do it, no dispute that if George became Regent, Pitt was done for. So much for the idea that William Pitt owed his position to a parliamentary majority or even popular support. George III insane, the Prince of Wales Regent, meant that the younger Pitt would have been out and Charles Fox in. To everybody's surprise and very much to Pitt's relief, George III recovered and Charles Fox had to wait another fifteen or so years, until 1806, before he saw office again. But this is a striking illustration that the Crown still counted and that therefore George III's threat of going insane was a catastrophic threat against Pitt. There was, therefore, a balance, more of a balance than there had been earlier. People could not have managed without the approval of George III, but equally George III could not keep himself independent of the politicians (and, to a great extent, of parliamentary interference) without going hand in hand with William Pitt or some other distinguished politician. The Crown could no longer stand aloof from the wrangles of the House of Commons or the great parliamentary discussions, as maybe it could have done in the early part of the century.

As Prime Minister, William Pitt had, you might say, two careers: a distinguished career as a peacetime Prime Minister and a less distinguished, though more famous, career as a wartime Prime Minister. In 1784, when he became Prime Minister, his task was recovery, to bring England back to peace, stability and prosperity after the loss of the American colonies, to get politics quiet, to get the finances in order, to re-establish the authority of Government. He did these things. In a certain sense, the younger Pitt, not Walpole, was the first Prime Minister. He was the first whose primacy was clearly recognized by his colleagues. We can speak of Pitt's government, of his Cabinet, in a way that we cannot speak so readily of the Cabinet of any of his predecessors. Pitt had not the slightest doubt that he presided in Cabinet. This was now a Cabinet which the King did not attend. It was a Cabinet which, somewhat to George III's annoyance, actually took the initiative, considered questions and problems even before the King had asked them to do so. It was a Cabinet which was moving towards the later position when it would be the governing committee of the country; and in this Cabinet, quite clearly, the younger Pitt was, both because of his personality and because of his political position, the dominant, the decisive figure. He not merely took his line over finance, he guided his colleagues in a way that no other Prime Minister had done.

We can speak of Pitt's foreign policy. We cannot speak altogether clearly because he was only fumbling towards it; but when, for instance, the French representatives were negotiating in England just before the outbreak of the war with revolutionary France, these representatives thought it quite as important to see Pitt the Prime Minister as to see the Foreign Secretary or the King, in order to influence what Great Britain would do. The same is true about the conduct of war. It is true about such things as Indian policy and colonial policy. Pitt had a policy with regard to all these things, a policy which he executed not only through his Cabinet colleagues but often independently. He ranks high also in his actual conduct of finance. Pitt ordered, systematized, the finances of this country as no previous First Lord of the Treasury had done. In Pitt's time for the first time the Treasury produced an actual statement of accounts. It is extraordinary that right up to the year 1787, the people of the country, Members of Parliament, even the First Lord of the Treasury itself, had no clear idea how the national finances were doing. You got an impression in time because, if the government was spending more than it got in from taxes, then it would have to borrow from the Bank of England; and on the other hand, if it was getting in income taxes more than it spent, it would pay off debt at the Bank of England. Just like any individual in modern times, this was the only way you could tell whether the final figure was in red or in black. But a proper breakdown of how much they were spending on what, what the taxes were being used for, was never made until the year 1787 when Pitt produced the most sensational thing, a statement of national accounts. Even in his time this was not an annual occurrence. You will have to wait until the year 1823 before what we now call the Budget became a regular feature of political life stated every year. Pitt had taken a vital step towards it.

Men have criticized him later, and some men criticized him at the time, because he had failed – once he became Prime Minister – to carry out the promises which he had given before of great reforms. He had talked of parliamentary reforms; he carried through no parliamentary reforms once he was Prime Minister. I think Pitt would have answered not merely that he would probably have lost office if he had tried to reform parliament but that his being Prime

Minister was itself a proof that parliament did not need to be reformed. If parliament put into power the greatest and most devoted man of the day – and by definition Pitt was this – then obviously this was a perfect parliament. I think that this was too defensive of Pitt, but at any rate this would have been the defence of the day. Pitt at any rate intended to make England more peaceful, more prosperous, to order her finances, to achieve, as he did achieve, great things in peacetime. He was overwhelmed in 1793 by the storm of the war with revolutionary France, and the rest of his life was spent in this war, first with France until 1801, then he was called back to office in 1804 to conduct the war against Napoleon.

He believed, he claimed, that he was also a great war minister. He tried to repeat the successes of his father. From the record, a record of failure and defeat, his claim was exaggerated. The revolutionary war was, from the British point of view, a disastrous war. A war in which Great Britain only just managed to survive and, although in the war against Napoleon which started in 1804 Pitt chose Nelson, placed him in command of the fleet, sent Nelson off to win the battle of Trafalgar, even here his diplomacy was a total failure. At the end, in 1806, there was nothing left. In 1806, when Pitt died, all his alliances on the continent had crumbled, Great Britain was in isolation, she had to face long years of holding out alone while Napoleon dominated Europe. This is hardly a successful record, and where we examine in detail the campaigns which the younger Pitt conducted we will say that he had none of the warlike genius of his father.

What was the war about? Pitt claimed to be fighting for the liberties of Europe. What he was fighting for was the liberties of princes and for the aristocracy. The decision to go to war with revolutionary France in 1793 was a catastrophe for free principles. Charles James Fox opposed the war with revolutionary France. He argued that you can't go to war against principles, that it was only the war which was driving France to terror. He preached all along that the government of this country would never have needed to go to war if it was firmly based on popular support. It was, he said, a mockery and hypocrisy that the British government should be claiming to fight for freedom and at the same time suspending habeas corpus, shutting people up in prison without any kind of trial, and persecuting reformers. Pitt, even if he had intended to go on being a reformer, destroyed all possibilities of reform in this country for many years because he had swung England on to the side of absolutism, monarchy and despotism. The causes which he claimed to serve perished in the war which he insisted on fighting. And at the end of his life, living in self-despair, he thought that everything had been destroyed, that he had lost the war. According to one story his last words were, 'My country, how I leave my country.' There is, however, another and, I think, more likely story recorded by Disraeli. The refreshment room at the House of Commons was at that time run by a man called Bellamy, and in Disraeli's version Pitt's last words were, 'I think I could eat one of Bellamy's meat pies.'

Benjamin Disraeli

Benjamin Disraeli (1804–81). Son of a Jewish man of letters. Mainly self-educated. Himself the author of frivolous romantic novels, which can still be read with pleasure. Began politically as a Radical and never became wholly respectable. MP 1837–76. Led the attack on Peel over the repeal of the Corn Laws, 1846. Led the Conservative Opposition in the House of Commons from 1849 onwards. Chancellor of the Exchequer in Conservative (minority) governments, 1852, 1858–9 and 1866–8. Carried household suffrage, 1867. Prime Minister, 1868 and 1874–80. Made Queen Victoria Empress of India. She made him Earl of Beaconsfield, 1876. Brought back Peace with Honour, 1878.

You may know the story of the man who saw a giraffe and said, 'There ain't no such animal.' This, I think, is the only adequate comment that one can make about Benjamin Disraeli, at the end of his life Earl of Beaconsfield. There are perhaps important general things in Disraeli's career, which indeed I have tried to discover, but the most remarkable thing about Disraeli is Disraeli himself. The way in which he refuses to fit into any of the patterns of the age – or indeed of any age. He was for much of his life the leader of the Conservative party – the party which was called 'the party of the gentlemen of England'. His colleagues in the Cabinet were all great landowners. He himself moved, so far as he moved in society at all, in the society of aristocrats.

And yet no man belonged less to the society of Victorian England. He was, first of all, by birth certainly not English. He was of Jewish origin; he was a baptized Christian, though he never troubled himself very much about this. He had no conventional education. Where every other Prime Minister, until David Lloyd George, had been to one of the older universities – with the exception of the Duke of Wellington, but obviously the Duke of Wellington belonged to the aristocracy – Disraeli went to no university. He had no background of the ordinary social kind. He had no wealth; well, he had a certain amount of money from his father but really a triviality, for most of his life indeed he was heavily in debt. It was only when he married a wealthy widow that he managed to escape the danger of being imprisoned for debt. And even after that, when he was a leading politician, most of the furniture in his house was already mortgaged, marked off, pledged because of the great debts which he had accumulated, and it is said that he never freed himself from debt to the very end of his life. He managed to acquire fairly late in life some landed estate, but he only did it by borrowing from one of his aristocratic friends and you cannot say that it was ever really his.

He was a man indeed who exaggerated, if that were possible, his own differences. He looked different. He appeared in the most exotic clothes. He was a dandy of the time. He had heavy black ringlets which hung down on to his shoulders. He spoke in an exaggerated, almost foreign drawl. He was never ashamed to say the most paradoxical things about his behaviour. He made it clear to his wife, who was much older than he was, that he had married her for her money, and yet at the same time he treated her with such attention and courtesy that he was able to say, 'You've been more a mistress than a wife to me.' Which of these were true it would be impossible to say. What is certainly true is that she was devoted to him and that he on his side derived strength from her care and attention which kept him going. Yet again, unlike most public men he did not like public life. Oh, he liked a battle at the House of Commons all right, and he liked scoring political success, he liked saying clever things; but he didn't like social life. He was that very rare thing, at any rate in this country, a man who was happy only in the society of women. Men's society, men's clubs – and after all the House of Commons was the greatest club of the time – bored him; he found no satisfaction in them. He was not interested in exchanging ideas or gossip or anything of that kind with other men. Public dinners, all the grandeur of public life, were not at all for him except purely as matters of display.

Then again, if we ask: what was he? Before he built himself up in politics, what had he to show? He was a successful, flashy novelist. I use the term 'flashy' because I think it's the only one that describes his books. They are still readable, though they are at the same time extremely trivial; no one could take them seriously as pictures of politics, as pictures of human beings, or as pictures of society. They are full of brilliant remarks, of fantasies. We could almost compare them, although they are not of the same level, with the twentieth-century novels of Evelyn Waugh. They are that far remote from real life. And it was these flashy, frivolous novels with which Disraeli first made his name.

In politics he first made his name, or first attempted to break into politics, as a Radical. In the early days after the great Reform Act, radical creeds urging further and more extreme reform, denouncing the aristocracy for maintaining their control over the state, commanded wide attention, and Disraeli was one of the most extreme radical writers. His early novels are in a sense radical tracts, although this is mixed up with all kinds of aristocratic romanticism. He attempted to get into Parliament as a Radical. It was only when he failed that he then attempted to get into Parliament as a Conservative. And he succeeded. He was – I cannot say an obscure back-bencher, nobody can say that Disraeli was ever obscure – but he was certainly a back-bencher without influence.

When in 1841 Peel formed his second Conservative government, Disraeli wrote abjectly asking for a post. Peel did not even answer him. It did not occur to Peel that Disraeli was a man of any importance. Nor indeed would he have been, except for an extraordinary event. The Conservative party stood for protection and in particular for the Corn Laws, which imposed tariffs on foreign corn in order to benefit the landed proprietors of this country. In the year 1845 Peel decided that the Corn Laws were wrong, that they must be repealed, that free trade must be established. This was a repudiation of some basic things that the Conservative party stood for. Nevertheless Peel's prestige was so great – he had been Prime Minister for years, he was the outstanding statesman at the time – that it looked as if he would carry his reluctant followers with him. Disraeli seized this opportunity and it was in his attacks on Peel that he first came to the front. And the gentlemen of England found themselves cheering this strange character and being led by him in order to defend the Corn Laws. Again, this is characteristic of Disraeli. He was not interested in the Corn Laws at all. A year or two later, when he had established himself more or less at the head of the Conservative party, he was publicly willing to say that this was a closed issue and that free trade was here for good. He never understood the arguments either for free trade or against them, or if he understood them he had no interest in them. What he disliked or claimed to dislike in Peel was lack of consistency. Free trade should be carried, yes, but it should be carried by a Liberal government, not by a Conservative one. This, I think, was the most important contribution which Disraeli made to our political history: the concept of a fully two-party system. Up to that time, men, even when they were out of office, were a bit ashamed to oppose what was called the King's or the Queen's Government. Opposition seemed, not quite treasonable of course, but seditious or at any rate disloyal. Now it was Disraeli who first fully formulated the idea that the function of an opposition is to oppose, that there should be clear-cut lines of distinction between the parties. If the Liberal party stands for one thing, the Conservative party stands for the other, and the prime duty of a politician, of a statesman, is therefore both to form a party and then to be loyal to the things that it stands for.

If we take the case of Peel, the Conservative party stood for the Corn Laws. Peel therefore had a duty to defend them. If he became convinced that the Corn Laws were wrong then it was simply his duty to withdraw from public life, but certainly not to lead his party into doing the opposite of what previously it had stood for. It was this doctrine of party consistency which Disraeli preached. Of course the idea of loyalty to the party, the idea that men should stand together, that they should be able to rely on each other to carry out a policy, if only they knew what it was, was attractive particularly to back-benchers. The back-bencher is less likely to be persuaded at any time by high considerations of reason or the needs of public policy. He understands crude simple issues, he is for the Corn Laws or whatever it may be, and he expects his leaders to be as simple and straightforward as himself. Disraeli, the most complicated figure of the nineteenth century, presented himself as the simple, straightforward leader of the English country gentlemen, not only back-benchers but one might say backwoodsmen, and he secured the leadership of the Conservative party simply because he was ready to defend its interests, to put the needs of party first all the time, to appear as an avowed leader of the opposition so that, whatever the government was doing, Disraeli would stand up and tear it to pieces. This of course was an enormously enjoyable role, particularly for an intellectual, and Disraeli, I think, comes in this category. The intellectuals are destructive, it is much easier to criticize. There is in Disraeli's speeches a wonderful anthology of destructive remarks. I think it is true that there are more quotations from Disraeli than from any other British statesman in all our dictionaries of quotations. He was always saying clever things, but they were all destructive things. They were all about how mistaken or foolish or confused the other people are.

Leadership of the party did not bring Disraeli to high office, or at least not for a long time. The Conservative party of the mid-nineteenth century had got stuck with a single interest, the interest of the landed classes. And even this interest was not desperately at stake. The Liberal governments at the time carried measures which, though they were not exclusively in the interests of the landed class, were making Great Britain more prosperous. The idea of an England run solely by the territorial aristocracy had been jettisoned even by most members of the aristocracy. Disraeli seemed to represent a romantic, decaying idea, a sort of political Jacobitism. His justification, and he put this forward often in his writings, was that to act at all he must have a hard, consolidated party behind him. And if this meant many years of minority position where, if he got into office at all (as he did as Chancellor of the Exchequer in 1852 and again in 1858), it was only in a minority government, this was worth while because, unless a statesman had a hard and united party behind him, you could never move forward. It was in this conception of making the party a solid organized thing, building it up in terms of organization and finance, of co-operation, the readiness of one man to work in with another, that Disraeli was important. Disraeli's Conservative party was the first which had real party funds, which had a central organization, which began to treat politics as a national affair which could be run from a centre. At a time when the Liberal party was hard put to it to raise £20,000 for a general election, the Conservative party could always pull in £100,000 by means of the organization which Disraeli had built up.

Disraeli had another tactic, another thing, which made him interesting and important. He was the only nineteenth-century statesman, I think, or certainly the outstanding nineteenth-century statesman in this country, who analysed politics not just in terms of ideas and principles but in terms of class. It was Disraeli who said: 'Liberalism is middle class. If therefore we give the vote to the working class they will go with the aristocracy, the party above the middle class, just as the workers are the party below.' This was why he himself carried working-class suffrage in 1867, what his then leader, Lord Derby, called 'a leap in the dark'; and six years later, seven years later in 1874 he was rewarded. The Conservatives then won their first majority since the time of Peel in 1841.

Disraeli became Prime Minister for the second time. He had been Prime Minister for a short time in 1868. This time he had a great majority behind him. He actually made two remarks when he became Prime Minister. The first was characteristic. Whereas Gladstone, when he became Prime Minister, talked about great public policies and his mission to do this or that, Disraeli merely said in a light-hearted way, 'Well, I've climbed to the top of the greasy pole.' His other remark was sadder; he said, 'Power has come to me too late. Once I could have reshaped empires, now I am old.' Whether he really could have reshaped empires when he was younger it would be difficult to decide.

He showed little in the nature of a constructive planned policy. He was a man of expedience, and the excuse that he was too old, that he had lost his zest, is one which he would have had to make, perhaps, in any case. This is not to say that Disraeli's government of 1874 was without importance. It was important in itself, it broke the long run of the Liberal governments and Liberal majorities. It showed that British politics were taking a different form. It vindicated after thirty years Disraeli's argument in favour of the two-party system. For the first time, when one party had become discredited, feeble, confused, another party was able to present itself, as it were, ready-made, not on the ruins of the old, but simply as an alternative to the other one, and to say, 'Well, we are ready to take over, with new men, fresh men, new ideas.' Whether the claim was justified or not, the existence of this second party was really established in 1874 and set the pattern for most of British politics thereafter.

Moreover, Disraeli's programme was not all pretence. When he talked about winning working-class votes he did not think solely in terms of class resentments. He was more receptive than Liberals to the policy of social reform. Liberalism was still an individualistic, a negative creed. Disraeli was able to envisage the mass of people as part of the community and to do things for them. The early years of Disraeli's government, 1874 to 1876, were marked by the first great advances in social reform in terms of welfare, in terms of housing and doing various other things for the mass of poor people. The trade unions, for instance, were given by Disraeli a privileged position which they still maintain. I am perfectly prepared to say that this was the first government genuinely sympathetic to the poor and needy as a distinctive element of society which Great Britain had held. This was one element of Disraeli's policy, the policy of welfare.

The other element, which in his speeches had been in the nature of window-dressing, was imperial grandeur. In terms of words Disraeli was the first imperial statesman of the nineteenth century, the first one who talked about the British Empire rather than simply the United Kingdom and the politics we conduct in this country. In practical terms his actions did not amount to much. Disraeli's imperialism was shelved. The only mark which he left in imperial history was to give the Queen the title 'Empress of India'. Nothing was changed except the title. Great Britain had been directly ruling India ever since the Indian mutiny and the Queen had been Queen of India too – but this was something just like Disraeli's clothes, his diamonds and his ringlets: the title 'Empress' was to give a glitter to the idea of empire. In terms of real colonial expansion or bringing the empire together, Disraeli contributed nothing. He bought, it is true, a majority or a considerable number of shares in the Suez Canal and this has often been pointed to as a beginning of imperialism in Egypt. Maybe it was, but very much only at the beginning. The significance of this has been overrated. It was more as a gesture than anything else.

To his surprise he was involved in a great crisis of foreign affairs. None of this had any solid background. You cannot trace a tradition in Disraeli's policy. He grabbed at an opportunity of display. He wanted to show that Great Britain was an independent power. He opposed Russia because he was fascinated with the glamour of the East. He moved fleets and sent Indian troops to Malta, not because any practical British interests were at stake but because these were sensational, glamorous things to do. When he was at the Congress of Berlin in 1878 he told Bismarck how he was planning to acquire Cyprus, and Bismarck said to him, 'Splendid, that is progress.' You see, these two old scamps, sitting around grabbing other people's territories, thought this was progress because it showed off, it hit the headlines. Everything that Disraeli did was designed in terms of sensation. When he came back from the Congress of Berlin he coined the famous phrase that this was 'peace with honour'. Well, really it did not amount to very much. The Congress of Berlin settled a relatively trivial issue for a relatively short time, but it was a sensational thing. It soon ran out. The last years of his government were marred by sensations which did not come off, by confusions in South Africa and by an aggressive war in Afghanistan. And in 1880 the Conservatives were defeated. At the end of his life Disraeli had only the consolation that he had done these sensational things, that, whether or not he had permanently altered the face of the British Empire, he had established the two-party system and that – what he perhaps attached most importance to – he had won the heart of Queen Victoria. I do not believe for a moment that this was of any political significance. But it is undoubtedly true that Queen Victoria rated Disraeli above all her other Prime Ministers and that Disraeli paid her with an exaggerated affection, respect; as he said, 'When you come to royalty you must lay on flattery with a trowel.' It was not only with royalty that Disraeli did this; when he came to any political issue he laid it on with a trowel, and he left therefore, if not solid achievements, a glitter, a sparkle, a demonstration which keeps his name alive.

W. E. Gladstone

*William Ewart Gladstone (1809–98). Son of a Liverpool merchant
who was also a considerable slave-owner. Educated at Eton and
Christ Church, Oxford. MP 1832–94. Started as a High Churchman and High Tory. Remained a High Churchman but ended
politically as a Radical. President of the Board of Trade in Peel's
Conservative government 1843–5. Followed Peel over Free Trade.
Chancellor of the Exchequer 1852–5 in coalition government of
Aberdeen. Refused to join Palmerston in 1855, did so in 1859 and
became Chancellor of Exchequer 1859–66. Liberal Prime Minister
1868–74. Retired from politics in 1875 and wrote theological
works. Returned to politics because of the eastern crisis. Prime
Minister 1880–85, and again in 1886. Failed to carry Home Rule.
Prime Minister 1892–4. Home Rule carried in Commons and
defeated in Lords. Resigned and left politics, 1894. Returned briefly
to politics because of the Armenian atrocities, 1896. Buried in
Westminster Abbey.*

William Ewart Gladstone was the greatest political figure of the
nineteenth century. I do not mean by that he was necessarily the
greatest statesman, certainly not the most successful. What I mean is
that he dominated the scene. When Victorians particularly thought
about political life they thought about what they called 'Mr G' or,
later on, 'the People's William' as the outstanding figure. This was
after all because he was a great man, he stood in stature and in
character above all his contemporaries. It was also because, of
course, he stood there for a very long time. No man has played a

leading role in politics for as long as he did. When he entered parliament, the Reform Act had only just begun to operate. When he last attended parliament in 1894, David Lloyd George was already an MP. So the two men together straddle all our political history from 1832 until 1945.

Another extraordinary thing about Gladstone was that he started as a High Tory, he finished as a Radical. Many men have taken the opposite course. Gladstone was almost alone in going increasingly radical, increasingly extreme, as he advanced into old age. His Tory period is not interesting to us. This is a period when he was a young man. He came from the merchant class. His father was a wealthy Liverpool merchant. Gladstone himself was educated at Eton and at Christ Church, Oxford. He had the scholarly distinctions of somebody of the old style, distinguished in Classics, distinguished in Mathematics. He had been in politics for a very short time when he began to move away from High Toryism to a more modern Conservatism. Under Peel, Gladstone became a Free Trader, and it was in economic matters in regard to free trade, in regard to taxation, that Gladstone first came to the front. In the early 1860s, when he held high office as Chancellor of the Exchequer, he made an enduring contribution to our life. The Gladstonian budget, the idea of a full statement of accounts every year, the strict balancing of the Budget on the basis of the economy, the belief that taxation, though inevitable, was a necessary evil, these things really dominated our financial system and most of our political life for eighty years thereafter, and it was only in the stresses of the Second World War that Gladstonian finance, with all its rigidity, was finally abandoned.

This, though striking and important, would make Gladstone merely a figure of historical significance. We should pick him out as the representative Victorian of the middle nineteenth century. There were many others of the same type, none of them perhaps so able, so rigorous, none perhaps so distinguished in personality; but he was not a man who stood apart from others of his generation. This was a highly educated, conscientious type of man, most of them High Churchmen, most of them either from the upper classes or upper-middle class, who came into the service of the state in the middle of the nineteenth century. Though men sometimes wondered where Gladstone's drive and personality would finally carry him, they hardly envisaged, I think, in the middle years of the 1860s exactly where Gladstone would be swept along, where he would carry so much of the country with him. These men were changing, not so much their outlook, but their political name. In the earlier nineteenth century, in the 1840s, they, like Gladstone, called themselves Conservatives. This was already a breach with Toryism. They were no longer reactionaries. By conservatism they meant ordered, cautious progress. The Conservative party, at the time when Peel founded it in the 1830s, aimed to combine all those who had a stake in the country, mill-owners as much as landowners, capitalists as much as members of the aristocracy. It was a party of resistance to wild and radical change, but it was certainly also a party of cautious reform.

By the 1860s most of these moderate Conservatives were changing their names and also their outlook. They were becoming Liberals. Now Liberal, too, was a moderate word. It was a word which had been coined earlier in the century in distinction to radicalism. Whereas radicalism stood for extreme, impatient, sometimes inconsiderate reform, Liberals were those who reformed always with the idea of maintaining the constitutional structure and the existing class order of society. The Liberals were essentially the creation of a middle-class industrial community, where the industrial leaders themselves were no longer in conflict with the old order but were beginning to co-operate with it as long as the old order on its side was prepared to change. Liberalism in the 1860s was a creed which could embrace men from the aristocracy down to, shall we say, trade-union leaders. Its old political leaders, with the exception of Gladstone, were usually aristocrats: Lord Palmerston, Earl Russell, and many others of old families. They accepted Gladstone, not because he was different, but because he had the most powerful personality and drive.

After the Second Reform Bill in 1867, Gladstone conducted a passionate campaign in the general election. Despite the fears that newly enfranchised workers would vote Conservative in order to vote against their employers, Gladstone won the majority of working-class constituencies and established his first Liberal government. Indeed, in a sense, though this may sound paradoxical, Gladstone's government (which lasted from 1868 to 1874) was the only purely Liberal government in our history, 'the one which concerned itself with measures of administrative and judicial reform. His government had a record second to none in the changes which it carried out in the administration of law, establishment of a ballot, the disestablishment of the Irish Church. None of these were things which struck at the roots of the existence of society. Indeed, none of them were things which greatly appealed to radical opinion. Gladstone seemed to be performing his essential function, the function of Liberalism, which was that of moderate reform in a stable society. These moderate reforms, carried out in great number, particularly between 1868 and 1872, seemed to have exhausted the Liberal programme. Indeed it was common throughout Europe – in Germany, Italy and France – that the party of moderate Liberals, the party that was essentially appealing to the educated classes and successful only in a limited electorate, ran down, and in most European countries the Liberal party in this narrower sense either disappeared altogether or at any rate dwindled into a small faction. Gladstone himself in 1874 believed that his purely Liberal work was done and a year later, after the Liberals had lost the 1874 general election, he resigned the leadership of the party and announced that he was withdrawing into private life in order to pursue theological studies. If he had done this he would have had a considerable reputation, he would have ranked with Peel as a great Prime Minister, but he would not have had the unique importance which came to him really only in extreme old age. It was in the years after he had passed the age of seventy that Gladstone acquired a new character.

What swept him back into public life was an issue of foreign affairs, the so-called Bulgarian horrors, when in 1876 the Turks attempting to restore order in the Ottoman Empire massacred some 12,000 Bulgarians. Gladstone was induced by Radicals to return to public life – not, he claimed, as a leader, purely as agitator, as a speaker. It was at this time that he began to make the great public orations for which he was famous. Indeed, he initiated this practice.

Before his time great statesmen never spoke in public – they spoke only in the House of Commons or to selected gatherings. It was Gladstone who first addressed the mass meetings in the way that demagogic orators in the past have done. And it was Gladstone's campaign that swept the country, disturbed, provoked the Tories, hindered their foreign policy; and in 1880, apparently against his will, Gladstone was once more returned as Prime Minister. This time he held office not with a purely Liberal party or majority, but with a party into which the new Radicals, such as Chamberlain and Dilke, had pushed themselves forward and were seeking to carry out a much more democratic, a much more ruthless programme. And in this government (which lasted from 1880 to 1885) Gladstone occupied an equivocal position. He was there really because he had caught the Radical temper and yet he spent most of his time opposing the ideas which the Radicals put forward. Few governments in our history really have had a feebler record: the things which the Radicals wanted to do Gladstone thwarted, the things which the Liberals wanted to do, as indeed Gladstone himself was aware, had already been done. Gladstone seemed to be occupying a position of negation, straddling between the Liberals and the Radicals, irritating them both and being irritated by them both. A man of power who had become powerless and ineffective.

His most important act in this second government was one which in retrospect was highly unwelcome to him. It was the occupation of Egypt by British forces in 1882. This inaugurated the late-Victorian policy of imperialism. It is strange to think that Gladstone, a man who disliked imperialism both because he thought we ought not to conquer other nations and even more because he thought it was expensive, was the man who started the process.

In 1885 he was once again, what Disraeli had called him previously, 'an exhausted volcano'. Now came the last, most dramatic turn of his career. Throughout both of his ministries Ireland had been in a disturbed state. Gladstone had offered concessions. He had disestablished the Irish Protestant Church. He had brought in new measures of land reform which gave the Irish peasants greater security. The basic thing which the Irish wanted was a measure of national freedom, the programme called (in the phrase of the time)

'Home Rule'. Gladstone had opposed this, he had opposed Parnell, he had put Parnell in prison. But he now became convinced that only Home Rule would satisfy the Irish and, though it might not be such a tidy or efficient solution as those that had been put forward before, it would be a more enduring solution because it would command the goodwill of the people of Ireland. Even now, in his equivocal way Gladstone did not openly advocate Home Rule. He hoped indeed, strange as this may seem, that a Conservative government would carry Home Rule and that he would merely appear behind the scenes to give it his blessing. His calculation failed. The Conservatives turned against him. In the general election held in November 1885 the Liberals once more were the biggest party, but the Conservatives with the Irish Nationalists held an equal number of seats.

Without warning Gladstone sprang on his followers the announcement that he had been converted to Home Rule. In his arrogance – there was in him a hardness, a belief in his own power and righteousness, which made it easy for him to sweep others aside – in his self-confidence he believed that Liberals who had always opposed Home Rule, who had been led by Gladstone to oppose Home Rule, would at a sign from him turn around. The first Home Rule Bill, which he drafted entirely alone, without any assistance from his colleagues, without any assistance from official advisers, produced one of the most famous battles ever fought in the House of Commons. Gladstone was deserted not only by his more moderate followers, he was deserted by some of the Radicals. Joseph Chamberlain, who had been the outstanding Radical, turned against Home Rule partly because he disliked the idea of breaking up the United Kingdom, but more, I think, out of jealousy of Gladstone. Here was this old man who had hampered radicalism in the past now coming forward with a radical solution which would interfere with Chamberlain's own leadership. Chamberlain hoped to drive Gladstone out of politics and substitute himself as Radical leader. He failed.

The Liberal party split asunder. Home Rule was defeated. The majority of Liberals followed Gladstone into opposition; a minority went with Chamberlain, took the title of Unionist Liberals and co-operated with the Conservatives. Gladstone by this time was nearly eighty, he was always saying that he wanted to withdraw from public life but that as long as Home Rule was not achieved he was determined to stay there. And so we have this extraordinary epilogue to his career when Gladstone found a new cause to fight for, a cause which he fought for much harder than he had ever fought for anything else; and in his zest for Home Rule he became radical on every other issue. If he could only win working-class votes for Home Rule by promising them social reform – a thing which he had always disliked, he called it constructivism and had never approved of it – then he was prepared to promise social reform. With these promises Gladstone pulled the working class, or a considerable part of it, back to support the Liberal party.

When we look forward to the early twentieth century, we find the Liberal party still surviving, largely with working-class votes, associated with social reform; what indeed was called at the time a Lib-Lab party, a coalition of Liberals and Labour. It was Gladstone, strangely, who created it, but not at all for purposes of social reform. He created this solely for the purposes of Home Rule. This tactic gave him a final government from 1892 to 1894, when he once more attempted to carry a Home Rule Bill, and he actually carried it through the House of Commons but it was defeated in the House of Lords. Gladstone wanted to challenge the House of Lords at a general election. His colleagues, who knew that there was no enthusiasm for Home Rule in the country, refused. Gladstone was angry and hostile to all his Cabinet; he often prevented it from meeting. He was even angrier when they proposed to increase the expenditure on the navy because public expenditure, in particular expenditure on arms, was the thing which most aroused his own Liberal conscience. And it was on this issue, in protest against the increased armament bill, that Gladstone resigned in the early days of 1894. Back to theological studies, as he supposed. Even then politics did not leave him alone. As late as 1896, when he was deaf and almost blind, he appeared on the public platforms to thunder against the ruler of Turkey, Abdul the Dammed as he was called, because of a new bout of massacres, Armenian this time.

John Morley, his devoted disciple, asked Gladstone once for an explanation of his career. Gladstone said this: 'I was brought up to fear and detest liberty. I came to love it. That is the secret of my whole career.' This was a noble epitaph, and in a sense a true one. But on another occasion Gladstone gave a more cynical explanation. When Morley asked him, 'Why, Mr G, did you hang on in politics so long, when you were eighty-four and exhausted, when you had earned the right to retirement? Why were you still battling every night in the House of Commons and subduing the greatest political masters of the day?' Gladstone opened his eyes in surprise and said: 'Why, to keep Joseph Chamberlain out of the leadership of the Liberal party.' This was the combination which made him a great and a strange man, a man full of noble ideas but also of personal animosities. A man who at any rate, for good or ill, changed the history of the nineteenth century and established a great Liberal party which was to be a dominating force in our political life from the 1860s until the days of the First World War, when it crumbled apart and was superseded by Labour as the second party in the state.

David Lloyd George

David Lloyd George (1863–1945). Born in Manchester. Brought up in North Wales by shoemaker uncle. Educated at Church of England primary school. Liberal MP for Caernarvon Boroughs 1890–1945. Opposed the Boer War and was nearly lynched at Birmingham Town Hall. President of the Board of Trade 1905–8 under Campbell-Bannerman. Chancellor of the Exchequer under Asquith 1908–15. Introduced People's Budget, 1909, and Health Insurance, 1911. At first reluctant to enter First World War, then supported it wholeheartedly. Minister of Munitions, 1915–16. Secretary for War, 1916. Overthrew Asquith and became head of coalition government 1916–22. Won the war and made the peace. Conducted civil war in Ireland and then settled Irish question, 1921. Overthrown in 1922 when Conservatives left coalition. Returned to Asquith's leadership, 1923. Quarrelled with him over general strike in 1926 and replaced him as Liberal leader. Offered constructive programme against unemployment, 1929. Refused to join National government 1931. Opposed appeasement before Second World War. Refused to join Churchill's National government. Created Earl Lloyd-George, 1945.

Lloyd George. By the way, that is a curious thing – about his name. His name was George. When he came into politics he was first known as George. Those who disliked him – many Tories, for instance – always used to refer to him as Mr George. He himself very much disliked this. He himself wanted to be called Lloyd George. Anyone who wanted to win his favour had to call him

Lloyd George. All his life he pushed this out, and at the end of his life he won; when he became an Earl in 1945 he slipped in the hyphen. So after eighty years of struggling to be called Lloyd George, he was in fact entitled to do so. George or Lloyd George was the greatest British statesman in the twentieth century.

Winston Churchill said, when the history of the first quarter of this century comes to be written it will be found that we owe more to Lloyd George than to any other one man. And we can say not only in the first quarter of the century, even at the present day, many of our modern institutions, the welfare state itself, we owe to Lloyd George. Health insurance, the National Health Service – Lloyd George; unemployment insurance – Lloyd George; housing as a public service – Lloyd George; Ireland as a contented and reasonably friendly neighbour – Lloyd George; the victory of the First World War – Lloyd George, the Man Who Won the War.

Lloyd George was a unique figure in British politics. The man who walked alone. He said himself, 'There is no friendship at the top,' and certainly that was true in his case. He had no associates who stuck to him all through, and he stuck to none. He was his own creation, far more than anyone else in modern times, a Prime Minister who rose because of his own merits, character, drive, and not because of party organization or even class associations. Lloyd George was a man of the people. There has been only one other Prime Minister of similar humble origin, and that was Ramsay MacDonald – but Ramsay MacDonald owed his rise to the Labour movement as much as the Labour movement owed its success to Ramsay MacDonald. Lloyd George was not associated with a movement; even though he called himself a man of the people, his was in a much wider and, in a sense, a less effective way. When Lloyd George talked about the people he did not mean – as one would expect anyone to mean in the modern industrial Great Britain of the twentieth century – the organized working classes. Lloyd George meant by the people shopkeepers like his own uncle, who brought him up. Men certainly of humble origin, but not in our modern sense formal, organized classes. Here too he stood alone.

Lloyd George was an exception to almost every rule. He had very little formal education. He had no interests outside politics.

He talked politics, thought politics, read politics. His only diversion was found in wild western thrillers. In comparison with other prime ministers he was not a man of wide general culture, he was the only Prime Minister, I suppose, we have ever had who spoke a native language (Welsh) other than English. He came from a remote part of Wales, not industrial South Wales but remote, backward, agricultural North Wales. He fought and pushed his way forward and in time, with the organization of parties and the developing strength of class feeling, Lloyd George felt himself left alone. In name he was a Liberal, and yet he had few connections with the Liberal party which existed in the early twentieth century. He did not belong to one of the great Liberal families. He was relatively uninterested in the ordinary Liberal ideas: the ideas of free trade, free enterprise, of standing aside. Lloyd George was an organizer, a man who wanted to do things, not a man who wanted to pull government away from activities. Yet at the same time he was an organizer without system. No man has done so much in modern political life with so few ideas to start with. He had no ideas except the idea of creation and activity. There are two striking instances which come to mind.

One is the origins of the health system, a great revolutionary act. You can imagine how this would happen in the ordinary way. People wanting to introduce national health insurance, there would have been committees of inquiry, material would have been assembled for months, perhaps for years, there would have been research papers submitted and so on. Not with Lloyd George. He commissioned a civil servant, Braithwaite, to visit Germany for three days, a country where there was an advanced system of social security. After three days in Germany, Braithwaite travelled to Nice in the south of France, where Lloyd George was on holiday. Lloyd George greeted him, took him out on to the front, they sat down (says Braithwaite), not too near the band, and Lloyd George said, 'Tell us all about it.' Braithwaite described for four hours how the thing worked in Germany. At the end of that time Lloyd George said, 'That's enough, I've got the whole thing.' He went back, devised a system all alone, produced a most elaborate Bill, carried it single-handed through the House of Commons, and the National

Health system was established as it remains, with certain modifications, to the present day. One four-hour conversation on the front at Nice.

Another example is the Ministry of Munitions, created in the First World War to provide munitions, particular shells, for the British Army. When Lloyd George entered the hotel which had been taken over as his headquarters, he found, he said, 'one table, three chairs, far too many mirrors and no secretaries'. Four years later, at the end of the war, a Minister of Munitions was employing a staff of over 200,000 civil servants and he had under his control something like three million workers. All created out of nothing, out of this empty hotel. Everything, you might say, with Lloyd George was created out of nothing until his energies began to play upon it. Most of our modern ministries, in many ways our modern system of government, was created by Lloyd George. When he came in he found a sleepy, amateurish system of Cabinet government. He himself was always restless under it, an unsatisfactory Cabinet minister. He gained his first appointment on the eve of the great Liberal victory of 1906, a victory which was based essentially on free trade. This was not a topic which profoundly interested him. He wished to move forward.

As Chancellor of the Exchequer in 1909 he introduced what is still known, perhaps with some exaggeration, as the 'People's Budget'. The first time, perhaps, when taxation had been deliberately designed in order to transform the social order, designed, effectively or not, as an attack on the rich and particularly on the landlords. It was the people's budget which provoked the conflict of the House of Lords and the great constitutional crisis which lasted from 1909 to 1911. But here again, Lloyd George was not particularly interested in the political conflict of the House of Lords, he was far more interested in the attack on the landlords and on the deliberate transfers of wealth from the rich to the poor. In 1911, soon after the height of the House of Lords crisis, he was busy piloting the Health Bill through the House of Commons.

He distinguished himself in the Liberal government in another way. He was the first minister who took an active part in settling industrial disputes. Before, of course, governments had intervened to bring strikes to an end because these strikes were disrupting the life of the nation. But the ministers who did this had acted only as aloof, impartial mediators, standing far above the battle trying to persuade the employers and the men to come together. Lloyd George took a far more active part when he settled the railway strike in 1911, the mining strike in 1912. He was himself on the side of the workers. After he had received a deputation of owners, all still carrying their top hats, and then a deputation of trade-union leaders with their cloth caps, he said to one of his civil servants, 'I know which side I'm on.' He was quite prepared to diddle, to manoeuvre the trade-union leaders, the owners. He was quite clear that the only way of producing a quieter, more settled industrial life was that there should be very great concessions to the working class.

The great surprise of Lloyd George's career is that he made his reputation as a man of war. In origin his first great period of independent fame was when he opposed the Boer War and, above all other Liberals (or Radicals, as they were often called), Lloyd George was distinguished as the anti-war statesman. In 1914, when war drew near, Lloyd George was the most emphatic that there was no real reason for conflict with Germany. It was expected to the last moment that he would oppose the war, that he would resign from the government. Even when, over the German invasion of Belgium, he dropped his opposition he did not for some weeks come out wholeheartedly in support of the war. When he did, his whole character and standing was changed. Instead of being the man who had opposed the war or instead of becoming the man who might have half-heartedly supported it, as so many Liberals did, Lloyd George, once he changed over, became thoroughly committed. In the Liberal government under Asquith and then in the coalition government which Asquith formed in 1915, Lloyd George was the driving force to use new methods, however ruthless, in order to carry the war on. His objections of principle were abandoned, no doubt because for him principles were far less important than achievement. Other Liberals groaned at the interference with industry, they groaned at the interference with financial policy, they groaned first of all at military compulsion. Lloyd George took the lead in all these things. He believed that the people of this country wanted to fight the war and therefore that it was his job to ensure that the war should be fought effectively.

At the end of 1916, many people believed that the war was being badly conducted. They turned against Asquith, the then Prime Minister, and Lloyd George was carried to the supreme position, by the support of back-benchers, by the support of popular opinion, by the support of the newspapers. He was forced into power. When he died, Churchill said, 'He seized power, perhaps it was his to take.' As soon as he came in, he transformed the system of government. He made the Cabinet efficient for the first time. During the war he cut it down to five or, at the most, six members. He provided it with a secretariat. There were Cabinet minutes. People knew what the Cabinet had decided. The secretaries ensured that the decisions of the Cabinet were going to be carried out. Lloyd George was able not only to give orders, he received for the first time clear and competent guidance as to the basis, the figures, on which these orders would be given. It would be wrong from this to say that Lloyd George was a wholly successful war minister. In mobilizing the country for war, in mobilizing industry, in introducing what many people rightly called 'war socialism', he was successful.

His great problem, his failure, was that he was unable to overcome the resistance of the generals. Lloyd George never established (as Churchill for instance did in the Second World War) the supremacy of the civil power over the military leaders. Lloyd George believed that the war in France, the whole process of mutual exhausting slaughter, was not the way to end the war. He had perhaps rather fantastic ideas of winning the war from behind, breaking in somewhere from the Mediterranean; but he was unable to enforce these ideas, or even to get the solid basis of information on which they could be enforced. In this conflict between the generals, particularly between Haig and Lloyd George, there was in a sense no winner. Lloyd George gradually advanced his power and his position, but he did not accomplish what he really wanted to accomplish, he never became the full director of strategy.

The end of the war brought him greater power. In the general election of 1918 there was something like a plebiscite for Lloyd George. Bonar Law, I think it was, said, 'He can be dictator for life if he wants to be.' What went wrong with Lloyd George after the war? Why did it happen that within four years of the end of the war he was driven from power, never to hold office again? One answer is that he was too successful, he did too much. He carried England through a period of social peril, carried it through successfully. He wound up the war with relatively little damage to this country. He achieved a settlement with Ireland which British statesmen had pursued for the past hundred years and had never been able to find. Lloyd George did better than Peel, better than Gladstone. He ended the Irish question. In 1921, looking at Lloyd George you would still say he was the supremely successful ruler.

Yet his popularity all the time was diminishing, perhaps not so much with the people. But in peacetime the people, the masses, public opinion in the vaguest sense, these things count for less and politicians count for more. Lloyd George politically was a wrecker. He wrecked parties. He wrecked the Liberal party. He looked as though he might well wreck the Conservative party. He looked forward to a time when he would even wreck the Labour party. None of these parties would tolerate this wrecking activity. His very readiness to improvise and do things disturbed people. There was a feeling that with Lloyd George there would always be something new, always be some new activity, some new drive, some new invention. People wanted a quiet life. They did not want any more to be a world power with this glamour and excitement. When in 1922 Lloyd George again seemed to be projecting a great war, he was thrown out.

He failed to return to office. He tried to crawl back into the Liberal party. He became for a short time even the leader of the Liberal fragment, but power had been snatched from him. He remained in his period of opposition in the 1920s still the most fertile mind among all statesmen. He alone faced the economic crisis of 1929 and subsequent years with constructive policies. He saw the opportunities for the New Deal which Roosevelt was to carry through in the United States. These ideas were too novel. Lloyd George's voice was not heard. In the later 1930s, when he again preached for a more active and effective foreign policy, he remained alone. His last great intervention in politics was in 1940

when his speech helped to bring down Chamberlain and put Churchill in. Lloyd George was invited to join Churchill's government.
He refused. Perhaps he felt too old. Perhaps he wanted to be the
war dictator but was not prepared to be dictated to by somebody
else. But his own criticism was also true. He said, 'Churchill's
government is a coalition of parties. I have always believed in
bringing individuals together.' It was because Lloyd George was a
great individual that he triumphed. It was because Lloyd George
was a great individual that he found himself, in the end, alone.

Yet it would be wrong to leave Lloyd George with this impression
that he was a failure. Even when he was alone at the end of his life
he commanded a unique position. He was still the great individual,
the man to whom people listened, the one to whom people turned.
But more than this, the transformation which he had effected in
his six years as Prime Minister and the transformation which he
continued to effect while he was in opposition or in a critical
position, these things left a lasting effect. It was Lloyd George's
work during his six years as Prime Minister which had started Great
Britain on the path of being a twentieth-century country. It was
Lloyd George to whom other people looked for inspiration. Nye
Bevan, for instance, when he took up the Health Service after the
Second World War, was treading consciously in the footsteps of
Lloyd George.

We are, I think, entitled to say another thing. He has left – and
this is strange for a man who was not a writer, with no literary
gifts and no literary background – a more considerable record of
his work in the form of books than any other prime minister. Other
prime ministers have written books, memoirs, autobiographies, but
Lloyd George sat down and tried, though not always successfully,
to give a full, coherent picture of what he did; far more revealing than
any other prime minister, perhaps because he was less concerned to
reveal himself. He wanted to describe his triumphs. He excited,
even in his literary works, more criticism, more hostility than any
other prime minister has done. This is perhaps the strangest thing
about Lloyd George: that with all this tremendous achievement,
with so much to admire and to praise, he was undoubtedly for most
of his life the most hated figure or distrusted figure in British

politics. The fear that Lloyd George was unpredictable, that he was unreliable, that he would always have some new trick up his sleeve, this turned men against him. One would see over and over again in his career how the most brilliant and subtle constructive ideas which he put forward were either rejected or had to be fought for in the most difficult ways because of this distrust and because there was some justification for it. Lloyd George was a rogue in more senses than one. A rogue in the sense that he did not come out of the ordinary political pattern, that he was something entirely different from others. A rogue also in the sense that he did not respect the ordinary political laws. He had no scruples; he did not observe the rules of the game; he was ready, not merely to sell honours as most prime ministers have done, but to avow that they had been sold. He was ready to jump from one policy to another and not claim that there was consistency in what he had done. To be the greatest improviser of the age, to have transformed the country over which he ruled: for these things a price had to be paid, and it was the price of distrust. Lloyd George, in the last resort, was always in danger because of his individual greatness, because he had no associates, because he stood alone. He was called in in the great emergency to save the country, but all the time what you might call the governing classes in the wider sense – by the 'governing classes' I mean trade-union leaders as much as business leaders – always regarded Lloyd George as expendable. And when his usefulness was exhausted, he was expended.

Stanley Baldwin

Stanley Baldwin (1867–1947). Son of Midlands ironmaster. Educated Harrow and Trinity College, Cambridge. Conservative MP for Bewdley 1908–37. President of the Board of Trade in Lloyd George's government 1921–2. Helped to end coalition 1922. Chancellor of the Exchequer under Bonar Law 1922–3, when he made unsatisfactory settlement of the American debt. Prime Minister of Conservative government 1923. Advocated Protection and lost election 1923. Renounced Protection and won election 1924. Prime Minister 1924–9. Resisted Beaverbrook's attempt to oust him as Conservative leader, 1930–31. Lord President of the Council in MacDonald's National government, 1931–5. Prime Minister of National government. 1935–7. Successfully arranged abdication of Edward VIII, 1936. Created Earl Baldwin of Bewdley. 1937.

The twenty years between the two wars are now regarded as a dark period in British history. In 1921 unemployment went to over a million and never fell to below the million mark again until the outbreak of the Second World War. Often it was over two million. Then in the 1930s the problems of foreign policy accumulated, the British government failed to measure up to them, failed to do anything about Hitler, failed (it is often said) to prepare Great Britain for the Second World War. In this dark period Baldwin has often become the symbol. He was for most of the time the leader of the Conservative party (from 1923 until 1937), and the Conservative party in its turn was usually the predominant party of the state.

Certainly a great responsibility rested on Baldwin and, if indeed there were failures, he cannot be acquitted of them.

On the other hand there is, I think, more to be said on Baldwin's side than is often appreciated nowadays. Baldwin was essentially the conciliator, the man of peace, the man who sought for quiet in our own affairs and abroad. And if indeed he was overwhelmed at the end of his public career by foreign affairs, we should also not forget that it was largely thanks to Baldwin that home affairs became less bitter. Baldwin and his counterpart, Ramsay MacDonald, were the two men who brought about reconciliation in British public life, who took the bitterness out of the class war, who made the British people more tolerant, more of a single community, and who, rightly or wrongly, maintained bolder standards of morality and respect when in other parts of the world these standards were falling to pieces.

Baldwin was a very unexpected person to be Prime Minister, also less unexpected to be a great man. There is a drawing by Max Beerbohm called 'The Old and the Young Selves'. It shows the young Baldwin, a boy at Harrow, looking up at Baldwin in the days when he was Prime Minister and saying to him, 'Prime Minister? You? Good Lord!' And you feel that Baldwin never got over his original surprise that he got so high.

He was in fact a less usual sort of man than he appeared, or claimed to be. In outward appearance he was very much an ordinary English gentleman. He used this term often; 'I was brought up', he said, 'among gentlemen.' He claimed to be the English country gentleman who liked pigs, who liked country life; but this claim was not altogether genuine. For one thing he did not belong to a great county family. On the contrary, he is the only industrial capitalist, genuine capitalist, who has ever been Prime Minister. Baldwins were and are a great steel firm. He himself was trained to be the head of Baldwins Limited before he went into politics. Nor was his background exclusively capitalist or industrial, or even bourgeois. Rudyard Kipling was his first cousin. Baldwin himself was by no means ungifted with words. Lloyd George once reminded people that Baldwin's origin was largely Celtic and that there was in him too the element of a dreamer. As a politician he was strangely formidable. Lloyd George once described him as the most formidable antagonist he had ever encountered. That was by no means a mean tribute from one who had fought many fierce battles. Baldwin is in fact the man who defeated and outwitted Lloyd George on more than one occasion.

His political origins were curiously accidental. He came into parliament almost by heredity. He took over the seat which his father had held before him. He was an undistinguished, reliable, back-bench Conservative until 1917 when Bonar Law, who was then Chancellor of the Exchequer, invited Baldwin to join him, mainly in order to do the entertaining at the Treasury, which Bonar Law disliked. Later on, in 1921, he was pushed up into the Lloyd George Cabinet, where he was a discontented and disillusioned member. The other members of the Cabinet he thought were all too clever, too smart, and also too unscrupulous. When in 1922 Lloyd George proposed to fight another general election on the coalition basis, Baldwin was the principal opponent, and it was largely thanks to Baldwin that the Conservative party reverted to independence. Baldwin attacked Lloyd George as a great dynamic force, and he said, 'A dynamic force is destructive.' This gives the pattern of the politics which Baldwin followed thereafter. He himself was certainly not going to be a dynamic force. He wanted that things should be conserved, that the old standards should be put back. Here again accident played its part in his advance. When Bonar Law formed his Conservative government, the most distinguished and brilliant Conservatives of the time were still associated with Lloyd George, and Bonar Law had to take in the second eleven. He had to make Baldwin Chancellor of the Exchequer. A few months later Bonar Law fell ill, and again, simply because there was no one else, in an undistinguished team, Baldwin, though undistinguished, was the one that became Prime Minister.

Within a few months of becoming Prime Minister in 1923 he led his party to defeat. It was the only initiative he ever took: deciding suddenly in the autumn of 1923 that there must be tariffs, protection. The Conservatives had a considerable majority, their government seemed secure, the problems were not particularly grave, and Baldwin flung himself into protection. Nobody quite knows why.

He once alleged that it was in order to dish Lloyd George. This was his obsession, with the clever men. Lloyd George was the cleverest of them. Lloyd George might take up protection. Baldwin wanted to get in before him. The result of this was the first Labour government, the government of 1924. The Conservatives turned against Baldwin. Almost at the beginning of his career as leader he was told that he ought to resign. He seemed to have very few supporters in the party. A few months later, in the autumn of 1924, the situation was reversed. Now it was the Labour government that was in trouble, there was another general election and the Conservatives won the biggest majority which they had had for over twenty years. Baldwin was vindicated.

The general election of 1924 was not fought on any great issue. No more talk about protection, no more talk about producing some new economic plan. It was fought on a straight ticket which Baldwin introduced, 'Surely you can trust me.' This was, incidentally, the first election in which radio played a part. Baldwin was the first politician of any standing who distinguished himself by giving a radio talk. Nowadays you can hear them occasionally. They sound slow and old-fashioned but, compared to the other public orators of the time, Ramsay MacDonald even to Lloyd George, Baldwin had the intimate manner which one trusts, the manner which people could listen to in their own homes. It is said that, so relaxed was he when he appeared before the microphone, he put a pipe in his mouth and struck a match just as the green light went on. I don't really believe this. He may have just taken a couple of sucks at the time but in the end put it down. But he was the first, how ironical, of the radio politicians. He was the English competitor – not a very striking one – against, shall we say, Hitler.

Baldwin's government of 1924–9 marked a return to party. It marked still more a return to a sort of complacency, to caution. These were the brief years when men believed that the old world, the world before 1914, could be restored. The outward symbol of this, strangely enough set up by Winston Churchill when he was Chancellor of the Exchequer, was the return to the gold standard. From 1925 until 1931 we actually had a gold pound. You could, if you went to a great deal of trouble, get gold sovereigns from the

Bank of England. Gold was freely exchangeable on the old basis that it had been before 1914. There was this brief period of illusion that the age of gold had come again, that all the terrible innovations of the war, all the burdens of high taxation and welfare, all these could be swept away and you could get back to the happy days of Queen Victoria.

This complacent, comfortable illusion was dispelled by the General Strike of 1926, the first great episode, really, of Baldwin's political life. In 1926 the trade unions of this country, wishing to support the miners, embarked upon what they called not a general but a national strike. The railways were stopped and road transport was stopped; not all industry was stopped, but there was a very widespread strike which, whether advisedly or not, was seeking to push the government into doing something for the miners. Baldwin was reluctantly driven into resisting the strike and the trade unions. He was driven indeed into insisting on complete victory. The General Strike ended in failure. Nothing was done for the miners, they remained an embittered element in the community and the coal mines went on being run badly by their private owners until after the Second World War. Nevertheless, in another aspect the General Strike was an extraordinary transformation in British life. For many years past – for the preceding twenty years of the twentieth century, one might say – men had talked about the General Strike as a great revolutionary weapon. They believed that it would initiate the social revolution. Instead it passed over harmlessly and, what is more, Baldwin ensured that it should pass over without lasting bitterness between the two sides. The General Strike in fact began the process of class collaboration. It began the new aspect of British trade-unionism by which the trade-union leaders were in fact co-operating with the employers far more than they were resisting them. Industry ceased to be a battlefield. Of course there were still strikes, there were still disputes between the two sides, but the old political atmosphere, the old class war, came to an end. Baldwin always regarded this as his greatest success. He had been able to carry through resistance to the General Strike and do so in a way that, after it, the working classes were not embittered. The union leaders themselves were not embittered, the General Strike in no time at all was forgotten on all sides. People never referred to it. They never dug up the hatreds that there might have been. This was Baldwin's great and lasting contribution to British life. He took the class war away. I cannot say he did much else in this government. It was a government which moved slowly, if it moved at all; but when it moved, it moved towards conciliation.

During this period Ramsay MacDonald and Baldwin drew closer together. The two of them collaborated in politics just as union leaders and employers were collaborating in industry. When the Labour government came in again in 1929, Baldwin and Mac-Donald secured that the government should not be constantly harassed, that there was no revival of the old savage political warfares that there had been, say, before 1914.

This, however, in other ways was Baldwin's period of greatest weakness. He had offered no constructive progress in the general election of 1929 and his only slogan was 'Safety First'. Many Conservatives felt that this was not enough. There was a fierce and organized drive against Baldwin's leadership. Lord Beaverbrook embarked on a policy of Empire Free Trade. He ran rival candidates against the official Conservatives. Many of the Conservative party favoured Empire Free Trade, or at any rate favoured the dynamic ideas of Beaverbrook against the sleepy Conservatism of Baldwin. Baldwin reached the point early in 1931 where he believed once again that he was going to be driven out. He referred to it as 'the year when my party wanted to get rid of me'. Then at the last minute he secured victory by presenting himself as the decent plain man harassed by press lords and by the way in which he switched public feeling against these press lords. He said that they wanted power without responsibility, 'the prerogative of the harlot throughout the ages'. This one phrase saved him. The campaign for Empire Free Trade died away. Baldwin was left still without policy, without ideas, without constructive drive, but the secure leader of the Conservative party.

Then, in the summer of 1931, the great economic crisis overwhelmed the country. Baldwin, if he had pushed hard, could have become Prime Minister, but he did not want to push hard. It suited him well enough that Ramsay MacDonald should become head of a national government with Baldwin, in a more obscure position, as the real controller of it.

After the general election of 1931, Baldwin, as leader of the Conservative party, commanded an overwhelming majority in the House of Commons but he did not seek to use this majority to force himself to the front. He kept up the national façade. Though this national government carried out reactionary measures in its cuts in unemployment pay and in many other ways, it also continued the policy of conciliation. It was at this very time, in a period of reaction, that MacDonald and Baldwin insisted on taking further steps towards the emancipation of India, towards the establishment of dominion status. Incidentally, it was over this issue that Winston Churchill broke with the official Conservative party and went into an opposition of his own. He was opposed to any concessions to India of any kind. It was Baldwin that prepared the way for the developments which ultimately produced Indian independence.

The national government had been formed in order to restore British economic life. It was not very successful at this. In so far as there was recovery in the 1930s, this was far more due to the ordinary energies of ordinary people than because of what the government did. Here again, it was quiet reform Baldwin was seeking. He believed that, if there was quiet, people could then bring about recovery themselves. He never applied himself to a serious study of problems. No prime minister ever read fewer papers. Where Baldwin was great was in the House of Commons. He spent his days and often his nights on the Treasury bench. It is probably true that no prime minister since Sir Robert Walpole has known the House of Commons so well or has spent so much time in it. Those on the Treasury bench would study the character of each member. When a crisis arose, Baldwin would interpret the feeling of the House of Commons more effectively than any other prime minister has ever done.

In one crisis of his second period of the 1930s Baldwin scored a great triumph. This was the strange story of the abdication. When Edward VIII wanted to marry Mrs Simpson and when it was held, rightly or wrongly, that most British opinion was against this marriage, it was Baldwin who stepped forward, who manoeuvred the King, kept Edward VIII away from any kind of public opinion, carried through the abdication so smoothly that in no time at all the prestige of the Crown was as proud as it had ever been before. This is one of the two things, perhaps, that he would most like to be remembered: the two smooth operations of the General Strike and of the abdication.

Unfortunately for Baldwin, British affairs could not be conducted in isolation. He was caught up in the storm of foreign dangers. When Hitler in the 1930s began to rearm, Baldwin was early forced to recognize that dangers were accumulating. He hated it. In one of his most notorious remarks he explained how, if he had advocated great armaments in 1933, he would have been swept aside and that therefore democracy is always two years behind the dictators. It was not until 1935, by which time he had become Prime Minister, that the British government began to suggest that more expenditure on arms would be necessary. Even then very little was done in the expenditure on arms.

Baldwin much condemned this. His argument was not altogether ill-founded. By keeping quiet at a time when most people in this country were against armaments of any kind, Baldwin was able to prepare the way for great armaments later on. He did not understand the great issues of foreign affairs, he disliked the League of Nations, he never visited the meetings in Geneva, though he spent his holidays quite near. He himself once attributed all his misfortunes to the League of Nations Union, which had pressed this unwelcome cause upon him. When he finally resigned in 1937, much admired, regarded as the great elder statesman of the day, it was his achievements in home affairs which people remembered. When, two years later, Great Britain was involved in war, when, still more in 1940, Great Britain was nearly overwhelmed by the German danger, people turned against Baldwin and blamed him, very often, for their own faults and failings. Baldwin had been perhaps only the representative man at the time and he had shared, indeed, its faults and failings. He had also shared in its good qualities. If this country, Great Britain, now is a more tolerant and easy-going place, if there is more understanding, readiness to co-operate between different sections of the community, it is very largely due to Baldwin, to his softness – his evasiveness if you like – that these things have come about. During the war he shrank from coming to London. He said, 'People hate me so.' I think he probably exaggerated this. There was a readiness to shift all the blame on to Baldwin. He himself was often crushed by the weight of it. Among all the prime ministers that one looks back on, none has had greater failures to show, and yet none has also had so much tolerance, good sense, patience – distinguishing qualities which have enabled Great Britain, for good and ill, to go on as a civilized country. Somebody once remarked that a very important thing about this country: we don't kill each other for political reasons. If this remains true of the twentieth century, it is largely because of Baldwin.

George Canning

George Canning (1770–1827), Foreign Secretary 1807–9 and 1822–7, Prime Minister, 1827, was notable for his Liberal Conservative foreign policy (1822–7). He was much admired by such later statesmen as William Ewart Gladstone (1809–98).

This essay was first published as a book review of Peter Dixon, Canning, Weidenfeld and Nicolson, 1976, in the Observer, *4 April 1976. In an earlier book review of Sir Charles Petrie's biography (second edition, 1946) he had delivered the verdict, 'Canning was probably the most striking personality in public life between Chatham and Churchill' (Manchester Guardian, 19 November 1946). On another occasion he commented that Canning was not a great Liberal statesman but 'was a thorough-going isolationist, with all the attractiveness and all the illusions of that school' (Manchester Guardian, 11 September 1951).*

George Canning called the New World into existence in order to redress the Balance of the Old. He also directed the seizure of the Danish fleet during the Napoleonic war, even though Denmark was neutral. And what else? The shadow of a great name and Canning Clubs at Oxford and Cambridge if they still survive.

Canning belonged to that small and distinguished class: the predestined Prime Ministers who did not reach their goal. True, he became Prime Minister in 1827, but he was already a sick man and died four months later. Yet no man was more fitted to be Prime Minister. He was the greatest orator of the age after the deaths of Pitt and Fox. He was a dynamic statesman of infinite courage and resource. His gifts were of no avail. He was out of office altogether during the years of victory, and the war was won by such dim figures as Sidmouth and Liverpool, the Arch-Mediocrity, not by Canning. This is a fascinating story of thwarted talents, only partially redeemed by Canning's tenure of the Foreign Office from 1822 to 1827.

Peter Dixon tells the story admirably. His book has used some new manuscript sources which provide interesting material on Canning's private life. Dixon handles firmly the political complexities of the time when the Tories, despite their confusions, clung to office and the Whigs panted after it in vain. Canning was a Pittite rather than a Tory, but he had no illusions about his hero. He wrote in 1808: 'we have now ... a maritime war in our power ... And we have (what would to God poor Pitt had ever resolved to have!) determination to carry it through.' It was with this determination that Canning launched the Peninsular war; others carried it to a victorious conclusion. Canning was perhaps too determined, forever proposing some new stroke of daring and wearing down the less daring much as Churchill did. Unlike Churchill he did not live long enough to learn restraint.

Canning was also too clever. Like Lord Birkenhead, it was easier for him to keep a live coal in his mouth than a witty saying. He was the only great statesman who excelled in satiric verse and used his talent to even more devastating effect than Disraeli used his talent as a novelist. Sometimes he directed his poetry against his Radical antagonists, as in his famous poem on 'The Needy Knife-grinder'. But often he used it against his associates, dismissing Addington in the lines:

> Pitt is to Addington
> As London is to Paddington

It was unreasonable to suppose that those whom he had wounded would welcome him as a colleague. His birth was also against him. His mother was an actress, and Earl Grey spoke for most of the aristocracy when 'he took it as axiomatic that no son of an actress should become Prime Minister of England'.

It was also alleged against him that he had been the lover of

Princess Caroline, the wife of the Prince of Wales. Dixon goes into this story at length. Canning was certainly in love with the Princess for a short time and always remained fond of her. Caroline was not one of those who would let such an opportunity pass. When Lady Bessborough discussed the question with Canning in 1806, he 'neither own'd nor denied, but on the whole I am staggered and afraid it is in great part true!' Whether true or false, the story did Canning no good with the Prince of Wales, later Prince Regent and then George IV.

Most of all, Canning would not work the system. Politics were at this time an affair of groups, each leader bringing in a useful body of supporters. Canning had a few political associates, but they were detached individuals like himself and carried little weight. He claimed office on the grounds of his superlative abilities. The run-of-the-mill politicians asked how many votes he would bring with him. Only Castlereagh's suicide in 1822 enabled him to become Foreign Secretary. Only Liverpool's death made him Prime Minister in 1827. In British politics great gifts are not enough.

Dixon provides light relief as well as politics. Thus, 'it is plausible to surmise a connection between the high-flown and grandiose oratory of Members of Parliament with the state of inebriation into which many would have passed after dining and drinking heavily'. Here is an interesting social note: Canning was a relatively poor man, but his tax return in 1801 'included an assessment for ten male servants, two four- and one two-wheeled carriages and a dog'. And here one that anticipates the equivocations over the Resistance during the Second World War: when the Spanish people rose against Napoleon, Canning was their enthusiastic supporter, but 'he objected to references to the "Patriots of Spain" as being too like the language of the Whig *Morning Chronicle*, and preferred the term "Loyal Inhabitants"'.

The best story is the last. On 12 April 1827 George IV received Canning 'who, according to Wellington, stood with a watch in his hand giving the King half an hour to make him Prime Minister'. Thus Canning had his triumph, however belatedly.

Lord Aberdeen

George Hamilton-Gordon, fourth Earl of Aberdeen (1784–1860)
was Prime Minister 1852–5. He was a special ambassador in Vienna
in 1813 and British representative at the Treaty of Paris, 1814. He
had been a Scottish representative peer 1806–14 and was created a
UK peer in 1814. He served in several Conservative administrations
between 1828 and 1846. He was Foreign Secretary 1828–30 and
1841–6 and Secretary of State for War and the Colonies 1834–5.
He remained with Sir Robert Peel after the Conservative party split
in 1846, serving as the Peelite leader in the House of Lords and
being the Peelite leader after Sir Robert Peel's death in 1850.

This essay was first published as a review of Lucille Iremonger,
Lord Aberdeen *(Collins, 1978), under the title 'Muddling Through'*
in the Observer, *10 September 1978.*

Lord Aberdeen enjoyed an unrivalled reputation among the political
leaders of the earlier nineteenth century. Croker said of him, 'Of
all the men I have known in my life, his regard for truth was the
most strict and scrupulous.' Gladstone was even more emphatic,
saying thirty-four years after Aberdeen's death, 'He is the man in
public life of all others whom I have *loved*. I say emphatically *loved*.
I have *loved* others, but never like him.'

Aberdeen had many diplomatic successes. As a young man he
helped to construct the union of the Allies against Napoleon. When
Foreign Secretary he established the first *entente cordiale* with
France and averted war with the United States over the disputed
Canadian frontier. In 1852 he became Prime Minister at the head

of a strong coalition government. There he seemed to provide stability after a succession of weak governments and the eccentricity of Palmerston.

Then this man of peace allowed Great Britain to drift into a quarrel with Russia and presided over the discredit that accompanied the ensuing Crimean War. In 1855 Aberdeen's government was overthrown by a revolt in the House of Commons. His place was taken by Palmerston, now belatedly hailed as the saviour of his country. Aberdeen faded from history as the Prime Minister responsible for the Crimean War.

Lucille Iremonger has set out to vindicate Aberdeen's record. As an accomplished biographer she has a sure touch in the treatment of individual characters. She has also developed a surprising gift for the details of diplomatic history, almost to the point of bringing some sense into the origins of the Crimean War. She has made no mistakes except for the unlikely statement that Lord Clarendon received a message by wireless in August 1853. Her book is a reliable work of scholarship. As an essay in vindication, however, I feel that it does not come off.

For one thing Aberdeen, despite his reliability, his industry and his strength of character, was a dull man. There is never a laugh in any of his sayings whereas Palmerston's have one in every line. Moreover his policies and achievements lacked definition. The Allies of 1813 were still at sixes-and-sevens until Castlereagh arrived and took over from Aberdeen. In 1846 he left enough loose ends in the affair of the Spanish Marriages for Palmerston to turn it into a first-rate, though highly comical, crisis. Above all he failed to take a firm grasp of negotiations before the Crimean War.

No doubt he wished to avert war. No doubt he was harassed by the irresponsibility of Lord John Russell and others of his colleagues. All the same there was something wrong when a Prime Minister, the only member of the Cabinet not in favour of war, allowed himself to be outvoted and then went along with the majority. Maybe, too, the disasters of the Crimean War were the fault of the British military administration and not of the Prime Minister. This is a plea that can be made at the bar of history, not in the House of Commons. Aberdeen became the man who had muddled into the Crimean War and ran it in a muddled fashion. Such was the inevitable verdict and he accepted it himself.

Lord Palmerston

Henry John Temple, third Viscount Palmerston (1784–1865), as an Irish peer was eligible to sit in the House of Commons. He did so as a Tory MP, 1807–31, and as a Whig MP, 1831–4 and 1835–65. He held office 1807–28 in Conservative governments, retiring with the Canningites in 1828. He was Foreign Secretary in Whig governments, 1830–34, 1835–41 and 1846–51, Home Secretary 1852–5, before becoming Prime Minister, 1855–8 and 1859–65. His second government has often been deemed the first Liberal government.

This essay was first published in History Today, *July 1951, and subsequently reprinted in* British Prime Ministers: A Portrait Gallery, *introduced by Duff Cooper, Allan & Wingate, 1953;* A. J. P. Taylor, *Englishmen and Others,* Hamish Hamilton, *1956; and his* Essays In English History, *Harmondsworth, Penguin, 1976. In his introduction to this essay on Palmerston in his 1976 selection, Alan Taylor wrote, 'It is no longer true that the brick fortifications behind Portsmouth are useful and effective, if indeed they ever were.'*

Among the surprising careers of British prime ministers, none has contained more surprises than that of Lord Palmerston. For twenty years junior minister in a Tory government, he became the most successful of Whig Foreign Secretaries; though always a Conservative, he ended his life by presiding over the transition from Whiggism to Liberalism. He was the exponent of British strength, yet he was driven from office for truckling to a foreign despot; he preached the Balance of Power, yet helped to inaugurate the policy of isolation and of British withdrawal from Europe. Irresponsible and flippant, he became the first hero of the serious middle-class electorate. He reached high office solely through an irregular family connection; he retained it through skilful use of the press – the only prime minister to become an accomplished leader-writer. Palmerston was not a member of one of the great Whig families or even connected with them. He was an Irish peer, moderately rich, who naturally entered politics to supplement his income. For a peer, he was an educated man. He went to Cambridge, which – even at the worst time – provided a solid grounding in mathematics, and he early absorbed the principles of political economy. Hence, he was not staggered, as Peel and Gladstone were, by the sudden impact of the Free Trade case; this had been a common-place of his thought for thirty years. Born in 1784, he entered the House of Commons at the age of twenty-three, without either strong convictions or defined party ties; simply a young man of the fashionable world who wanted a good appointment and – rarity enough – was qualified to hold one. Having a reasonable grasp of figures and of economics, he was offered his choice among the junior financial offices;* he chose that of Secretary at War and retained it for twenty years. This was the equivalent of the present-day financial secretary to the War Office, a post strictly administrative and financial without a seat in the Cabinet. Though Palmerston ran his office competently, he did not trouble much with politics and seemed to care only for life in society. Good looking and fickle, he established himself as 'Lord Cupid', a name which tells everything. But the years of obscurity were not wasted: he served a more prolonged apprenticeship in

---

* Spencer Perceval is said to have offered him the post of Chancellor of the Exchequer. Even if he did, this was not the important office that it has subsequently become. The First Lord of the Treasury himself conducted the financial affairs of the country, and – if he sat in the House of Commons – held also the office of Chancellor. Spencer Perceval must have thought better of his proposal to Palmerston, for he adhered to the usual arrangement and was his own Chancellor. Peel in 1841 was the first to sit on the Treasury bench, as First Lord, with a Chancellor beside him; Russell, in 1846, the first to leave financial business to a Chancellor of the Exchequer.

administration than any other prime minister has ever done and, when he came to sit in Whig Cabinets, was distinguished from his colleagues by his ability to run an office. It was this ability, not his policy or his personality, which finally made him Prime Minister in 1855.

Though Palmerston served a Tory ministry, it would be wrong to describe him as a Tory; he was simply a 'government man'. Nor was he a Canningite until late in the day. What brought him over to the Canningites was his support for Catholic emancipation. With his gaiety of spirit and his easy-going morals, he hated tyranny and oppression wherever they occurred. After twenty years of comfortable office, he left it for the sake of the Catholics, just as, at the end of his life, he threatened to resign as Prime Minister rather than relax the struggle against the slave trade. In 1828 Palmerston, out of office, found himself associated with Melbourne and Huskisson, the Canningite remnant who had broken with Wellington and were drifting over to the Whigs. There were also personal grounds for this tie. After a good many adventures, Palmerston had settled down with Lady Cowper, Melbourne's married sister. He lived with her more or less openly; had children by her; and married her in the late 1830s after Lord Cowper's death. Melbourne was a more important man than Palmerston, more influential and better connected. When he joined the Whig Cabinet in 1830, he carried his illegitimate brother-in-law with him. Without the Melbourne connection, Palmerston would hardly have reached the Cabinet rank which started him on the path to the premiership, and Melbourne was to sustain him against the criticism of the orthodox Whigs at the end of the 1830s. In the last resort, Palmerston owed his position as Prime Minister to the odd chance that the sister of one of his predecessors had become his mistress.

Palmerston was to make his name at the Foreign Office, but this was neither intended nor expected. Lord Grey, Prime Minister in 1830, had been Foreign Secretary in a remote era and meant to conduct foreign policy himself. All he wanted was a competent underling in the House of Commons. Lady Cowper was again of service. Princess Lieven, her closest friend, recommended

Palmerston to Grey as presentable and well-mannered. For some time it was believed that Grey supplied the policy. Palmerston was held to be 'frivolous' and failed to establish a hold over the House of Commons. The peaceful solution of the Belgian question was primarily a triumph for Grey. When Melbourne became Prime Minister, Palmerston had things more his own way, and his conduct of British policy during the eastern crisis of 1839–41 was brilliant, perhaps the most perfect in the records of the Foreign Office. But it was a performance for experts. It did not make him popular with the general public, and it made him much disliked by many of the great Whigs, such as Holland and Durham. In 1841, when the Whig Government declined into collapse, Palmerston was still a relatively little-known figure. His frequent evocation of Canning, whose policy he neither understood nor followed, was an implied confession that he could not stand on his own feet.

The five years between 1841 and 1846, when Peel was in office with a Conservative government, were decisive for Palmerston's future. The succession to Melbourne as Whig leader was open. Lord John Russell assumed that it would automatically be his as political representative of the greatest Whig family, and he thought he had done all that was necessary when he secured the allegiance of such Whig managers as 'Bear' Ellice. Palmerston could hardly play his family connection against Russell's, even if it had counted for anything. He therefore decided to play the British public. He built himself up deliberately as a public figure, established relations with the press and himself wrote leading articles in his forthright, unmistakable style. At the end of 1845, when Peel first resigned, the third Earl Grey made it a condition of his taking office under Russell that Palmerston should be excluded. The condition wrecked Russell's Cabinet-making. The episode was at once an unconscious recognition by the great Whigs that they had taken a cuckoo into the nest, and a sign that the cuckoo was now too strong to be ejected. Later, in 1846, Russell formed the last Whig government of our history, and Palmerston went undisputed to the Foreign Office. This feeble government had a record of failure broken only by Palmerston's dazzling display in foreign policy. His policy had its serious side and can be defended, as it were, on technical grounds, but there was a flamboyant touch as well – Palmerston was deliberately playing Russell off the centre of the stage. His triumph came in 1850 with the Don Pacifico debate, when he held his own against the greatest speakers of the age – Peel, Gladstone and Cobden – held his own and worsted them. The triumph was not one of oratory in the conventional sense. Palmerston was always a bad speaker full of 'hums' and 'haws', his voice trailing away before the end of the sentence, and the pause filled up by a flourish of his handkerchief. Rather it was a triumph of character. With his dyed whiskers and his red face, Palmerston exemplified British self-confidence and bounce.

Still, it needed the impact of war to finish the job for him. At the end of 1851 Russell finally got rid of Palmerston. Early in 1852 the Russell government fell in its turn. Then, at the end of the year, Russell and Palmerston found themselves together again in the coalition of Whigs and Peelites brought into being by Prince Albert and presided over by Aberdeen. Palmerston was relegated to the Home Office. He was rescued from it by the disasters of the Crimean War. Though he shared the common responsibility of the Cabinet, public opinion seized on him as the man of destiny, the man who would win the war. This was the moment of crisis in Palmerston's life and, for the historian, the most interesting point in his career. Again and again in modern history, Great Britain has drifted unprepared into war; then, after early failures, has discovered an inspired war-leader. How does public opinion make its choice? And what is it that Palmerston had in common with the elder Pitt, Lloyd George and Winston Churchill? It was not done merely by advertisement, though all four made skilful use of publicity. It was not even done by brilliant speeches in the House of Commons or outside. It turned rather on the impression of resolution and courage laid down in the House of Commons over a period of years. During a crisis the Members of Parliament broke away from the conventional pattern – whether of family connection or party organization – and acted according to their patriotic duty. Curiously enough, the popular choice has always been right: on all four occasions it hit on a leader who was not only more colourful or more dramatic than his peace-time predecessor but also more efficient technically.* This is puzzling. The general public or even the members of the House of Commons could hardly deduce from Palmerston's speeches that he was an administrator of the first quality who could challenge the Peelites on their own ground of efficient government without any of the high moral tone which they found necessary to accompany it.

The government which Palmerston formed in 1855 was neither a party government nor a coalition; it was an association of individuals, united only to win the war. The old system of family connections was in decay; the new system of defined parties had hardly begun. The Conservatives were on the way to becoming a party in the modern sense; but they were doomed to perpetual minority so long as there was a middle-class electorate. Those acceptable as ministers were in confusion. The Peelites broke with Palmerston and disintegrated. When Russell bungled the conference at Vienna shortly afterwards, Whig solidarity also dissolved. Palmerston's personality was the only stable point in a fluid political system. It would be absurd to claim that his government was a war Cabinet of the highest order. Though it began the reform of the British military system, these reforms stopped half-way like the Crimean War itself. Opportunity had come to Palmerston too late in life: he was seventy-one when he became Prime Minister. More important, opportunity came at the wrong time: Great Britain could not be turned into a military nation only four years after the Exhibition of 1851. Still, in one way, Palmerston did better than his peers, those other great men who have saved their country. He not only won the war that he had been called on to win, he actually survived his success. The elder Pitt, Lloyd George, Churchill, were all ruined by victory. All three were ejected from office before the end of the war or shortly after it. Palmerston stayed safely in office and, even more remarkable, won a general election a year after the war was over.

* On one occasion the public choice was flagrantly and persistently wrong. The younger Pitt, 'the pilot who weathered the storm', was not a good war-leader; the nonentities who succeeded him did much better.

The general election of 1857 is unique in our history: the only election ever conducted as a simple plebiscite in favour of an individual. Even the 'coupon' election of 1918 claimed to be more than a plebiscite for Lloyd George; even Disraeli and Gladstone offered a clash of policies as well as of personalities. In 1857 there was no issue before the electorate except whether Palmerston should be Prime Minister; and no one could pretend that Palmerston had any policy except to be himself. Of course, we know very little about the general election of 1857 (or, for that matter, about any other in the nineteenth century), and it may turn out on detailed examination that the result of it was really determined by less obvious factors. Still, there was in it, at the least, a plebiscitary element, as though even the British had to be in the fashion and had caught the taste from Louis Napoleon. In the same way, Neville Chamberlain in the 1930s got as near the *Führerprinzip* as an Englishman could.

The political victory of 1857 was not the end of Palmerston's career. He had presided over, and in part caused, the end of the old political order; he was destined to inaugurate the new. His period of personal government lasted only a few months after the general election of 1857. The rather cantankerous patriotism which had sustained him against the Peelites and the pacifists turned on him when he tried, sensibly enough, to appease Louis Napoleon after the Orsini plot. Since no one could form a government with majority support, the Conservatives – as in 1852 – formed a government without one; this in turn was bound to be followed, again as in 1852, by a coalition. But the government which Palmerston organized in June 1859 was a coalition of a different kind: not a coalition of groups which looked back to the past, but a coalition which anticipated the future. Had it not been for Palmerston himself – too individual, too full of personality to be fitted into a party-pattern – it would have been the first Liberal government in our history. Everything that was important in it was Liberal – finance, administrative reform, its very composition: the first government with unmistakable middle-class Free Traders as members. Palmerston would have included even Cobden, if he could have got him. It was Cobden who had scruples against tolerating the irresponsible survivor from an older world, and not the other way round. Of course, tolerance and good nature had always been Palmerston's strong points, not virtues for which Radicals are usually distinguished.

Palmerston was too strong a character to be swamped by Liberalism even in old age. It was not so much that he resisted reforms; he himself had welcomed and often promoted the administrative reforms of the preceding thirty years. It was rather that he thought a government had other tasks than to be always reforming: it should conduct a forceful foreign policy and strengthen the national defences. Palmerston is one of the few prime ministers who has literally left his mark on the face of the country: all those odd-looking brick fortifications behind Portsmouth are his doing – they are still useful and effective, which is more than can be said for Gladstonian finance. But Palmerston in his last ministry was fighting, and winning, the wrong battle. For nearly a hundred years – ever since Dunning's famous motion in 1780 – self-confident British aristocrats had aimed to reduce the powers of the Crown and to prevent its interference in the course of government and policy. Melbourne and Palmerston had had four blissful years on the accession of Queen Victoria when the Crown seemed on the point of becoming politically null. The process had been reversed by Prince Albert, and when Palmerston was at the Foreign Office between 1846 and 1851 he had to contend with ceaseless royal interference – the more galling for being justified by every historical precedent. The years of the Crimean War had been too serious to allow of constitutional squabbles, but these began again in 1859. Between 1859 and 1861 the Crown fought persistently the policy of Palmerston and of Russell, now Foreign Secretary; intrigued, as George III had intrigued with members of the Cabinet behind the Prime Minister's back; dreamt of ejecting Palmerston as the Fox–North coalition had been ejected in 1784.

Then, in 1861, the Prince Consort suddenly died. Victoria was both unwilling and unable to carry on the contest; she became again and remained the political nonentity that she had been before her marriage. Palmerston had fulfilled the highest Whig ambition, though after the death of the Whig party: the Crown had been eliminated from politics. It turned out almost at once that the victory was of no use at all. The Whigs had evoked public opinion against the Crown; Palmerston had played off public opinion against his Whig rivals. Now public opinion interfered more effectively than the Crown had ever done. Though Palmerston had been much harassed by the Crown when he was at the Foreign Office, he had always got his way in the end; and this was equally true of Palmerston and Russell in the severe disputes between 1859 and 1861. Despite the Prince Consort's Germanic enthusiasm for Austria, they managed to back up Italian unification from start to finish. Things were very different between 1862 and 1865. Russell, for instance, would have liked to recognize the southern states in the American Civil War and go to war for the sake of Poland in 1863; Palmerston would have threatened war for the sake of Denmark in 1864. They were overruled by the majority of the Cabinet,* itself reflecting the opinion of the majority of members in the House of Commons, and they in their turn accurately voicing the opinion of the middle-class electorate. It is often said that Palmerston's foreign policy was a failure at the end of his life; it would be much truer to say that he was not allowed to have a foreign policy. Public opinion had pulled off the feat that was beyond the Prince Consort or even George III. Palmerston, the first – perhaps the only – prime minister to owe his success solely to public opinion, ended his life its prisoner.

Yet he was very near hitting on the method by which public opinion would be tamed. At the time of the general election of 1859, party organization meant nothing at all except perhaps among the Conservatives. Whig grandees put up money to fight a few constituencies, from a mixture of family and party motives; all the rest still depended on local initiative. By 1868 the Liberal Whips were handling a party fund, and were seeking subscriptions much more widely than at Brooks's. The transition took place when Palmerston was Prime Minister. He it must have been who decided to leave these matters to the Whips, and to keep the Prime Minister out of the financial side of the party-system; it may even have been

---

* Six members of the Cabinet out of fourteen favoured going to Denmark's aid in June 1864.

Palmerston who first, though unwittingly, recommended men to honours in return for their contributions to the party chest. Gladstone found the system settled when he took over the leadership of the Liberal party in 1868. After all, it was the only way to run a party once the moneyed men pushed aside the members of the great families, and Palmerston no doubt acquiesced in it more easily since he had never belonged to these select Whig circles. Thus, without knowing it, he invented both the Liberal party and the modern party-system, no mean achievement for an individualist adventurer.

This is the essential point about him, the secret of his failures as of his success. He was never dependent on connection or on party, and rather disliked both; he was self-made. Men have written many books about his foreign policy and will write more. Very little has been written, or ever will be, about his place in British political life, for it is an empty one. The British political system has no room for the rogue elephant. Though he may ruin others – as Palmerston ruined the Whigs or as Lloyd George wrecked the Liberal party sixty years afterwards – he will certainly ruin himself. He will be barren as Prime Minister; he will not create. Our system is admirably suited to represent interests and to voice general ideas; it does not like independent characters, except as an eccentric adornment. In war both interests and ideas are pushed aside; hence, as an exception to the rule, the great individuals then triumph. Once peace comes, their power is ended, even if they cling to office as Palmerston managed to do. The steady men of solid principle and mind are the ones who achieve effective success, but the adventurers are more fun. Palmerston was not the spokesman of a class, though he defended the Irish landowners towards the end of his life, and he did not voice any great principle or idea. He was simply an individual of strong personality – resolute, self-confident and with great powers of physical endurance. As Foreign Secretary he was always too independent of the Prime Minister and the Cabinet; as Prime Minister, though he stood loyally by his colleagues, he failed to dominate the Cabinet or even to lead it.

He was not an Irish peer and an Irish landowner for nothing. He had the Irish jauntiness which always wins English hearts. He could never rein in his irrepressible high spirits; even his best speeches have here and there a touch of flippancy. He would rather make a good joke than win a debate. He was not, as is sometimes alleged, a survivor from the eighteenth century. Rather he had 'Regency' written all over him – in his clothes, his morals, even in his way of talking and his metallic laugh. Nor did he 'represent' the electorate of the Reform Bill, if this means that he resembled the middle-class voter. The men of the time delighted in Palmerston just as Churchill is now admired by millions who would never vote for him, but their serious taste was for Peel and Gladstone – these were the truly 'representative men'. Palmerston was certainly the most entertaining of Queen Victoria's prime ministers. Though there have been greater prime ministers, there has been none more genial and, for that matter, none so good-looking.

Lord Salisbury

Robert Arthur Talbot Gascoyne-Cecil, third Marquess of Salisbury (1830–1903), was Secretary of State for India 1866–7 and 1874–8, Foreign Secretary 1878–80, and Prime Minister 1885, 1886–92 and 1895–1902 (combining the premiership with Foreign Secretary 1886–92 and 1895–1900).

This essay was first given as a talk in a series on 'British Prime Ministers', broadcast on BBC Radio's Third Programme in April 1947. It was first published in the Listener, *24 April 1947, and subsequently reprinted in A. J. P. Taylor,* From Napoleon to Stalin, *Hamish Hamilton, 1950, and his* Essays In English History, *Harmondsworth, Penguin, 1976. In his introduction to this essay in the 1976 Penguin selection, Alan Taylor wrote, 'The Lord President of the Council referred to was Herbert Morrison who described another talk of mine on British foreign policy as "anti-British, anti-American and not particularly competent", a rebuke echoed by R. C. K. Ensor, the historian. When this talk was given, the British government had not yet transferred the guardianship of anti-Communist Greece to the United States.'*

Lord Salisbury was a consistent Tory. He never wavered in his principles and never deserted them: in 1867 he risked his political future rather than agree to the democratic Reform Bill with which Derby and Disraeli hoped to 'dish the Whigs' and twenty years later he took office as the uncompromising opponent of Home Rule. He came of one of the few genuinely Tory families – and one of the few, too, which went back beyond the Glorious Revolution, a family which had never joined in the hunt for honours under the Hanoverians. Two great Cecils, William and Robert, served Elizabeth and James I, then came an unbroken row of nonentities for more than two hundred years. Here is the strange thing about Salisbury: he was distinguished from his ancestors by his intellectual gifts, which were very great; he had the political and religious outlook of a slow-witted countryman. His own thinking was ruthless – he spared nothing and nobody; the political creed to which he held had been hammered out by generations of Englishmen who distrusted thought in politics. He hated society and social functions, he was impatient with hereditary distinctions; the party which he led existed to preserve the social order and valued hereditary claims. He arrived at his own conclusions by private thought, locked away in his study behind double doors, never consulting others until his mind was fully made up; yet he spoke with contempt of the study-made conclusions of political thinkers. His followers cared for the English countryside and country pursuits; he disliked horses and preferred the villa which he built at Dieppe to his historic house at Hatfield. The Tory party has been called the stupid party (and not unfairly, to be stupid and to be sensible are not far apart. The Progressive party, Radical and Socialist, is clever, but silly). Strange indeed: the most successful leader that the stupid party has had since the Reform Bill was an intellectual, supremely clever.

This contrast gives Salisbury's character a special fascination. Most prime ministers would not be interesting unless they had been prime ministers (and some are not interesting even then): most of their biographies are heavy going even for the historian – think of the dead-weight of Morley's Gladstone, or Monypenny and Buckle on Disraeli. Lady Gwendolen Cecil's life of her father is a work of art, a great biography which can be read for pleasure by someone with no interest in political history at all. Salisbury would have been a remarkable man even if he had never been Prime Minister or even if he had never gone into politics at all. He was a character as Dr Johnson was a character and on the same scale. Think of his monumental absent-mindedness which led him to greet his own son, encountered in the grounds of Hatfield House, as an important but unrecognized guest. Once at a breakfast party, sitting on his host's left, he asked in an undertone who was the distinguished man on the host's right. It was Mr W. H. Smith, Salisbury's Chancellor of the Exchequer, who had sat at Salisbury's side in Cabinet for years. Equally delightful was his scientific enthusiasm, which led him to put glaring and erratic electric light into Hatfield House; it worked from the river and sank to a dull red when the stream was low. Hatfield was also wired for a primitive telephone, with a sort of loud-speaker attachment, by means of which Salisbury could boom into every room: 'Hey diddle diddle, the cat and the fiddle; the cow jumped over the moon.'

He was a first-rate writer. His letters and dispatches are still, after half a century, a delight to read – no one could say the same of Peel or even of Gladstone. His political journalism is as fresh now as when it was written. His essay on the Polish question, for instance, written in 1863, is the most sensible thing ever written on Poland and Russia; it was heavily drawn on by Eden during the debate in the House of Commons which followed the Yalta Agreement of 1945. Eden jibbed however at the conclusion that the best one can hope for Poland is that she should enjoy a limited autonomy under Russian protection. He was a master of the telling phrase. 'Backing the wrong horse' – the policy of propping up Turkey instead of co-operating with Russia in the Near East. 'Splendid isolation' – not, as is often supposed, a description of his policy, but a reminder that only a Power whose vital interests are not involved can examine a problem in an 'emotional and philanthropic spirit'. Some of his most telling phrases had a jaunty air which would have brought the wrath of Mr Ensor and the Lord President of the Council down on me if I had used them. Thus he described the Cape-to-Cairo railway as 'a curious idea which has lately become prevalent', and the conflict of the Great Powers in China as 'a sort of diplomatic cracker that has produced a great many detonations, but I think the smoke of it has now floated into the distance'. When the Russians occupied Port Arthur in 1898 he wrote that the British public would demand 'some territorial or cartographic consolation in China. It will not be useful, and it will be expensive; but as a matter of pure sentiment, we shall have to do it.' Once, defending an agreement which assigned to France a large part of the Sahara, he said: 'This is what agriculturists would call very "light" land' – not a tactful way of recommending the agreement to French public opinion.

All these dazzling phrases are about foreign affairs, and foreign policy was his consuming interest. He first stepped into the front rank in politics in 1878; he became Foreign Secretary in place of Lord Derby and got British foreign policy out of the mess into which it had been landed by the conflict between the pacifism of Derby and the erratic, unpredictable bellicosity of Disraeli. Sitting in the House of Lords – he was the last prime minister to sit in the Lords and I don't suppose we shall have another, the peerage is not likely to produce a man of Salisbury's genius in centuries – he had few parliamentary cares and, except for a few months in 1886 and again for a few months at the end of his life, he combined the jobs of Prime Minister and Foreign Secretary. He was very much the senior, too, in his Cabinets. He could conduct foreign policy virtually uncontrolled – not checked by a prime minister, not interfered with much by the Cabinet and remote even from questions in the House of Commons. Add to this that Rosebery, the Liberal Foreign Secretary in the short break between Salisbury's governments, was virtually imposed on Gladstone by the Queen, at Salisbury's prompting, and that Rosebery was Salisbury's obedient pupil. As a result, Salisbury had fifteen years, from 1885 to 1900, of directing foreign policy, a record in our history; moreover, it was really a policy he directed. He was fond of saying that a British Foreign Secretary could have no policy. In his own words, 'British policy is to drift lazily downstream, occasionally putting out a boat-hook to avoid a collision.' But this apparent planlessness was really a device to keep his hands free and to conceal his plans from foreigners. There is nothing in the history of our foreign policy to compare with the prolonged and patient way in which Salisbury solved the difficulties of the British position in Egypt, isolating Egypt first from one country and then another, and finally staging the open challenge to France at Fashoda in 1898. Indeed, I would say that Salisbury laid down the lines on which British foreign policy was to develop for many years after his death: he saw that so long as we were quarrelling with France and Russia all over the world – in Egypt, in Persia, in the Far East – we were dependent on German favour, and he was determined to escape this favour. Therefore, slowly and persistently, he prepared the way for the Anglo-French entente, which matured in 1904, and the Anglo-Russian entente, which matured in 1907. At the very basis of his thoughts was the fact that has been brought home to us by two great wars: if England and Russia, the two Great Powers on the edge of Europe, fall out, they will have Europe, in the shape of Germany, on their backs. That is why Salisbury, greatest of our Foreign Secretaries, was the greatest advocate of Anglo-Russian co-operation.

In comparison with these great world affairs, Salisbury had less interest in the humdrum tasks of a prime minister. He was too outspoken to be a good manager of men and could never have been a successful leader of the House of Commons. But, to his surprise, he found that he could compete with Gladstone as a public speaker at mass meetings: like many intellectuals, an impersonal mass audience drew him out where a few dozen individuals did not. He spoke in the fine Victorian way without notes, sometimes pausing for as much as thirty seconds between sentences; the effect was ponderous, absolutely sincere, like the strokes of a great hammer. But, with this sincerity and greatness of character, what had he to say? Very little. The only question on which he felt strongly was the defence of the Established Church. This marks him off from other Victorian prime ministers: most of them were lukewarm in religion. Glad-stone, on the other hand, was so devout that he desired to disestab-lish the Church so that it could develop the virtue of apostolic poverty. Apart from this, Salisbury excelled at exposing the follies of others, but had little to advocate himself. Though a good landlord in private life, he had no social philosophy: he accepted private enterprise and Free Trade like any Liberal. When Disraeli urged that the Conservatives ought to take the lead in social reform, Salisbury complained that Disraeli was 'feather-brained'.

The truth is that this great man, so free from illusions, had one great illusion: fear of democracy and belief in the virtue of resisting for resisting's sake. During the American Civil War, when he was, of course, strongly on the side of the slave-owning South, his mind was so agitated that he took to sleep-walking, and one night his wife saw him rise from his bed and stand at the open window, warding off an imaginary attack; the forces of democracy were trying to break into Hatfield House. He spoke all his life as though democracy was a sort of germ people catch, much as people now talk of Communism as a germ that will get into the Western world unless we keep the Greek window closed. Instead of the process of compromise between parties which has been the normal pattern of our political life, he wanted to make a sharp division between them and have a fight. The issue he found to fight on was Irish Home Rule. Gladstone had hoped that the Conservatives would carry Home Rule as Peel had carried Free Trade. Instead Salisbury – it was his decision that mattered – made it the matter of political conflict for a generation. In one sense it did the trick: it gave the Conservatives almost twenty years of office. But at a high price. It left the Irish question to be settled later at a terrible cost in bitterness and bloodshed. It taught the Conservatives to value violence and pugnacity as a policy and so led them to the follies of defending the House of Lords in 1910 and to the worse-than-folly of the Ulster rebellion in 1914. What is more, it made Salisbury himself the prisoner of all the violent men prepared to resist Home Rule, the prisoner of Joseph Chamberlain and of the unscrupulous Imperialists, the prisoner even of Cecil Rhodes.

Salisbury had begun as the leader of devout country gentlemen with centuries of honest tradition behind them. He ended as the leader of the Unionists, the party of the City and high finance. He took the lead in the partition in Africa in order to end the slave trade; this was not the motive of his party-backers in the Chartered Companies. His last great act was to lead this country into the Boer War. Undoubtedly he hoped to establish the British ideal of racial equality in South Africa. The Boer War made the gold and diamonds secure for the city companies; it has not, so far, benefited the South African natives. And here, I think, we have got to the secret of his strange personality, of the contrast between his private charitableness and the bitterness of his public expression: he loved the joy of battle, but found no worthy cause for which to fight. He fought for victory; he expected defeat. His two great ancestors had founded the greatness of the British Empire; Salisbury heard from afar the notes which announced its end. When Salisbury resigned in 1902, old England too passed from the stage of history.

Lord Rosebery

Archibald Philip Primrose, fifth Earl of Rosebery (1847–1929), was one of the few leading Whig peers who did not defect from the Liberal party over Home Rule or other Irish matters in the 1880s. He was Gladstone's host and supporter during Gladstone's famous Midlothian campaigns (1879–80), was Gladstone's Foreign Secretary (1886 and 1892–4) and his successor as Prime Minister (1894–5) and Liberal leader (1894–6). He was a Liberal Imperialist and an advocate of 'national efficiency', who drifted away from the Liberal party in the early twentieth century.

This essay was first published as a review of Robert Rhodes James, Rosebery, Weidenfeld & Nicolson, 1963, in the Observer, 17 February 1963. Later, Alan Taylor named it as one of his books of the year.

Lord Rosebery had ambition of an unusual kind. His lifelong dream was that, without effort or preparation, he should be offered the post of Prime Minister, and that he should then gracefully refuse.

He nearly attained this ambition. He was duly invited to become Prime Minister; but, to his great misfortune, he could not refuse. He spent his fifteen months of office lamenting his position, his colleagues, and himself. His government and his party were brought to ruin. Yet even after this failure he went on hoping that the call would come again and that this time he would refuse in earnest.

Politically his was a wasted life. He had superlative gifts. He was the most elegant orator of his time, uniquely popular in Scotland and widely admired by Liberals everywhere. He had great wealth, an irresistible social presence, wide knowledge of literature and history, particularly of the eighteenth century. He was the only Prime Minister to win the Derby while in office. For twenty years he was confidently named as the Man of the Future: then it appeared that he had not even a past. He had it in him to be a great man, and he achieved nothing except to add Uganda to the British Empire.

Bernard Shaw said that Rosebery was a man who never missed an opportunity of missing an opportunity. Others accused him of wanting the palm without the dust. This was not quite true. He never shrank from the labour of public speeches. He worked hard on his papers when Foreign Secretary. No man conducted more correspondence or preserved it more carefully, though unsystematically. But he lacked the ability to work with others. Entering the House of Lords early and with grandeur, he never learnt the art of political co-operation or of compromise. He remained aloof and isolated, like his hero, the great Earl of Chatham. He expected men to divine his secret thoughts and to follow them without question. Yet he would not reveal what these thoughts were. Men had to chase him, as he moved restlessly among his four great houses. When found, Rosebery would captivate his visitor with lighthearted conversation, and dismiss him before the serious topic had been raised.

He was first stirred into political excitement by the Midlothian campaign. He served Gladstone with romantic devotion, actually rejoining Gladstone's government after the death of Gordon, as a gesture of suicidal loyalty. Yet he groaned under the servitude, and regretted, at the end of his life, that he had not followed Disraeli.

Rosebery's life could be told as a portentous essay in political biography. Great things were happening in the world. Home Rule was transforming the Irish question; social reform was pushing to the front: the old Liberal party was disintegrating; the great European Powers were creating their empires and moving towards conflict.

Rosebery played a part in all these affairs. Others bore the real burden. What Rosebery contributed unwillingly was entertainment. His life provides material for comedy of the most refined type. This is how Mr Rhodes James has treated it, as though Meredith had turned to writing biography. His book is the richest comedy to be produced for many years. I cannot remember when I have enjoyed a book more.

Outwardly the presentation is scholarly and solemn. Rosebery's own papers are reinforced by the papers of others, and particularly by the diaries of the preposterous Loulou Harcourt, son of Sir William. Intrigue is the dominant theme: intrigue by others to get office, and by Rosebery to avoid it. Rosebery was made a junior Minister at the outset of his political career. He demanded to be admitted to the Cabinet. Once in, he insisted on going out. He fought against becoming Foreign Secretary, and accepted with the laconic telegram: 'So be it. Mentmore' (one of his country houses). He resented the efforts of others to become Prime Minister, and then counted the days until his own government fell. 'He loves me. He loves me not' was the dominant thought in the minds of Liberal politicians for many years.

Gladstone is the richest figure in the book. Rosebery had a skin too few; Gladstone half a dozen too many. He wrote to Rosebery on one occasion: 'I seem to be like the juror, who sat with eleven most obstinate men, that he could not convince of the truth he himself saw.' Rosebery described Gladstone, presiding over his last Cabinet, as 'pale old croupier in midst with passion seething in his face'.

As a special element of farce, Loulou was determined to make his father Prime Minister without Sir William's knowledge, and the old gentleman had to pay the price for Loulou's manoeuvres.

The social revelations are also fascinating. The Prince of Wales and the Duke of Edinburgh wished to borrow Rosebery's town house in order to entertain their 'actress friends'. Rosebery refused on the ground that the house was too small. Later, Edward VII quarrelled with Rosebery for turning up to dinner in the royal yacht in a Yacht Squadron mess jacket. Gladstone took Rosebery to the theatre to see Lily Langtry, and explained that he was busy 'rescuing' her. Later, when Rosebery was Prime Minister, four of his colleagues pursued the same admirable mission. He rebuked them in a Cabinet circular, and suggested alternative entertainment: 'A public visit to inspect their own effigies at Madame Tussaud's would be both pleasing and popular; while for those to whom this might be too great a strain it might be useful to bear in mind that Mr Haldane, QC, MP, lectures on "Schopenhauer and the Ideal London," at the George Odger Coffee Tavern, 3 Cowslip Terrace, Clerkenwell Green, at 8 precisely (there will be a collection).'

The whole book is on this level – a memorable contribution indeed to the innocent gaiety of nations.

A. J. Balfour

Arthur James Balfour (1848–1930) was the successor (1902–5) of his uncle, Lord Salisbury, as Prime Minister. Balfour served in most Conservative Cabinets between 1886 and 1929, latterly from 1922 as the Earl of Balfour. He also served in the coalition governments of Asquith and Lloyd George (1915–22).

This essay was first published, under the title 'Trickery as a fine art', as a review of Alfred Gollin, Balfour's Burden, *Blond, 1965, in the* Observer, *21 November 1965. Alan Taylor disliked Balfour, commenting in one review that he 'appears a detestable man, cynical, unprincipled and frivolous' (Observer, 11 August 1968) and in another, 'Intellectual foolery was Balfour's incurable weakness. Intellectual policy was intermittently his strength' (New Statesman, 15 March 1963).*

Dr A. M. Gollin has an unrivalled achievement as a researcher in recent history. He discovers new and startling material, binds it into a skilful narrative, and tops everything with a style of remorseless repetition. He has written two very long books. His new book is shorter and slighter. Indeed, a more economical writer could have brought it within the compass of a scholarly article. There is much incidental entertainment, including, for instance, Northcliffe's pre-Gallup soundings of public opinion, which led him to denounce 'Stomach Taxes'. There is elaborate background over a prolonged period.

But the core of the book is the political crisis of September 1903, when Joseph Chamberlain resigned from the Unionist Cabinet in order to preach Tariff Reform. Balfour, the Prime Minister, allowed the Free Trade members of the Cabinet to resign, without telling them that Chamberlain was about to go. Then Balfour won over the Duke of Devonshire, chief of the discontented, by telling him about Chamberlain after all. The Duke withdrew his resignation. Victory for Balfour. The Duke was reproached by his former associates and resigned. Defeat for Balfour. That is all. Funny no doubt, but rather thin.

Dr Gollin thinks that Balfour was a marvellous political tactician. Can this really be said of a Prime Minister who led his party open-eyed into its greatest electoral defeat? To quote Campbell-Bannerman: 'Enough of this foolery.'

H. H. Asquith

Herbert Henry Asquith (1852–1928) was Home Secretary under
Gladstone and Rosebery (1892–5), Chancellor of the Exchequer
under Campbell-Bannerman (1905–8) before becoming Prime Min-
ister (1908–16) and leader of the Liberal party (1908–26).

This essay was first published as a review of Stephen Koss,
Asquith, Allen Lane, 1976, in the New Statesman, 3 September
1976. Alan Taylor did much to revive David Lloyd George's repu-
tation. He was much less enthusiastic about Asquith. He observed
on one occasion that Asquith was 'muddled and lethargic' (New
Statesman, 6 May 1966), and Asquith comes near to being the
villain of the early part of his volume in the Oxford History of
England, England 1914–1945 (Oxford University Press, 1965).
Perhaps Taylor's personal background contributed in a small way
to his downgrading of Asquith. Taylor's parents had been Lloyd
George supporters as members of the pre-1914 Liberal party, leav-
ing for the Independent Labour Party in the latter part of the war.
Also, Lloyd George was remembered as a much more dynamic
figure by Alan Taylor's friend, Lord Beaverbrook. Nevertheless,
these were relatively minor influences to the major matter of Alan
Taylor's professional judgement as a historian.

Most prime ministers provide good material for historians to fight
over. Now that the disputes over Baldwin and Chamberlain have
somewhat died down, Asquith heads the field. How did he reach
'that narrow street so many desire to tread, yet so few deserve to
enter, the path that leads to No. 10'? How did he become the most

powerful peacetime Prime Minister of the twentieth century? And how, after this achievement, was he ejected from office so ignominiously, bringing down the once-great Liberal party with him? Though his policies were often radical, he also enjoyed the reputation of a patrician – 'the last of the Romans'. When he fell, D. H. Lawrence lamented: 'It is the end of England. It is finished. England will never be England any more.' Others however saw him as a befuddled old man – in Churchill's phrase, 'supine, sodden and supreme' – who spent his time in Cabinet writing letters to his young lady friends.

Asquith has had a good press biographically, culminating in the sympathetic life of him by Roy Jenkins, which has been sometimes hailed as a classic. Jenkins perhaps resembled Asquith too much to see his faults as well as his virtues. Stephen Koss is more detached. He provides no references to his sources – a decision I applaud if the alternative was to have the notes at the end of the book. In fact Koss has used many new sources – the diaries of Liberal politicians and of course Asquith's letters to Venetia Stanley, which like other closely guarded secrets prove to be less sensational than was expected. Koss's book is not perfect. As is the way of historians, he sometimes overrates the importance of his own discoveries. He fights battles with other historians who are not worth his powder and shot. He also goes astray occasionally on details, attributing to Balliol non-existent cloisters and to the elder Pitt alcoholic habits that belonged to his son. On a larger scale I think Koss fails to emphasize how really great the Liberal party was in its last tenure of power and how great Asquith was as its leader. After all, Asquith presided unchallenged over a true Ministry of All the Talents. There has been none since. However, this is the best biography of Asquith yet to be written and a book indispensable to every lover of political history.

Koss makes a good personal point about Asquith at the outset. There were two Asquiths. The first was 'Herbert', the stolid Yorkshire Nonconformist who married a Yorkshire girl of equally humble origin. Margot, Asquith's second wife, said of her predecessor: 'Helen was no wife for him. She lived in Hampstead and had no clothes.' Asquith was on the way to becoming 'Henry' even before Helen Asquith died of typhoid. His marriage to Margot

Tennant completed the process. Many thought Margot had ruined him. Campbell-Bannerman, for instance, said: 'Asquith *qua* Asquith is a fine fellow, an honest man and a sincere Liberal. But Asquith *cum* Margot is a lost soul.'

This was not all Margot's doing. Asquith wanted to be 'a lost soul'. He liked the high life and the social round that Margot provided, even if it sometimes exhausted him. He lived lavishly and assumed the airs of a patrician. He had an income of between £5,000 and £10,000 a year at the Bar; Margot had £5,000 a year of her own. Even so, Asquith lived beyond his means. He had a house in Cavendish Square with fourteen servants, including a pair of footmen, and kept a stable for his wife. It was a considerable achievement to remain even a somewhat lukewarm Liberal under such conditions.

Yet undoubtedly Asquith was a sincere and even resolute Liberal all his life. Though he did not care much for the Home Rule cause he had inherited from Gladstone, he was a stalwart Free Trader who could rout even Joseph Chamberlain in argument. He was also determined to get to the top. Few stories are more entertaining than the Relugas Compact, by which Asquith, Grey and Haldane agreed to relegate Campbell-Bannerman to the House of Lords. At the first whiff of high office Asquith deserted his two friends and left them to fend for themselves. Thereafter his rise to the premiership was certain. He had only to wait for Campbell-Bannerman to die; meanwhile he was Campbell-Bannerman's loyal supporter. In 1908 Asquith kissed hands as Prime Minister, appropriately at Biarritz. He had become 'the indispensable man'.

Morley complained, in his feline way, that Asquith as Prime Minister, 'although he discussed every proposition advanced by others with great intelligence and force ... never submitted any ideas of his own for consideration'. This was always Asquith's way. He let the storm of argument rage in Cabinet or in parliament and, when it had blown itself out, sailed placidly forward in calm waters. He had many great achievements to show. He introduced old age pensions, one of the first steps towards the welfare state. He secured the building of a great navy despite the reluctance or outright opposition of a good many of his followers.

He enabled Grey to conduct a foreign policy which many admire and which at any rate landed England in the First World War. He reduced decisively the powers of the House of Lords. This was a long and bitter struggle which Asquith fought impeccably. It can even be argued that he had brought the Irish problem to the verge of an agreed solution when success was snatched away from him by the outbreak of war in August 1914. If he had died then or left office, he would have had an undisputed claim to rank as one of the greatest prime ministers in our history.

The First World War was Asquith's undoing. 'Wait and See' had proved the key to success in peacetime. It was no way to run a war, particularly when the war went on so long. Asquith had really nothing to offer except his own unshakeable retention of office. Moreover, just when he should have become more resolute and determined, he became more pleasure-loving and easy-going than ever. Lloyd George called him rightly 'a soft-nosed torpedo'. Koss quotes Lytton Strachey's description of Asquith at Garsington in 1916: 'I studied the Old Man with extreme vigour, and really he's a corker. He seemed much larger than he did when I last saw him (just two years ago) – a fleshy, sanguine, wine-bibbing mediaeval Abbot of a personage – a gluttonous, lecherous, cynical old fellow ... On the whole, one wants to stick a dagger in his ribs ... and then, as well, one can't help liking him – I suppose because he *does* enjoy himself so much.'

The surprise is not that Asquith fell from power but that he held on so long. Even a dead oak takes a lot of chopping down. At his fall he showed an arrogant and mistaken pride. Unlike Neville Chamberlain in 1940, he refused to serve under his successor. As Koss says, 'Asquith was acting out of pique, which he asked contemporaries to accept as principle.' Not only contemporaries have done so. After the war he lingered on as leader of the declining Liberal party with Lloyd George as his unwilling and unwelcome second. He made no attempt to arrest the decline and, though Lloyd George made many, he was equally unsuccessful. Both men had outlived their time.

Asquith accepted this fate without demur. He never repined. Perhaps he did not even realize what had happened to him. It was reported that, reading a novel by his younger daughter Elizabeth Bibesco at the Reform Club, he sighed: 'another nail in the Asquith coffin'. Frank Swinnerton asked Vivian Phillipps, Asquith's secretary, whether the story were true. Phillipps laughed and replied, 'Mr A doesn't even know there is an Asquith coffin.' Asquith was a little distressed when he was not elected Chancellor of Oxford University. He was not at all distressed at being the leader of an almost non-existent party. As long as he could conduct amorous correspondence with his lady friends, Asquith was content. He remained complacent to the end. This had always been his great fault and also his great virtue.

Lloyd George

Though there is another essay on Lloyd George in this collection, this essay is an interesting assessment of the Welsh statesman in his last phase of office. It is also interesting as an assessment of one of Beaverbrook's books. Max Aitken, Lord Beaverbrook (1879–1964), was a friend and even father figure to Taylor from the late 1950s until his death.

This essay was first published as a review of Lord Beaverbrook, The Decline and Fall of Lloyd George, Collins, 1963, *in the* New Statesman, 8 March 1963. *The review was entitled 'Big Beast at Bay'.*

Lloyd George, for most of his life, was the Goat of British polities – agile, solitary, unpredictable. He succeeded by craft, not by force. After the First World War, he acquired a new nickname. Men called him now the Big Beast of the Forest. He was no longer the Goat. He was a Lion, the king of beasts. He commanded a great majority in the House of Commons. He was supreme in Cabinet as no statesman had been since the great Lord Chatham, and as none has been since. The greatest figures of the day cowered before him.

Many resented his dominion, and feared where he might lead them. None dared to go out and shoot big game. Dramatically the scene changed. In October 1922, Lloyd George, the dictator, was suddenly Out – despised and rejected, with a handful of followers, never to hold office again. How was the king of beasts brought down? This is Lord Beaverbrook's theme. His new book has no rivals except its predecessors, *Politicians and the War* and *Men and*

Power. Like them, it is a unique combination of political history and personal recollection. There is the same sparkling style, an equally rich stock of anecdotes, and the same endearing frankness of Lord Beaverbrook about himself. *Politicians and the War* has the tightest narrative. Also it has the most important subject: the story of how Lloyd George became Prime Minister in order to win the war. *Men and Power*, being designedly episodic, has the most sustained portraits of individuals. *The Decline and Fall* is slighter and sometimes diffuse.

But the new arrival has qualities of its own. It deals with an almost unknown topic. Many men have contributed to an understanding of Lloyd George's rise to power. Few have illuminated his fall – least of all Lloyd George himself. Further, Lord Beaverbrook now reveals much from the political archives which he has acquired – the papers of Carson, Curzon, Bonar Law and Lloyd George himself. He is indeed embarrassed by his own wealth; and has had to stuff letters and other material which he could not use in his text into sixty pages of appendices. The most valuable new information comes from the unpublished diaries and autobiography of Miss Stevenson, Lloyd George's secretary and second wife. We can follow the tactics of Lloyd George as well as the tactics of his enemies.

There is a personal theme in this book, which is also more than personal. Beaverbrook was one of the first to turn against Lloyd George. He had a mission in public life, the cause which he has always served, if not wisely, at any rate with devotion. This cause was Empire Free Trade. Empire Free Trade meant, in practice, taxes on British food imports, Stomach Taxes. Beaverbrook did not shrink from these. Lloyd George did. Not that Lloyd George was a Free Trader by conviction – he was rarely troubled by convictions on this or any other subject. He was tied to Free Trade by his Coalition Liberal followers. They were essential to him, so that he could continue to ride high above the Conservatives; and Free Trade was essential to them, as the only guarantee of their separate existence. Hence Lloyd George often listened to Beaverbrook's temptations, and never succumbed to them. Hence also Beaverbrook sought for someone who would overthrow the Big Beast and carry Empire Free Trade to triumph.

The champion existed: the one man who did not fear Lloyd George and was himself a believer in the great cause. This man was Bonar Law. He had fallen ill early in 1921, and had withdrawn from politics. Much of this book is the story of Beaverbrook's efforts to bring him back. Bonar Law was reluctant, as always. Indeed this very reluctance made him the greatest giant-killer of his age. Balfour, Asquith, Lloyd George all fell beneath his axe – slaughtered after much hesitation and protest, but slaughtered all the same. This time Bonar Law's withdrawal seemed final. He was weary of politics, and would not return unless the nation, or the Conservative party, were in danger. Beaverbrook had to look elsewhere. There seemed to be plenty of material. The leading members of the government all had their grievances against Lloyd George, and were tempted to desert him. Both Churchill and Birkenhead dreamt of becoming Prime Minister. Then 'the Plot' dissolved. The Conservatives would not follow Churchill, the Free Trader. Lloyd George said to him brutally: 'To be a party you must have at least one follower. You have none.' Birkenhead was cajoled back into obedience. It is strange what flattery could achieve with one so arrogant. Soon Birkenhead was telling Beaverbrook: 'It is no good trying to upset Lloyd George. There would be no one to put in his place, and in any case you will not succeed.' Beaverbrook replied: 'No, but I can *try*.'

Lloyd George was not idle. Where he had once intrigued for great purposes, he now intrigued to survive. The manoeuvres, chronicled in this book, were conducted in obscurity. These glittering birds of paradise behaved as though British destinies rested solely with them; as though back-bench MPs hardly existed, and the electorate not at all. The struggle for power was fought with scarcely a hint that an alternative claimant to power was waiting round the corner, in the shape of the Labour party. Lloyd George evaded the nets which were being spread before his feet. He sacrificed Dr Addison, his devoted follower, the man who had helped to make him Prime Minister in December 1916. Addison was blamed for the failure to provide Homes for Heroes. There was a price to pay for this escape. Previously men had laughed with Lloyd George. Now they laughed at him. He had demonstrated only too clearly that there was no friendship at the top. Others, too, shook off the sense of obligation which Lloyd George had disregarded. His prestige was going; he could no longer survive by sounding the great trumpets of his reputation. Yet even now Lloyd George was not dismayed. He showed new zest, fresh ingenuity. He was game to the last. He had been swept to the top by his achievement in winning the war. Now he wanted some new achievement, some new pinnacle of success dazzlingly attained, which would make men accept him once more as dictator.

He seized the chance to end at last the Irish question which had tormented British politics for centuries. Lloyd George pulled off a characteristic stroke. He invited Churchill and Birkenhead to join the Irish negotiations. They were won over and, from that moment, became again his loyal allies, upholding the hands of Moses. Beaverbrook watched the negotiations from an unusual point of vantage. Tim Healy had come over from Ireland, ready to advise the Irish delegates. He stayed at Beaverbrook's house. Healy's advice was soon needed. Lloyd George posed the dreaded question: 'Do the Irish government concede to the British Admiralty control of the ports and harbours of Ireland?' The Irish delegates were dismayed. Healy was not. He advised: 'Ask Lloyd George – what is Ireland? What will be the jurisdiction of the Irish government?' Thus the ultimatum was evaded: the conference was back at the problem of Ulster.

Beaverbrook went to the Conservative leaders. They were expecting the conference to break down. He told them that the corner had been turned. The Conservative leaders demanded to know his source of information. Beaverbrook could not reveal it. He bethought him of George Barnes, one-time member of the war Cabinet, who 'lived up to every Pauline injunction'. Rashly Beaverbrook replied: 'Barnes's mistress!' 'This was greeted with shouts of laughter and also perhaps another black mark against me because of my ribald conduct.'

Lloyd George carried the Irish treaty. What is more, every prominent Coalition minister was associated with it; every possible rival thus compromised – with the exception of Bonar Law. The Conservative rank and file were resentful. Lloyd George needed new triumphs. His opportunity came unexpectedly when Kemal, leader of nationalist Turkey, drove the Greeks out of Asia Minor. Lloyd George saw himself once more as the great war minister. Even those colleagues who had been pro-Turk rallied round him. 'So Samson pulled down the pillars of the temple and was buried in the ruins.' Beaverbrook opposed him once more, this time successfully. During the summer of 1922, Beaverbrook had been in Turkey. He knew an honourable peace was possible. The essential move was to bring Bonar Law back into politics. The task was hard. Bonar Law disapproved of Lloyd George's policy, but he showed all the old reluctance to strike. He hesitated until the last moment.

On the night before the meeting at the Carlton Club where the Conservatives were to decide their attitude to Lloyd George, Beaverbrook went to Bonar Law. Bonar Law produced a letter to the chairman of his constituency at Glasgow, declining to stand at the next general election. Beaverbrook refused to comment. He merely said: 'The letter is too long.' Bonar Law pleaded for his opinion. Gradually Beaverbrook warmed to his task, 'concluding on a high Imperial note'. Bonar Law refilled his pipe and said quite simply: 'I am going to the meeting.' Beaverbrook, suffering from a fever, 'went hotter and colder'. He fled, and passed the news to the Press Association. The next morning Bonar Law telephoned: he had not slept all night, he wanted another talk at once. Beaverbrook replied: 'Have you seen the morning newspapers?' Bonar Law went to the meeting. The Conservatives resolved on independence. Lloyd George fell. The great Coalition was at an end.

Beaverbrook's work was not over. Lloyd George and the ex-Ministers who followed him did not believe that Bonar Law could win a general election. Bonar Law doubted it also. The Conservative Central Office sought Coalition Liberal support. It did not back candidates against them. Beaverbrook defied this pact. He stirred up local Conservative Associations. He financed some candidates himself. The move worked. 'Out of fifty-six seats where Conservative candidates were launched against Lloyd George's party men, only two of the Lloyd George candidates were successful.' Bonar Law triumphed. The Conservatives won a clear majority of over seventy seats. Lloyd George was ruined for ever. He and his associates blamed Beaverbrook – rightly. 'From that day of conflict the mistaken opinion persists that I seek after power without respons- ibility. It is not true. There have been times when I have taken too much responsibility.' Beaverbrook had succeeded, and his success turned to dust. He had worked for the victory of Empire Free Trade. He forgot Lord Derby. Derby, for once, failed to behave like the feather pillow. Though Beaverbrook sat upon him, Derby did not show the marks. He insisted on Free Trade, and Bonar Law agreed. The Conservative ministry was as much pledged against Stomach Taxes as its Coalition predecessor.

There is a moving epilogue. In September 1923 Bonar Law was out of office, a dying man. Lloyd George was also out of office. Beaverbrook invited the two men to lunch. They were reconciled. They talked over old quarrels, now forgotten. Lloyd George put forth all his charm, and brought a last flash of gaiety into Bonar Law's sad eyes. 'They parted in an atmosphere of companionship. They were two friends destined never to meet again.'

Empire Free Trade was never brought to triumph. But Lord Beaverbrook has had great consolations. He has been at the heart of events for over fifty years, at once observer and doer. He has appreciated every moment of drama, and often provided the drama himself. He has been the greatest newspaperman since Northcliffe. Now, on top of this, he writes books which are the admiration and envy of the professional historian.

Bonar Law

Andrew Bonar Law (1858–1923) was leader of the Conservative party, 1911–21 and 1922–3, and Prime Minister 1923, after serving loyally as Lloyd George's deputy in his coalition governments (1916–21), until retiring due to ill-health. Bonar Law was born in New Brunswick, Canada, the son of an Ulsterman, a Presbyterian minister. Max Aitken, Lord Beaverbrook, also the son of a Presbyterian minister who had emigrated to Canada, was helped by Bonar Law to achieve selection for a marginal parliamentary seat, which he won in the December 1910 general election. Thereafter, he was a noted supporter, friend or even acolyte of Bonar Law.

This essay was first published under the title 'Iron Merchant' as a review of Robert Blake, The Unknown Prime Minister, *Eyre & Spottiswoode, 1955, in the* Observer, *9 October 1955.*

Bismarck described Lord Salisbury as lath painted to look like iron. Bonar Law was iron not painted at all. No harder man has risen to the top in British political life. All statesmen are ruthless, and have to be if they are going to succeed; but English statesmen usually obscure this in a haze of easily stirred emotion. Not Bonar Law. He never shed tears over any public issue: and he was unmoved by the tears of others. When Churchill pleaded to be allowed to retain the Admiralty in 1915, Bonar Law replied curtly: 'Believe me, what I said to you last night is inevitable.' Or again, having driven Asquith from power, he made no attempt to apologize or to smooth things over, but merely said: 'When a man has done another a serious injury no good can come from explanations.'

When later he overthrew Lloyd George in the same way, he made no comment at all.

Tariff Reform took him into politics. Ulster kept him there. All the rest was 'the game', as he confessed later. He did little even for his chosen causes. Tariff Reform did not move an inch in the years when he led the Conservative party, and he made no reference to it when he became Prime Minister. Austen Chamberlain, or even Baldwin, would have been less forgetful. He defended the cause of Ulster unflinchingly and indeed brought the United Kingdom to the edge of civil war. But he agreed to the partition of Ireland as a surgeon detaches a limb without a sign of interest in the patient.

His overriding aim was to keep the Conservative party together: and if he has a place in history it is as the man who carried this party through the stresses of the early twentieth century. The Conservative party nearly split over Tariff Reform; nearly split over Ireland; nearly split over the House of Lords. It was on the brink of being eaten up by Lloyd George, and then lost all its leaders save one in getting rid of him. It survived all these dangers to become the dominant force in British politics between the wars. This was all Bonar Law's doing. But what else? Where is the great speech, the creative doctrine, where even the witty remark? Nowhere. He never said anything either original or memorable; he gave no lead in policy; he stirred no generous emotions.

He was as dull in private life as he was drab in politics. He disliked the beauties of nature (the only Prime Minister to refuse the use of Chequers); he had no interest in pretty women, or in literature, or in art. He was a teetotaller who gobbled his commonplace food. He played bridge and golf, competently, without enjoyment. His one oddity was to play chess 'with great recklessness, flashes of brilliance, but in a manner dangerously unsound by ordinary standards'. Perhaps it was the same oddity that made him welcome colourful, erratic friends – Lloyd George, F. E. Smith, Lord Beaverbrook. It is strange to think of him sitting cool and unyielding through their gay evenings.

How is one to write the life of such a prosaic figure? Mr Blake must have been tempted to overplay his hand and to present Bonar

Law as a statesman of genius, particularly as he had Lord Beaver-brook at his elbow supplying material and, no doubt, inspiration. Mr Blake has withstood temptation nobly. Apart from a few rhetorical passages, his book is as sober as its subject: but also, like its subject, extremely competent, a much more admirable production from the historian's point of view than the last horse from Lord Beaverbrook's stable. The book is packed with new material, and Mr Blake uses it admirably, though sometimes watering his revelations with stuff that we knew already.

There are many questions in recent history which this book answers decisively, so that they need never be asked again. How did Bonar Law become leader of the Conservative party when he had markedly less backing than either of his rivals? Would the Liberal government have gone to war if the Germans had not invaded Belgium? How did Lloyd George overthrow Asquith? Or, for that matter, how did Bonar Law overthrow Lloyd George? Whom did Bonar Law expect to succeed him? On a different plane: where did the Conservative party get its money from (and presumably still does)? What was the price of a baronetcy, of an earldom? What happened to Lord Astor's £200,000? – the last a question easier to ask than to answer.

There is certainly much entertainment here for those who like to see below the surface of politics, and for all our academic exponents of the subject who think that they have exhausted it when they explain how the machine works. But where is the fuel of enthusiasm, of passion, of belief? Not in the life of Bonar Law. It is all as significant as the story why Mrs Smith became president of the local women's institute instead of Mrs Brown – important enough to Mrs Smith, perhaps even interesting as a case history, no more.

Mr Blake could have written a book in exactly the same tone, though not perhaps of the same length, if Bonar Law had remained in Glasgow as a partner in the firm of William Jacks and Company, iron merchants. The story might even have been more exciting, for as Bonar Law remarked shortly before becoming Prime Minister: 'I was in the iron trade, a highly speculative business with frequent violent fluctuations in prices.' He never fluctuated though his fortunes did. He was always a business man, dealing in the destinies of men as he had dealt in pig-iron. But at any rate he was a good business man, which is more than can be said for some of the later Conservative ventures in this class of goods.

Ramsay MacDonald

James Ramsay MacDonald (1866–1937) was Prime Minister 1924 and 1929–35. He formed the first Labour governments (1924 and 1929–31) but broke with his Labour party colleagues when he formed the National Government and consolidated it by holding and winning the 1931 general election.

This essay was first published as a review of David Marquand, Ramsay MacDonald, Cape, *1977 in the* Observer, *6 March 1977.*

Alan Taylor was often very critical of MacDonald but went some way towards rehabilitating his reputation in his English History 1914–1945, *Oxford University Press, 1965. Yet he remained sceptical of Ramsay MacDonald being radical. In 1971 he observed, 'Ramsay MacDonald was less of a danger to society than Lloyd George had been. With MacDonald as Labour leader the old ladies of the Conservative party could sleep quietly in their beds.'(Observer, 25 April 1971). He also remained very critical of MacDonald in the 1931 financial crisis. He commented, 'MacDonald now appears as totally at a loss, with no understanding of economics, no idea of what to do and more bewildered than the most ignorant speculator' (Observer, 10 September 1978).*

> Oh no, we never mention him;
> His name is never heard.

Such until recently was the attitude of all good Labour men towards Ramsay MacDonald, first Labour Prime Minister and incomparable Socialist orator, who unwillingly left his party in 1931 to become

Prime Minister of the so-called National Government. Conservatives who followed his lead then were subsequently not proud of what happened. MacDonald became a scapegoat for the failures of the 1930s, a man better forgotten.

Now at last Ramsay MacDonald has received full and fair treatment from David Marquand, a distinguished historian and himself until recently a Labour MP. This is a first-rate biography, the best, I think, of any prime minister between the wars. The book is inevitably very long, just on 800 pages. But every page is relevant and endowed with the powerful clarity of which Marquand is a master. Marquand does not conceal MacDonald's faults and failures, but he also does justice to MacDonald's great achievements.

For they were great. MacDonald created the British Labour party and defined the social democratic outlook which still keeps it going. He established Labour instead of Liberal as the predominant party of the Left. The successes of British foreign policy between the wars, and these were not few, were mostly his doing. His oratory rivalled that of Gladstone. As Prime Minister he proved that Labour was fit to govern. Until his lapse in 1931 he was regarded almost universally as the greatest Socialist leader in Great Britain.

MacDonald was a Scotsman of humble origin. He was a true romantic, always inclined to melancholy and self-pity, particularly after his wife's death in 1911. At the same time he was a canny tactician, bargaining over seats and guiding quarrelsome Cabinets to agreement. Marquand offers two brilliant phrases to characterize MacDonald's outlook. One is 'principled opportunism', the other 'vehement moderation'. MacDonald could rant like any revolutionary, but his purpose was to promote caution and patience. Whereas Marxists expected socialism to spring from the collapse of capitalism, MacDonald held that socialism would follow almost imperceptibly on capitalism's success. His was a fair-weather socialism and in practice he was often more concerned to make capitalism succeed than to supersede it.

Before the First World War MacDonald formed an electoral alliance with the Liberals and even contemplated entering the Liberal Cabinet. Once the Liberals were split by wartime events, MacDonald changed his line. The very unpopularity he acquired by opposing the war made him popular after it. He was one of the few not besmirched by the discredit of wartime failures. He alone seemed to offer a better future. The Labour government of 1924 was MacDonald's greatest victory. After it Labour was firmly established as the only alternative to the Conservatives, and from this position Labour has never looked back. By 1929, when MacDonald again took office, a Labour government had become natural and acceptable.

MacDonald had another concern during his leadership of the Labour party. He was determined that the political party should become independent of the trade unions even though they provided most of its funds. He opposed the First World War when the trade unions supported it. In the great crisis of 1931 one motive for his action was a resolve that financial policy should not be dictated by the TUC. This provoked resistance from Arthur Henderson, who put loyalty to the unions first. The rivalry between the two men shaped much of Labour's history. Though Henderson ultimately won, his victory did not at the time do Labour much good.

MacDonald was a rhetorician, not a clear thinker. He often equivocated and muddled in face of conflict. He was shifty over the Campbell case in 1924 and got the Zinoviev Letter scare into hopeless confusion. But many others were often as muddled as he was. The story of the financial crisis in 1931 brings this out dramatically. Everyone, including even the Keynesian economist Hubert Henderson, agreed that the gold standard must be saved. Otherwise there would be a *dégringolade*. The Labour Cabinet agreed. It also agreed that there must be cuts in government expenditure. The TUC intervened, condemning all cuts and those in unemployment benefit most of all. A strong minority of Labour Ministers responded to the crack of the TUC whip, which incidentally made more sense economically. The position of the Labour Cabinet was that the cuts must be made, but that Labour could not make them.

MacDonald assumed that a Liberal–Conservative coalition would follow and that he would support its policy from the back benches. Intense pressure from George V drove him into becoming National Prime Minister. George V had a high opinion of Mac-

Donald, telling him later, 'You have been the Prime Minister I have liked best.' MacDonald expected the National Government to last only a few weeks. It never crossed his mind that Labour leaders, who had accepted the cuts when in office, would oppose the same cuts once they were in opposition. But so it proved. MacDonald was stuck with the National Government. He was struck off the lists of the Labour party. He became the prototype of political traitor and made his public image worse by his platonic friendship with Lady Londonderry. MacDonald lamented that the National Government was 'nae my ain hoose' and never ceased to mourn his breach with the Labour party. If indeed he betrayed the Labour party, his rewards for this were singularly few.

MacDonald was a pathetic, almost a tragic figure. Yet it is difficult to be sorry for him. He was the architect of his own downfall. Despite his genuine humility, he was also a vain man, eager for popular acclaim and delighting in the finery of a privy councillor's uniform. He was impatient with criticism or disagreement and saw himself as a lonely maligned hero, carrying all the cares of the world on his shoulders. Far more than Gladstone he was inebriated by the exuberance of his own verbosity. Gladstone often stopped to think; MacDonald never did so. Words came easily to him; ideas were not his concern. In this he did not differ from most Labour leaders of the time. But, being carried to the highest place, he bore the greatest responsibility. His failure was in intellect, not in character. Marquand concludes with this moral:

A radical party requires, not merely high ideals and skilful leadership, but intellectual coherence and a willingness to jettison cherished assumptions in the face of changing realities. It is an easy moral to formulate. Half a century bears witness to the fact that it is not so easy to practise.

Neville Chamberlain

(Arthur) Neville Chamberlain (1869–1940), the son of Joseph Chamberlain (1836–1914) and half-brother of (Joseph) Austen Chamberlain (1863–1937), was the only one of the three to achieve the premiership (1937–40), although his father was a major national political figure from the 1880s until 1906, and his half-brother a major figure in the Conservative party and briefly its leader (1921–2).

This essay was first published as a review of Iain Macleod, Neville Chamberlain, *Muller, 1961, in the* New Statesman, *1 December 1961, and subsequently reprinted in his* Politics in Wartime, *Hamish Hamilton, 1964, and* Essays In English History, *Hamish Hamilton, 1976. When reprinting the essay in 1976, Alan Taylor added the remark: 'Chamberlain's system of local government has now been superseded, alas.'*

Napoleon used to ask of a man: 'Has he Luck?' Ability, experience, integrity were important; without luck they were useless. Neville Chamberlain had many great qualities. He had courage and industry. His intellect was clear and sharp. No politician this century has had a finer administrative brain, nor used this gift better. When he became Minister of Health in 1924 he set out his reforming programme in twenty-five draft bills, and carried twenty-one of them in the following four years. His Local Government Act of 1929, devised almost wholly by himself, had 115 clauses and twelve schedules. It shaped the structure of English local government to the present day. As Chancellor of the Exchequer, he recast the fiscal system, again with lasting effect. He commanded for a time the unquestioning allegiance of the Conservative party as none other of its leaders has done this century, not even Bonar Law. In Chamberlain's case, the allegiance was as strong on the front bench as among the rank and file. Yet it was all to no avail. The decisive element of luck was lacking.

Neville Chamberlain was without luck from the beginning. In the period of imperialist expansion, he stumbled on one of the few products, sisal, which failed to show a profit; and after five years of hard work in the West Indies came out with a loss of £50,000. In the First World War, he was saddled with the hopeless task of organizing National Service, and failed again, though he was abler than most of those who reaped high honours. Lloyd George called him 'not one of my lucky finds'. When the Conservative leadership became vacant after the death of Bonar Law, Chamberlain found ahead of him a man of few administrative or creative gifts, easygoing and evasive: Baldwin, constantly threatened by party revolt, yet repeatedly surviving, perhaps by innate political skill, perhaps by the essential quality of luck.

Chamberlain's reforms were dwarfed by other events. Not many cared about local government during the great depression; protective tariffs were less important in the 1930s than quotas and currency management. As Prime Minister, Chamberlain intended to be the initiator of domestic legislation. Instead he was caught by foreign affairs, and then led his country lamenting into war. His fall was a further irony of no luck. The Norwegian campaign was inspired and directed by Winston Churchill. Its failure brought down Chamberlain and put Churchill in his place. Even then Chamberlain could have been in charge of administration at home. He was struck by cancer, and died.

Neville Chamberlain has also been without luck after death. He has had to carry the sole blame for the failure of British foreign policy, despite protests from his more honest colleagues such as Hoare. By now one would imagine that Chamberlain conducted appeasement single-handed against an almost unanimous Conservative and an entirely unanimous Labour Party. In 1946 Dr (now Sir Keith) Feiling published an authorized biography. This was soundly based on the material then available: Chamberlain's letters to his sisters and his rather dry diary. There was a full and carefully drawn picture of Chamberlain's life in its various aspects, though Dr Feiling did not claim to be a specialist on the period. The book attracted less notice than it deserved. Maybe Englishmen were stunned by recent events, or did not wish to disrupt the new national unity against Russia by arguments about the past.

Still, Chamberlain's life was a subject which had been covered. Apart from writing a polemical tract, a new biographer would need to strike a fresh hoard of private material (or be able to prove that Dr Feiling had suppressed really important evidence). Alternatively, the new writer would use the material published since 1946 from the official records of the Foreign Office and the Cabinet; he might even get permission to see records not yet published, as some others have done. Even without new information, he might provide a new perspective and show wisdom after the event. But once more: no luck. It is excessive even in Chamberlain's run of bad luck that a biography claiming to vindicate him should neither vindicate him in any serious sense nor contain new information of importance.

Even an author who is a Cabinet minister and, like so many figures now forgotten, a future prime minister has a duty to his readers; in this case a duty to explain why they should read a second biography when a first, satisfactory, biography exists. This duty is not performed. The earlier biography is not mentioned, though the name of Sir Keith Feiling appears occasionally in the text. There is no hint that the diaries and private letters have been examined before, and have already yielded practically everything. The most interesting quotations all appear in Feiling's book; indeed for the period when Chamberlain was Prime Minister there are many more of them. When Mr Macleod has a new scrap to offer, this is produced with exaggerated emphasis. Thus a memorandum of 25 February 1931 from the Director of the Conservative Central Office, stating the dissatisfaction of the party with Baldwin as leader, is described as 'never before published'. Correct, but the gist is accurately summarized by Feiling.

Again Mr Macleod prints in full from Chamberlain's diary the story of the events which led to Eden's resignation as Foreign

Secretary in February 1938, and asserts that this 'makes clear much that has hitherto been conjectural and contradicts much that has hitherto been accepted'. In fact, Feiling printed five extracts from the account in Chamberlain's diary, which made the story clear, though passing over some details. Feiling's book is superior on nearly every point.

A few omissions are rectified. Feiling concentrated on Chamberlain and left out some episodes which might embarrass others, particularly when they were Fellows of All Souls. It is, for instance, odd that Sir John Simon, then a Liberal, should have drafted the Conservative vote of censure on the first Labour government over the Campbell case, when the Liberals were only asking for a committee of enquiry. Again, during the outcry over the Hoare–Laval plan, some members of the Cabinet, including Chamberlain, felt that, since they had in fact endorsed the plan, they should not make a scapegoat of Hoare. One member of the Cabinet however insisted that 'unless Sam went, the whole moral force of the government would be gone'. Hoare went. In 1940, when Chamberlain proposed to move Hore-Belisha from the War Office to the Ministry of Information, a Cabinet minister objected that 'it would have a bad effect on the neutrals both because H. B. was a Jew and because his methods would let down British prestige'. As Mr Macleod says, 'to all intents and purposes Hore-Belisha's career was broken'. On both occasions, the Cabinet minister concerned was Lord Halifax. Such new information, though welcome, does not justify a book. Many writers have the experience at some time of taking up a subject which seems rewarding, only to discover that it has been adequately treated already. It is usual in such cases to abandon the subject with regret.

We might at least have expected that the passage of time would bring a more detached judgement, if not a more effective defence. In this, too, we are disappointed. There is little here which was not said better by Chamberlain at the time. Mr Macleod does not much explore public opinion. He has a good quotation from the Labour spokesman at the time of the German reoccupation of the Rhineland:

It is only right to say bluntly and frankly that public opinion in this country would not support, and certainly the Labour party would not support, the taking of military sanctions or even economic sanctions against Germany at this time.

The speaker was Dr Hugh Dalton. Generally Mr Macleod is content to reiterate two points. First that 'Hitler was insatiable, war inevitable, and appeasement therefore a forlorn hope': second, that Chamberlain, knowing the weakness of British armaments, was concerned only to buy time. Both points have become the current orthodoxy, so much so that any attempt to question them, or even to examine them dispassionately, is met not with argument, but with cries of abusive rage. Of course Hitler was bent, as other German statesmen had been, on making Germany again the dominant Power in Europe; and this undoubtedly made some war probable, if not inevitable, at some time. This is far different from saying that the war which started in September 1939 was inevitable, a war in which Great Britain found herself fighting Germany without any effective ally. Once Germany recovered from her defeat in the First World War, the only choice was between her domination over eastern Europe and Russia's; and the only clear-headed opponents of appeasement were those who preferred Russia to Germany. Most of those who condemn appeasement are even more indignant at the consequence of its failure, a consequence which was, in their own favourite word, 'inevitable' – the eclipse of the British Empire by Russia and America.

Chamberlain perceived some of this, though he did not perceive all of it. He certainly appreciated the weakness of British arms, and indeed exaggerated it. He supposed, as the experts did, that bombing was a decisive weapon and that more bombing was the only answer to it. Mr Macleod waves aside the suggestion that Hitler was 'bluffing' in 1938. At this time, the Germans had forty divisions, only one armoured; the Czechs alone had thirty-six, four armoured. Hitler placed two divisions on his western frontier against eighty-two French divisions, and planned to send two more later. What was this if not bluff? It is too simple to say that Chamberlain merely aimed to buy time. He did this, but also hoped, and even believed, that appeasement might succeed.

Men, particularly statesmen, do not always think with precise and rigorous logic. Yet Chamberlain was not muddled or an appeaser by nature. On the contrary, he was more hard-headed than most of his contemporaries; he liked to get things settled one way or the other. At the beginning of the Abyssinian crisis, he was the Cabinet minister most insistent for oil sanctions, though he was also the first to demand the ending of sanctions when they had obviously failed. Again, during the Abdication crisis, Chamberlain wished to present Edward VIII with formal Cabinet advice to the King that he should end his association with Mrs Simpson, together with a warning that the Cabinet would resign if the advice were not taken. It was not that, as a Unitarian, he had religious principles against divorce; but the uncertainty was 'holding up business and employment'.

So, too, in foreign politics. Chamberlain did not have the emotional dislike of 'Versailles' common to most Englishmen at that time. He was merely irritated by the instability of the existing order, and regarded revision as an unpleasant necessity. And he was not taken in by Hitler. He found Hitler detestable, but not much more so than most foreigners except musicians. Chamberlain was neither blind nor stupid, least of all was he a coward. On the contrary, his courage was his undoing. He wanted to end uncertainty, to speed things up. In this he succeeded. His policy helped to produce in 1939 the war which everyone else, including Hitler and Mussolini, expected in 1943. His aim was to avert war. He failed; and failure on this scale cannot be excused by a plea of good intentions. Chamberlain is now beyond defence or condemnation. He needs a biographer who will try to understand him. Probably none will be found. Neville Chamberlain is fated to go on being the man of no luck.

Winston Churchill

*Alan Taylor greatly admired Winston Spencer Churchill (1874–
1965) and wrote much about him.*

When he reviewed Lord Moran, Churchill: The Struggle For
Survival, Constable, *1966, in the* New Statesman, *27 May 1966,
Alan Taylor wrote, 'Anyone can run up an account of Churchill
and find plenty of faults. They weigh not a feather in the balance.
There has never been anyone like him, and that is all there is to it.
He was the saviour of his country, at the most critical moment in
its history . . .'*

*The first group of essays are the reviews of the official biography of
Winston Churchill; the first two volumes were written by Randolph
Churchill and the subsequent volumes by Sir Martin Gilbert. He
reviewed the first five volumes of* Winston S. Churchill, Heinemann,
1966, 1967, 1971, 1975 and 1976 in the Observer, *23 October
1966, 22 October 1967, 24 October 1971, 8 June 1975 and 24
October 1976.*

*The sixth essay, 'Daddy, What Was Winston Churchill?', was
first published as an assessment of Churchill's record in the Second
World War, marking the centenary of Churchill's birth, for the*
New York Times *magazine, 28 April 1974. It was reprinted in
A. J. P. Taylor,* Essays In English History, Harmondsworth, Pen-
guin, *1976.*

*The final piece on Churchill was Alan Taylor's tribute on Church-
ill's ninetieth birthday, first published in the* Sunday Express, *29
November 1964.*

Winston S. Churchill: Volume I Youth 1874–1900 by Randolph S. Churchill

In 1932 Randolph Churchill, who was not yet of age, telegraphed to his father in America: 'Have been offered £450 advance on substantial royalties for biography of you have you any objection to my accepting.' Winston Churchill replied: 'Strongly deprecate premature attempt hope some day you will make thousands instead of hundreds.' The advice was accepted and has proved wise. The projected biography, of which the first volume now appears, will no doubt be a highly profitable venture.

Five large volumes, each with a Companion Volume of documents, may seem a bit much even for a great man whose public life extended over half a century. But the objection is irrelevant. Just as railways fixed their rates on the principle of what the traffic would bear, so books are geared to the appetite of readers and, as the public will buy ten volumes on Churchill, it is right that they should have them. At any rate, if the biography had to be done on this scale, it could hardly be done better. The author says that he has long aspired to write 'a filial and objective biography'. To judge by this volume, he has succeeded. Though the 'research assistants' have been by no means idle, the author has added many characteristic touches and given shape to the whole. There is much admiration, sometimes extravagantly expressed. But there is also courageous frankness, both about Churchill and about those around him.

The later volumes will have their fill of public affairs. This one tells a private story, apart from somewhat perfunctory references to the political activities of Lord Randolph, Churchill's father: the story of schooldays and adventurous early manhood. The documentary material for the story is almost unbearably rich, though one is tempted to add that what is new is not interesting and what is interesting is not new. The new material deals with Churchill at school and at Sandhurst. He seems to have preserved all his parents' letters to him, and his mother preserved most of his letters to her. The author writes resignedly at one point: 'A number of unimportant letters to his mother treat of such subjects as visits to his doctor, his goldfish, his riding and his stamp collection.'

We are also given in full the invitation of the Jerome family to a reception at Cowes, where Lord Randolph first met his future wife. Some of the information given is curious, and some, particularly as Churchill begins to grow up, illuminating. At one moment he contemplated taking Holy Orders; he also proposed abortively to learn the cello. He early showed a capacity for organizing the train journeys of others and developed a strong, though not always successful, desire to get his own way.

Churchill was a neglected child, at any rate by modern standards. Lord Randolph rarely noticed him except to rebuke him occasionally for idleness, and he saw little of his adored mother, whose time was consumed by an extravagant social life. He strove to please and often failed. He wrote from Sandburst: –

If I write a descriptive account of my life here, I receive a hint from you that my style is too sententious and stilted. If on the other hand I write a plain and excessively simple letter – it is put down as slovenly. I never can do anything right.

The rotund style of later years was, however, already in the bud, as in this phrase: 'A Remittance would not be altogether misplaced.' Churchill, though by no means stupid, was, in the author's words, 'obstinate, rebellious and mischievous'. The author also suggests that unhappy schooldays strengthened his character. Churchill himself thought so. He wrote about the Mahdi:

Solitary trees, if they grow at all, grow strong; and a boy deprived of a father's care often develops, if he escapes the perils of youth, an independence and vigour of thought which may restore in after life the heavy loss of early days.

He was sent to Sandhurst and then passed to regimental service in India. He played polo, which he regarded as 'the emperor of games'. He also played bezique, but not whist – 'a most uninteresting game and one at which I have but little luck'. Randolph adds: 'A game at which he did not prevail was naturally a bore. He was already developing that egocentricity which was to become such a predominant characteristic, and to which must be attributed alike his blunders and his triumphant successes.' Churchill was determined to prevail in the great game of Life. He wanted money. He wanted to write in the spirit of his models, Gibbon and Macaulay. He wanted to rise to the top in politics.

He shook off his Army career and went wherever he could see action – Cuba in rebellion, the North-West Frontier, the Sudan, and the Boer War. Each of these enterprises produced much profitable journalism, and all except the first provided material also for profitable books. Randolph Churchill states the theme of his work on the first page: 'He shall be his own biographer,' and that is indeed the difficulty. Churchill has been his own biographer in volume after volume. It is perhaps of some interest to learn that Churchill wrote of Kitchener: 'He may be a general – but never a gentleman,' and there is a detailed examination of the story, probably legendary, that Botha himself took Churchill prisoner during the Boer War. But most of all this has been described by Churchill long ago.

His first ventures into politics are a different matter. Here the theme was stated by Churchill in a letter to his brother: 'This is a pushing age, we must push with the best.' He made full use of the political friends inherited from his father, though he did not always respect them. He wrote to his mother:

Among the leaders of the Tory Party are two whom I despise and detest as politicians above all others – Mr Balfour and George Curzon. The one – a languid, lazy lackadaisical cynic – the unmonumental figurehead of the Conservative Party; the other the spoiled darling of politics – blown with conceit – insolent from undeserved success.

Lord Salisbury was 'an able and obstinate man, who joins the brain of a statesman to the delicate susceptibilities of a mule'. His own creed was Tory Democracy, a phrase learnt from his father:

1. *Reform at Home.* Extension of the Franchise to every male. Universal Education. Equal Establishment of all religions ... A progressive Income Tax.
2. *Imperialism abroad.* East of Suez Democratic reins are impossible.

India must be governed on old principles ... Also we must combine for Tariff and Commerce.

3. *European Politics.* Non Intervention. Keep absolutely unembroiled – Isolated if you like.
4. *Defence.* ... A mighty navy must keep the seas. The army may be reduced to a training depot for India with one army corps for petty expeditions.
5. To maintain the present constitution of Queen – Lords – Commons – and the Legislative union as at present established.

Peace and Power abroad – Prosperity and Progress at home.

Some parts of this creed Churchill later abandoned; to most of it he remained constant. There are some curious minor notes:

The Russians are bound to get Constantinople. We could never stop them even if we wished. Nor ought we to wish for anything that could impede the expulsion from Europe of the filthy Oriental.

As to women's suffrage:

It is contrary to natural law and the practice of civilized States – those women who discharge their duty to the State – viz marrying and giving birth to children – are adequately represented by their husbands – every kind of hysterical fad would gain strength – religion would become much more intolerant, etc.

Churchill taught himself politics by reading old volumes of the *Annual Register* – a neglected and most rewarding discipline. He sought constantly for a constituency and wrote to his mother after one such attempt:

The conclusions I form are these – with practice I shall obtain great power on a public platform. My impediment is no hindrance. My voice sufficiently powerful, and – this is vital – my ideas and modes of thought are pleasing to men.

In 1900 success at last opened its door. Churchill was elected for Oldham as a Conservative. He also delivered profitable lectures on the Boer War, making £3,782 15s. 5d. in England and £1,600 in America. He wrote triumphantly to his mother: 'I am very proud of the fact that there is not one person in a million who at my age could have earned £10,000 without any capital in less than two years.'

He had now to face a greater test: whether in fact his ideas and modes of thought were pleasing to men.

Winston S. Churchill: Volume II
Young Statesman 1901–1914
by Randolph S. Churchill

Winston Churchill had many careers, so various that he seemed to be, not one, but all mankind's epitome. His most brilliant, until his belated rise to supreme power in the Second World War, was before 1914, when he was second only to Lloyd George among Radical leaders.

There was a profound difference between the two champions. George's radicalism was in his blood: he could not shake it off even if he tried. Churchill's radicalism sprang from his pugnacity. It was provoked in him by the opposition of others and by his own tempestuousness of phrase. Asquith said: 'Winston thinks with his mouth.' It would be truer to say that Churchill often went where his mouth, and still more his pen, carried him. His radicalism, like all his other feelings, was sincere. But there was something odd about a Radical who denounced dukes during the week and spent his weekends at Blenheim.

Five volumes of biography are a heavy prospect even for the most devoted admirer of Churchill's, and in this volume there are times when the interest flags. Compared to its predecessor, it contains comparatively little of a personal nature. Churchill was now less close to his mother, who provided him with little except money difficulties. In 1908 he found lasting happiness in his marriage with Miss Clementine Hozier. He wrote to her a year or so later:

I am so much centred in my politics, that I often feel I must be a dull companion, to anyone who is not in the trade too. It gives me so much joy to make you happy & often wish I were more various in my topics.

Still the best is to be true to oneself – unless you happen to have a very tiresome self!

And when a tiny cloud of suspicion once appeared:

I could not conceive myself forming any other attachment than that to which I have fastened the happiness of my life here below ... You ought to trust me for I do not love any woman in the world but you and my chief desire is to link myself to you week by week by bonds which shall ever become more intimate & profound.

The reader will be glad to learn that Diana Churchill, when a baby, was known as the Puppy Kitten, and Randolph, most appropriately, as the Chum Bolly.

However, it is politics that we want to hear about, and there is plenty of material, not all of it novel. Churchill's speeches are often worth recording again, particularly such passages as his description of the Tory party which ends:

Sentiment by the bucketful, patriotism by the imperial pint, the open hand at the public exchequer, the open door at the public-house, dear food for the million, cheap labour for the millionaire.

Or his dismissal of Milner:

Lord Milner has gone from South Africa, probably for ever. The public service knows him no more. Having exercised great authority, he now exerts none. Having held high employment, he now has no employment. Having disposed of events which have shaped the course of history, he is now unable to deflect in the smallest degree the policy of the day.

Randolph Churchill's comments are not always felicitous. Thus, on the failure to consider the vote for Africans in 1906, he remarks: 'It has only been in much later times that it has been thought desirable and profitable to accord the franchise to people who cannot read or write.' Again, he dismisses Churchill's opposition in 1908 to the building of more battleships with the slighting phrase: 'On foreign policy he took the same wrong-headed position as other Radicals on the Left and in the Liberal party.' Later he attributes to Churchill a clear grasp of Germany's threat to the Balance of

Power. In fact, Churchill was less consistent. Even in 1914 he thought Anglo-German hostility rested on misunderstanding and believed that all could be put right if he had a talk with Tirpitz – an episode which Randolph Churchill ignores.

Often he brings new information and illumination, as much from anecdotes as from the written record. He shows that Campbell-Bannerman did not alone swing the Cabinet to immediate self-government for the Transvaal. Churchill's persistent memoranda aided the process. Lloyd George supplied a remarkable story of how the Cabinet accepted his land taxes. Asquith went round the table and, according to Lloyd George, 'everyone spoke against them, including your father'. Asquith then said: 'We have had a very full and frank expression of opinion from every member of the Cabinet and it seems to me that the weight of the argument rests with the Chancellor.'

There is another picture of Asquith of a less creditable kind. On 22 April 1911 Churchill wrote to his wife:

On Thursday night the PM was vy bad: and I squirmed with embarrassment. He could hardly speak: and many people noticed his condition. He continues most friendly and benevolent, & entrusts me with everything after dinner. Up till that time he is at his best – but thereafter! It is an awful pity, & only the persistent freemasonry of the House of Commons prevents a scandal.

Churchill's Radical activities are carefully described, but in somewhat muted vein. There is not enough emphasis on his creation of unemployment insurance, though this is perhaps as much Lloyd George's doing as the author's. Irish affairs are treated in a separate chapter, detached from Churchill's work at the Admiralty, though the two were happening at the same time. Churchill's plans for disarming Ulster, which provoked the Curragh mutiny, were in part an attempt to restore the Radical reputation which he had forfeited by his demand for more battleships. On his last great dispute in the Liberal Cabinet, there is a striking story from Lady Megan Lloyd George. Her father had resisted the Admiralty programme. He invited Churchill to breakfast and greeted him with the words:

Oddly enough, my wife spoke to me last night about this Dreadnought business. She said, 'You know, my dear. I never interfere in politics; but they say you are having an argument with that nice Mr Churchill about building Dreadnoughts. Of course I don't understand these things, but I should have thought it would be better to have too many rather than too few.' So I have decided to let you build them. Let's go in to breakfast.

Perhaps things really happened like that.

By August 1914 Churchill had brought the Royal Navy to full fighting-pitch, or so he thought – wrongly as events proved. His last thoughts before he became a war-leader were characteristically conflicting. On 28 July 1914 he wrote to his wife:

Everything tends towards catastrophe and collapse. I am interested, geared up & happy. Is it not horrible to be built like that? The preparations have a hideous fascination for me. I pray to God to forgive me for such fearful moods of levity. Yet I wd do my best for peace, & nothing wd induce me wrongfully to strike the blow . . .

You know how willingly & proudly I wd risk – or give – if need be – my period of existence to keep this country great & famous & prosperous & free. But the problems are vy difficult. One has to try to measure the indefinite & weigh the imponderable.

In such passages as these Churchill transcended his erratic impulses and revealed his true greatness.

Winston S. Churchill: Volume III
1914–1916 by Martin Gilbert

When war broke out in 1914 Winston Churchill stood in high esteem. Many acclaimed him as 'the greatest First Lord of the Admiralty of all time'. Kitchener praised him: 'The Fleet was ready.' Fifteen months later Churchill left office with his reputation shattered. He served on the Western Front, was promised a brigade and was fobbed off with a battalion.

In the spring of 1916 he returned to Parliament, confident that he would make a great impact and again grasp the reins of power.

His oratory in full spate, he was interrupted by an Irish member: 'What about the Dardanelles?' The question dogged Churchill throughout the war and for long afterwards. Indeed, it took him thirty-five years to recover from the failure at the Dardanelles. Yet, as Martin Gilbert shows, he was brought low by blunders in strategy and execution for most of which he was not responsible. Kitchener, the Secretary for War, was most at fault. Fisher, the First Sea Lord, gave erratic counsel. Asquith, the Prime Minister, gave no firm direction. Churchill alone carried the blame.

This is a stupendous book, almost too much so. It devotes on average a page to each day of Churchill's life between August 1914 and December 1916. If Martin Gilbert treats the rest of Churchill's public career on this scale, he will need 16 more volumes, not counting the companion volumes of documents with which we are also threatened. Gilbert has consulted seventy-three collections of papers. He quotes 1,446 documents. The writers range from Cabinet Ministers, generals and admirals to ordinary soldiers in the trenches. Gilbert has been meticulously through the proceedings of the War Council and the Dardanelles committee. He is the first to use without restriction the staggeringly indiscreet letters which Asquith addressed to Venetia Stanley. The result is a general history of British politics in the first year of the war rather than a biography of Churchill. As Churchill ran most of the war, perhaps the two things are much the same.

The seat of government was empty. Asquith, according to Churchill, was 'supine, sodden and supreme'. The Cabinet and the War Council drifted leaderless. Kitchener had sole military authority and did not know what to do with it. Churchill's energy frothed over into every sphere. He repeatedly crossed to France and advised Sir John French on strategy. He instructed Sir Edward Grey on foreign policy. He took over the air defence of England and inspired the building of the first tanks. When Antwerp was threatened, Churchill went to its aid with his private force of the naval brigade and proposed to take command of its defence. Kitchener was ready to make him a lieutenant-general. Asquith and the Cabinet merely laughed.

The Dardanelles affair takes up nearly half the book. Arthur

Marder really got everything clear in his great history of the Royal Navy during the First World War. Gilbert adds more detail and drama. At the end of 1914 many ideas were aired for circumventing the deadlock on the Western Front. Fisher wanted to send a fleet into the Baltic. Churchill proposed a landing on the island of Borkum. Lloyd George favoured an expedition to Salonika or the Adriatic. Kitchener asked for something which would be of direct aid to Russia. Churchill suggested an attack on the Dardanelles. He insisted that it must be a joint military-naval operation. Kitchener said he had no troops to spare. Churchill answered that the Navy would try what it could do on its own. Far from thrusting the Dardanelles campaign on the Cabinet, Churchill was himself pushed into it by Kitchener.

Once action started Churchill became confident of victory. The distant fire of the naval guns intoxicated him. German howitzers had reduced the Belgian forts. Therefore it was assumed that naval guns would reduce the Turkish forts. This assumption was totally wrong. The naval guns had a flat trajectory and were ineffective against land batteries, as some gunnery experts pointed out. Their opinion was disregarded. No real consideration was ever given to the problem of sweeping the mines. The War Council never discussed these practical problems. Its members took success for granted and spent their time discussing how the spoils of the Turkish Empire should be divided.

Churchill not merely assumed success. He also convinced himself that forcing the Dardanelles would win the war. Greece, Bulgaria, Romania and perhaps even Turkey would join the Allies. Their united armies would march up the Danube Valley and break into Germany – of course under British direction. Churchill wrote to Grey: 'I beseech you at this crisis not to make a mistake in falling below the level of events.' He himself strode far above them. These fantasies were shattered when the Fleet failed to force the Straits. Reluctantly Churchill had to wait for the Army. The Gallipoli campaign was none of his doing. Generals without experience of war failed to show the dash and initiative which the operation demanded. Fisher resigned in protest against sending more ships to the Mediterranean. A coalition government was formed and Churchill was the chief victim.

He passed this verdict on his fate: 'My one fatal mistake was trying to achieve a great enterprise without having the plenary authority which could so easily have carried it to success.' Here was the mixture of truth and error which he maintained thereafter. With plenary authority he might have done better. He might also have failed even more disastrously. The Dardanelles campaign required for success stronger forces than were available, equipment of a kind no one had thought of, and generals with an aggressive spirit such as did not exist at that time in the British Army. Churchill had the will for victory. He lacked the means.

Churchill down was not fundamentally different from Churchill up. Though he had never held even the humblest command in the field, he assumed that he could direct a brigade as efficiently as he had directed the Royal Navy. In a richly comic scene he delivered to his front-line infantry words of command suited only to cavalry in India almost twenty years before. But there was also nobility in his action. No other fallen minister went straight from the Cabinet to the trenches. Asquith promised Churchill a brigade. When a question was set down in Parliament, he told French not to carry out the promise – 'Perhaps you might give him a battalion.' Churchill wrote of Asquith: 'His conduct reaches the limit of meanness and ungenerosity.'

Churchill's wife urged him to remain in France until a political opening showed itself. Churchill refused: 'Manoeuvring for position is only a minor part of war; a strong army and a good cause and plenty of ammunition drives ahead all right.' Churchill's idea of driving ahead was extraordinary, almost as great a folly as the Dardanelles campaign itself. Fisher's resignation had brought Churchill down. Churchill wrote truly: 'Considering that he had agreed to every step taken and issued every order, it seems to me his conduct was rather treacherous.' Yet when Churchill returned to Parliament in the spring of 1916, the climax of his speech was that Fisher should be brought back as First Sea Lord. The House of Commons dissolved in laughter. Churchill was humiliated. Yet he would not give up the idea. He pressed for and obtained a commission of inquiry into the Dardanelles. He devoted all his time to preparing his evidence and encouraged Fisher to do the same. This was a strange partnership. Churchill demonstrated that Fisher had supported the Dardanelles campaign. Fisher demonstrated that he had opposed it. Yet both demonstrated their approval of each other.

In the autumn of 1916 the political storm blew. Asquith was overthrown. Lloyd George took his place. Churchill was not involved. He was thinking only of his evidence for the Dardanelles commission. It was not surprising to anybody except himself that he was left out of the Lloyd George government.

Martin Gilbert, I am sure, believes that he has vindicated Churchill. He has not. His historian's conscience has been too much for him. Unwittingly perhaps he has told the truth. This is the Churchill we all remember – sometimes heroic, sometimes comic, often mistaking words for deeds, his wise judgements ruined by impulsiveness, and in the last resort always confident of victory. In the First World War he pined in vain for 'plenary authority'. Here was the secret of his many failures and his ultimate success. He was *capax imperii* and of nothing less.

Winston S. Churchill: Volume IV *1917–1922* by Martin Gilbert

At the end of December 1916 Churchill was in despair. No place had been found for him in the Lloyd George Coalition. Six months later Lloyd George felt strong enough to defy the Conservative ban, Churchill became Minister of Munitions until the end of the war and was then in succession Secretary for War and Secretary for the Colonies.

The relationship between Churchill and Lloyd George is a fascinating one and the hidden theme of this book. Churchill professed the utmost admiration for and devotion to Lloyd George. In practice he was less wholehearted, wrangling with Lloyd George and even defying him. Lloyd George on his side professed to rely on Churchill. His private judgements were less favourable. 'He has spoilt himself by reading about Napoleon.' 'The two great qualities for a Prime Minister are patience and courage. Winston will be defective in patience.' And again: 'The PM compared Winston to a chauffeur who apparently is perfectly sane and drives with great skill for months, then suddenly he takes you over the precipice . . . There was a strain of lunacy in him.'

During the war all went well. Lloyd George often sent Churchill on unofficial missions to the western front, much to the indignation of other ministers who thought Churchill should stick to munitions. At the time of the German offensive in March 1918 there was an explosion. Lloyd George sent Churchill to see Haig. Wilson, the CIGS, and Milner, the Secretary for War, protested, and Churchill was only allowed to visit Clemenceau. Churchill, however, found a way round. He persuaded Clemenceau to visit Haig and went along with him. Churchill rejoiced to be at the heart of the crisis. During the German offensive he usually spent the night at his office, though it is difficult to understand what he could contribute. On 24 March 1918 he wrote to Lloyd George:

Courage & a clear plan will enable you to keep the command of the Nation. But if you fall below the level of events, your role is exhausted. I am confident you will not fail. Lift yourself by an effort of will to the height of circumstances & conquer or succumb fighting.

These were hardly words to address to a Prime Minister who was showing plenty of courage without them, and for once Churchill did not send the letter. But Churchill was often a wise counsellor. He preached Tanks persistently, which contrasts with some foolish words by General Sir Henry Rawlinson: 'All you have to do is to keep our infantry up to strength and not waste manpower in tanks and aviation. They won't win the war for you as the infantry will.'

After the war Churchill became obsessed with intervention in Russia against the Bolsheviks. Time and again Lloyd George tried to pull him back. Time and again he broke loose. As late as September 1920 he was still confident of success. He wrote to Lloyd George:

Nothing can preserve either the Bolshevik system or the B regime. By mistakes on our part the agony of the Russian people may be prolonged. But their relief is sure.

Lloyd George finally lost patience:

The reconquest of Russia would take hundreds of millions. It would cost hundreds of millions more to maintain the new Government until it had established itself. You are prepared to spend all that money, and I know perfectly well that is what you really desire. But as you know that you won't find another responsible person in the whole land who will take your view, why waste your energy and your usefulness on this vain fretting which completely paralyses you for other work?

In private Lloyd George said Winston was a greater source of weakness than of strength to the government and described him as like the counsel employed by a solicitor, not because he is the best man, but because 'he would be dangerous on the other side'. There was a wiser, more conciliatory Churchill, as he showed on other occasions. His speech defending the condemnation of General Dyer after the massacre at Amritsar was a masterpiece of generosity. Over Ireland he began badly, announcing in September 1920: 'I see no reason why, with patience and firmness, we may not wear the trouble down in the course of a few years.' Many Englishmen have made the same mistake at each stage of the Irish problem. But with the truce and the negotiations for a treaty, Churchill worked loyally with Lloyd George. Michael Collins came to trust him. Lloyd George, Birkenhead and Churchill shared the credit for the Irish treaty on the British side. Credit for the establishment and consolidation of the Irish Free State is due to Churchill alone. Lord Knollys, once the King's private secretary, said Churchill's conduct of Irish affairs had been a great proof of good *judgement* and added: 'I think this exercise of judgement brings him nearer to the leadership of the country than anyone would have supposed possible. It will modify a great many views.'

These are only a few of the themes developed by Martin Gilbert. Another which bulked large at the time was the settlement of the Middle East which Churchill as Colonial Secretary carried through all on his own despite the protests of Curzon, the Foreign Secretary.

The National Home for the Jews was preserved in Palestine. Transjordan and Iraq became Arab States under a British mandate. When the Arabs continued to complain Churchill wrote of Faisal, the new ruler of Iraq:

Six months ago we were paying his hotel bill in London, and now I am forced to read day after day 800-word messages on questions of his status and his relations with foreign Powers. Has he not got some wives to keep him quiet?

The final explosion came with the Chanak crisis when the Turks challenged British control at the Straits. Churchill had previously opposed Lloyd George's support of the Greeks, but once the crisis came he was all for a strong line. The crisis ended peacefully, much to the regret of both Churchill and Lloyd George. Mrs Keppel reported: 'Winston is longing to drop the paint brush for his sword and L. G. murmuring at every meal, "We will fight to the end".' Later Churchill 'frankly regretted that the Turks had not attacked us at Chanak, as he felt that the surrender to them of Eastern Thrace was humiliating, and that the return of the Turks to Europe meant an infinity of troubles'.

The Chanak crisis ended Lloyd George's government. The Conservatives abandoned the Coalition. There was a general election with the added trouble for Churchill of an operation for appendicitis. From his sick-bed he fought the election as a devoted supporter of Lloyd George. His main ticket was the danger from the Labour Party 'behind which crouched the shadow of Communist folly and Bolshevik crime'. Not surprisingly he lost his seat. Churchill's second political career was over. Few thought he would ever have another.

Martin Gilbert has done very well to get all the twists in this stage of Churchill's career into a single volume, even if a very long one. The story is told very much from Churchill's side, but with a full display of original evidence. There is perhaps a bit too much on the Middle East settlement, which has now become past history. There is also too much reliance on Churchill's imaginative work 'The World Crisis'. We might for instance have been warned that when Churchill described his feelings as he sat waiting for the eleven strokes of Big Ben on 11 November 1918 he must have waited in vain. Big Ben had been silent since early in the war.

Winston S. Churchill: Volume V
1922–1939 by Martin Gilbert

The Fates played Snakes and Ladders with Winston Churchill between the wars. In 1922 he landed on his biggest Snake. He was out of office; he lost his seat in the House of Commons; he was generally unpopular. Two years later a Ladder carried him to the post of Chancellor of the Exchequer. At the end of the decade he was down again and estranged from his party. Throughout the 1930s he sought Ladders that proved to be Snakes. His campaign against the proposed constitution for India was a total failure. His championing of Edward VIII was a catastrophe. Even his warnings against Nazi Germany and his demands for greater armaments caused widespread irritation and seemed to have been in vain. Beaverbrook voiced the general opinion when he called Churchill 'a busted flush'. A final throw of the dice carried him once more into office and the way was clear for him to become the saviour of his country.

Martin Gilbert tells this long and complicated story with the ruthlessness of a devoted biographer. The volume has over 1,100 pages. Each topic is thoroughly explored even when it has now lost all significance. Gilbert is very much Churchill's man and sees everything from Churchill's point of view. For instance he discusses the return to Gold at the pre-war parity without any mention of recent investigations of the subject. In the prolonged wrangles between Churchill and the Air Ministry over the size of the Luft-waffe, Gilbert repeatedly emphasizes that German statistics confirm Churchill's larger estimates. Post-war research has established that these figures were deliberately inflated and that the Luftwaffe was almost as ill-equipped as the RAF for a prolonged bombing campaign.

Again, on a non-political subject, Gilbert describes how Churchill composed, usually after midnight, his two great historical enterprises: the *Life of Marlborough* and *The History of the English-Speaking Peoples*. However, he makes no attempt to estimate the scholarly merits of these two works, though he is well qualified to do so. The reader is left to conclude that everything Churchill wrote was a masterpiece. Perhaps Gilbert decided that his book was long enough already. Certainly it is a monument of industry and an historical feast for those with an insatiable appetite.

Churchill's casual remarks are often the most interesting. For instance in 1924: 'The existing capitalist system is the foundation of civilization and the only means by which great modern populations can be supplied with vital necessities.' And in 1937: 'Of course my ideal is limited and narrow. I want to see the British Empire preserved for a few more generations in its strength and splendour.'

Other remarks foreshadow Churchill's outlook during the Second World War. What he wrote in 1924 helps to explain the loss of Singapore in 1942:

A war with Japan! But why should there be a war with Japan? I do not believe there is the slightest chance of it in our lifetime . . . The war would last for years. It would cost Japan very little. It would reduce us to bankruptcy . . . We could never do it. It would never be worth our while to do it.

In 1925 he prophesied unwittingly his Finest Hour. Discussing a possible German control of the Channel ports, Churchill wrote:

If in addition to sea superiority we had air supremacy, we might maintain ourselves as we did in the days of Napoleon for indefinite periods . . . It should never be admitted in this argument that England cannot, if the worst comes to the worst, stand alone.

Of course this view did not prevent Churchill's sounding an alarm over the Channel ports later when he advocated alliance with France.

Gilbert puts the record right on many questions. He plays down Churchill's role during the General Strike. Churchill breathed fire and slaughter against those who dared to challenge the British Constitution. But he was no more extreme than his colleagues, including Baldwin, except in his choice of words. Once the General Strike was called off, Churchill swung round and was eager to coerce the intransigent mine-owners. Left to himself Churchill would have tried to impose a compromise favourable to the miners. It was Baldwin who allowed the owners to dictate their own terms.

Churchill's line before the abdication of Edward VIII is also made clear for the first time. It is generally supposed that he championed the King's right to marry Mrs Simpson. This is not so. Of course he spoke emotionally in his usual fashion. But essentially, like almost everyone else from Baldwin to Beaverbrook, he wished to prevent the marriage. His difference with the other political leaders was in believing that, given sufficient time, the King would change his mind and that there would be no need for abdication. As he wrote afterwards, 'I believe the Abdication to have been altogether premature and probably quite unnecessary.' Baldwin judged differently, and Baldwin was right. The King was set on marriage and it is unlikely that delay would have shaken him.

These are relatively minor topics. There are three which occupied most of Churchill's attention. The first was derating, a matter of great fiscal complication and now of little interest except for the irritation Churchill's insistence provoked in Neville Chamberlain. The second was the constitution for India, now also a pretty dead subject. Churchill blindly ignored the development of Indian nationalism and imagined the Raj as it had been in the days of his youth.

The third and most important was the threat from Nazi Germany. Churchill fought for greater armaments. Also he gradually developed an independent view of foreign policy. What he always wanted was a Grand Alliance against Hitler. At first he put this in the form of collective security, an outlook which shared all the illusions of the League of Nations. Gradually he became more realistic. Towards the end he advocated alliance with Soviet Russia, the policy that was ultimately to bring total victory. But even Churchill was not always clear-sighted. Gilbert does not quote the article of 15 September 1937 in which Churchill wrote, 'I declare my belief that a major war is not imminent, and I still believe there is a good chance of no major war taking place in our time.' Even the greatest man cannot be always right.

Churchill's personality dominates the book despite all the political details. He was inexhaustible and overpowering. In office he instructed his colleagues how to conduct their affairs. Out of office he still poured out advice. This interference was not always welcome. Baldwin tolerated Churchill, was amused by him and even said, 'If there is going to be war . . . we must keep him fresh to be our war Prime Minister.' Hoare detested him, particularly after the interminable rows over the India Bill. Neville Chamberlain was exasperated and took no notice of his promptings. Outwardly the political leaders remained friendly to him. Their private correspondence confirms the general rule, 'there is no friendship at the top'. Churchill never grasped this. He fought hard and bore no malice. His estimate of men changed overnight. He once dismissed Eden, later his blue-eyed boy, as 'a light-weight'.

Churchill lived for the moment, although he often wrote history, and his moment came only when he attained supreme power. This will be the theme of Gilbert's next volume and is certainly something to look forward to. Churchill was totally self-centred. He was erratic, plunging wildly from wisdom to error. He espoused many mistaken causes. He was a great man all the same.

Daddy, What Was Winston Churchill?

On 24 January 1965 there died Winston Spencer Churchill, Knight of the Garter and, if he had not refused the title, Duke of London. Six days later he was given a state funeral in St Paul's Cathedral, an honour previously reserved for two great men of war – Admiral Lord Nelson, victor at Trafalgar, and the Duke of Wellington, victor at Waterloo. What brought Churchill into this select company? The men of the time had no doubt as to the answer. He was the saviour of his country, the first Englishman to be so hailed since King Alfred the Great.

How does Churchill look now, nine years after his death and 100 years after his birth? The Second World War, in which Churchill won his fame, has receded into history. Its memories are fading; the antagonisms that it inspired are almost forgotten. The British

Empire that Churchill championed has vanished, and Great Britain is no longer numbered among the World Powers. Was Churchill's policy mistaken and his victory barren? Future historians may give a confident answer. One of the present generation cannot speak with detachment. He sees the consequences of the war but he also remembers the circumstances in which it was fought.

Success and achievement came to Churchill late in the day. If he had died in 1939 at the age of sixty-five, he would now be regarded as an eccentric character, sometimes a Radical, sometimes a Tory, and running over with brilliant ideas that were more often wrong than right. In the years before the Second World War he reached the height of his unpopularity. He had only two supporters in the House of Commons and was disregarded in the country. He was almost alone in advocating great armaments and steadfast resistance to Nazi Germany. Underneath the surface there was always a current of opinion on his side. It may well be that Hitler never wanted war against Great Britain and was willing to respect the British Empire. But the British people, despite their anxiety to avoid war, would not tolerate a German domination of Europe, even if it had been less barbarous than the Nazis made it. In September 1939 British public opinion forced a reluctant government into war, and Churchill entered the war Cabinet as a symbol of the national resolve.

Seven months later, when the Germans invaded Norway, Churchill was already directing operations as Minister of Defence. It was on his orders that a weak, ill-armed expeditionary force was sent to Norway and that the British attempted a strategy beyond their strength. Nevertheless when the House of Commons revolted against the Chamberlain government, it turned to Churchill. Though he had made mistakes, they were mistakes of action, not of caution. On 10 May 1940 Churchill became Prime Minister and thus attained supreme power. He held this position, virtually unchallenged, throughout the war.

June 1940 was the moment of decision for Churchill and for the future of the British Empire. When France was defeated and fell out of the war, it could be plausibly argued, and was argued by some, that Great Britain should accept the compromise peace which

Hitler offered and watch with detachment while Germany and Russia tore each other to pieces. We now know that this policy was advocated in the War Cabinet by Lord Halifax and, more cautiously, by Neville Chamberlain. Churchill rejected it. He told his colleagues: 'Of course, whatever happens at Dunkirk, we shall fight on.' His first speech in the House of Commons as Prime Minister defined all that was to follow:

You ask, What is our aim? I can answer in one word: Victory – victory at all costs, victory in spite of all terror; victory, however long and hard the road may be.

This was a rash promise to make when Great Britain stood alone against a European continent united under Hitler. But it was what the British people wanted to hear. They did not feel like a defeated people, particularly after the German Air Force had been thwarted in the Battle of Britain. Churchill was their guarantee that somehow total victory would be achieved, and this is what gave Churchill his hold over the British people. He and they had made a pact with death. They would win the war or perish in the attempt.

And something more. Unconditional surrender by Germany and her associates did not have to wait for President Roosevelt at Casablanca. It was already implicit in Churchill's speeches in 1940: 'All, all shall be restored.' This insistence on unconditional surrender has often been condemned. Yet what was the alternative? Presumably to deal with Hitler or some other German government. At whose expense were the British and later the Americans to buy peace for themselves? Was Poland to remain under Germany? Was Czechoslovakia? Perhaps Belgium would have made a suitable bribe? It has been suggested that an offer of generous terms would have led to the overthrow of Hitler. But even the leaders of the so-called resistance in Germany assumed that she would keep some of Hitler's conquests as a reward for getting rid of him. In any case, the German people, apart from a few generals and politicians, remained solidly behind Hitler until the very end of the war. Hitler aimed at total victory. Unconditional surrender was the only possible answer to him, and any idea of negotiated peace is too nonsensical to merit serious discussion.

Churchill was, therefore, never in search of a policy. The policy of defeating Hitler was imposed upon him by events. His sole problem was how to apply this policy, a hard nut to crack in the circumstances of 1940. At home his position was never endangered though he often thought it was. His critics were an impotent handful. Despite grumbles and discontents, Great Britain was never so free from political controversy as during the Second World War. National unity was complete, particularly after Hitler attacked Soviet Russia and so turned the British Communists into enthusiastic supporters of the war. This unity rested on a partnership between Churchill and the British people. His speeches, a mixture of old-fashioned rhetoric and homespun humour, struck the right note and made him uniquely popular. Even those most harassed by him always ended by asking: 'What should we do without him?' There have been many great British leaders. There has only been one whom everyone recognized as the embodiment of the national will.

Great Britain's task was to survive. As Stalin said later, accurately summing up the record of the war, 'Great Britain provided time, the United States provided money and Soviet Russia provided blood.' Churchill recognized this in his cooler moments and always worked to call in the New World to redress the balance of the Old. But he was not content to wait. As Minister of Defence he was a war lord, directing strategy, and he often talked as if Great Britain might overthrow Hitler all on her own. This was a fantasy, though it was what the British people wanted, and Churchill often attempted too much with limited resources. The strategical decisions that he took when Great Britain stood alone continued to shape the war even when the United States had joined in.

The first of these decisions was for the bombing of Germany. Churchill wrote in July 1940: 'There is one thing that will bring Hitler down, and that is an absolutely devastating, exterminating attack by very heavy bombers from this country upon the Nazi homeland . . . Without this I do not see a way through.' This strategy was applied. German towns were laid waste. Over half a million Germans were killed. Yet all the time German war production went up and German morale also. Much of British and later American production was devoted to heavy bombers, and the strategic bomb-ing offensive did more harm to the Allied than to the German economy. Yet, once started, it could not be stopped, a striking illustration of the rule that in wartime it is better to do the wrong thing than to do nothing. In the end Churchill grew ashamed of what he had initiated and turned against Sir Arthur Harris, the chief of Bomber Command. But he could not shake off the respons-ibility for indiscriminate bombing and all the decline in morality which that implied.

The second legacy which Churchill passed on to Anglo-American strategy was an obsession with the Mediterranean and the Middle East. Here again there was nothing else Great Britain could do in the circumstances of 1940. She had a fleet in the Mediterranean and an army in Egypt. She could win battles against the Italians, which gave the British people a sensation of victory. But it was a side issue. Hitler never had offensive plans in the Middle East, though perhaps he should have had. Italy was a burden to Hitler, not an asset, and later became a burden to the Allies. Vast demands were made on shipping and military resources for a campaign that never engaged more than a handful of German divisions. The back door into Europe about which Churchill had dreamed even in the First World War remained firmly closed against the Allies. Yet when America entered the war, the Mediterranean front alone was active. President Roosevelt wanted some immediate stroke to influence the Congressional elections – though in fact it came too late to do so – and the American forces, therefore, followed where Churchill had led. This persistent commitment to the Mediterranean postponed any landing in northern France for two years and so helped to prolong the war.

Churchill's third decision was negative and, therefore, less obvi-ous, though perhaps even more fateful. With the British Army engaged in Egypt and the Royal Navy engaged in both the Mediter-ranean and the Atlantic, Great Britain had no forces to spare for the Far East. Churchill had to gamble that Japan would not go to war. This gamble rested on a fundamental misjudgement. Churchill always exaggerated the strength and the prestige of the British Empire. With his mind rooted in the past, he did not appreciate that its strength had crumbled and that the Japanese were not impressed by a prestige that existed only in name. Even when Churchill grew alarmed, he imagined that the Japanese would be overawed by what he called 'the vague menace' of two capital ships. The battleship *Prince of Wales* and the battle cruiser *Repulse* were sent to the Far East. The aircraft carrier allotted to their support scraped her keel in Jamaica and never joined them. Thus defenceless against air attack, the two great ships were sunk by Japanese torpedo-bombers on the third day of the Far Eastern war. So much for the vague menace. Moreover, the defences of Singapore were neglected by Churchill as much as by his predecessors. When Singapore fell, Great Britain's empire in the Far East fell with it and was never to be effectively restored.

Churchill's achievements in the eighteen months between the fall of France and Pearl Harbor were outstanding. His strategy was not always successful, and some of the mistakes, particularly at Singapore, were his personal responsibility. But he worked closely with the Chiefs of Staff and, despite many wranglings, never overruled them, as Hitler did with his generals and as President Roosevelt often did later with General Marshall. Churchill was also the driving force, even if less directly, in home affairs. All the great decisions stemmed from him, and some of the lesser ones also. At the height of the war, for instance, he concerned himself with the question of whether the transport of cut flowers from Cornwall to London should be permitted.

Churchill went through the charade of consulting the war Cabinet. He recognized one member of it as a formidable figure: Ernest Bevin, trade-union leader and Minister of Labour. Thanks to Bevin, the industrial workers remained loyal, co-operative and productive, and Churchill was the first to acknowledge Bevin's achievement. All the other ministers were Churchill's agents and subordinates, however politely this was disguised. When criticisms were voiced in the House of Commons, it was always Churchill who answered them and secured a parliamentary majority.

From the first Churchill was also his own foreign minister, with Anthony Eden as his loyal associate. It was Churchill who conducted the harrowing negotiations with the French government when the

German armies were overrunning France, and thereafter it was Churchill who handled General de Gaulle. Though Churchill often complained that his cross was the Cross of Lorraine (de Gaulle's symbol) he never doubted that de Gaulle would be the saviour of France at some time in the future, and it was solely thanks to Churchill that de Gaulle subsequently attained greatness.

Churchill's hopes for victory were based on the prospect of American aid – at first economic and ultimately military. When the American fleet was attacked at Pearl Harbor, he exclaimed: 'So we have won after all.' He even felt that his work was done and is said to have contemplated retirement. He soon thought better of this. He had now a new task: to cement what he called the Grand Alliance and to assert Great Britain's claim to a place in it. Anglo-American partnership was closer than any alliance in modern history. There was a combined Chiefs of Staffs' committee, directing a common strategy, and Supreme Commanders over Anglo-American forces. Without any formal agreement, this alliance rested on the personal intimacy between Churchill and President Roosevelt.

Yet it is hard not to feel that Churchill misunderstood the spirit of American policy. Certainly Roosevelt was wholeheartedly engaged in the war. He was not equally engaged in preserving the British Empire or even in preserving Great Britain as a great power. Lend-Lease enabled Great Britain to keep going; but the Americans drove a hard bargain. The American financial authorities stripped Great Britain of her gold reserves and her overseas investments before they would institute Lend-Lease. As a condition of Lend-Lease, British exports were restricted, American officials supervised and checked all British foreign trade and American exporters moved ruthlessly into overseas markets that had hitherto been British. Moreover, a post-war abolition of imperial preference and con-trolled exchanges was dictated to the British. As an independent financial centre, London ceased to exist. There was here a sharp contrast with Canada, whose mutual aid was given without strings or conditions. Keynes said truly: 'We threw good housekeeping to the winds. But we saved ourselves and helped to save the world.' Great Britain was just as essential to the United States as the United States to Great Britain. Churchill accepted without demur the stern terms of Lend-Lease. He gave to the Americans all the British scientific secrets and asked for nothing in return.

Churchill received from President Roosevelt a formal promise that Great Britain, having revealed how to make a controlled nuclear explosion, should share equally in all further nuclear discoveries. The promise was subsequently evaded by President Roosevelt and was altogether repudiated by President Truman. Churchill counted on 'the special relationship' and put his trust in American generosity. The trust was misplaced.

Churchill's relations with Soviet Russia were inevitably more remote and took longer to ripen into intimacy. When Hitler invaded Russia, her defeat was expected within a few months. The German generals told Hitler the defeat of Russia would be easier than that of France. Sir Stafford Cripps, the British Ambassador, gave the Russians a month. Sir John Dill, Chief of the Imperial General Staff, said six weeks. American intelligence told the President: We can count on a minimum of one month and a maximum of three. Even Stalin believed on the outbreak of war that Russia was facing disaster and exclaimed: 'Everything that Lenin worked for has been destroyed for ever.' Naturally Churchill hailed Soviet Russia as an ally, but it did not occur to him that any great decision of principle was involved. Russia was fighting Germany and so giving the British a breathing space. Her victory seemed so remote as not to be a matter of speculation. The British and Americans sent Russia what aid they could, but geographic obstacles prevented them from sending much. The situation changed when the Russians halted the German armies outside Moscow in December 1941, and still more when they defeated the Germans at Stalingrad in the autumn and winter of 1942. It gradually became clear that Russia was not merely going to survive. She was going to win. Once Germany was defeated, Soviet Russia would emerge as the only Great Power on the continent of Europe.

In theory the British and Americans were faced with a vital question: should they allow Soviet Russia to step into this great position? In practice, the question was never considered, least of all by Churchill. Great Britain and the United States were at war with Germany and welcomed any power that aided them. As Churchill said: 'If Hitler invaded Hell I should make at least a friendly reference to the Devil in the House of Commons.' Roosevelt in his usual way evaded the problem by postponing any discussion of the post-war world until the war was over. Or maybe he assumed, too easily, that American power would then be overwhelming. Churchill was more direct. He tried to establish relations of personal intimacy with Stalin, the Soviet dictator. He tried to secure some limitations on Russian power while the war was on. In the first task he largely succeeded, certainly more than any other man could have done; with Churchill, Stalin became a human being. The second task was one impossible to accomplish. In concrete terms, how could Poland, Russia's essential concern, be both friendly to Russia and a democratic country? The answer was that it could not be done, and the Polish government was as great an obstacle to this as the Russian.

As the war proceeded, the magnitude of Soviet Russia's coming victory became ever clearer and with it Churchill's anxiety to limit it. In October 1944 he seemed to have succeeded. He went to Moscow and proposed to Stalin a division of Europe into spheres of interest. This proposal later came in for much condemnation and was regretted by Churchill himself. Yet in fact it provided the answer. Certainly it handed over Eastern Europe to the Russians. But equally it handed over Western Europe to the British and Americans.

Soviet forces have remained in Eastern Europe to the present day. Similarly, British and American forces have remained in Western Europe. Each party has justified or excused itself by pleading an invitation from the government concerned. The Russians were constantly asked to compromise. The Anglo-Americans would have been awkwardly placed if the Russians had responded and offered to abandon, say, the secret police and the labour camps on condition the Anglo-Saxon powers abandoned private property in land and the means of production.

As it was, the British were able to suppress the resistance forces in Greece by armed force, the only such action by any Allied power in the course of the war. In Italy, Togliatti, the Communist leader, returned from Moscow with orders to co-operate with the Allied authorities. And the Italian resistance, composed of 150,000 fighters, surrendered their arms uncomplainingly. Thorez, the French Communist leader, accepted de Gaulle's authority and helped to preserve the French state. Even in Eastern Europe, Communist governments were a consequence of the Cold War, not its cause. In the Far East, Stalin aided the recovery of China by Chiang Kai-shek, and the subsequent victory of Mao Tse-tung was highly unwelcome to him.

With the war drawing to a close Churchill became increasingly anxious. As is well known, he urged Eisenhower to abandon his strategy of a broad advance and to march on Berlin ahead of the Russians. Eisenhower rejected this prompting and has sometimes been criticized for doing so. But what was the purpose in the Americans incurring 300,000 casualties for the sake of Berlin when the Russians were eager to do so? Churchill's immediate apprehensions were exaggerated and misplaced. The Russians had no intention of penetrating further into Germany. Their momentum was exhausted; their losses in men and material were beyond all counting. At the moment of unconditional surrender by the Germans, it was Anglo-American forces, not Russian, that were often a hundred miles beyond the agreed zonal boundaries. On the other hand it was a fantasy to suppose that the Anglo-Saxon powers could suddenly switch sides and oppose the Russians with the aid of the defeated German armies.

The end of the war brought an anti-climax in Churchill's career. Though the British people supported him wholeheartedly as the wartime leader, they had bitter memories of Tory rule during the 1930s and now put their faith in the Labour party. Churchill was cast down, but not for long. His speech at Fulton, Missouri, in 1946 proclaimed the coming of the Cold War. Yet a few years later, with his physical powers failing, he clung to office as Prime Minister in the belief that he was the only man who could win over Stalin's successors to a policy of peace and reconciliation. It must be said that Churchill's mind was not constructive. Despite his radical outbursts, he was essentially conservative. He wanted to preserve Great Britain and the British Empire as he remembered them from his romantic youth. He understood nothing of the social and political forces that were changing the world. Fundamentally, his outlook was sombre. He did not share the contemporary belief in universal betterment nor did he await the coming of some secular Heaven on Earth.

Late in life, Churchill pronounced a gloomy verdict on his career. He remarked that the final verdict of history would take account not only of the victories achieved under his direction, but also of the political results which flowed from them, and he added: 'Judged by this standard, I am not sure that I shall be held to have done very well.' Churchill did himself an injustice. The results were not his doing; the victories were. The results were foreshadowed when the British people resolved on war with Hitler. From this moment it followed inexorably that, unless Hitler won, Soviet Russia would establish her domination over Eastern Europe and become a World Power.

Was the price worth paying? The men of the time had no doubt that it was. When we consider the barbarities of Nazi rule – the tyranny, the gas chambers, the mass exterminations – we must agree that Hitlerism had to be destroyed whatever the cost. No one can contemplate the present state of things without acknowledging that people everywhere are happier, freer and more prosperous than they would have been if Nazi Germany and Japan had won, and this applies even to the countries under Communist control. Future generations may dismiss the Second World War as 'just another war'. Those who experienced it know that it was a war justified in its aims and successful in accomplishing them. Churchill defined his policy once and for all when he said: 'Victory at all costs.' The British people agreed with him. How right they were.

The man who gave us our finest hour

At a tense moment in the First World War Herbert Henry Asquith, the Prime Minister, sat unruffledly in Cabinet, placidly composing a letter to his lady friend. He wrote about one member of the Cabinet: 'He will never get to the top in English politics, with all his wonderful gifts; to speak with the tongue of men and angels, and to spend laborious days and nights in administration, is no good if a man does not inspire trust.'

A damning verdict. Who was it pronounced on? On none other than Winston Spencer Churchill.

Asquith, the Prime Minister who was driven from office in the First World War, failed to foresee the triumphant Prime Minister of the Second World War.

A singular misjudgment. An error in prophecy of the first magnitude. Yet Asquith was proved wrong only late in the day. If Winston Churchill had died in his sixty-fifth year he would now be forgotten or, at best, remembered only as a brilliant failure.

Sir Winston Churchill, at ninety, is universally loved and honoured. Yet there was a time when he was hated throughout the land.

And not only by his opponents. Churchill had a unique gift for provoking equally great bitterness among those who were nominally on his own side.

First cause of bitterness was the way in which he changed sides in politics.

Churchill was of ancient lineage, the grandson of a duke. He first took his seat in Parliament in 1900 as a Tory, champion of the Empire and of the Boer War.

Yet he soon found himself beside Lloyd George, pro-Boer and man of the people. Churchill and Lloyd George were the two most aggressive Radicals in the years before the First World War.

Together they soaked the rich. Together they denounced the House of Lords. Together they created National Insurance and founded the Welfare State.

Tories hated Churchill. Retired Army officers longed to horse-whip him. One leading Conservative, in uncontrollable rage, threw a book at him across the floor of the House.

The First World War increased Churchill's unpopularity. He championed the expedition at the Dardanelles. He was saddled, most unjustly, with all the blame for failure at Gallipoli.

He was driven from office by universal outcry. When the Conservatives agreed to serve under Lloyd George in 1916 they made one implacable condition: *Churchill must not become a Minister.*

Churchill was not satisfied to offend the Conservatives. He was equally ready to challenge organized labour. He sent troops against the miners at Tonypandy, and the reproach was to dog him for thirty years afterwards.

Not sated by war against Germany, he preached intervention in Russia against 'the baboonery of Bolshevism'. He spent £100 million of British money in this vain crusade.

Brought down in 1922 by the ruin of Lloyd George, Churchill slipped humbly back into the Conservative party. Soon he took the aggressive line again.

When the General Strike threatened, Baldwin, then Prime Minister, wanted to compromise. So too did other Conservative ministers, including even the fiery Birkenhead.

Churchill insisted on a fight to the finish. He demanded 'unconditional surrender' on the part of the TUC. He sent food through London in armed convoys and announced triumphantly: 'The convoys reached their destination without attracting the notice of the enemy.' The enemy, in this case, was the British working class.

Churchill added his own contribution to the hardships of these years. He put the pound back on the gold standard. The famous economist, J. M. Keynes, wrote a pamphlet: 'The Economic Consequences of Mr Churchill'. The consequences were mass unemployment and general poverty.

Hatred and distrust mounted against Churchill. He quarrelled with Baldwin, the Conservative leader, over India. Alone among leading Conservatives, Churchill was left out of MacDonald's National Government.

Throughout the 1930s Churchill stood entirely alone, pursuing romantic impossibilities.

He championed the Indian princes. He denounced the League of Nations and disarmament. Worst of all, in the eyes of most politicians, he became the defender of King Edward VIII.

When he rose to plead for delay on the King's behalf, he was shouted down by the Conservatives around him and had to sit back with his words unspoken. No front-bench figure had suffered such humiliation for many years.

Churchill's voice rose unrepentant against Neville Chamberlain's policy of appeasement. Few heeded his words, and these few were helpless. He was approaching sixty-five, the end of his active career. He could be dismissed as an empty echo from the past.

Turn back to the yellowing newspapers of 1939. What do we find? The Conservatives hated Churchill. Labour distrusted him. He was alone, finished, disregarded.

Then overnight he was vindicated. Hitler invaded Poland. Great Britain declared war on Germany. Churchill returned to the Admiralty. But still in a humble position, serving under Chamberlain.

In April 1940 came disaster in Norway, a disaster for which Churchill was largely responsible. It was Gallipoli all over again. This time with a very different result.

Men turned against Chamberlain. A new government had to be formed. All the leading politicians, as we now know, strove to keep out Churchill. Chamberlain, Attlee, King George VI, favoured Halifax.

Only the people wanted the man who had stood alone. Winston Churchill became Prime Minister. When he first entered the House he was received, as he himself has recalled, with stony silence on the Conservative benches.

Not for long. The German armies overran France. The shattered British forces withdrew, as by a miracle, at Dunkirk. Great Britain stood alone. Churchill became the undisputed national leader.

He declared in imperishable words: 'If the British Empire and its Commonwealth last for a thousand years, men will still say, "This was their finest hour."' It was Churchill's finest hour also.

Nearly a quarter of a century has passed since those summer days of 1940. The younger generation listens sceptically, or not at all, to the tales of old men in the chimney corner. Yet they must believe us. This was the most inspiring and most united moment in the history of the British people.

Looking back, it all seems easy. Victory was to follow: in the air, at sea, ultimately on land. Hitler's Reich, with its tyranny and barbarism, was brought to the ground.

This was far off in 1940. Then death and conquest seemed on the horizon. No one faltered.

But what if Churchill had not been there? What if he had not been raised to supreme power in time?

Hitler counted confidently that Great Britain would sue for peace. He was wrong, but he might have been right. Other nations crumbled and fell. All for lack of resolute leadership.

Only Churchill could give it. Churchill had stalwart associates: Bevin, the strongest man the Labour movement has ever produced; Beaverbrook, the master of improvisation. But no one else could speak for and to the nation.

Churchill not only spoke rousing words. He announced at once a rousing policy. The British people, one might suppose, were hard-pressed even to survive. Churchill did not talk of survival. He talked from the first of victory.

In his first speech, when he offered 'blood, toil, tears, and sweat', he announced his policy: 'It is victory, victory at all costs, victory in spite of all the terror: victory, however hard and long the road may be.'

These words are often overlooked. Later writers have sometimes lamented the lost opportunities for a compromise peace. There were in fact none. The British people had announced, through Churchill, that they would be content with nothing less than unconditional surrender.

From that moment Hitler knew that he was fighting for his life. He might well have left the British Empire alone if he could have ruled Europe according to his will and had a free hand against Soviet Russia.

Instead, Churchill defied Hitler. He compelled Hitler to prolong and to extend the war. Despite inadequate means, Churchill carried the war into the Mediterranean and into the air over Germany.

The British people were buoyed up by these blows against Germany. No doubt mistakenly. It is hard to believe, in cool retrospect, that Great Britain could have defeated Hitler if she had remained alone. The essential British task was to keep the war going, until Hitler ruined himself by his own mistakes.

Hitler created the Grand Alliance against Germany, first by his attack on Soviet Russia, then by his declaration of war on the United States. Churchill reaped where Hitler had sown.

He declared solidarity with Soviet Russia. He made the only fit comment about Pearl Harbor driving the United States into war: 'So we had won after all.'

Churchill's solitary leadership became a partnership. Three great men – Churchill, Roosevelt, Stalin. All intent, whatever later cavilling may suggest, on the destruction of Hitler and Nazi rule. They won. Look round the world today. With all its faults, the world is far brighter, cleaner, saner than it was thirty years ago. All because of victory in the Second World War.

The decision against Hitler was taken when the British people resolved to fight on and when they fought alone. The decision was taken by Churchill and could have been taken by no other man.

He was the saviour of his country and the saviour of freedom throughout the world. We bless his name on his ninetieth birthday and on every day when we draw breath as free men.

Clement Attlee

Clement Attlee (1883–1967) was leader of the Labour party (1935–55) and the first Labour Prime Minister to form a government with the support of a majority of the House of Commons (1945–51), Ramsay MacDonald's premierships being minority governments (1924, 1929–31). His background was of the professional middle class, social work in the East End of London and substantial war service in the First World War (ending as Major Attlee).

Alan Taylor was exceptionally skilled at delivering, with very little time to prepare, excellent short obituaries on radio or television. This brief tribute to Attlee was broadcast by the BBC on Radio 4 in the programme 'The World This Weekend', broadcast at 13.00 on 8 October 1967. It was first published in the Listener, *12 October 1967.*

Attlee was the one who stayed at home, who looked after the Cabinet when Churchill wasn't there, who would accept the responsibility while Churchill was, as it were, doing the glamorous and exciting things. It's also said that Attlee was a much more efficient Chairman of the War Cabinet, that the only hope of really getting business through was in the days when the old man was off. But Attlee was intensely loyal to Churchill throughout the war. They'd had their conflicts before the war, and after the war Attlee was to show that he wasn't a bit afraid of Churchill, but he quite consciously accepted the view that Churchill was the inspired war leader and that it was his job to stand beside him and to support him in everything.

The Labour party always has a restless and idealistic Left. The difficulties of the Attlee time were no greater than they are now – perhaps less. After all, Attlee always managed to give the impression – perhaps a misleading impression – that he himself was in sympathy with the Left to some extent. He said – and I don't think that it would be true in the same sense of either Gaitskell or Harold Wilson – that he led the Labour party from somewhere left of centre. However much he disapproved of the Bevanite emotionalism, he had in his time belonged to it. He had also seen the Labour party and socialism as a movement towards Utopia, to the building up of a new world and so on. He also had a far deeper hostility towards – what shall I say? – the capitalists, the Tories, than Labour men have at the present time.

I think history will have to say that Attlee made the decisive contribution to the Welfare State and, particularly of course, to the independence of India, which was very much his doing. But in this period when the Labour party was moving from being a party of romantic idealists to a party of practical achievement, it was Attlee who did more than anybody else to bring about the transition and to change the character of the Labour party. It was in Attlee's time and not before that the Labour party became fully a party fit to govern. A very significant prime minister – a prime minister who did great things often by keeping quiet, by keeping out of the way, by his strength of character and his readiness to take decisions, and to support others when they were making the decisions. I think that it will give him a place in history, perhaps not as a great prime minister, but as a prime minister whose period of office made a very great difference to British and Commonwealth affairs.

Anthony Eden

(Robert) Anthony Eden, Earl of Avon (1897–1977), was Foreign Secretary (1935–8, 1940–5 and 1951–5) and Prime Minister (1955–7).

These essays were published as reviews of Lord Avon, The Eden Memoirs, Volumes 2 and 3, Cassell, 1962 and 1965, in the *Observer, 18 November 1962 and 21 March 1965. Alan Taylor had strongly opposed Britain's Suez operation in 1956. He roundly condemned Eden in his introduction to Sidney Aster,* Sir Anthony Eden, *Weidenfeld & Nicolson, 1976 (a volume in a series of books entitled* British Prime Ministers *which he edited). He commented there, 'Eden, if anyone, not Nasser, was the Hitler of 1956 with the same cloud of words and the same unscrupulousness of action.' Alan Taylor's first feature article for the* Manchester Guardian *had been on Eden's resignation from Neville Chamberlain's government. In 'The Case of Mr Eden: An Historical View' (23 February 1938) he had discussed possible historical parallels of Foreign Secretaries resigning or staying in spite of friction with their Prime Ministers. These ranged from Palmerston in 1851 to Derby in 1878, Rosebery and Gladstone in 1892–4 and Grey in 1909–12, but his conclusion was that the greatest similarity was with the French minister, Théophile Delcassé (1852–1923), in 1905.*

The Eden Memoirs, Volume II: Facing the Dictators

On 27 November 1936, Anthony Eden, then Foreign Secretary, recorded his doubts about the proposed Gentleman's Agreement with Mussolini. He wrote: 'No amount of promises or understandings or even humble crawlings on our part will affect Mussolini's course. On the other hand, a little plain speaking may.' Now Lord Avon, in retirement, presents the same doctrine in a volume of over 600 pages.

His book is an important contribution to historical knowledge. It begins in September 1931, when he became an Under-Secretary at the Foreign Office. It ends with his resignation on 20 February 1938, when he had held the post of Foreign Secretary for more than two years. Lord Avon, or his research assistant, has had free access to the Foreign Office archives, and prints many papers from them, apparently without restriction. The official volumes on British foreign policy between the wars have at present a gap between the middle of 1934 and March 1938. Lord Avon's book is therefore our only source of documentary information for this period, and of course welcome. Yet it provokes doubts. Lord Avon has been allowed to select the documents which vindicate him. Simon, Hoare and Neville Chamberlain are dead. There is no one to perform the same service for them; and no detached historian is given access to the archives. This is one-sided justice. Sir Horace Wilson is still alive. But he remains resolutely silent even when presented, as here, in an unfavourable light.

Again, Lord Avon prints many minutes by himself and others. The editors of the official volumes decided to exclude minutes; and Lord Avon was actually Foreign Secretary, responsible for this decision when it was made. The result of this is that his version, and only his version, will hold the field until the archives are opened in some twenty-five years' time. Charles Beard, the great American historian, laid down a better rule: 'Official archives should be opened on equal terms to all, with special privileges for none.'

Lord Avon presents the case against appeasement. That is easy.

Appeasement failed; and everyone now is readier to condemn than to try to understand it. He also seeks to show that he was not tarred with the appeasement brush. This is less convincing. For instance, he was strenuous for a disarmament convention in 1933. He implies now that this was merely to acquire a moral advantage when Germany broke it, though it is difficult to understand what gain yet another moral advantage would have brought. At the time he believed, as nearly everyone else did, that agreement might satisfy Germany.

In 1935 he was eager to stop Italy's oil before he became Foreign Secretary. He did not support the 'oil sanction' as Foreign Secretary. By then apparently it had become ineffective or dangerous. In reality the case had been the same all along; only the position of Anthony Eden had changed.

Lord Avon skates over the difficulties which confronted British ministers in the Abyssinian crisis. The British people wanted 'all sanctions short of war' – maybe foolish, but that is what they wanted. The Chiefs of Staff were insistent that Italy should not be added to the enemies of Great Britain, in view of the dangers from Germany and Japan. The French were apprehensive for the Rhineland; they believed that Great Britain would not support them over this, and therefore wanted to keep on good terms with Italy. French fears were correct. When Germany reoccupied the Rhineland, Eden offered them only 'a steady and calm examination by all those interested'. Even the military conversations with France were a gesture; as Eden told Ribbentrop, 'it was not a question of their military value'.

The Spanish Civil War dominated Eden's time at the Foreign Office. Eden was a leading protagonist of non-intervention. Yet he knew that Italy and, to a lesser extent, Germany were cheating all the time. He took no action. Why? For exactly the same motive as the appeasers appeased – fear of war. The motive was in fact mistaken. Hitler and Mussolini, as we now know, had both decided to run away if the Western Powers backed the Spanish Republic. Lord Avon writes: 'From the early months of 1937, if I had had to choose, I would have preferred a Government victory.' He did not choose. The one good chance of defeating the dictators was thrown away. Eden faced the dictators, as the title of his book implies: he did not oppose them.

Eden broke with Neville Chamberlain only in February 1938. The dramatic conflict between them established Eden's position as an opponent of appeasement. It is fully described here with the aid of many documents never published before. Chamberlain behaved badly, intriguing with the Italian Ambassador against his own Foreign Secretary. Chamberlain's associates behaved badly also. Sir John Simon tried to make out that Eden was looking ill so that his resignation could be put down to ill-health. Horace Wilson threatened that 'he would use the full power of the Government machine in an attack upon A. E.'s past record with regard to the dictators and the shameful obstruction by the FO of the PM's attempts to save the peace of the world'.

All the same, the dispute was of narrow compass, a dispute over words, not between resistance and surrender. The first topic was in regard to the United States. Eden still had faith in gestures. He regrets that he did not visit President Roosevelt in 1937. 'For if the meeting had met with some success, its steadying effect upon the dictators could have been important.' Could it? Would Hitler and Mussolini really have been deterred because Eden and Roosevelt had had a quiet talk? In January 1938, Roosevelt proposed to approach the Heads of all Governments with 'the suggestion that they should agree on the essential principles to be observed in the conduct of international relations'. Eden thought that this was a great chance to associate the US with the Western Powers. Chamberlain thought that it would irritate the dictators, and gave Roosevelt little encouragement.

No doubt Chamberlain did wrong to go against his own Foreign Secretary. But was a great opportunity lost, as Lord Avon still claims? Professors Langer and Gleason have examined American foreign policy in great detail with the aid of the records. They describe Roosevelt's proposal as 'very modest, very general'. They conclude their account with these words: 'Conceivably a really strong stand by the US Government in support of the British might have changed the course of events, but the foregoing narrative should suffice to show that nothing of the kind was ever remotely considered in Washington.' Thus no great opportunity was lost; there was none to lose.

The final break between Eden and Chamberlain came over Italy. Chamberlain wished to get on better terms with Italy by immediate negotiations. Eden refused to negotiate until the Italian 'volunteers' were withdrawn from Spain. Here again Chamberlain was no doubt wrong to go against his Foreign Secretary, and foolish to suppose that Mussolini could be won over by soft words. Was Eden any more sensible to suppose that he could be deterred by hard ones? Eden did not propose action of any sort – a blockade of Franco's ports, for example, or intervention on the side of the Spanish government. He relied solely on gestures.

The dispute was once more over words. Chamberlain proposed to give *de jure* recognition to Italy's rule in Abyssinia. Eden opposed this. That was all. Was the refusal of *de jure* recognition really a threat to make Mussolini cower? The choice in the years before 1939 was between appeasement and resistance. Chamberlain chose appeasement. Eden chose hard words. He spoke against the dictators. He did not resist them, in this resembling many other English people. Eden did not even oppose the Chamberlain government after his resignation. He abstained.

Vansittart once remarked: 'Anthony says the right thing so often that it becomes monotonous.' This remark perhaps explains why, as revealed in this book, Eden, not Chamberlain, kicked Vansittart upstairs. Words were Eden's stock-in-trade – words once marshalled against the dictators, now used with equal fluency to captivate the reader. This book lacks one thing: a motto on the title page. This lack is easily supplied:

> Sticks and stones
> May break my bones;
> But words will never hurt me.

When, many years later, Anthony Eden attempted action, the unaccustomed exercise was his undoing.

The Eden Memoirs, Volume III:
The Reckoning

On 20 February 1938, Anthony Eden (now Lord Avon) resigned as Foreign Secretary. He rejoined Chamberlain's government as Dominions Secretary on the outbreak of war, was Secretary for War from May to December 1940, and then Foreign Secretary until the end of the war. He became Leader of the House of Commons in November 1942, and was, as well, Churchill's designated successor. No man other than Churchill himself stood nearer the heart of British war policy, saw more, or was more responsible for decisions.

Unlike Churchill, Eden kept a daily diary and has used it as well as his correspondence in writing this volume of memoirs. The book ought to be of great importance: informative and tingling with life. It is curiously disappointing and, in general effect, elusive. Despite the laborious detail on many points, the great events seem remote, and there is a querulous tone, pitched in a minor key. Perhaps the Foreign Office remained cloistered, even in wartime, or perhaps Eden was overshadowed by the grandeur of his position. At any rate, this book hardly claims a place among the literary memorials of the Second World War.

In 1938 Eden, out of office, was also at a loss for a policy. He would not support the government and hesitated to oppose it. The Eden group, he thought, amounted to perhaps thirty. At the time of Munich, Richard Law judged that a minority of Conservatives were opposed to Chamberlain. 'A still smaller minority maintained that the Prime Minister was right, while the majority were miserably unhappy and would now follow an alternative lead, if given one.' Eden did not give this lead. When Members cheered Chamberlain, Eden walked out, or, in his own phrase, 'I did not feel I could take part in this scene.' As late as 12 August 1939, Eden was still speculating what he and his friends should do: 'These questions require urgent thought.' The outbreak of war resolved his problem. He rejoined the government in an ineffective position:

I was back again, not because my former colleagues wanted me to join them, but because the country had judged me to be right and them to be wrong in the controversy over my resignation. I was only there on condition that I took no effective part in anything outside the work of my department.

Eden's opportunity came with the Churchill Government. As Secretary for War he was at once caught up in the battle for France. On 19 May Ironside, the CIGS, said to him: 'This is the end of the British Empire.' Even in this dark hour, Eden was anxious to sustain the Middle East – perhaps because of his old antagonism to Mussolini. Churchill was less eager. Thus, on 25 July: 'Dined with Winston. Violent tirade about Middle East.' On 16 September: 'Winston was vehement against sending anything more to Middle East. "I do not know what you are thinking of, etc., etc." ' Churchill had no faith in Wavell: 'a good average colonel' and 'would make a good chairman of a Tory association'. Even Neville Chamberlain said: 'I'm sorry, Anthony, that all your generals seem to be such bad generals.'

Churchill had, however, great faith in Eden. On 30 September 1940: 'Winston reiterated that he was now an old man, that he would not make Lloyd George's mistake of carrying on after the war, that the succession must be mine.' On 5 December: 'Winston proposed I should go out to command in Middle East.'

Instead Eden became Foreign Secretary. As such, he went to the Middle East with Dill, the CIGS, and the two men largely determined the calamitous British expedition to Greece. Eden hardly refers to the warnings from Churchill and the War Cabinet. But he marshals the support of Wavell and Dill. When Eden arrived, Wavell said: 'As you were so long I felt I had to get started, and I have begun the concentration for a move of troops to Greece.' Eden also records a later judgment by Dill: 'He was quite unrepentant that we were right to go there. Politically no doubt: militarily, on balance, "yes".'

Greece was Eden's only excursion into strategy. Thereafter he had his hands full conducting foreign policy and restraining Churchill's impulses. There runs through the diary a monotonous refrain: 'Great wrangle, but we stood firm and Winston gave in . . .

Prolonged wrangle . . . We wrangled throughout the evening . . . A shouting match . . .' Others, particularly Alanbrooke, have described their controversies with Churchill. Their accounts, however bitter, imply that there was serious argument and debate. Eden's picture is one of crude brawling in an impatient, ill-tempered way. Occasionally he admits the inspiration which went with the difficulties:

A Cabinet as conducted by Mr Churchill could be a splendid and unique experience. It might be a monologue, it was never a dictatorship. The disadvantage to those with specific duties to perform or departments to run, was the time consumed.

Other Ministers shared Eden's dissent.

Mr Churchill declared that, if it came to the point he would always side with the United States against France. I did not like this pronouncement nor did Mr Bevin, who said so in a booming aside.

Again:

Attlee rang me up during the day. He didn't like W.'s reply to FDR. Nor did I much, but I had secured one amendment and failed to secure more. I therefore suggested he should try. He did, and secured another.

Churchill, it seems, was always eager for the Grand Alliance. Eden, or more often 'Attlee and I', raised objections. They were reluctant to see Great Britain taken in tow by the two great Allies. Eden listened with alarm when Roosevelt casually redrew the map of Europe. There should be a new State called Wallonia. 'This would include the Walloon parts of Belgium and Luxembourg, Alsace-Lorraine and part of northern France . . . In the Balkans, Mr Roosevelt favoured separating Serbia from Croatia and Slovenia.' Relations with Soviet Russia alarmed Eden even more. On 29 May 1945, he talked with Davies, Truman's emissary, and commented:

He is the born appeaser and would gladly give Russia all Europe, except perhaps us, so that America might not be embroiled. All the errors and illusions of Neville C., substituting Russia for Germany.

Even Churchill was not sound. At Potsdam:

He is again under Stalin's spell. He kept repeating 'I like that man.' I am full of admiration of Stalin's handling of him. I told him I was, hoping that it would move him. It did a little.

Eden was less sceptical about Germany. On the news of the attempt on Hitler's life:

Ernie Bevin at once said that it was Nazi stunt to popularize H. Brendan [Bracken] said it was Goebbels's work. I said it was hard to tell so far, but I didn't think so.

Eden was not surprised when the Conservatives lost the General Election:

I told Winston that his place in history could have gained nothing by anything he might have achieved in the postwar years. That place was secure anyway. This he accepted.

There is a bitter final paragraph:

It is a common happening that those in power, as their tenure of office continues, find themselves less and less able to contemplate relinquishing it. The vows they made earlier that they would give way to a younger man when the years begin to blunt their faculties . . . these they choose to ignore. Power has become a habit they cannot bear to cast off. Mr Churchill, by his indubitable stature and his weighty talents, belied this process. What neither he nor I could have foreseen was that when at last I stepped into his place, I should have so short a run. Thirty years of political work and a feckless disregard for my health were to claim their forfeit.

An epilogue remarks that Attlee, not Churchill, announced the surrender of Japan.

Mr Churchill had not been asked to say any word to the nation. We went home. Journey's end.

HOW WARS BEGIN

Introduction

Six major wars have been fought in Europe since the French Revolution. A seventh was fought all over the world, though Europe contributed to its outbreak and provided one field of combat. Since then there has been one major conflict which, without leading to actual war, had many of its characteristics. Two major wars – the American Civil War of 1861–5 and the Russo-Japanese War of 1904–5 – being fought entirely outside Europe, do not fall into the pattern of the others and I have therefore omitted them from my survey of how modern wars begin.

This has long been fertile ground for historians. Many of the wars had a long background or, as Renouvin wrote, profound causes. Two were presented as wars of creeds: the French revolutionary wars as a conflict between Jacobinism and reaction, the Second World War between Fascism and democracy. The Austro-French War of 1859 and the Austro-Prussian War of 1866 were inspired in part by the principle of nationalism. Imperialist rivalries are often cited as contributing to the First World War. The overweening ambition of a single man – Napoleon at the beginning of the period and Hitler towards its end – has sometimes bulked large.

Public opinion, inflamed by a jingo press, has not escaped censure. Diplomats, too, have been made responsible. The First World War was widely attributed to secret diplomacy and to the European alliances that were its outcome. Militarism, preaching the glories of war, has played its part. Sometimes, it is said, the guns went off of themselves. On a more prosaic level wars were allegedly provoked or at least encouraged by armament manufacturers, 'the merchants of death'.

Historians themselves might be added. In the nineteenth century, though perhaps less at the present day, they were fervent patriots, 'chaplains of the pirate ship' as Beatrice Webb called them. They presented the expansion of empire as the noblest chapter in the history of their particular country. English historians glorified Queen Elizabeth I or the great Earl of Chatham; French historians glorified Napoleon I, though less unanimously; German historians made do with Frederick the Great or even Julius Caesar. On a slightly more academic level historians presented international relations as a series of conflicts between sovereign states, shaped by the ever-changing Balance of Power and leading inevitably, even admirably, to major wars.

All these explanations have some validity. But there is also another more prosaic origin of war: the precise moment when a statesman sets his name to the declaration of it. The statesman is no doubt a creature of his time and shares its outlook. But the actual act of signing his name has often little relation to the profound causes, as I discovered to my surprise when developing my theme. The Jacobins certainly hoped to carry the Rights of Man across Europe, but they were forced into war by the declared intention of the conservative powers to destroy the French Revolution. Napoleon may well have aspired to found a great European empire. But all his wars except the last were preventive wars, provoked by the preparations that others were making to attack him. The Japanese wished to dominate the Far East but they, too, were forced into war by the prospect that otherwise the American embargo on their oil would strangle them.

Public opinion has more often trailed after policy rather than determined it. Italian nationalists showed little enthusiasm for the Austro-French War of 1859, and German nationalists showed little for the Austro-Prussian War of 1866 until after Bismarck had achieved his victory. In 1870 Parisian crowds called 'à Berlin' only when war had been declared. In 1914 there were frenzied demonstrations for war in every European capital again only when war had been declared. We have no idea whether they would have cheered as widely if peace had been preserved; British crowds certainly did so after the conference at Munich in 1938. The only case to be set on the other side is the Crimean War, where popular hostility to Russia made it difficult for the British government to follow a conciliatory policy. Even so, diplomatic muddle contributed more than an excited public opinion to the outbreak of the Crimean War.

Militarism, or rather the opinion of the military authorities, has of course always counted for something. Napoleon presumably knew what he was doing when he declared his wars, though in 1812 at any rate he judged wrongly. The Prussian general staff were confident of victory in 1866 and still more in 1870, though they did not actually provoke the declarations of war. The French generals should have advised against war in 1870 if they had understood their profession and instead urged war for purely emotional reasons. In 1914 all the general staffs reported that they were ready for war, but only the German general staff pushed for its declaration and then at the last moment. Both Hitler and the Japanese intended to avoid a major war until later and were lured into it by the minor wars that they undertook. Perhaps the British and French general staffs of 1939 reported that war, though unwelcome, could be at any rate tolerated, but even this is doubtful.

Wars in fact have sprung more from apprehension than from a lust for war or for conquest. Paradoxically, many of the European wars were started by a threatened Power which had nothing to gain by war and much to lose. Thus Austria started the Austro-French War of 1859 by her declaration of war on Sardinia. She started the Austro-Prussian War of 1866 by promoting the condemnation of Prussia at the Federal Diet. She started the First World War by her declaration of war on Serbia. Yet in each case she was almost bound to be the loser. Apprehension was reinforced by exasperation – with Austria the harassment of nationalist propaganda. Similarly France in 1870 was exasperated by Bismarck's successes and started the war by her declaration of war on Prussia.

England and France acted in much the same way in 1939 when they transformed the German invasion of Poland into the preliminaries of the Second World War by declaring war on Germany. The French expressed this when they said, '*Il faut en finir.*' Even the Japanese acted more from apprehension than from aggression when they attacked Pearl Harbor in 1941. As to the Cold War between Soviet Russia and the United States, this seems in retrospect to have been motivated by mutual suspicion, at any rate for most of the time, rather than by any conscious design of one party to destroy the other.

Every Great Power is suspicious of any likely or even unlikely rival. What seems defence to one will always appear as an aggressive preparation to another. This has nothing to do with human nature, which is infinitely variable. It is the inevitable consequence of the existence of sovereign states. Every Great Power relies on armaments as a means of deterrence. This deterrent has often worked and has given Europe long periods of peace. There comes a moment of impatience or misjudgement, and the deterrent fails to work. With nuclear weapons the Balance of Power has been replaced by the Balance of Terror. This only means that the chances of war are less, not that they have been eliminated. In the old days the deterrent worked nine times out of ten. Now presumably it will work ninety-nine times out of a hundred. But if past experience is any guide – and as I have suggested in my conclusion it is not a certain one – the hundredth occasion will come.

Even so, the nuclear weapons will not go off of themselves. In the last resort some human being will have to press the button just as in the past some statesman had to sign the declaration of war.

The First Modern War:
From French Revolution to
French Empire

How do wars begin? This is perhaps the most constant theme of the historian. Wars make up most of European history. In every civilization there have been wars, at any rate until, we think, our own time. Wars caused in all kinds of ways – wars of conquest, wars of imperial rivalries, wars of family disputes, religious wars.

In the eighteenth century they had settled down into almost legalistic wars, wars as to who had the right to the throne: the War of the Spanish Succession, the War of the Polish Succession, the War of the Austrian Succession, and indeed you could say in the early eighteenth century, though we don't call it such, the War of the English Succession which brought the Hanoverians to the throne. In the last 200 years there has been a profound change. Wars have changed from being wars between rulers to being wars between nations, and it is these wars of the last 200 years or so that I shall talk about. This was where modern history began. More than this, as I looked into the French Revolution and the wars that it caused, I realized that in some ways it was the most modern of all wars, a war brought about by rival systems of political outlook.

Undoubtedly, the French Revolution of 1789 was the most formidable event in modern European history. Charles James Fox said of it, and I think he was right, 'How much the greatest event since the beginning of the world and how much the best', though not everyone would agree about the second part of the phrase. What made it so different? There had been revolutions, plenty of them, including incidentally a revolution in England which overthrew the monarch, but basically changes of family. The French Revolution was different because it brought into the world, and Europe in particular, a new idea, the Rights of Man, and with the Rights of Man went the Rights of Nations. Where previously states had been based on dynastic power they were now based on national existence. In the old days, right up to 1789, a state was simply the property of its ruler; Madame de Pompadour called Louis XV 'France' even when she was in bed with him. Then suddenly there appeared the French people who said, 'We are France.' This was a challenge to all the dynasties of Europe and there was a competition of propaganda and of assertion, with, as the French Revolution developed, first the liberal and then the radical, and then the revolutionary leaders staking out more aggressively the claims of the people of France and in time of course the claims of others. After all, if France had the right to be a nation, if France was composed of its peoples and not just of its king, this applied to others.

One of the factors which produced the revolutionary war was the provocative declaration which the French legislative assembly made on 19 November 1792, promising help and fraternity to every nation seeking to recover its liberty. The word 'recover' is curious. Most of these nations had never had their liberty, but it was already a myth that there had been a distant time when peoples had all been free and had then been enslaved by their kings. In answer to this, or in rivalry to this, the kings and emperors of Europe had met as early as June 1791. They met at a place called Pillnitz and warned the French that, unless they behaved better, unless they treated their king better, the great powers of Europe would call them to order. The Declaration of Pillnitz marked the real beginning of the revolutionary war, because here were these kings seeking to display their authority, to rebuke the French, to push them back into discipline under Louis XVI. Instead it provoked them forward.

Something else was curious about it. Although two great forces, the one of monarchy, of tradition, of conservatism, the other of liberalism and nationalism, were moving against each other, neither of them looked at it in practical terms. The armies of old Europe, although they were competent professional forces, were not at all equipped to occupy a foreign country and to suppress it. They thought that warnings would be enough. For that matter, with the revolution in France the French army practically collapsed and none of the violent statesmen who were preaching war or at any rate resistance to the rest of Europe had the slightest idea what the French army was like. Each side thought that phrases would be enough. That is a common case before a war; that if you assert conservatism or revolutionary principles this in itself will shape things.

Strangely enough, though France was the one threatened, it was the French revolutionary government which finally plunged into war, declared war – threatened Austria in April 1792, and then actually went to war, though unable to do very much.

Why? Because as one of them said, 'The time has come to start a new crusade, a crusade for universal liberty.' There was a more practical consideration. King Louis XVI was intriguing with the other kings, and the revolutionaries hoped that with war it would appear how he had been disloyal to his own country. The revolutionary leader Brissot said, 'What we want is some great treason.' This worked. When the French revolutionary armies encountered the armies of the old regime and were defeated, the cry arose, as it does in a war, of 'Treason' ... 'We are betrayed.' The very same cry that the French raised in 1940 when they were again defeated. People find it difficult to imagine that a defeat can happen for perfectly practical causes and not because of treason. At any rate Louis XVI was overthrown.

One date is memorable as the beginning of the modern world. On 20 September 1792 the French troops, who up to that time had hardly fought at all, stood in line at a place called Valmi where the Prussian army advanced against them. There was no really heavy fighting, there was a cannonade and for the first time the new French revolutionary troops did not run away. The Prussians pulled back and Goethe, who was with the Prussian officers, said, 'Gentlemen, you have this day taken part in the birth of a new world.' Birth only, there was a great deal more to come. The French revolutionary wars were much more ragged than modern wars; they came here a bit and there a bit. It was not until the beginning of 1793 that this war began to extend all over Europe. Even then there was a great deal of muddle about it.

In 1792 the English government had claimed that they would

stand aloof since, although England was not by any means a revolutionary country, she had a constitution and could not join with the absolute monarchs. At the same time there was increasing apprehension, not only about France but about the movement of revolutionaries and Jacobins inside the country. There was an anti-Jacobin panic. After all, the greatest of all revolutionary statements of principle, the greatest statement of democratic principles ever made, although it was called the 'Rights of Man', which was a French idea, was written by an Englishman, Tom Paine. Increasingly the British government, faced with discontent and with demands for parliamentary reform, used France as the excuse for a policy of repression. It is always tempting, when you have political discontent in your own country, to say it is the fault of some other country and not of your own government. Early in 1793 the British government demanded that the French revolutionaries should withdraw their support for peoples who wished to recover their liberty.

Two things marked the last days of January 1793, both of them assertions of revolutionary principle. Louis XVI was executed. Danton said, 'The Kings of Europe challenge us, we throw down to Europe the head of a King.' It was defiance, a complete breach between revolutionary France and the traditional states of Europe, and at the end of the month revolutionary France declared war on Great Britain. This began the first of the coalition wars. It seemed to be a war of principles. On the one side, the allies, the great powers, the kings and emperors were concerned (or so they said) to save civilization, by which they meant themselves. The French revolutionaries were concerned to carry through new and universal principles of enlightenment. Never for a moment did they suggest that the Rights of Man were simply something for France. They were something for others, and more than this – others must have them whether they wanted them or not. When the French invaded Belgium, the Belgians deeply regretted that the churches were secularized and the monasteries and convents all closed. But the Belgians ought not to have done this; they ought to have welcomed liberation from the Church, liberation from their traditional rulers. French enthusiasm for liberty easily became French dogmatism for liberty.

On both sides also there were more practical considerations.

When the allies started their crusade to save conservatism and civilization, they also worked out the bits of French territory which they hoped to annex. On the other side, the French revolutionary armies, when they began to achieve victories, certainly brought with them liberation of a sort; liberation from the traditional institutions, liberation from the kings and princes, liberation from the Christian religion. At the same time they brought demands of a very practical nature. 'After all,' the French said, 'we have done the fighting, we have liberated you, we have presented you with the Rights of Man, we not only had to pay the money for these armies, we had actually to do the fighting for you as well. Therefore you must pay us.'

Wherever the armies of liberty went in Europe, they imposed indemnities. They collected so much that there was a time when the French revolutionary wars were practically paying for themselves. Moreover, as the armies grew greater and more powerful, the apprehensions of the civilian politicians in Paris grew greater also. What they wanted was that these revolutionary armies, splendid as they were in their spirit, devoted as they were to liberty and equality and fraternity, should not exert power in Paris itself. As one of the revolutionaries said, 'We must get these scoundrels to march as far away from France as possible.' Revolution had become something for export.

So far as we remember these first wars at all, we think of them as one great block, a twenty-year war which lasted from 1792 or 1793 until 1814 or 1815; throughout the nineteenth century it was called The Great War. But when I looked at it more closely, I realized that it was not a continuous war, in a sense not even a continuing story. There were in this war two entirely different epochs which became confused afterwards but which were quite distinct. The revolutionary wars, which asserted the independence of France and destroyed (or at any rate defeated) the crusade for conservatism and reaction, lasted a comparatively short time. By 1794 all the territory of France had been cleared. By 1795 France had reached what were called the natural frontiers. That is another curiosity, by the way, which was to be repeated all through the nineteenth century – the way in which a nation starts by claiming its national freedom, then says, 'God or providence not only created

this nation but created natural frontiers for it, and there they are.'
Always, you will find, natural frontiers mean more territory than
you can claim for any other reason.

By 1795 France had reached the natural frontiers of the Rhine
and the Alps. By 1796 the French armies had swept into northern
Italy and had established satellite republics there. This first wave
of revolutionary wars asserting French power ended with the eighteenth century. There was a short and very important period of
peace. In 1801 there was, although we forget it, universal peace in
Europe; even England and France were not at war. And when war
started again in 1804, it had taken a different character. The French
revolutionaries who had conducted French affairs were replaced
by a single man who in 1804 made himself emperor – Napoleon
Bonaparte. The most powerful European emperor since Roman
times. Napoleon achieved power not on a promise of universal war
and conquest, but on the promise of restoring order.

When I looked at this history, the record of these Napoleonic
wars, I realized how different they seem in the perspective of 150
or nearly 200 years. To those who experienced the wars and looked
back to them, they were purely wars of French aggression – or shall
we say, as many French people said afterwards, 'pure Napoleonic
aggression'. After all, Napoleon's victories carried French arms and
French authority right across Europe, and historians have constantly
speculated – what kind of an empire did he want to achieve? Surely
he was aiming at some kind of universal monarchy?

But when you look at Napoleon's war in detail, there emerges a
striking contradiction of the traditional story. I hesitate to say this
because if you venture an opinion of this kind and say, 'Well, it
really wasn't Napoleon who started these wars,' this is felt to be
somehow heterodox and provocative. But I think that is how it
was.

Take the first of them, the war which was resumed between
England and France after a very brief period of peace just when
Napoleon had become emperor. What was the technical reason?
The technical reason may not be why a war starts, but it is at least
the spark. The technical reason was simply this: that during the
revolutionary war the Royal Navy occupied Malta. It was not

theirs, it was not British; if anything, it belonged to the Knights of Malta who had been there for the last 400 years, and one of the terms of the Peace of Amiens between England and France was that the British would give up Malta. When the time came they refused to do so. They said to Napoleon, 'You have not withdrawn from certain territories you have occupied in Europe – therefore we are going to stay in Malta.' The British are entitled always to mistrust other people but others are not entitled to mistrust the British. That is why England is known or was known abroad as '*Perfide Albion*', because the British have two standards, one for themselves and one for other people.

This was the actual origin of the renewal of the war. And from this time on, it was British policy to stir up new coalitions against Napoleon. The British had much more gold than anyone else and used it to ensure that the Austrians or the Prussians, or whoever it might be, did the fighting. The French used to refer to these subsidies as 'the Cavalry of Saint George'. Right at the beginning of these ten years, the pattern was set for wars which occurred at regular intervals: British attempts to create a coalition; Napoleon, partly with his instinctive shrewdness, partly with his greater intelligence service, getting his blow in first. One of the things that the British greatly objected to about Napoleon was that, just when they were conspiring to produce a coalition against him, he would destroy the coalition instead before it was ready. Unfair, it was often claimed to be, that Napoleon moved too fast.

The first and most dramatic occasion was in 1804 when Napoleon had assembled 'the Army of England' with which he proposed to cross the Channel and occupy London. The project was not going well. Napoleon had not got command of the seas, in fact he was very soon to lose command of the seas altogether. And while the French army was still at Boulogne, Napoleon heard that an Austrian army, propped up by British subsidies, was being built up on the Danube. He broke camp, the entire 'Army of England' moved across Europe – remember it was a much more formidable thing in those days; no railways, indeed not very good roads. And yet Napoleon, entirely under his own direction, was able to carry this army right across Europe and to surround the Austrian army at Ulm in October

1805, before the Austrians knew that he had even left Boulogne. In the further battles that followed, the coalition crumbled. The story was repeated in 1808, a second Austrian army accumulated, a second Austrian army surprised. The Napoleonic empire was carried across Europe by war, not because this was the aim, but because this was its result. Napoleon was left more and more as the dominant factor in Europe simply because he had to defeat the other countries which were conspiring against him. It would be foolish to suggest that Napoleon was a man of peace or of a kindly, gentle nature. Nevertheless in 1805, in 1808 and, should one say, in 1812 he was provoked into war. The last and most dynamic of the wars followed on Napoleon's decision to invade Russia. Statesmen often decide to invade Russia. And when they do, it is always the same puzzle, why on earth did they do it? Russia was remote from Europe. The idea that Russia would join in to Europe and take part in these conspiracies, though the Russians had taken part in the coalition of 1805, seemed a little speculative. Napoleon absolutely dominated Europe, could he really believe that Russia would raise Europe against him? Not at all; in fact, he claimed he was going to Russia simply in order to win the friendship of Alexander, the Tsar. His other idea was that once he had taken Moscow he would march straight on to India, which I think was a bit ambitious.

This was the first time when Napoleon deliberately decided to take the offensive, to commit an act of aggression without suspecting any coalitions or combinations, conspiracies against him. And it was 1812 which, again for the first time, produced universal European war. Up to this time there had been little patches here and there; they got bigger and bigger. 1812 produced first of all Napoleon's arrival in Moscow; he spent weeks there waiting for the Russian emissaries to come and make peace, but none came. Even then, this was still a war only between France and Russia. But with Napoleon driven out of Moscow, driven out of Russia, there came a coalition of the conservative European powers against him. So what we think of as the great war with all the powers involved was a very short war between 1813 and 1814 and, incidentally of course, the British contribution was always peripheral, on the edge. The

British army in Spain did not arrive in France until Napoleon had already been defeated.

There was an epilogue after Napoleon had been exiled to Elba, the last of the Napoleonic wars, which started simply because Napoleon turned up and said he wanted to be emperor again. At which all the powers of Europe put him to the bar of Europe and declared that he was an international criminal. And it was with this, which we remember as the wonderful battle of Waterloo, that the Napoleonic wars ended.

In appearance it seemed that nothing had been achieved by this twenty years of fighting, that the old order had been restored, and the Rights of Man forgotten. But all the same something had been achieved. It was for a very short period that, as Elizabeth Barrett Browning said, '. . . kings crept out to feel the sun again'.

Two Contrasting Wars:
Crimea – The Diplomatic War
Italy – The War of Liberation

The Crimean War is of particular interest to English people. It was the only European war that Great Britain took part in between the battle of Waterloo in 1815 and the battle of Mons in 1914. It was also, incidentally, the first war that left behind it memorials to the ordinary soldiers killed and not merely the generals who led them.

The beginning of the conflict was a rivalry between two sets of monks in Jerusalem over the keys to the Christian Holy Places. France backed the Latin monks, the Russians backed the Greek monks.

As it was the Turkish government that had to allot the keys, both France and Russia put pressure on Turkey. France sent a battleship through the straits to Constantinople, and the Latin monks got the keys.

Russia sent an army to the frontier of Turkey, and the Latin monks lost the keys, or some of them.

The tension was mounting, each country putting on the pressure and each beginning to suspect the other. By this time it was commonly accepted by the British and French governments, and by many ordinary people too, that Russia, this tyrannical power, was hoping to overthrow Turkey and establish control of Constantinople. On the other side, the Russians were convinced that England and France were hoping to close the straits, making it impossible for Russian trade or Russian ships to get out into the Mediterranean.

There was a competition of suspicion, both lots of suspicion mostly unfounded. Then the European Powers, behaving sensibly, tried to settle the dispute and held a conference at Vienna of the five great powers involved: England, France and Russia, with Austria and Prussia. They reached an agreement, something which would satisfy the Russians, a legitimate Russian protectorate over the Greek Church without interfering with the sovereignty of Turkey. Something went wrong. It has been well said that the Crimean War was caused by the fact that there was a telegraph line from most places to Vienna but no telegraph line from Constantinople to Vienna. The five great powers had agreed, but they could not ask the permission of Turkey because they could not get to Turkey in time over the wires; it took something like a week or ten days to get a message through.

When the Turks saw the agreement, they said, 'It won't do at all, this deprives us of too much of our sovereignty.' It took another ten days for the message to come back. By this time Russia felt thoroughly cheated. The Russians had agreed to what the other powers in Europe had insisted on, and now they were told they could not have it. They therefore moved a stronger army up to and even across the Turkish frontier.

Then something quite extraordinary happened. Turkey, the weak power, the power that was supposed to be on the brink of dissolution, declared war on Russia and moved the Turkish army up against Russia, although there was no fighting.

The war had in a sense started. It had started without any serious consideration of what was at stake. The Russians had not the slightest idea that they were going to get involved in a war over the Russian protection of the Greek Church throughout Turkey. It had been started to some extent deliberately by Turkey because the Turks thought, 'The more we can get the war going, the more England and France will get involved.'

The Turkish fleet in the Black Sea was a very creaky old fleet, quite unfit for action. The Russians came out from their naval base at Sebastopol and sank the entire Turkish fleet at Sinope. There was a tremendous outburst of public opinion in England. This perfectly legitimate Russian action of war against a country that had declared war on it was described as 'the massacre of Sinope'.

There were protest meetings all over England and demands for war. Here was something new in European history, a deep involvement of what was called public opinion. Perhaps it did not go so deep down into the population but it certainly existed.

The Crimean War indeed was the first war which was helped on by the newspapers. In earlier wars the newspapers had had to catch up afterwards. *The Times* in particular led public opinion, and public opinion was led to believe that Russia was not merely seeking to encroach on Turkey or to destroy Turkey, but was seeking to be the tyrant of Europe.

In 1849 Russian troops had intervened to suppress the national revolution in Hungary. Russian troops held down Poland and also sustained the two reactionary powers, Prussia and Austria. Russia prided herself on sustaining what was called the Holy Alliance of Reaction. In England, which was then in its liberal phase, it was widely believed that if Russian power could be destroyed then Europe would become free.

The other powerful factor making for war was the ruler of France, Napoleon III, who had become emperor in 1852 and hoped, though with little justification, to repeat the successes of his uncle, Napoleon I, perhaps not by means of universal war but by establishing a great political influence.

Here were the two quite different factors pushing to war: in England the desire to see a movement of liberation, and in Napoleon the desire to see a movement, maybe of European liberation, but one led entirely by himself.

The body which was most unwilling to go to war was actually the British government, or some sections of it. The Prime Minister, Aberdeen, was so determined to remain at peace that he refused to take any precautions and when in fact he had to lead the country into war, he believed he had committed a great sin. Later in life, after he had retired, he refused to build a church on his estate because, like David, he had committed a great sin and God had said: 'Thou shalt not build an house in my name, because thou hast been a man of war and hast shed blood.'

There was no consideration of what was at stake, or whether even after this first engagement they could not go back to the arrangement which had been made before, which did not involve anything about the break-up of Turkey or indeed any Russian influence in Turkey other than that the Turks should show reasonable sympathy with the members of the Greek Orthodox Church.

The British and French had said they were going to protect Turkey. They had sent their fleets to the Near East, and yet the Turkish fleet had been destroyed. The British and French fleets therefore went through into the Black Sea and issued an ultimatum, ordering the Russian fleet to withdraw to harbour and not to come out again without British and French permission. This technically was the cause of the Crimean War as we understand it, that is to say in which the great powers were involved.

The Russian fleet, although in fact it withdrew to Sebastopol, did not respond to the order as such, and in May 1854 the Crimean War was declared. Even then the war did not actually begin because, although the British and French had got their fleets in the Black Sea, how could they get at Russia? They were maritime powers, Russia was a land power.

By August considerable British and French armies had accumulated at Constantinople which needed no defence. There they faced the problem which often arises in war: 'Where shall we go? What shall we do with these armies that we have brought here?'

They could not march overland all the way from Constantinople to Moscow. So they said, 'Let's take Sebastopol.' This was the main Russian naval port. At the time it was ill defended and there were very few Russian troops there. The British and French said, 'It will be easy, we shall take it in a week. Then we shall have a considerable military achievement and public opinion will be satisfied.' The British and French landed successfully. They moved towards Sebastopol and did not move fast enough. In fact they were so pleased at landing, they thought it was not worth while to do anything else. Instead of its taking a week, it took eighteen months for the British and French to capture Sebastopol. That was the Crimean War.

What happened about the keys to the Holy Places I have no idea, whether the Latins got them or the Greeks got them or they shared them. Whether the Crimean War helped to preserve Turkey I also have no idea, although Turkey still exists. But in one sense the Crimean War was of great importance. It eliminated Russia as a great power in Europe for many years to come. You could argue that until the outbreak of the First World War – indeed, I would argue that until 1941, nearly 100 years – Russia did not count in Europe to anything like the extent she had counted before the Crimean War. This enabled liberal movements which sought for national independence and freedom to go forward without fearing Russian intervention.

The whole balance, not so much military but political, was changed. The conservative, reactionary powers which stood in the way of German nationalism and Italian nationalism were now very much on the defensive. The principal consequence of the Crimean War was that the question of the unification of Italy could be raised. This produced the second war of the 1850s, the war with the humdrum title of the Austro-French War, but one with very significant results for Italy and for the history of Europe.

In 1848, the great year of revolutions, the Italians had tried to liberate themselves. At that time Italy was divided into a great number of states and the whole of northern Italy was inside the Austrian empire. Both Lombardy and Venetia were ruled directly from Vienna.

In 1848 there were risings everywhere. The Austrians were driven out of Lombardy and out of Venetia. The little kingdom of Piedmont, sometimes called Sardinia, sent its army to the assistance of the liberal nationalists and was defeated. Austria re-conquered Lombardy and Venetia, and Austrian rule was restored. It was restored more harshly than before because now there was complete estrangement between the Austrian rulers and the Italian ruled.

There were new conspiracies, there were bomb plots. Austrian soldiers were shot at and killed. It is the kind of thing which happens under alien rule, but the kingdom of Piedmont on its own was not strong enough to create Italy or to liberate northern Italy. In 1852 Piedmont acquired one of the great statesmen of the nineteenth century, Camillo Cavour. He decided that the right way to unite Italy was not by national passion and idealism but by hard-headed diplomacy. He set out to win Napoleon III for the Italian cause.

Napoleon III on his side believed that a united or a liberated Italy would be a grateful client state and that France would be able to dominate the Mediterranean. Also he wished to repeat the achievement of his uncle, who had set up a kingdom of Italy of a sort. Moreover, Napoleon III as an absolute ruler had to establish a reputation. Although by no means a distinguished soldier or general, he wanted to show that he was.

Napoleon III and Cavour met more or less in secret at Plombières, a spa, with very good spa water which I can recommend. While they were drinking the spa water, they made a deal. France would join Piedmont and get the Austrians out of northern Italy. In return, France would be allowed to acquire what were called the national frontiers of Savoy and Nice which at that time belonged to the King of Sardinia.

They had agreed on the war. Their problem was how to get it. Wars are expected to have a technical legal cause. You have to have grievances, you have to have claims to territory, but Piedmont had no claims to Austrian territory. By every treaty right in the world, Austria was the rightful ruler of northern Italy. Any international tribunal would have been bound to say: 'Austria is totally justified. There is no conceivable maxim of international law by which Austria should be compelled to withdraw from northern Italy, or for that matter that France and Piedmont be allowed to go to war with her.'

Cavour was a very clever man; he said he would provide some respectable cause of war, some frontier grievance. Napoleon III and Cavour racked their brains over the problem.

On the other side the Austrian government grew increasingly exasperated by the more or less open preparations that were being made. Here was Piedmont preaching nationalism, subsidizing Italian national propaganda in northern Italy, providing a refuge for Italian nationalists who had to escape from Lombardy, even although Piedmont was a monarchy providing a refuge for Italian republicans.

There was a free press in Piedmont, the only one in Italy which talked in liberal terms. There was even a parliament, two chambers meeting in Turin and claiming to speak in the name of Italy. It was very exasperating for a great imperial government that it was now being challenged by a miserable little jumped-up state and with the implication that Austrian government was imcompetent and tyrannical. The Austrians had insisted that, because they had legitimate right behind them, they were the moral party. Now it was being suggested that for an empire to rule over people of a different nationality was actually immoral. This was particularly dynamite for the Austrian empire because all its territories really were non-national. The emperor did not belong to any nationality; his statesmen did not belong to any nationality, although most of them spoke German. They were above nationality and, once you raised the cry of national rights and national freedom, the Austrian empire might well break up, as happened indeed in 1918 for exactly this reason.

The Austrians, therefore, felt that they must not only stand out against these national claims but must get their blow in first. This is a fascinating paradox. Austria could not conceivably gain by war. Austria could not annex Piedmontese territory; that would give her more discontented Italians. She was not likely to be able to annex French territory. The Austrian line surely should have been to remain firmly at peace and to give no possible excuse or opening for war. Instead, the Austrians began to speak in increasingly bellicose terms. Then, rather as before the Crimean War, the other powers tried to prevent a war.

The British government offered to mediate. The British ambassador in Paris went to Vienna and discussed the estrangement between Vienna and Paris. The Austrians said that they merely wished to be left alone. The British ambassador took the message back.

Then the Tsar thought he would like to play some part and proposed a European congress. A European congress was summoned though it never met. The Austrians mistakenly believed that European opinion was moving on to their side. They thought, if they got their blow in first, they would knock out Sardinia-Piedmont and that this would solve their problem.

Just at this moment Napoleon III deserted Cavour and said, 'We cannot risk a war, you must disarm.' While he was saying this in secret, the Austrians said it in public. They sent an ultimatum, demanding that Piedmont should disarm, without promising that Austria would do so as well. Cavour refused. The Austrians invaded Piedmont and were driven back. This was the beginning of the

Austro-French War because France came to the aid of Sardinia-Piedmont.

How ironical that if the Austrians had waited another few days, Napoleon III would have compelled Piedmont to disarm and the Austrians would have achieved their aim. As it was, they were defeated and lost Lombardy.

This is not the end of the story about the Italian wars of this time.

1859 was one sort of war. In 1860 there was quite another war, a war that does not come into the history books as a war. It was in fact the only guerrilla war in history, or one of the very few, that succeeded. This was an unofficial war. Garibaldi wanted to go somewhere to liberate some part of Italy. What he really wanted to do was to liberate Rome, which at that time was ruled by the pope. Garibaldi had defended Rome in 1849 at the time when it was a republic and he wanted to repeat his success.

Cavour was desperately anxious that Garibaldi should go somewhere else, anywhere rather than go to Rome, which would cause an international crisis. Fortunately there was a peasant revolt in Sicily, such as there often was. Cavour persuaded Garibaldi to go off with a scratch force of 1,000 men, incidentally most of them middle class. When they were on their way, Garibaldi said to an Englishman: 'There is one curious thing about this expedition, I am the only working man on it.' I am not sure that he was a working man himself.

To everyone's astonishment, this irregular force of 1,000 men managed to land in Sicily and overcame the army of the King of Naples which held Sicily. This army, 70,000 men, were driven out by 1,000.

Now Garibaldi decided to go ahead again. At any rate he could get into Rome, he thought, from behind, by marching on Naples. He swept right through Naples, and now there was the fear that he really would go on to Rome. The only way to stop him was for the regular Piedmontese army to come down, as an ally or as an antagonist, who could say?

It advanced down Italy and encountered Garibaldi just as he was preparing to march on Rome, and at this moment he made his great sacrifice. Garibaldi was a republican – but even more, he was an enthusiast for Italian unification. He had fought for this cause. Indeed, for its sake he betrayed the peasants whom he had inspired and led. He did not support their land claims. He was a man of the people. He felt deeply for them but the thing which was absolutely dominant in his mind was unification.

Garibaldi immensely distrusted and disliked Cavour but he had a curious sentimental attachment to Victor Emanuel II, the King of Sardinia-Piedmont, who was very much a man of Italian character. At this dramatic moment they met each other on horseback, Garibaldi at the head of his revolutionary army riding north from Naples, Victor Emanuel II coming down from the north. Garibaldi rode up to the King and said, 'Hail to the King of Italy.' With this, Italy was born.

On the way back into Naples, the King said, 'How are you, *caro* Garibaldi?'

'Excellent, Majesty, and you?'

'Very well.'

Victor Emanuel asked Garibaldi what he would like: 'I will make you a duke, give you a great estate.'

Garibaldi said, 'All I want is a bag of seed corn for my farm at Caprera,' and with that he went back to his little farm.

Such are the things which make Garibaldi the most wholly admirable man in modern history.

Bismarck's Wars

In 1862 Otto von Bismarck became Minister President (Prime Minister, that is) of Prussia and within the next few years Prussia was involved in three wars. I think one must call them Bismarck's wars although he was not solely responsible for them.

The first was a war by Prussia and Austria combined against Denmark over two duchies, Sleswig* and Holstein. Its causes were extremely complicated. Indeed, Lord Palmerston said that there were only three people who could understand the problem. One was the Prince Consort, who was dead; the second was a German professor, who had gone mad; and the third was Palmerston himself, who had forgotten about it. I think we had better leave it forgotten, but it was a curious beginning: an alliance between Prussia and Austria, an alliance which was soon to be severed by Bismarck's own work.

Bismarck's achievement of course was to unite Germany. From 1815 onwards, the German states were brought together in a loose confederation – something like the EEC, both in its complications and in its ineffectiveness.

Technically Austria was the presiding power; Prussia, though a great power, had to play a secondary part. For German Liberals and Nationalists this was an exasperating situation. The German Confederation had been created by the Congress of Vienna. It was a part of international law and, while it was easy for a revolutionary like Garibaldi in Italy to defy international law and make Italy, it

* The old English fashion, which avoids favouring either the German or the Danish spelling.

was very different for Bismarck who was a conservative and the leading minister of a very conservative king.

Bismarck's achievement was to maintain conservative principles without abandoning the aim of liberal unity. What Bismarck would have liked, I think, was to reach a peaceful agreement with Austria. After all, circumstances often change, despite international law, and circumstances had changed since 1815. In 1815, at the time of the Congress of Vienna, Austria was the greater power and an empire, whereas Prussia was only a kingdom.

By the mid-1860s Austria had fallen behind. Prussia had become the greater power, greater in wealth and greater in industrial resources. Prussia was a prospering modern kingdom. Austria was a decaying or stagnant empire. Maybe the wise course for a stagnant empire is to hitch itself on to some other great power rather than run into troubles, but it is very difficult when you have been one of the greatest powers in Europe to renounce some of your grandeur and step down. The Austrian statesmen and the Austrian emperor, Franz Joseph, were well aware of Austria's problems, conflicts of nationalities and an ineffective economic system, and Austria's weakness in Europe.

The Austrians had relied on allies, principally on Russia, but Russia had ceased to count in Europe after the Crimean War, and Great Britain, who at one time had called Austria 'the natural ally', had also lost interest in Europe. Austria was very much on her own with the exception of France, and here was another problem: Napoleon III, the semi-revolutionary emperor, could not make up his mind whether he was on the side of the conservative power or on the side of the liberal and quasi-national power.

There is one other point to bear in mind. Austria depended essentially on her army. In 1848, at the time of the revolutions, the great Austrian poet Grillparzer, addressing Radetzky, the Commander-in-Chief in Italy, wrote 'In deinem Lager ist Österreich' (in your military camp lies Austria). To confess the weakness of the army would be to confess a weakness of the monarchy altogether.

From 1864, the time of the Danish War, for the next two years there was ceaseless diplomatic manoeuvring between Bismarck on the one side and the Austrian statesmen on the other.

Bismarck gave the impression, as many people do when they are seeking a gain, that he was the conciliatory one. He offered compromises, he offered to sustain the Austrian empire elsewhere in Europe if Austria would renounce her position in Germany.

He expressed a solidarity with conservative principles, but at the same time he was always demanding that Austria should recognize equality between Prussia and Austria. If not, he threatened, there would be a Liberal revolutionary nationalism in Germany which would destroy both the conservative Prussian kingdom and the empire of Austria.

These negotiations had the strangest twists. In the middle of 1865, the King of Prussia and his ministers met at Gastein and held a council of war to decide whether they should go to war with Austria the next week. The delightful thing about it is that Gastein was actually in Austrian territory. Fancy going on holiday in your enemy's territory and discussing whether you should go to war with him. That is how they did things in those more-or-less civilized times.

The situation grew tenser and the problem – Cavour had it also in Italy, but Bismarck had it much more – was how without infringing international law it was possible to challenge a system, such as the German Confederation, set up by international law. The only hope was that the country which benefited from international law, in other words Austria, could be herself provoked into war, and Bismarck's persistent offers of peaceful settlement were, I think, intended to push the Austrians into impatience.

There is another fascinating thing: this was the first time that the actual time of mobilization came to count. Instead of armies acting once a war had been declared, it was the movement of armies which brought the war on.

The technical point was this. The Prussian army could mobilize in three weeks, the Austrian army took six weeks; therefore, unless Austria started to mobilize first she would be at a disadvantage. But if she mobilized first she would appear to be the aggressor, so the Austrians tried to turn the trick by offering simultaneous disarmament. The King of Prussia thought he was caught and agreed. Bismarck was heartbroken, he had missed his war.

Then the Austrians were afraid of Italy at their rear: if they disarmed, then perhaps Italy would attack them. They considered partial mobilization. Then they said, 'If we do partial mobilization we shall not be able to have full mobilization.' So they mobilized fully. When Bismarck heard this, he exclaimed, 'God Save the King,' because from that moment William thought that Austria was the aggressor. Even then, though Austria was mobilizing, the Prussians could sit back for a fortnight and let Austria mobilize and thus appear to be the aggressor, and still have their three weeks to catch up. As a matter of fact, all this business about a mobilization race turned out to be pointless because both sides were fully mobilized when the war of 1866 began.

In the end, at the beginning of July 1866 the Austrians lost patience. They took the first step to war by getting the German Confederation to denounce Prussia. This gave Prussia the opportunity to withdraw from the German Confederation and declare that the Confederation was at an end. With that the Prussian armies could perhaps invade other German states, but they had no real conflict with Austria. Indeed, when it came to the point, even Bismarck with all his ingenuity could not think of a reason why they were at war.

The Prussian army advanced through Saxony. When they reached the Austrian frontier, a junior Prussian officer was sent with a letter which he handed to the nearest Austrian officer. It said, 'I beg to inform you that a state of war exists.' That is how one of the greatest wars of the century began: no ultimatum, no declaration of war, it just got going.

The war produced the desired result so far as Bismarck was concerned. Austria was excluded from Germany, northern Germany was put under Prussian hegemony and Prussia had become a greater power. Bismarck himself made a rather different comment, a comment which I think is particularly apposite to all the discussions which go on about war origins and about who is the aggressor, which country started it. When the King wanted to have revenge on Austria and said, 'Austria started the war, therefore Austria should be punished,' Bismarck replied, 'Austria was no more in the wrong in opposing our claims than we were in making them.' That, I think, is all that there is to be said about charges of aggressive war or war guilt.

If ever there were a planned war, a war of purpose, it was Bismarck's war against Austria. That war had fulfilled a programme which the Liberals had had for many years of virtually uniting Germany. It fulfilled Bismarck's programme because it had united or largely united Germany and established Prussian leadership in Germany without upsetting the conservative order. It had been a war defined in its purpose and limited in its achievement. The moment that Bismarck got what he wanted he stopped, and although he may have hoped beforehand to get these results without war, possibly by bluff, possibly by negotiation, possibly by conciliation, at any rate it was quite clear in his mind that something like this was necessary if Prussia were to retain her leadership in Germany.

Relations between Prussia (or, as it was now called, the North German Federation) and France were of quite a different character and, although Bismarck was to be blamed for this war also, his responsibility was much less, responsibility at any rate only in the sense perhaps that he failed to foresee events. After all, Prussia and France had no conflict. France – technically at any rate – did not claim to dominate Europe, let alone Germany. Prussia had no territorial claims on France. Any such claims sprang out of the subsequent war; they had not been formulated beforehand.

Napoleon III on his side had claims of a sort against Prussia and Germany. Napoleon III had been Emperor of the French since 1852. He had arrived at this position largely because he possessed his uncle's name. As one of the great French historians said: 'His origins condemned him to success.' As a Napoleon he had to succeed, otherwise he would be discredited and people would say, 'Why should we bother to have a Napoleon? We might just as well have a republic.'

He succeeded in Italy in 1859 when he had acquired Savoy and Nice, but he needed more success. He had a very enlightened view that France would be a stronger country if, instead of divided countries, there was a national Germany and a national Italy where they could all combine together. He was one of the many who saw a vision of a united Europe, a Europe which would be bound together on liberal national principles. He had welcomed therefore the national unification of Italy. He was not opposed to the national unification of Germany, but there the other side of his position came in.

If Germany were to be united and stronger, then, according to all the calculations of traditional diplomacy, France would be weaker, and indeed Thiers, one of the French statesmen, said about the Prussian victory at Sadowa in 1866, 'It is we who were beaten at Sadowa,' because France was not now as strong as when Germany was disunited. Therefore France should receive compensation. Napoleon III duly demanded these compensations and Bismarck very reasonably refused them. There was no earthly reason why, because Germany had become united, France should be compensated. The discussions tailed away, leaving resentment on both sides. Napoleon tried by means of diplomacy, by threats of alliance, alliance – how paradoxical! – with Austria, the country which he had turned out of Italy in 1859, or even alliances with both Austria and Italy to seek revenge, to hold up the advance of German power, to undo the unification of Germany which was now under way. None of these things achieved any success, and the general impression of observers in the years before 1870 was that, although Germany was not united yet because southern Germany had not been brought in, she was on the move to unification and that Bismarck would accomplish the miracle of doing it not only without an international war but without social upheaval or revolution at home.

It was a slow process and Bismarck was perfectly patient and was prepared to wait. At the same time he was naturally anxious to increase the prestige of the King of Prussia. If the King of Prussia was to become the head of a united Germany, then he must rank along with the other great powers, perhaps take on an imperial name. This seems to be the explanation of a very strange story which started the conflict of 1870.

In 1868 there was a revolution in Spain. Queen Isabella was dissolute, she had been married to an impotent husband and took the not surprising way out of having many lovers who rather filled up the royal castle. In time the expenditure of maintaining these royal lovers exasperated the politicians. There was a revolution and Isabella was dethroned.

A Spanish general became temporary regent and there was a republic, but the Spanish rulers did not want to remain republican and the throne of Spain was hawked around Europe. This raised a big problem. They did not want anybody who was too closely connected with any great royal house. Napoleon ran one of his cousins, but there was a general outcry that this would be putting France in power in Spain. Then Bismarck had a bright idea.

Spain was a Catholic country. There was in the house of Hohenzollern, that of the Kings of Prussia, a separate family line who were Catholics. Now here was a young man, Leopold, a prince of Hohenzollern, who had all the qualifications. He was a liberal so that he would co-operate with liberal Germany. He was a good, loyal but not over-patriotic German and he was a Catholic, a beautiful answer, you would think, to the problem. Moreover, his brother was already Prince of Romania and had been nominated to this post by Napoleon III himself, so obviously Napoleon did not dislike the Catholic Hohenzollerns.

Bismarck appreciated that there would be some French protests and he therefore meant to rush the thing. I should warn you there has been over 100 years of discussion and dispute and it is often alleged that Bismarck deliberately organized the Hohenzollern candidature in order to provoke France into war. It is also alleged that he did it in order to strengthen the German side against France during the war.

I think that these views are mistaken. Bismarck certainly said that if there were a Hohenzollern king in Spain, France would have to keep some army on the Pyrenees and this would make war less likely, not more so. He never imagined that Spain would go to war on the German side. So I think, if anything, his consideration was simply, 'This will make France more reluctant to threaten us.'

It does not seem as if he was considering mainly this. He was considering largely the prestige of the Prussian royal house and also more practical things. He thought it would be good for trade between Germany and Spain because Bismarck was a very modern man and thought a lot about economics. He thought the Spaniards would be keener on buying things from German industry than French industry if they had a German king. The essential thing was to get Leopold to Spain and on the throne before the French could protest.

The Spanish representative in Berlin sent a telegram on 26 June 1870 saying, 'I will be back in three days with Leopold's consent.' The Spanish Parliament or Cortes was in session; it would meet on 29 June; Leopold would be in and the French taken by surprise. But a cypher clerk in the German legation in Madrid read the cyphers wrongly. He reported that the Spaniard coming from Berlin would only arrive on 9 July. This was too long for the Cortes to wait during the summer heat, and its members went away. By the time Salazar, for that was his name, arrived, the Cortes had dispersed. The members had to be summoned back. It had to be explained why they were being brought back: they were being brought back to elect a king and therefore the news became public.

Leopold in fact never got to Spain at all. The surprise was never sprung. Instead, the news arrived in Paris and there followed a decision which made war more than likely, inevitable.

The Bonapartist dynasty, Napoleon III and his family, were losing prestige. Napoleon III was harassed by the demands of Liberals to turn his empire into a constitutional monarchy. He had only a young son who was not old enough to take over from him. He himself was a very sick man; he died three years later and had been sick for a long time before that.

The tough old guard who had put him on the throne, the Bonapartist adventurers who had made a fortune out of the empire and were a set of scamps for the most part, were anxious to restore the prestige of the empire – and how could this be done? Why, by humiliating Prussia. Far from hesitating and saying, 'This is a plot of Bismarck's to catch us in a war,' they – if it were a trap – jumped straight into it, they welcomed it because they thought they had a strong case.

If the French government had merely wanted to stop the candidature of Leopold, they could have protested at Madrid and it would have been dropped. But with this there would be no prestige, therefore they must protest in Germany, protest to King William. The protest was made, to the great delight of Napoleon III and his advisers.

William I, who had disliked the idea of Leopold going to Spain all along, agreed at once to drop him. The reason why William wanted Leopold not to go was not at all that he was worried about France; he thought Leopold might get killed and that in any case the job of being King of Spain was not an attractive one for a cousin of his. He said, 'Gladly. I never liked the idea. I will have a word with the boy and he will withdraw.'

This was no good for the French ministers. They had not humiliated Prussia. Instead, William I had been conciliatory and friendly. The French foreign minister therefore sent another note, insisting that William must apologize, although he never had anything to do with the candidature. Not only must he apologize, he must promise that Leopold would never try to run as candidate again. He must give guarantees that no such thing should ever happen again.

Bismarck had no idea that the war would blow up as it did and was taken as much by surprise as everyone else. Bismarck was far away in the country. When the first French demand was made, he felt this was humiliating but he was rather relieved. Bismarck was a great one for putting the blame on others. Now the humiliation had fallen on William I, not on himself.

Just at the time when the second French demand was under way Bismarck came back to Berlin. He was depressed that he had missed a great chance. Prussia could have asserted herself by answering sternly. Instead the king had let them down. We have a description of Bismarck having supper with Moltke, Chief of the General Staff, both of them very gloomy and speaking very unfavourably about William, about how feeble he had been just because of the threat of war or worrying over Leopold.

Then there came the second message from William, describing the meeting where he had been ordered to apologize. He had said, though in a very gentle way, 'I told the French ambassador I had nothing more to say to him. Leopold has withdrawn. I have nothing more to say.'

Bismarck said, 'That's it.' He seized a pencil and edited the king's telegram. It is called the Ems telegram because William sent it from Ems. Every word Bismarck put in the telegram was correct but it was arranged in such a way that, instead of the King saying, 'Well, Leopold had withdrawn, there is nothing more I need to say,' the King merely said, 'I have nothing to say to you.' Bismarck's version was published the same day and with this the French press was in an uproar. The streets of Paris reverberated with the cry, 'To Berlin,' and Napoleon III prepared to go to war.

One extraordinary thing about this story is the total lack of consideration displayed by the French and by Napoleon III as to the possibilities of going to war. It seems very late in the day that men, when they are moving on the edge of war, look at it and say, 'Can we win, is there any sense in it?'

As a matter of fact the French army was in a very bad state. Napoleon III, who had certain training as an artillery officer, was aware of this and reform of the French army had begun. This reform was still dragging behind. People earlier had despised the Prussian army. Its victory in 1866 showed that it was the first in Europe but, when it came to the point, Napoleon and the Council of Ministers relied solely on their prestige, the prestige of the great name of Napoleon I. Thus, for a cause which they themselves had trumped up, they launched a great war in which France suffered defeat after defeat and at the end blamed Bismarck for it.

As for Bismarck, he drew a striking moral from having laid on three wars: to have no more wars.

The First World War

The Great War, the First World War as it was later called, broke out at the beginning of August 1914 and it followed on a month of intense activity.

Indeed, the month of July 1914 has probably been more studied than any other month in history. Thousands of documents have been published – British documents, French documents, German documents, Russian documents, Italian documents. Only the Serbs have not revealed their documents, although they are said to be in print. Hundreds of historians have laboured, one book after another has been written.

During the war, of course, each side blamed the other. The Germans said it was caused by entente aggression planned by Russia or France. The Allies said that it was caused by German aggression, and the Treaty of Versailles repeated this statement.

Gradually, as historians worked, these sharp interpretations were rejected and there grew up something like a general agreement. There were still qualifications that one power had made more mistakes or was more at fault than the other, but broadly by the time the Second World War came along historians were agreed that there had been no deliberate plan for war on the part of any power and that there had been a series of mishaps and mistakes and misunderstandings. As Lloyd George said, 'We all muddled into war.'

Just when historians thought, 'Well, that is one subject I can talk on for ever and never have to add anything new,' there came along a German historian, Fritz Fischer from Hamburg, who studied first of all the German war aims actually during the war. They were (as you can imagine) to hold on to all the territory that they had conquered and get more if they could. Then Fischer turned back to the period before the war and identified these aims as having already been formulated, perhaps not in the highest places but in very influential circles where the talk was of the conquests to be made. Other historians joined him, some of them arguing that the Russian army was outstripping the German and that the German generals had agreed that in 1914 was the last chance when they could fight a favourable war.

In recent years the younger generation of German historians has come more and more to the belief that the Imperial German government was actually a driving force for war and that the war which broke out in August 1914, far from being a war of accident, was a war of design: a war, as one of them said, long prepared for.

The Imperial government, it was alleged, was anxious for war in order to prevent the victory of social democracy and the transformation of Germany into a democratic country. It was fought in the interests not only of the imperial authorities, the officers and the army, but of the German landed class. The historians who say this are not Marxists, they are historians from Western Germany.

In fact, the Marxists in Eastern Germany are very jealous that they did not hit on this. They said, of course empires cause wars, but they had not done the work in detail; it was the development of purely liberal German historians. Others laid more emphasis on the military side, the actual fear that Russia was going to get too strong.

The only way one can answer this, I think, is to describe what happened – or some of it.

On 28 June the Archduke Franz Ferdinand visited the town of Sarajevo in Bosnia. Bosnia is a Slav, Serbo-Croat province, only acquired by Austria-Hungary in 1908, and there was a good deal of discontent there. Franz Ferdinand did not however go there in order to make a demonstration against the discontent; he went because he had married beneath the permitted degrees. His wife was only a countess, so she did not rank as an archduchess, but if he went to Sarajevo, which was still under military occupation, he could go as Inspector General of the army and she would rank right at the top. It was to give his wife a treat that he went to Sarajevo.

The Serbian government certainly did not want to provoke a crisis, of that we can be quite sure. There were of course, as there have been in later times, plenty of national conspirators. Half a dozen of these were schoolboys working for what we now call their A-levels. They said, 'We ought not to let the archduke's visit go without some sort of demonstration.' Although they did not in fact belong to the secret society, the Black Hand, which was supposed to organize conspiracies, they got a couple of revolvers and a couple of bombs and they turned up on the day. As the archduke drove along, the first conspirator could not get his revolver out of his pocket because the crowd was too tight, and the second thought a policeman was looking at him; the third felt sorry for the archduke's wife. The fourth simply went home. The fifth threw his bomb, which missed, though it injured one equerry. The sixth, Gavrilo Princip, having heard the bomb go off, thought, 'Ah, it has succeeded,' and stepped aside. At that moment the procession drove by. Princip realized that it had failed. He sat down in a café, very gloomy.

The archduke drove on to the town hall, arrived in a great rage and said, 'I come here and you greet me with bombs. I am not stopping, I am driving straight out. I am not going back through the old town.' However, the chauffeur had not been told that they were driving straight on, not turning; when they came to the turn where the original route had been, he turned; and there was Princip sitting on the edge of the pavement in a café. To his astonishment he saw an open car with the archduke and archduke's wife stationary in front of him. He walked out of the café, stepped on to the running-board of the car, took out his revolver, shot the archduke and then aimed at the Governor of Bosnia, who was sitting in the front of the car, and hit the archduke's wife, who was sitting at the back. That was the assassination at Sarajevo.

An empire cannot allow the heir to the throne to be assassinated without doing something about it. The obvious thing to do was to blame the nationalists and particularly to blame Serbia, who really had nothing to do with it. The Austrian government were anxious to do this but they ran a shaky old empire and dared not go ahead without the support of their German ally.

An Austrian representative went to see William II, the German Emperor, at Potsdam. Nearly everyone had gone on holiday. All the generals were on holiday. Moltke was somewhere in the country, having an agreeable time. William II himself was just off to the North Sea. However, he had time to see the Austrian, and in the afternoon the Imperial Chancellor, Bethmann Hollweg, arrived as well. William, supported by Bethmann, gave a firm response: Germany would support Austria in her claims against Serbia and would stand by Austria even if Russia, the patron of Serbia, intervened.

Neither William nor Bethmann consulted a single general of any importance. They did not turn to the general staff and say, 'Is the time right for a war? How long do you want before there is a war?' More than this, William had never been told the earlier arguments, such as they were. He had no acquaintance with the military details.

We have quite recently got some new information. Somebody has investigated the reports of the German military intelligence for the whole month, which curiously no one had looked at before, and what do they tell us? They tell us that on 5 July, which was when the meeting took place, military intelligence was not given any warning that war might be imminent. During the whole month of July, German military intelligence recorded no special activities. No general was consulted, no troops were moved, no preparations for war were made. Indeed, if this was a decision for war it was a very haphazard one and, from what the reports of German military intelligence reveal, you would imagine you were in a completely peaceful country, as indeed I think you were.

There was then a long gap, very characteristically Austrian. Having decided to act at once against Serbia, it took the Austrians three weeks to draw up an ultimatum. One reason perhaps was that President Poincaré was visiting St Petersburg and the Austrians did not want a fuss while the French President was with the Tsar. For another reason, the Austrians were solemnly working away, trying to discover – and totally failing to find – any kind of proof that Serbia had been involved.

In the end the Austrians felt that they really must do something so they hotchpotched an ultimatum and sent it to Serbia. The Serb government was extremely anxious not to have a war; Serbia had just been involved in the Balkan Wars and the Serb army was in no condition for a war. Pasič, the Prime Minister, very characteristically said he was going on a holiday and would leave his colleagues to draft an answer. However, at the last minute he was brought back, and the Serb answer accepted every Austrian demand. Then, before it was handed over, the ministers revised it and cut out a number of concessions. This is another puzzling little point. Why did the Serbs, instead of simply accepting every humiliation, alter the answer to the ultimatum so that it would be unsatisfactory? This we do not know. It is sometimes alleged that the Russians told them to do it because Russia wanted to provoke a war. There is no evidence to this effect. The Russian minister to Belgrade, Hartwig, had been in such a state of excitement over this tense situation that, when calling on the Austrian representative, he fell down dead. Thus Russia had no representative in Belgrade.

My own guess is that the Serbs wanted to prolong the negotiations. They thought, 'If we accept everything then that will be it, but if we put in some hesitations then the Austrians will have to come back and make the demands again.' Instead of this, the Austrians, knowing how dilatory and hesitating they themselves usually were, acted resolutely for once. The Austrian minister looked at the answers, said, 'Not complete acceptance,' and broke off relations.

At this, for the first time there was a chance to negotiate. Sir Edward Grey, the British Foreign Secretary, suggested there should be negotiations between Serbia and Austria-Hungary. To prevent negotiations, Austria then declared war on Serbia, fearful that, if there were negotiations, concessions would be imposed on Austria as well as on Serbia.

Grey's line by the way was that all the concessions should be made by Serbia. He said, 'Peace is more important than justice and therefore Serbia as the weaker power must give way.' It was fortunate perhaps that he never got the negotiations started.

The Austrian declaration of war on Serbia was pure theory; no action followed it. Now this gives the essential factor in the outbreak of the First World War. All the Great Powers, of whom there were five, or six counting Italy, had vast conscript armies. These armies of course were not maintained in peacetime. They were brought together by mobilization. This factor had already counted before in the Austro-Prussian War of 1866, but this time there was a further complication.

All mobilization plans depended on the railways. At that time the automobile was hardly used, certainly not as an instrument of mass transport, and railways demand timetables.

All the mobilization plans had been timed to the minute, months or even years before, and they could not be changed. Modification in one direction would ruin them in every other direction. Any attempt for instance by the Austrians to mobilize against Serbia would mean that they could not then mobilize as well against Russia because two lots of trains would be running against each other. The same problem was to arise later for the Russians and in the end for the Germans who, having a plan to mobilize against France, could not switch round and mobilize again against Russia. Any alteration in the mobilization plan meant a delay not for twenty-four hours but for at least six months before the next lot of timetables were ready.

The Austrians could not mobilize against Serbia because this would mean that they were defenceless against Russia, so they did not mobilize at all.

The Russians then thought they ought to stake out some claim to prove that they were going to support Serbia, so the Tsar and his advisers contemplated mobilization but only against Austria, and this was actually ordered. Then the Russian generals who knew about the timetables pointed out that if they began to mobilize against Austria, they would then be totally defenceless against Germany because they could not then mobilize against Germany. Partial mobilization was scrapped. The next day the Russian generals said, 'But this is terrible. We have done nothing. Right, we will have general mobilization.' They were still hesitating and the Chief of the General Staff himself said that this was rather pushing things beyond what they wanted. They had no idea of a war against

Germany or even against Austria. They wanted a threat, not a real preparation for war. Mobilization was a mere gesture.

The Chief of the General Staff rashly said in the Tsar's presence, 'It is very hard to decide.' The Tsar, who was one of the most weak-willed men there had ever been, was roused by this and said, 'I will decide: general mobilization.' He then, according to his diary, having made this decision, went out, found a pleasant warm day and went for a bathe in the sea. His diary does not mention mobilization.

Now with Russia mobilizing, the problem moved to Germany, and here again this was entirely a matter of timetables. It was said afterwards that mobilization meant war. Technically, for most countries this was not true; it was merely a step towards war. Mobilization after all took place within the country. The Royal Navy had mobilized as late as 1911. Russia mobilized in 1913. There were occasions when other powers had mobilized and because war did not take place the armies could be dispersed. With one country, however, this did not apply. The German general staff, ever since the creation of a united Germany in 1871 under Bismarck, had contemplated the possibility of war on two fronts: France on the one side, Russia on the other.

It is the function of general staffs to plan for wars. Germany had two great neighbours, France on the one side, Russia on the other. Moreover, in 1894 France and Russia made an alliance which was technically defensive in nature, that each would help the other if attacked. Thus Germany might have a two-front war. Successive German chiefs of general staff, Moltke, Schlieffen, the younger Moltke, all laid down: 'Germany cannot fight two great wars at the same time.'

As often happens with chiefs of the general staff, they were quite wrong. In 1914 Germany fought a two-front war and continued to fight it successfully until 1918. This was a false alarm, but it was an alarm which absolutely dictated their policy.

If you are faced with war on two fronts and have not got the resources to conduct both wars, what should you do? By definition you cannot eliminate one of the dangers by diplomacy because if you did there would not be a two-front war, in fact there would not be a war at all. You must assume that diplomacy has failed.

The German answer was to get in one blow first and so decisively that they would have eliminated one enemy. At first they thought of doing it against Russia, then decided that that was too difficult. Russia was too big; the German army would go rambling into far remote places. The other answer therefore was to eliminate France. Ever since they began planning this, the idea had been, 'We must beat France first.' But France had a strongly fortified frontier. After about 1890 the Germans decided they could not rush this frontier in the way that they had rushed the French frontier in 1870. A way round must be found, and it must be through Belgium. The Germans arrived at this conclusion as early as 1893, although it took a long time before the full plan was developed. Its most detailed form was laid down in 1905.

One essential part of this plan was to go through Belgium. The other essential part, which was equally important, was that there could be no delay between mobilization and war because if there were delay then Russia would catch up and the Germans would get the two-front war after all. So the moment that the Germans decided on mobilization, they decided for war or, rather, war followed of itself. The railway timetables which in other countries brought men to their mobilizing centres, in the Schlieffen Plan continued and brought the troops, not to their barracks but into Belgium and northern France. The German mobilization plan actually laid down the first forty days of the German invasion of France, and none of it could be altered because if it did all the timetables would go wrong. Thus the decision for mobilization which the German general staff made and which Bethmann endorsed on 29 July was a decision for a general European war.

There was no deeper consideration in the background. Nothing was weighed except the technical point: if Russia mobilizes we must go to war. Serbia and Austria-Hungary were forgotten. The Germans declared war on Russia simply because Russia had mobilized.

The Germans were very stuck over France; they had no conceivable grievance against France. They demanded that France should promise neutrality, to which the French prime minister merely replied, 'France will consult her own interests.' The Germans then invented an allegation that Nuremberg had been bombed by French planes. This was untrue. Whether there had ever been bombing I am not clear. It may be that a German plane had dropped bombs, but who did what did not matter; the thing was to get the war going. Thus the war came about mainly because of railway timetables.

There was one further and, in the long run, perhaps the most dramatic and decisive consequence. The continental powers were at war; Great Britain was not. The whole trend of British policy – or certainly the desire of the British people – had been to stay out of war.

The Liberal government asserted that Great Britain had given no pledges. In secret the British had already arranged a railway timetable to take the British army to the left flank of the French army, but this had been concealed from the British public. Assertions were made constantly by the Prime Minister and by the Foreign Secretary that no commitment had been made which would limit the freedom of Parliament and the British people to decide.

Now this was very awkward because the French had been told over and over again, 'Yes, yes, we shall stand by you if you are threatened by German,' and the Cabinet was divided. It looked as if the Liberal government would break up; perhaps the Conservatives would take over, there would be even more controversy than there had been during the Boer War, more than there had been during the revolutionary wars against France. Then came the news that the Germans had demanded the right to go through Belgium.

It is often said that this had been known for a long time beforehand. That the Germans had such military plans was indeed known, but the diplomatic consequences were not realized. Indeed, Bethmann Hollweg himself, the German Chancellor, had no idea until 29 July that he would be setting his name to a demand that the Germans should go through Belgium.

British Liberal ministers later on claimed that they had hung back and said, 'Don't worry,' because they knew Belgium would solve the problem. However, it came as a complete surprise to most people and produced a tremendous reaction. Great Britain, it seemed, went to war not in order to play a part in the balance of power, not in order to aid France or to destroy Germany as an imperial rival or to destroy the German navy. Great Britain went to war, in the phrase used from the very first, 'to fulfil her obligations to Belgium and in defence of the rights of small nations'. This did the trick in the House of Commons. It did the trick with British public opinion. In a sense it has done the trick with people ever since.

Very few people looked at the treaty of 1839 which established Belgium as a neutral country. The guarantor countries were given by this treaty the right to intervene in order to defend the neutrality of Belgium. There was no obligation laid on them to do so. I am not saying for a moment that there was no obligation of a moral kind. Belgium was a small country and Belgium was very wrongfully invaded – just as, for instance, in 1916 France and Great Britain invaded Greece in exactly the same way, though with less fighting than when the Germans invaded Belgium; but the treaty obligation was something invented for the sake of public opinion.

All the Great Powers had relied in fact on the deterrent, the deterrent of great armaments. Previously the deterrent had worked. On this occasion the deterrent did not work and so it will be again.

The Second World War

The problem with the Second World War is not so much how did it begin but when did it begin. The Second World War was not some precise, sudden event like the First. The First World War, as we now call it, was perfectly simple in its beginning.

In July 1914 all the Great Powers were at peace, and a month later at the beginning of August 1914 they were all at war, and you can really describe that, as I have tried to do, in terms of a week or a month at most. But the Second World War, exactly when did it become a world war? When in fact did it become a war at all?

Suppose you said that a declaration of war indicates that the world war has started, then you would have to go back to April 1932 when Mao Tse-tung and Chu Teh declared war on Japan in the name of the Kiangsi Soviet.

For the Abyssinians the war started in 1935. For the Spanish Republicans it started in 1936; for the Czechs, even though they were defeated without an actual war, it started in 1938. For us English people it started on 3 September 1939. Indeed, I was once mistaken enough to write a book called *The Origins of the Second World War* which worked up to 3 September 1939, which was the day Great Britain declared war on Germany. In my last paragraph I realized I had been writing on the wrong subject and finished up by saying: 'What I have described is the origins of a minor conflict in Europe, the effects of which have been lost without trace and were only a preliminary to the real world conflict which came later.'

At any rate I thought I would try to present it in different terms, accepting that there were a series of wars which seemed of course very serious and great to those who were involved in them. The actual Polish war for instance lasted a fortnight so far as the serious fighting was concerned, but it was a great war while it was on and in its effects for the Poles.

The war between France and Germany, in which British troops were involved to a lesser extent in May to June 1940, lasted for something like at most six weeks – from any dynamic point of view, a fortnight. The Germans in conquering Europe between 1939 and 1940 suffered fewer casualities than they had suffered, say, during the battle of the Somme in 1916.

These were all preliminaries and no more than this. From June 1940 until June 1941 there was virtually peace in Europe and, for that matter, generally in the world. There were minor aggressions, there were minor conflicts and there was a running undercurrent of conflict. When I say that there was no great war I mean predominantly that there was no land war, apart from a very short-lived engagement in Greece. British troops were not in conflict with the Germans at all in Europe during that period and only to a very slight extent even in North Africa.

The only striking episode in this period of British history was a war between England and Italy in North Africa, which, although a very dramatic and sensational affair, had little relevance to the world struggle. Unlike the First World War, where we still have doubts what the issues were, whether it really was a conscious struggle for the mastery of Europe or of the world, the Second World War had a more defined character. Some of the Great Powers possessing empires or protected zones of their own could derive adequate resources from what they possessed. That was true of the United States; the whole, really, of the American continent was America's and nobody else's. This was also true of the British Empire and of the French Empire.

Two of the great industrial countries of the world did not possess such zones, they were short of resources and background. Quite apart from other things – their nationalist feeling, and their political aims such as German Nazism – they were discontented with their lot and were seeking to break into the monopoly of the other Great Powers. This is a pattern which occurred all through the 1930s. On the one hand, the contented empires; on the other, the discontented aggrieved powers, Germany and Japan.

Japan throughout the 1930s was aspiring to make first China and then the whole of the Far East, as they called it, the Greater Asia Co-Prosperity Sphere. When people use the term 'co-prosperity' of course it does not mean it is going to benefit those they conquer; it means it is going to benefit the conquerors. Co-prosperity is just a name for grabbing other people's resources, though it sounds very impressive.

In the same way, German leaders (and particularly Hitler) looked forward to a greater Germany with greater resources and more land. Essentially they aimed to break the structure of monopoly which penned them in. This is quite different from saying that they necessarily aspired to world war, still less to world conquest. Germany and Japan sought a secure recognized place at the table of the great. They wanted to sit down with the great empires as equals. Of course when people say that, they always want to be superiors too.

One of the things which historians have seen more clearly with the passing of the years is how closely the European question and the Far Eastern question were linked. For instance, the policy of appeasement which Chamberlain followed from 1937 to 1939 was largely designed to get Europe settled so that the British forces could move to the Far East and resist Japan. On the other side, the reluctance of the United States to get involved in the European theatre sprang to a great extent from the consciousness in Washington that the Far East was their most pressing concern and one where, with the European countries too busy in Europe, they had no associates.

Therefore, it seems to me the story of the Second World War begins as a practical proposition in June 1940. In June 1940 the readjustment of Europe was complete. It had been achieved at fantastically low cost in men and in equipment. There had never been an imperial conquest which had been achieved so easily as the way in which Hitler established German domination over Europe. In June 1940 Germany dominated the entire continent of Europe, either directly through her power or indirectly, as with the few remaining neutrals, by her influence and requirements. Indeed, you can go further and say Europe was united for the only time in its history, and there seemed little likelihood that this situation could be reversed from within Europe. We know that in fact any resistance in Europe, although sometimes very honourable, was ineffective in pushing the Germans back.

The only remnant of this earlier war, the war which had started in 1939 and terminated in the railway carriage at Compiègne when the French signed the armistice, was that Great Britain remained in the war. Indeed, this was the basic contribution which Great Britain made to the world war that came later. As Stalin put it, at a much later time, the Russians gave blood, the Americans provided money, the British provided time. They ensured that something like a war-like situation would remain.

After the attempt by Hitler to invade Great Britain in August–September 1940, neither side could strike decisively against the other. There were ineffective bombing raids. That again sounds ironical to anyone who lived through the blitz but, compared to any really heavy air bombardment, the blitz carried no weight and achieved no result.

The one factor which might have changed the war and which threatened Great Britain and brought her to the brink of defeat was the struggle in the Atlantic between the German U-boats against the British convoys, and this provided a link with the war that was to come after. Otherwise British and German armies were not fighting.

In 1941, when we in this country were already facing fairly limited rations, much of the German army was demobilized and German munitions production was cut down. There was a feeling that the war was over, yet it was not over because of the theoretical fact that Great Britain maintained the war, and this was one of the things which imposed a strain upon Hitler. He could not say, 'The war is finished.' He often talked about how he would like to make peace with Great Britain but he never attempted it seriously, and probably any attempts he made would have been rebuffed.

One of the fascinating topics still well worth studying is why did the British keep going so well? I do not mean to say effectively.

They were not having any effect against Hitler at this time until they could bring a greater war to bear. Why did they hold out when their cause seemed impossible, when everybody said, 'Well, Hitler can't invade Great Britain but then Great Britain will never be able to defeat Hitler'? What kept them going? Some hope for the future? I often think an echo of the past, a memory of earlier times when they stood alone against Napoleon, dragging on for ten years. In the end something would come right.

What should Hitler do, faced with this position that Europe was his? Should he just rest on his laurels? It is fairly clear that he anticipated further struggle. It may be also that, having once mobilized his army, he felt he must use it, and we know that after twelve months of deliberation and preparation Hitler's decision was to invade Russia.

Here is one of the very rare cases of how a war begins. There are wars which have been planned, in the sense that countries have built up their armies and envisaged that there would be a conflict. For instance, when the Germans built a navy against Great Britain before 1914, they assumed that one of these days there would be a naval war. But here Hitler and his staff sat down months beforehand and said, first of all, 15 May and then, with weather and other things interfering, 22 June 1941 as the day they would start their next war. It is very rare that there should be such an absolutely precise timetable. Why 22 June? Not because there was anything dramatic happening then but because it would fit in with their timetable. Unlike most wars – unlike, I am prepared to say, Hitler's earlier wars – this was a war of absolutely clear-cut determination with no argument, with no hesitations.

Why did Hitler do it? People have talked about this a lot, I think too much. Some people say he wanted to destroy communism. Some that he wanted to acquire great stretches of Russia, what he called 'Lebensraum', living space. Others say in more practical terms that he feared the ultimate strength of Russia. He argued, 'We are the stronger now, but as soon as Russia gets the stronger, the Russians will attack us.'

We have no idea what Russia's intentions were, except of course a clear-cut intention to survive. There is no indication at all of preparations to attack Germany or even to take precautions. Stalin, we know, was absolutely fixed on the doctrine that, until Great Britain had been defeated, Germany would not attack him.

When we look at the records it is clear why the decision was taken. The German generals and Hitler were absolutely confident they would win, so why not go ahead? How simple it would be. In an earlier stage there had been arguments about whether they should attack France. Many of the generals doubted whether France could be defeated. Hitler insisted it was possible, and it was. The French army was supposed to be the greatest in Europe. If France could be defeated within a month, Russia could be defeated within a few weeks. The very practical, simple, straightforward answer to the question, 'Why did Hitler invade Russia?' is because he was confident he would win and, with this, all serious threat to the German domination of Europe would disappear for ever. Indeed, he said as much very often: 'Once the British have lost all hope in Russia, they will make peace and the German empire will be secure.'

At the same time Hitler was becoming, as victors always do – as Napoleon did for that matter, but even more so – more confident and greedier with each success, and even before he attacked Russia he was making the next jump. Earlier he had said: 'The final battle for the world will be between Europe, led of course by Germany, and the United States, but it will not happen in my time. It will happen in a hundred years' time.'

After he had conquered France he still said, 'The battle between Europe and America will happen in my time, it will happen in twenty years,' but the moment he had decided that Russia could be eliminated in the early days of 1941, he said, 'The battle for the world will start in 1942 or thereabouts. We want to get Russia out of the way and acquire Russia's resources, and then for the great war against America.'

There is no doubt why the Germans went to war with Russia; they went to war with the absolute blind confidence that they would win. It would be such an easy war that it was inconceivable to turn it down.

This was a decisive step towards world war. It was a more decisive step than the Germans expected, of course, because Russia survived instead of being defeated within a month as everyone had expected, as the German generals had expected, as the British general staff had expected, as the American army had expected. Germany was faced with, if not world war, at any rate a conflict of the greatest size and with it the implication that German power would not necessarily be sustained on this level.

We must also bring in the other side. It is not possible to understand the origins of how the Second World War actually came into being without considering the similar story of Japan in the Far East. Here too the Japanese had great successes, they had successes before the war in which they established their control over most of the coast of China and most of the Chinese ports. Here again there was a parallel with Great Britain; just as Great Britain kept a war going by merely existing, so Nationalist China kept a war going by merely existing. The Chinese did virtually no fighting against Japan between 1938 or early 1939 and the end of the world war, but they were still theoretically in existence. Incidentally, China did not declare war on Japan until after Pearl Harbor, but there they were, and this tempted Japan to go further along the coast. Moreover, with the collapse of the European powers and their empires, the Dutch empire and the French empire, these were wide open. The Japanese saw the opportunity to break the ring and acquire raw materials for themselves.

In the background, the factor which more than anything else shaped and conditioned the Second World War was the United States, indisputably at that time the greatest industrial power in the world, a power with a stake in European affairs and also in Far Eastern affairs, a power torn between the overwhelming desire of a great many of its people to keep out of war and, on the other hand, a similar desire to assert American principles of democracy and of what one could call free trade or, more truly, free investment for American money. That was the basis of America's liberal economy.

It was very much in America's interest to keep Great Britain going, not only interest in the economic sense but interest in the strategic sense. Ever since the Declaration of Independence in 1776, Great Britain had, willingly or not, supplied a strategical buffer between the United States and Europe. It was for this reason to a great extent that the United States had entered the First World War in 1917.

More than this, Great Britain now represented the only way in which American power, if it were going to be reasserted, could get back into Europe. From very early on in the war, American strategists, envisaging that there would be a war between Germany and the United States, pointed to Great Britain as their impregnable aircraft carrier from which American troops could get into Europe. The struggle in the Atlantic therefore directly involved the United States.

For American battleships and destroyers, the Second World War began a long time before Pearl Harbor. It began in the summer of 1941 when Germany and the United States were unofficially at war in the Atlantic. On the other side, America was following a similar policy of holding back Japan. Here again we can point to a precise moment when the Second World War in the Far East became inevitable, when it was decided on. This was not a Japanese decision; it was an American decision.

In August 1941 the US government imposed a total embargo on supplies to Japan, particularly supplies of oil and of credits. From that moment Japan was doomed either to surrender at discretion or to go to war. The Japanese had six months' supply of oil. Actually, as usual they overstated their distress. They could have lasted out for a year or two, but the doctrine was 'We have only got six months – before that we must break through the ring.' In anything but a technical sense the United States had declared war on Japan by thus attempting to close the ring.

By the autumn of 1941, therefore, the situation was changing, in some ways for the better, in some ways for the worse. On the one hand, the German predominance in Europe, which had seemed so complete and so unshakeable in the summer of 1941, was now gravely threatened.

In June 1941 everybody virtually – there were a few exceptions, of whom I was one – said, 'Russia will be defeated.' By the autumn, most strategical experts were still shaking their heads and saying, 'Well it has been tougher for the Germans than we expected, but

Russia is bound to collapse.' By November it looked as if Russia was going to survive, and there was a short period when the Russians themselves thought they had already won and Stalin was talking about complete victory in 1942. This was a fantastic turn of events.

The other aspect of this was the tense situation in the Far East. Did the Americans, did Roosevelt, deliberately turn the screw on Japan in the confidence that Japan would go to war?

We shall never be able to answer this absolutely clearly. I am inclined to think 'No'. I am inclined to think that, until October 1941 or perhaps early November, the Americans still thought that the Japanese, faced with this rigid blockade, cut off from their oil, would compromise, would draw back from some of their conquests and would seek a settlement, not quite a surrender but at any rate a withdrawal, with the Americans.

The Japanese on their side had no hesitation. They had decided they were going to break the ring. Where they hesitated was exactly how to do it; but we know that quite a long time before Pearl Harbor they had decided that the American fleet must be eliminated.

Hitler may have talked about dominating the world. The Japanese had no such fantasies; they wanted to establish the Far Eastern Co-Prosperity Sphere, and with that they would be content.

They undertook the attack on Pearl Harbor on 7 December 1941. This was not linked up with the European war. In fact the Japanese got their timing absolutely wrong because on 7 December the Soviet armies began a counter-offensive.

Maybe if the Japanese had hesitated one more day, they would have pulled back and realized they had missed the bus. As it was, they started the world war – not quite. Hitler finally launched the Second World War by his declaration of war on America. Why did he do this? Why did he give this most extraordinary assistance to the Allies? We shall never know.

Perhaps that marks the moment when the Second World War began, but perhaps not. Churchill certainly thought it was later, because he said after the battle of El Alamein in October 1942, 'This may not be the beginning of the end but it is the end of the beginning.'

The Cold War

I suppose 'How the Cold War Began' is rather a contradictory title because the essence of the Cold War is that it was a war which was expected to begin but never actually began. However, I suppose we know roughly what we have in mind by the term 'Cold War'. It applies to some parts of the international relations between Soviet Russia and the United States in the thirty years or so since the war – periods of tension.

Now international tension is nothing like so unusual as people imagine. Indeed the normal relation of sovereign powers is to distrust each other and to pursue rival ambitions. All through the nineteenth century, for instance, Great Britain was running in rivalry to either Russia or France or, in the early twentieth century, to Germany. Nor is it unusual for former allies to quarrel. In fact, the normal thing at the end of any great war is that the alliances break up and they fall out.

In 1815 England and Austria, the victors, made an alliance with France, their former enemy, against Russia, their former ally who had indeed delivered Europe from the conqueror; and if something the same happened in 1945 this was only to be expected.

There were, however, and still are, deeper elements than the normal rivalry and distrust which great powers show for one another. For one thing, Russia, even when a great power, has never been fully accepted as part of Europe. There has always been an assumption that Russia was just on the fringe of Europe. She was indeed quite often in the nineteenth century referred to as an Asiatic and almost an inferior power.

In 1856, after the Crimean War when somebody objected that the terms imposed on Russia were very harsh (much harsher incidentally than those imposed by Bismarck on France in 1871), Palmerston replied, 'Well, what can an Asiatic power expect?'

When Russia has claimed that she should be treated on the same level, has the same rights to make claims as other great powers, this produces not only indignation but surprise.

In 1945, for instance, at the end of the Second World War, when the victors were first speculating as to how things should be shared out, the British, who were hoping still to maintain the whole of their empire and their domination of the Mediterranean, were astonished to learn that Russian statesmen hoped to acquire Libya. If the Americans had come along and said, 'We should like a colony in the Mediterranean and have decided that Libya should be the one,' nobody would have minded. It would have been regarded as the normal thing for a great power to do. For Russia to do it was an outrage, an uncivilized, an Asiatic thing.

Similary in 1945, the British still controlled both ends of the Mediterranean, the Straits of Gibraltar and the Suez Canal, and this was said to be essential to their national security, although the Mediterranean, heaven knows, is quite a long way from this country. The Russians said that they would like to control the Straits of Bosporus and the Dardanelles. This would give them an outlet – it was a good deal more important to them than Gibraltar and Suez were to the British. Immediately the talk began of Russian aggression, but of course this was strengthened by many other things.

There is a greater division of ideology between Russia and the Western powers than between any of the Western powers themselves. This did not begin with communism; it began with the religious cleavage. The Russians have the Orthodox Church and are very arrogant about it. Their church is officially called 'the Orthodox Church', so what does that leave the rest of us with? I suppose we are all some kind of heretics, second-rate Christians, compared to the truly Orthodox. Add to this Marxism, which again claims to know all the secrets of the economic system. Russian statesmen, writers, have a determination to be right, a self-confidence which is asserted the more because others by no means always recognize it.

There are considerations of a more practical nature. Russia in the nineteenth century had great conflicts with Great Britain, particularly in the Middle East. With the Russian Revolution there followed a very great increase in the cleavage when, a thing often forgotten in the West, Great Britain and France, with some co-operation from America, conducted wars of intervention on a very considerable scale against the Bolshevik government.

What the British and French did in 1919 was very much what the old reactionary powers had done against France in 1793. In this case the wars of intervention were a failure and, though they did not provoke an actual counter-war on the part of Russia, they certainly created hostility on both sides. Throughout the inter-war period there had been this antagonism and a deep-based suspicion. Here again, suspicion is the normal relationship between great powers. That is particularly true, of course, of the military advisers. After all, it is the job of generals and admirals and air marshals to prepare for wars. They can only prepare for war at all sensibly if they envisage an antagonist and when they cannot see an obvious antagonist then they find unlikely antagonists.

In the 1920s, for instance, when Germany had almost ceased to exist as a military power and Russia had been forgotten, the British air staff in order to justify a large air force invented the French peril. They argued that because France had a large air force, this was inevitably bound to be used against Great Britain and therefore we must build a large air force in return. The large air force was not built, but the alarm was sounded.

I was reading just the other day a fascinating account of American military and strategic plans between the wars, at a time when neither Germany nor Russia was a danger. The American strategists had to justify themselves, so they sounded the alarm that America – as always – was in danger. After all, if your country is not in danger you would not have an army or an air force or a navy, and that would never do for the people who are running the army, the air force and the navy. So what did the army strategists in America discover in the middle of the 1920s? They discovered that a country called Red, which was in fact the United Kingdom, was preparing to invade White, which was the United States, with an army of eight million men in order to destroy the whole of American industry. This was not some fantasy of a novelist. It was the work of a serious strategical planner, trained in the staff colleges and setting down in genuine alarm that any day a new Armada might be sighted crossing the Atlantic, landing in Canada, and then eight million British troops marching, I suppose, on Chicago. 'Ah,' you may say, 'a fantasy; they didn't take many steps about it.' In fact they did. The Americans recast their strategical thinking entirely in face of the supposed danger from the British on the one side and Japan on the other, and the reason why in 1941 the Americans put Germany first was simply that they had put the other European danger – England – first fifteen or twenty years before.

The suspicion and rivalry between Soviet Russia and the Great Powers turned then on the historical record, on Russia's geographical position and, most of all, on the transformation of Russian society which we call the Bolshevik Revolution.

No such cleavage had existed in Western civilization since the time of the French Revolution, and even at the time of the French Revolution the cleavage was, though fierce, relatively short. The cleavage which started in 1917 between the state which claimed to be Communist and the countries which called themselves 'Democratic' or 'Capitalistic' or 'Liberal' has endured to the present day. It may be argued that the cleavage is now less, that all Western countries are becoming more communized, at any rate run by great corporations and not by individual enterprise, perhaps becoming less democratic too. It could hardly, I think, be argued that Soviet Russia is becoming more democratic. It is possible, however, that she is becoming less rigidly communistic. Nevertheless, the cleavage is still there, and I sometimes think that what people in the West dislike about Soviet Russia, or what many people dislike about Soviet Russia, is not the bad things in Soviet Russia but the good ones. It is not so much that people dislike the labour camps, the suppression of freedom of thought, the constant thought control, the secret police. What many people really dislike is that Russia has no capitalists and no private landlords. Marxism – which is after all a perfectly legitimate and coherent system of economic thought – is now used as a term of abuse and it is supposed that anyone who is a Marxist can hardly be British at all, even though Marxism was after all invented in the British Museum. No system of thought is more fully integrally British than Marxism, but this is not how people think of it nowadays. How far this crusade of ideas still persists it is difficult to say.

In 1918, though the Western powers wanted to grab Russian territory as well, there is no doubt that they regarded Bolshevism as a really barbaric idea. Now I think this is confined to theoreticians – most practical people take it as an oddity and not very much more – but in so far as Russia is a socialist state, this still provides a cleavage and a cause of tension which can flare up in the most unlikely places.

These, however, are not the practical considerations. At the end of the Second World War there was a suspicion on both sides, simply beginning with the very extent of the victory. Ever since 1941, the victors, the three Great Powers, had been held together by the need to defeat Germany and this need imposed tremendous demands on them. Despite whatever people have said, in my opinion none of the three Great Powers had any reservations about waging the war against Germany. They put the defeat of Hitler and Nazi Germany above everything else. Then suddenly, you see, Nazi Germany was defeated, suddenly Hitler was not there. The danger which had forced them together had disappeared and, although they talked at their Potsdam meeting and later of the possibility of a revived German danger, the fact is that the German danger has, I think, disappeared. I did not think that for a long time. I went on for a long time after the war being apprehensive of a revived Germany but I now admit that Germany has become a pacific country, thoroughly integrated into Western democratic ways. Equally true, of course, in the Far East Japan has ceased to be a political and military danger, although in a sense she is still an economic rival, as Germany is for that matter.

A wide range of misunderstandings began in 1945, some of which have continued to the present day. For instance the Russians had had the most terrible experiences, twenty million dead, nor was this the first time that such a thing had happened to them. In fact Russia has been invaded by one European country or another five

times since the beginning of the nineteenth century: by Napoleon
in 1812, by the British and French in 1856, by the Germans in 1914
to 1917, by the British and French again in 1919, and by the
Germans in 1941. Russia has never invaded Europe except in answer
to the conqueror and, one can say, as a liberator. Russian troops
came to Berlin in 1945, just as they had come to Paris in 1814, not
as conquerors but simply to drive the conquerors back, or so it
appears in retrospect. At the time, men feared that they had come
as conquerors.

We shall never know in our lifetime (and perhaps we shall never
know) what were the secret counsels of the Soviet leaders in 1945
or indeed now. All those who claim to know about Soviet policy,
Kremlinologists they are called, guess; that is all you can do about
Russia. I differ from them, but only because I guess slightly differently. No one has any solid information about Soviet policy from
inside.

There are many who think that in 1945 Stalin and his hordes
wanted to sweep right across Europe. In my opinion, and I am as
entitled to my opinion as others are, this was not the case. Soviet
policy wanted security: the defeat of Germany, and then the building up of a ring of satellite states which would ensure Soviet Russia's
security.

Far from wanting the spread of communism, and this is something
we know from the evidence before us, Stalin deliberately prevented
the possible victory of communism in both Italy and France; and
it is now, I may say, much against the will of the Soviet leaders that
communism is growing in strength in Italy and to a lesser extent in
France. My guess is that the last thing the Soviet leaders want is to
see the success of European Communist parties, because if any great
European country went Communist it would eclipse Soviet Russia.

This, however, is not how it seemed to others at the time. The
extensions of Russian power into Czechoslovakia and Poland were
deplored by Great Britain and still more by the United States, even
though the United States' policy and influence were being extended
by different means into Western Europe. How did Western Europe
recover and be saved from communism? By American economic
aid, because America attached importance to preserving Western

Europe as what it still is – an American outpost. Europe was divided into, on the one hand, American outposts and, on the other hand, Soviet outposts – neither possibly with any aggressive intention.

There was, I think, one period of genuine Cold War. I mean with one of the powers planning to take aggressive moves to drive the other back, not necessarily by war but by overwhelming pressure, and that was in the years when the United States alone possessed nuclear weapons. We know quite well that from the moment the atomic bombs were dropped on Hiroshima and Nagasaki American policy became tougher. There was a time when President Truman and others were envisaging that Russia would be pushed back to her 1939 frontiers. After all, President Truman (who succeeded Roosevelt only by the accident of Roosevelt's death) said on the outbreak of war between Russia and Germany in 1941, 'We should stand aside and let each of the two scoundrels cut each other's throats, supporting whichever happens to be the weaker at the moment.' So he showed little appreciation for Soviet Russia as an ally and, I would speculate also, that the Berlin airlift, that is to say the Russian blockade of Berlin, was in part an answer to this atomic alarm.

It is worth bearing in mind that the Berlin airlift could not have been continued for twenty-four hours unless the control towers, all manned by Soviet observers and operators, had been kept going, so that it was the Russians who really conducted the Berlin airlift, as it were, or patronized it.

The world situation undoubtedly changed when the Russians acquired nuclear secrets of their own, secrets I think which owed a great deal more to the work of Soviet scientists than to British or American defectors. From this moment there began a balance, sometimes called the balance of terror.

As with other weapons, it is not necessary to be as strong if you are on the defensive as on the offensive. In the Second World War it was said that the offensive had to be five times as strong as the defensive if it were to succeed; and something the same can be said about nuclear weapons. Russia until recently has not been as strong in nuclear weapons as the United States but has been strong enough to pose some threat; and in all these years, although there have been apprehensions, there has been only one alarm, in my opinion a mistaken one. This was called the Cuban missile crisis of 1962, often represented as an American victory. What it secured certainly was the withdrawal of Soviet rocket bases from Cuba, but the Americans paid a price. They acknowledged Cuba's independence and never repeated the attempt to destroy it as they had done in the Bay of Pigs affair. Cuba is really under a Soviet guarantee to the present day. Altogether an interesting experience of how near one could go to war.

Other Russian activities come, in my opinion, under the heading of defensive answers, answers which were very tiresome to those upon whom they were inflicted. There was a tendency for each side to nibble, hoping that there would be cracks in the lines of division. This was true in regard to Czechoslovakia in 1948, it was true in a different way in regard to Hungary in 1956.

The last time I saw President Beneš of Czechoslovakia, which was in 1947, he said to me, 'I have always hoped that Czechoslovakia would be a link, a hyphen between the Western powers and the Eastern powers. If now East and West quarrel, Czechoslovakia must go with Russia.' When I asked him why, he said, 'Because it is our only secure defence against the Germans.' This is a theme which is sometimes forgotten in the West. Maybe the alarm is now artificial, but it certainly existed at that time.

The Hungarian case is more contentious. The Hungarian revolution or rising could be depicted as a movement of good democrats. It could also be depicted as having been captured by those who looked back to the fascist, aristocratic, clerical-run Hungary of the inter-war years. Though the Soviet intervention was a move in the Cold War, it was specifically designed to ensure that this did not turn into hot war.

What is happening in other parts of the world is a different matter. Though we can look forward – for some years – to a reasonable balance between Russia and the United States, I think the most likely warlike events will sound like echoes from the nineteenth century. Wars of liberation have been fought in the last thirty years: the liberation of Vietnam, the liberation of Algeria, and it may well be, though much regretted, wars of liberation in

Africa, but these will not deeply affect the world balance. The Americans talked a lot of nonsense about the domino theory and asserted that if Vietnam went, the whole of South East Asia would be lost. So far the only consequence of the defeat of America in Vietnam is that the reunited Vietnam is stronger and more independent than it was before.

On the whole we have done pretty well since the war in not producing any great men. Great men are splendid in wartime, maybe essential, but they can be dangerous in peacetime. Great men have produced wars as Napoleon did. All the world statesmen now are rather humdrum secondary people who are unlikely to aspire to be world conquerors. The one force which still aspires to conquer the world is the planning staffs. They will produce the alarms and frights.

People often ask historians to tell them about the future. Heaven knows it is difficult enough to know about the past. The historian is no more competent than anyone else to foretell the future. In fact, in many ways he is less competent because he understands the infinite variety of what might happen. When people ask me, 'Will there be another world war?' I am inclined to answer, 'If men behave in the future as they have done in the past there will be another war.' But of course it is always possible that men will behave differently.

As a personal hunch I think it is unlikely and that there will be a Third World War. One day the deterrent will fail to deter.

HOW WARS END

Napoleon's Last Great War

Napoleon I invaded Russia in June 1812. At this time, Napoleon really dominated the whole of mainland Europe. Everywhere was either part of his empire or a satellite. Prussia had become a satellite, even Austria had become a satellite; all that was left of independence was Spain, which was fighting against the French, and Great Britain, which was of course independent and hostile to France. Russia had been something like a satellite, although a high-minded one. The object of Napoleon's invasion of Russia was not to conquer Russia but to win Russia's friendship back and make it once more a satellite. The remarkable thing about this war is that if you define a general war as a war in which more than two great powers take part, this was the last general war until 1914. There was not a general war in the whole of the nineteenth century, except possibly the Crimean War, which hardly counts.

But certainly Napoleon's object was not conquest. One of his objects was to detach part of Russia. In the late eighteenth century, Poland had been partitioned, and most of Poland was now in Russia.

One of Napoleon's many objects in life was to make Poland once more an independent country, and if he had had his way in this last war, Poland would have become independent, Russia would have become dependent on Napoleon, and he really would have dominated Europe.

As it was, the more he advanced into Russia, the more silent the Russians became on the other hand. They did not make an elaborate resistance, although they kept up a resistance, but what they did was to refuse to acknowledge Napoleon's existence. Napoleon never meant to go to Moscow. He thought that once he said, 'I'm going to Moscow,' the Russians would take fright and at once give way to whatever he wanted. In past times he had always gone for the capital. Once he had got to the capital, he had won. This time he reached Moscow by September, and the first thing he said to his agents, who were already in Moscow, was, 'Has the emissary from the Tsar arrived?' He thought: Now I'm in Moscow, Alexander will send a message of surrender. No emissary came. For a whole month, or very near it, the vast French army, probably the biggest army which had ever been mobilized in European history until that time, was scattered in and around Moscow, with conditions getting worse – Moscow burning – and at the end of September Napoleon made his first gesture, not quite of surrender, but of retreat. He withdrew from Moscow. And the retreat from Moscow, unlike the advance, was a catastrophe.

All the way back to the frontier, the French had to fight their way. They suffered terrible casualties. The Russians suffered great casualties as well, but they seemed to have endless resources. And there was a moment when it looked as if the French were all going to be cut off when they couldn't manage to cross the Beresina. It was only the work of sappers building temporary bridges that got them back over the Beresina and out of Russia.

In December 1812, the Napoleonic empire had already begun to shake. Its prestige was going. In the middle of December, Napoleon left his army still on Russian territory and, with one associate, mounted in a curious sort of box sledge in which he drove right across Europe. It took him something like a fortnight to get to Paris. And it was not until the very end of December that he announced in Paris: 'The Grand Army has been lost.' He was still confident that he could build up a new army, and in the early days of 1813 Napoleon returned to his army; he brought new forces together and in the first months of 1813 inflicted defeat on Russia and also on Prussia who, very cautiously, had now gone over to the Russian side. After these two French victories, there was again a pause, because Napoleon had no idea what to do. What was he aiming for? He was aiming for a reconciliation with Russia. But the more he defeated or challenged Russia in the field, the more unlikely the Russians were to become partners with Napoleon. He was in a deadlock. His short period of victories was not followed by further new advances by the French. When they were exhausted, the Russians came back and built up new forces. Incidentally, they now cast off the military leadership of Alexander and for some time had Kotusov, the last of the great Russian generals, who, however, died in March 1813.

What Napoleon wanted was negotiation. He proposed an armistice, which came into force and continued for most of the first part of 1813. He said later in life, when he was on St Helena, that the greatest mistake he ever made in his life was that armistice, because during the time of the armistice his army did not increase, but the Russian and the Prussian armies did. More than that. Technically, until this moment, Austria was an ally of France. Napoleon himself was married to an Austrian archduchess, he'd only just been married to her, and the Emperor was his father-in-law. But now, with Russia (and, to a lesser extent, Prussia) appearing on the field, Austria began to waver.

There was a celebrated meeting between Napoleon and Metternich, the Austrian statesman, which went on, it is said, for nine hours. Napoleon never yielded on anything. He insisted that Russia must come back within his sphere of influence. And after these nine hours, Metternich said to Napoleon as he was going, 'Sire, you are a ruined man.' Not much later, Austria too joined in the coalition against Napoleon.

Napoleon was at his best in facing apparently difficult circumstances. And combining, or trying to combine, negotiations and renewal of war. There is another very odd thing about this war of 1812 to 1814. It was a war in which conflict was interrupted constantly by negotiations. After the meeting between Napoleon and Metternich, they agreed that there should be a European conference in Prague of all the powers involved in the war. Although desks were made, and ink pots put out, the conference never got going. But somewhat later the conference actually moved to Frankfurt, and there they began to negotiate.

Already Napoleon was having to yield. No doubt he thought he would get it all back later. He made a supposedly generous offer that France should retain the natural frontier controlling Western Germany, and of course Italy as well, then there could be peace. At the same time as they were having peace conferences in Frankfurt, war was being resumed in Germany.

In August of 1813 the war was renewed, and once more Napoleon was victorious, defeated the Prussians and even made the Russians retreat.

But these victories led to nothing, because all that happened was that the Prussians and the Russians retreated, and then when Napoleon pulled up his army *they* came back.

In October there was the first great battle of the war – or the greatest battle since Borodino in 1812. This was when Napoleon was drawing his troops back and had to retreat through Leipzig. He was confident at first that, not only would he carve his way through Leipzig, but that he would inflict a defeat on the allies as, when he challenged them, he had always done. And this time, after a three-day battle, the French were defeated.

This is a landmark in European history. It was the first time, since France had become the military leader of Europe, that there was not merely a defeat, but a complete disaster to the French army. There had been disaster in Russia because of the horrible conditions of the retreat; but this was the first, the very first test in warfare when the French army suffered a vital defeat.

The French pulled through enough to be able to retreat to the Rhine, but the prestige of Napoleon was shaken and never restored. It was a turning point in European history.

For the Germans particularly, it became a national triumph. Prussia was the only German power which had really recovered its independence and had put into the field an effective army. The Austrians counted for something. But, historically, the battle of Leipzig became, in German history, the battle of the nations, because it was not merely the regular forces; now volunteer forces poured in to support Prussia and the other German states in their resistance to Napoleon.

Despite the defeat of the French, the conference at Frankfurt went solemnly on with its discussions, and seemed to have reached a conclusion that France should have what were called the natural frontiers, in other words the Alps and the Rhine. This would have left France with a good deal more territory than she had possessed before the Revolution of 1789. It was very characteristic that Napoleon, just having been defeated in battle, was confident that he would turn the scale next time, and therefore rejected the very favourable compromise which his negotiators had made for him. The Frankfurt conference broke down. Then there was a further pause and, early in 1814, Napoleon had gathered an army again together and he celebrated the opening of the year by a victory over the Russians who, having first attempted to invade France, withdrew again.

Now they were back at a peace conference once more, at a place called Châtillon, where they went over the ground and where the allies tightened up their terms. They now no longer offered the natural frontiers, but merely what were called the Old Frontiers, the frontiers which France had in 1789.

Napoleon thought this really not worth discussing. He merely allowed the conference to go on. As a weapon of war, in the two years between 1812 or the beginning of 1813 and the fall of Napoleon, international negotiations went on with an intensity for which there was very little parallel. Conference after conference; meeting and discussing and producing solutions, and everyone heaving a sigh of relief except Napoleon, who, at the last minute, would repudiate them. And just as he celebrated 1813 with a victory over the Prussians, he celebrated 1814 with a victory over the Prussians and over the Russians.

But these were matters of ingenuity, they were not matters of greater resources. The truth is that if the allies, now including Austria, assembled all their forces, ultimately Napoleon would be beaten. But he relied on quickness of manœuvre and he had quite a considerable record in 1814 of victories over the Prussians, over the Russians at one time; and the Austrians were so cautious and so anxious not to be defeated that they didn't attempt to invade France at all, but remained cautiously on the frontier, out of the range of Napoleon's armies.

In March 1814, the Prussians reassembled their forces and

prepared to march on Paris. Napoleon actually welcomed this. For one thing, he felt he must keep the allies separate, that he could move his own army against the Prussians, and against the Russians, and then possibly against the Austrians. And he was delighted when Blücher, the Prussian general, marched on Paris, because he said, 'Now I can cut off his retreat,' and he thought the situation was going in his favour.

At this time, even the Russians speculated on the idea that it would be wiser to give up, that a compromise with Napoleon would be possible, that Napoleon could be offered, not only France of 1789, but perhaps, after all, the natural frontiers.

The thing which stiffened the resistance of the allies was the arrival of Castlereagh, the British Foreign Secretary, who had no troops to offer, but could offer what was more important – lots of money – and tempted the allies back into action.

By the end of March 1814 the Prussians were well established in Paris. Napoleon prepared his master stroke. He would march away from Paris, leave it exposed to the allies, and when they had gone into Paris he would cut their communications, leave them high and dry, and would win after all.

And now one new factor came into play, a factor which was going to ruin Napoleon, and this was the resistance of the French marshals. The great French marshals had been at war, on and off, for something like twenty years. They had become very rich, they had become dukes and princes, they had great estates, and they did not want to fight any more. They had concentrated back in the Palace of Fontainebleau, and Napoleon arrived, having just carried out a successful manoeuvre to cut off Blücher's communications, and said, 'Now we can go into action against them.' The marshals all struck. Even Ney, who was the bravest of the brave, the man who had forced the passage of the Beresina and who, incidentally, was to go over to Napoleon again at the time of the Hundred Days, even Ney said, 'Emperor, we have done too much, it must end.' This brought down Napoleon's plans completely. Napoleon shrugged the marshals off, saying, 'I can perfectly well conduct a war without all of you. As long as I am in command and have someone to send messages, I can win this war.' And then he received the disastrous news that one of the marshals had carried the argument further. Marshal Marmont, commander of 50,000 men, the nearest force to Paris, had gone over to the allies. With that, Napoleon hadn't a fighting force at all.

In Paris there were fascinating developments. Alexander had arrived, and his problem was the question of whom they should recognize as a French government. He thought they might take Napoleon's son, or Napoleon's wife, or perhaps Bernadotte; but Talleyrand, who had been French Foreign Minister, and a very influential, very skilful politician, put forward the answer: the only alternative to Napoleon was the legitimate king, Louis XVIII, who'd been living in England, or sometimes exiled in Russia, ever since 1792. Alexander agreed and, long before the technical end of the war, Louis XVIII was recognized – though it took him some time to arrive from England. Meanwhile the question arose as to what should happen to Napoleon.

Every now and again, Napoleon would reject the negotiations and say, 'Let us carry on with the war.' But after Marshal Marmont had deserted, there was really no hope that he could do so. On 3 April 1814 he abdicated.

This was the end of the war so far as Napoleon was concerned, and you can't really say that there was ever an end to the war by means of a treaty. There was a treaty, but it was simply a stopping of the fight, because the person who fought was no longer in power. The only agreement that was made was an agreement between the allied powers and the former Emperor Napoleon, making him Emperor of Elba.

The great Napoleonic empire had come to an end. And instead there followed one of the most curious peace treaties in the record of modern times: a peace treaty with Louis XVIII. But the allies had never been fighting Louis XVIII. He had been in exile and had claimed to be king from 1795 onwards. Now he was king, but there was no way in which the allies could make a peace treaty with him because they had never been at war with him. What followed was, probably, the most generous peace treaty ever made by victors regarding a country that had been such a nuisance to them. France was not asked to pay any indemnity, she was not asked to return any of the works of art which Napoleon had plundered, she was not asked to reduce her army, and she was even allowed to take some of the territory which the French Revolution had gathered. France returned to the ranks of the great powers without any atonement, because it was a different France.

This was not quite the end of the story. Eighteen months later, Napoleon had another go; he returned for the Hundred Days. But he was quickly defeated at Waterloo and withdrew. Just to make the record complete, the second Peace of Paris was a little harsher. France had to pay a small indemnity and, in particular, had to return the works of art. And that is why the four horses of St Mark are on St Mark's church in Venice and not in the Louvre in France.

The Congress of Vienna, 1815

When Napoleon fell, in April 1814, there was no independent authority in Europe; for some years, everything in Europe had turned on Napoleon. The only state on the continent of any magnitude was of course Russia. That was why Napoleon had gone to Moscow so unsuccessfully. Great Britain was really independent, but she was not on the continent of Europe. Suddenly the Europe that had known so many changes was left alone to be arranged. The four allies – Russia, Austria, Prussia and Great Britain – decided that a *great* congress should be held in order to settle the future of Europe.

The invitations were sent out by the Emperor of Austria. The four allies held a preliminary meeting in Vienna at the beginning of October 1814. They were just beginning to settle down on an agenda and what they would decide, when the door opened and Talleyrand, the French Foreign Minister, came in and expressed surprise at seeing them. He said, 'Who are you?' They said, 'We are the four great allies.' 'Not at all,' he said, 'the alliance came to an end the moment Napoleon signed the treaty of peace and abdicated. So it must be, simply, the great powers. France is a great power, so I'm going to sit in with you and, as a matter of fact, I've brought the representatives of Spain, Portugal and Sweden as well, that makes up the eight who are the great European powers. We won't bother much about Poland.' In fact, the Spaniard was a great nuisance too. But the character of the meeting was changed, because here were delegates who had not been involved as an alliance, but representing the independence of many countries.

The conference worked partly with committees, partly with the direction of the great five, and partly by ideas being put up. Some things the Congress leaders were quite clear about. They did not like republics. They restored most of the monarchs who were knocking around Vienna. A lot of them were not much good as monarchs, but all the same they had the title of king or grand duke or archduke, and they had been dethroned by Napoleon, so here they were put back again. But where Napoleon had destroyed a republic, the directors of the Congress of Vienna did not restore it. Out of the 300 free cities in Germany, the great majority disappeared. In fact, before long, there were only two free cities left in Germany. Frankfurt was one, Hamburg was the other; and Hamburg has retained some of the characteristics of a free city to the present day.

In Italy the prejudice against republics was even more striking. Venice, Venezia, was a state far older than most of the monarchies or grand-duchies of Italy but, because it was a republic, it was simply given to Austria and lost its independence for ever. The same thing happened to Genoa, which was incorporated in the Kingdom of Sardinia.

When they met, there was one problem which the Congress leaders had not contemplated. It was the problem which, in a sense, caused Napoleon to go to Moscow – the problem of Poland. And now, with Napoleon gone, the problem of Poland raised its head. Until the year 1772, Poland was a great, independent state, not very well run; with an elective monarch, usually the Elector of Saxony, but still elected in a confused way; and while the neighbours of Poland – Russia, Prussia and Austria – had grown stronger, Poland had grown weaker.

In 1772 there was a partition of most of Poland. Russia took the central part, Prussia took one of the edges, Austria took Galicia. There was a further partition in 1792, and a final partition in 1795 when Poland disappeared altogether. But there was still a sense of Polish nationalism. And in 1809 Napoleon resurrected a small independent Poland as the Grand Duchy of Warsaw.

Alexander had cast himself as a new saviour of Poland. What he wanted was to resurrect a kingdom of Poland which would include the whole of Poland, would all be under him as Protector and Tsar, in fact would be a Russian satellite state – a phrase which you may have heard suggested in more recent times. The others obviously did not like this.

Nevertheless, when the great powers first met, Alexander was much the most powerful in armies, in background, and in the fact that he'd been able to fight Napoleon and defeat him. More than any other, it was Russian armies which defeated Napoleon and, if you like, liberated Europe.

Now Alexander was threatening to use this same great army in order to impose his will. Prussia was quite prepared to fit in. Prussia would surrender – hand over her share of Poland – if the King of Prussia could have Saxony instead. And there was a good argument for this, because the King of Saxony had stayed with Napoleon too late and was still an ally of Napoleon when Napoleon fell. So obviously he wasn't entitled to keep his kingdom, or so it appeared. But there he was, hanging around Vienna, hoping to insert himself.

In the autumn of 1814 it looked as if the Congress of Vienna was going to break up in dispute. And then a very sensational thing happened. Talleyrand raised his head again.

On 2 January 1815, Talleyrand, without any authority from his government, signed on behalf of France an alliance with Great Britain and Austria against Russia. Whether it would have ever operated, whether the French armies would have marched, whether the British and Austrian armies would ever have worked together, we cannot say. But it was enough to do the trick. In the course of the spring of 1815 Alexander compromised and finally agreed that, while he was entitled to resurrect Poland in the share that he had received in the original partitions, Austria would retain her share, Galicia (which she retained until the end of the Austrian empire), and Prussia would retain her share of Poland (which Prussia, or alternatively Germany afterwards, retained until 1945, if not later).

There still was a sort of kingdom of Poland because, although Poland was now only the central part of Poland under Russian control, it was still given a Polish character. Indeed, from 1815 to 1830, Poland had an autonomous government. The brother of Tsar Alexander, Grand Duke Constantine, acted as Viceroy of Poland, married a Polish countess and thought of himself as more Polish than Russian.

In 1825, when Alexander died, or is supposed to have died, Constantine, the next heir, refused the Russian throne because he said, 'I wanted to stay as ruler of Poland.' And it was the next heir, Tsar Nicholas, who became the tyrant of Russia from then until the Crimean War. There is a curious little point about Alexander. He went on tour in southern Russia in 1825, he developed a serious illness and then, presumably, he died. He was buried at a place in southern Russia where a tomb was erected. And in 1855, when they opened the tomb, there was nothing there. Legend has it that Alexander abdicated his throne and became a hermit. Members of the Imperial house used regularly to go down to southern Russia to sit at the feet of this hermit until he died in the due course of nature. How much truth there is in this story I've not the slightest idea. I suspect none, but what happened to Alexander's body we shall never know.

The Polish affair was the great crisis of the Congress of Vienna. It was settled peacefully and Alexander was able to reassert his leadership over the Congress by presenting a plan of his own that the allies, indeed all those who were associated with the Congress of Vienna, should continue to maintain a system of co-operation and to recognize an all-European organization.

Alexander wanted to build this on high Christian principles, and indeed called it the Holy Alliance: a resurrection of the Holy Roman Empire which had existed in Germany in the Middle Ages. The Holy Alliance not only took high-minded religious views, it took strong political views, in other words, that really good Christians did not believe in constitutional governments but in the control of absolute monarchs. This was not a theme which was at all acceptable to the British government or, for that matter, to Castlereagh, the British delegate.

The Holy Alliance put forward the framework, for the first time since the Middle Ages, of how states should co-operate together, in particular with an implication that if any monarch was in trouble from liberalism, from constitutionalism, the other members of the Holy Alliance would come to his assistance.

In the first few years, after the Congress of Vienna, much of its work seemed satisfactory. There were liberal movements in Germany which were arrested within the German confederation, under the guidance of Metternich. There were liberal conspiracies in Italy, particularly in Naples, where indeed the Austrian army ultimately intervened. After the first few years, it seemed that the Congress of Vienna had established a firm, lasting Europe and that the Holy Alliance was an essential part of it which brought the conservative powers of Europe together and made them a formidable force.

In 1819 there was a second congress at Aix-la-Chapelle (which people nowadays call Aachen). It dealt with fairly routine things, but some much to the good. It arranged for the withdrawal of the foreign armies which had, after the Hundred Days, occupied France. It also terminated the payment of an indemnity from France to the allies and made France a completely independent country, and one which was recognized for good and all as one of the five Great Powers.

Later there was a congress about giving a blessing to Austria for intervening in Naples. And then there came something they hadn't expected – there was a liberal movement in Spain. And with this liberal movement there were the beginnings of a civil war. Alexander at once claimed that here was the great opportunity for the Holy Alliance. There should be a strong military intervention against the liberal leaders in Spain, and the strong intervention should be provided by the Russian army. This did not meet with British approval at all. Not for the first time and certainly not for the last, the British government took the view that, if there was a liberal government out of hand somewhere, it should be allowed to lead its country to destruction, but there should not be an intervention by the Great Powers against this liberal movement.

After a lot of controversy they had yet another congress, this time at Verona. It was the last. Castlereagh was now dead and the Duke of Wellington, a somewhat taciturn man, was the British delegate. When it came to his turn, he just said, 'My instructions are that we're against intervention in Spain.' And every time the discussion went round and it came to him, he just said, 'Against.'

This wrecked the congress. Not only did Verona not arrive at any firm conclusion, but the congress system, as it was set up in 1815, and as people had anticipated it would go on and on, broke down. The old congress, as envisaged in the Holy Alliance, never met after 1822.

As a matter of fact, a very simple way of dealing with the Spanish liberals was then discovered. It was found that Great Britain had no objection if a neighbouring state intervened. The French, at that time being very conservative and also somewhat anxious to use their army which had been out of work ever since 1815, intervened in Spain and restored the absolute monarchy. The British made no complaint and Spain went on its peculiar way, which led to a great many liberal governments in Spain during the nineteenth century and also to a great many risings of resistance against these liberal governments and a confused history of Spain throughout the nineteenth century. But the decisive thing which happened in 1822 is that the congress system broke down.

Alexander provided a certain element of high morality for another two or three years but then disappeared off the scene.

The 'balance of Europe', as it was called, had been created. England and France represented, sometimes they call it the Liberal Alliance, sometimes simply the Western Alliance; they were able to throw their own weight into the balance against Russia. But by this time Russia had lost interest, particularly under Nicholas, in European affairs. It was a landmark when Alexander died. He had been an obsessive European; Nicholas was a Russian, and when he turned his interest to foreign affairs he was interested in the Near East, in Turkey.

He intervened in Turkey more than once, finally being led into the Crimean War, where one sees a perfect pattern of west and east. The two Western powers, England and France, opposed Russia, the Eastern powers, over the question of Turkey. They fought a rather futile, ill-planned war, the Crimean War, which, though it led to the defeat of Russia, did not change the situation at all, except that Russia was somewhat weaker. But there is one thing worth mentioning about the Crimean War, because here was a last echo of the Congress of Vienna.

When England and France, the two Western, supposedly liberal, powers, went to war against Russia, the revolutionaries of Europe urged them to take the war, not only into Turkey but into continental Europe by raising the standard of a free Poland; and though that standard was never raised between 1854 and 1856, there was something like a Polish revolution and an attempt to restore free Poland in the Polish rising of 1863.

More remotely, the Italian revolutionaries had a fantasy that Italy could be liberated as a result of the Crimean War. Indeed, they hoped for some sort of congress, and they were right. One of the rare congresses was held in Paris in 1856. It was a sort of thin resurrection of the Congress of Vienna. It laid down quite a lot of international law, particularly maritime law about when ships could be arrested at sea, and things of this kind. This was not welcome to Great Britain, which wanted to extend British naval power all over the world. It was supported by France but it did not go very far. Nevertheless, the Congress of Paris did achieve something. There was one other congress which also sprang out of the Eastern question. When Russia once more went to war with Turkey in 1877, the whole thing was wound up by a congress at Berlin in 1878, where there was a great European gathering and where, incidentally, Disraeli, Lord Beaconsfield, made a great speech, or so it was said. He was proposing to speak in French. Lord Salisbury had to persuade him to speak in English because he said, 'Everyone is wanting to hear your wonderful English oratory.' What Salisbury and other English people did not want to hear was Disraeli's dreadful French.

That was the last congress until after the First World War. The Congress of Berlin stands out because, in the whole history of the nineteenth century, after the Congress of Vienna it was the one time when all the Great Powers came together and reached some conclusions of value.

The First World War: Armistice

The Great War, as it was called at the time, what we now call the First World War, curiously started without any war aims except, of course, to win. It wasn't until the end of 1916 that the German Chancellor put forward a public pronouncement that the combatants should meet to settle the war, and he had already defined his war aims, though he did not tell anyone what he was going to ask, which was simply that Germany should keep forever all the territory which she had overrun, including Belgium and most of northern France. The following month, Lloyd George also talked about a settlement of war aims, but what he meant was that the Germans should give up everything they had conquered and pay a good deal of compensation into the bargain. So war aims had rather got stuck, and it was not for some time later that anyone discussed seriously how the war should end.

1917 was the first time when general public opinion moved towards the idea that there should be a discussion and a settlement of war. In August 1917 the German Reichstag, which had broken with Bethmann and was moving to the Left, carried a peace resolution. This was the first formal time when the idea of discussing peace was considered. There was no response from the Allies, although they in their turn were worrying that they must bring the war to an end somehow. The other great change which happened in 1917 and raised the question of war aims was the entry of the United States into the war, because from the very first the United States had been fighting for some wider aims than merely victory, because if they wanted victory they could just stay out. They had to stand for something, and this was President Wilson's first attempt to formulate war aims, which he did entirely differently from his associates. The United States was never an ally but simply an associated power, and Wilson felt that he should decide the settlement of the war without considering what England and France felt about it. This was the first occasion when this arose. What happened in 1917 was a development of public opinion rather than a statesmanlike activity.

In the summer of 1917, when the German Social Democrats were getting influential, they proposed a meeting of all Socialists or representatives of all Socialist parties at Stockholm. The Germans were able to go and the Russians were able to go because they had just had a revolution. Neither the British nor the French Socialists were allowed to go: the French Socialists were forbidden by their government, the British Socialists, who were such moderate persons as Ramsay MacDonald and G. H. Roberts, simply would not have been carried by the sailors. They said, 'Whenever we go to sea our ships are sunk by German submarines – we're not going to have anyone going talking to them.' In the end the Stockholm conference did not take place. Still, there was an assertion that something should be done about ending the war, and indeed this was the first time that there was something like a serious discussion. The new Emperor Charles of Austria-Hungary, the Habsburg monarch who had succeeded Francis Joseph in November 1916, put forward proposals for ending the war. He never got down to direct negotiations, this was done at second hand. What he proposed was that Austria-Hungary should act as a mediator and should be rewarded by being given a large slice of Poland, in general conducting the negotiations as though it was a completely impartial power. The Emperor Charles said he hoped to be able to get Alsace and Lorraine for France, giving away, one might say, German territory without ever asking the Germans.

As soon as this story reached the ears of the Germans, they protested and Charles backed down. But it had an effect on both the British and French governments. Throughout 1917 there were constant efforts to come back to Emperor Charles and to stir him up, to encourage his pacific thoughts. He had pacific thoughts all right, but when it came to a programme he ran up against the obstacle that anything he proposed would have to be forced on the Germans, and they were much too strong for him. There was a time when the Western allies said to Charles, 'We're quite prepared to make peace with you if you join with us, or let us through Austria, to invade Germany from the south.' But this would have meant war between Germany and Austria-Hungary and, although the Emperor was certainly stating ideas that he had expressed already, Germany was too strong for him; so that although this business of Austrian negotiations ran on as late as the summer of 1918 and General Smuts, a member of the British War Cabinet, was in Switzerland negotiating with an Austrian delegate, nothing came of it.

In 1917 Russia had a revolution, at first a moderate, democratic revolution and then, in November 1917, the Bolshevik revolution which put the Bolsheviks in power, as they remain to the present day. The Bolsheviks, Lenin in particular, held a clear view that if he offered no indemnities and no annexations, this would capture public opinion in the democratic countries of the West. In any case, he simply declared that the war with Germany was at an end; he said, 'We're not going to fight it any more.' There was then an attempt at a peace conference. It was held in Brest Litovsk, then in Russia, later in Poland, and it ran over the whole winter. Trotsky made his reputation there for the first time because he argued persistently with the Germans that any attempts to annex Russian territory were against democratic principles and the wider principles that the Germans themselves claimed to support. In the end the negotiations simply broke down because, though Trotsky could argue much better than the Germans did, the answers, particularly of the representatives of the German General Staff, were to say, 'Well, we don't care whether what we're doing is right or wrong, we're going to do it, and we're going to take a lot of Russian territory.' Trotsky then hit on another solution – as he thought – where he simply said, 'We proclaim neither peace nor war. We stop fighting but we are not going to make a peace with you because you're asking too much. So I just announce the war is over. Good morning.'

And he went back to Moscow. He calculated that the German High Command would not have the nerve to break off peaceful relations and march further into Russia. He was wrong. The German army began to roll forward. Lenin, who had always foreseen this, insisted that Trotsky must go back to Brest Litovsk and sign the Robbers' Treaty, which he did. Russia lost a lot of territory. As things turned out, it was for a comparatively short space of time. But sensationally one part of the war was over, that is to say Germany was no longer fighting Russia and the German army was not needed in the east – though as a matter of fact it was needed to hold down the difficult peoples of European Russia. But it left Germany free for a last offensive, and from March 1918 until August, the Germans were rolling forward and many people anticipated a complete defeat for England and France.

In August things turned the other way. The Germans had run out of strength, and when the Allies, that is to say Haig and the French Commander-in-Chief, sent their armies forward they achieved something that they had never done in the preceding three years: they broke through. From August onwards the allied armies were advancing, driving the Germans back, and the Germans very soon would have to anticipate complete defeat. Meanwhile the German front was collapsing in the east. In September 1918 Bulgaria made peace, which meant that the Allies could roll forward into southern Austria-Hungary and that the Austrians too were facing collapse. This was very sensational. On 29 September, Ludendorff's nerve broke. He said that the Germans must make an armistice at once.

By this time there had been an advance towards democracy in Germany and a democratic Chancellor called Prince Max of Baden. Prince Max insisted that they should approach the United States first because, he said, 'If we can settle the United States it doesn't matter about the others, but we will negotiate with them not on terms of an armistice but on general terms for the future.' And for nearly a month the Germans and President Wilson negotiated. Wilson had devised a whole set of peace principles called 'The Fourteen Points' and did not bother to consult the associated powers. Indeed, when he had got the Germans to accept the Fourteen Points, as he did at the end of October, he assumed that the Allies would accept them too. There were bitter meetings of the allied leaders, the British, the French, the Italians. When they first met, Clemenceau, the French Premier, said to Lloyd George, 'Do you know what the Fourteen Points are?' Lloyd George said, 'I've never read them.' But in the two or three days that were left to them they had to go through these points, decide on them. In theory, of course, the Allies were as much committed to the Fourteen Points as the Americans were, because Wilson had put them out. There remained the armistice to settle. This too was negotiated with President Wilson, and when the time came for the Allies to settle the armistice – it was Foch particularly who conducted the armistice negotiations – there again he had not known what the terms were that President Wilson had agreed with the Germans, he just had to accept them.

Meanwhile there was a revolution in Germany. The Kaiser was overthrown and a government of Social Democrats was established which accepted the principle that at once the war must be brought to an end. But this was only part of what happened in Europe.

The main decision certainly was between Germany and the conflicting powers, but the European war during the past two or three years had spread more widely. Firstly there was Austria-Hungary fighting both in the Balkans and in Italy, and then there was Turkey, or the Ottoman Empire, involved in fighting in Europe and also in Asia, and up until now they had been kept in line by the Germans. There was a gradual breakdown of German powers. Up to September 1918 Austria-Hungary, and the Turks for that matter, imagined that if they were in difficulty German forces could come to help them. By September of 1918 Germany had not the forces with which to assist her allies. Everything was breaking down and the allies of Germany had to face their own problem of making armistice, which they did with whichever of the Allies happened to be on the spot. For instance, the Sultan of Turkey made an armistice with the commander of a British battleship which got up to Constantinople when the Straits became opened. The armistice was duly signed, but Clemenceau was furious at this and said the Sultan should have signed with France as well. So the armistice was cancelled until a French battleship could go up to Constantinople so that the Sultan, or his representative, could sign their armistice too.

The first formal armistice between the Allies and what were called the Central Powers was at the end of September, when Bulgaria signed with the French commander and opened the door, as Ludendorff complained, to the allied armies. By the beginning of October the whole situation was moving towards a German collapse, with the additional factor that the Habsburg monarchy of Austria-Hungary not only agreed to armistices with its various contending allied forces, but collapsed – it broke altogether. Earlier in the year, when the British and French had been asked about a war aim, they had replied, 'One of our war aims is national self-determination' – that every area which was inhabited by a separate nationality could claim its own national state. This was a tremendous encouragement to the nationalities of Austria-Hungary and, as soon as the chance came, at the end of October, the Czechs proclaimed the Czecho-slovak Republic and the Croats, Slovenes and Serbs all put themselves under the authority of the King of Serbia in a federation which became Yugoslavia. Finally in October the Italians negotiated with Austria-Hungary and on 3 November the Austrian commander in Italy, because he was fighting still on Italian soil, signed an armistice of complete surrender. The Austrian armies broke up. The soldiers went back as best they could. Austria-Hungary ceased to exist and what remained, on 10 November, was the Austrian Republic, the republic which still exists. (This was not the end of the break-up for Austria-Hungary. In November the French armies operating from Salonika reached the frontiers of Hungary and imposed a stern, crushing armistice on the new republican state of Hungary because Hungary was regarded as an ally of Germany, not one of the peoples struggling to be free. This was quite wrong.)

Back to November 1918: the Germans accepted that they would seek for an armistice. The situation was very confused. There was a revolution in Berlin, there was fighting in the streets. Somehow a peace delegation was got together. It crossed the allied lines in the dark and was confronted in a railway carriage at Rethonde with the allied Commander-in-Chief, Marshal Foch. Foch is reputed to have asked, 'What are these persons doing here?' and the officer who brought them in said, 'They've come to seek an armistice', to which Foch merely said, '*Très bien.*' He then dictated the terms. There was no clear negotiation, simply a statement of terms, and the German delegation was in no position to turn them down. Erzberger, the leader of the delegation, attempted to make some impression and to say that with the terrible conditions of food shortage in Germany, he hoped that as soon as the armistice was signed food supplies could be sent through to the German people. His request was ignored.

There was one other aspect. Foch and his staff negotiated without any authority on behalf of all the allied powers, particularly, of course, of Great Britain, and for that matter of Belgium, and even the United States. There was one non-French representative, Admiral Wemyss, who spoke for the British because they attached importance to the surrender of the German fleet, and this was inserted as one of the terms of the armistice.

The negotiations for the armistice took about eight days. First of all the German delegation had to hear it all, then they had to take it back to Berlin, then they had to come back. It was only at 11 o'clock on 11 November that the armistice actually came into force. And when it came into force, it was one of a great number. Broadly, the fighting stopped all over Europe and indeed all over Asia Minor. It did not mean that the fighting stopped for long. Already British and French troops were moving into Russia and preparing for the war of intervention against the Bolsheviks which they tried to conduct, ineffectually, until 1921. But in this hugger-mugger of a way, a war which had started in confusion, with no clear definition at the beginning of what the war aims were, ended with no clear idea of war aims either. Everything was passed over to the great peace conference in Paris which was to follow in 1919 to make a new world. Whether they succeeded in that is a different matter, but what is certain is that with the general signature of armistice the Great War was over and with it the connection of Europe with its past.

The First World War:
The Peace Conference

The Paris Peace Conference of 1919 was the most ambitious peace conference there had ever been to date, although it has been eclipsed in later days. It was a conference not only to settle one peace, the peace with Germany, but to make peace with all the powers and to deal with a lot of things that were never involved in the war at all. People often refer to the peace settlement as the Settlement of Versailles. That really is technically wrong. The peace conference met in Paris, it met all over the place, wherever they could get people into committee rooms; but when they were actually having the signature of a peace treaty, they needed some bigger assembly hall, somewhere that Paris could not provide. The French, fortunately, had a number of palaces scattered round Paris, and they took over one of these for the day. The most important was, of course, the peace treaty with Germany, which was signed at Versailles. So one is entitled to refer to the Treaty of Versailles, but one is not entitled to refer to the Congress or Conference of Versailles.

There were plenty of other moves out to palaces. The peace treaty with little Austria was signed at Saint-Germain, the peace treaty with a very much curtailed Hungary was signed at the Trianon. The peace treaty with Bulgaria was signed at Neuilly and the peace treaty with Turkey would have been signed at Sèvres, but they never got it off the ground as a peace treaty because the Turks turned against it.

Another interesting point – the peace conference of 1919 was not a congress even though far more people attended it than attended the earlier congresses. The difference is this. The Paris Peace

Conference drew up the peace treaties with the enemies. When a particular peace treaty was ready, the defeated foe sent delegates who turned up at a meeting, not to argue, but solely to sign the peace treaty. In other words, what met at Paris was a conference, and because the enemy was never represented at this conference, it never became a congress. In 1878, for instance, the Turks who had been defeated in the recent war turned up for the congress just as much as the Russians turned up. But no congress has ever been held since. In 1945 the Germans did not get much of a look in to say what they had to say.

What we had was an enormous gathering of diplomats – committees of all kinds, committees dealing with this point, committees dealing with that point and a directing body which started with about twelve Foreign Secretaries from the main countries and swelled up sometimes to twenty or so. But after the conference, which met originally in January, had been meeting for a little while, quite without authority from anyone except themselves, the really great men took it over and became the directing bodies. The great men were originally the big three – President Wilson, the most important because he was a sovereign in himself, he was a directing power, Lloyd George who was a Prime Minister at any rate, and Clemenceau from France. After about a month or so, Orlando the Italian Prime Minister, who really had not had much to do with the war except in Italy – he had never been involved in the French war – came from Italy and became one of the big four, though his standing was nothing like as great as the others. And after that again, there came a representative from Japan. This was awkward, as it made the numbers up to five. The question was raised with the Japanese: 'What will happen if the European delegates vote two each?' To which the Japanese delegate replied, very ingeniously: 'Japan always goes with the majority.' How you get a majority when it's two-all is difficult to say, but that is a course that Japan followed thereafter.

The Supreme Council, as it was called, was more than merely a negotiating body. It took over the Supreme War Council, which had run the war in its latter stages, so that it was both an executive body – deciding where armies should go to, what steps should be taken of a purely practical kind – and a negotiating body. The big three, or big four, were not very well instructed, say, in the techniques of European geography. Harold Nicolson describes going to a meeting of the big four in President Wilson's private flat – that is another thing about the Supreme Council, it did not have an official meeting-place, it just met in Wilson's flat – and Nicolson describes going in to give some advice to the big four and finding these great men, all men in their fifties or older, crawling about over the floor, studying maps and discovering places they had never heard of before, of which they were going to decide the fate, move the frontiers and do things of this kind.

Their predominant problem, it was true, was peace with Germany. Germany was the only great power among the enemy powers. Austria-Hungary had been a great power, but it had dissolved into pieces: it had become Austria, a republic, Hungary, another republic (and at that moment a left-wing republic, at that), and then new states which had been carved out of the old Austrian empire, particularly Czechoslovakia and Yugoslavia, much of which had been Austrian.

Hungary had not ranked as a great power, but it had been a significant power. It lost far more territory than it should have lost because whenever one of the succession states, as they were called, claimed Hungarian territory, it got it, even though it was inhabited by Czechs or Romanians – when the Hungarians tried to put up the same case, they were pushed aside as former enemies.

But the basic question was to make a peace treaty with Germany. The determining factor was the series of principles which Wilson had laid down just before America entered the war – the Fourteen Points. These were to lay down a pattern not only for the world, for the League of Nations and so on, but particularly for dealings with Germany. The Germans, in September 1918, had accepted them. The allies had not been told of them at all until about a fortnight before the war ended, and both England and France made some – though not very important – reservations about them. When they got to the peace conference they just tried to avoid them altogether. The first thing they had to deal with Germany was to determine the new frontiers. It was quite easy for France to recover

Alsace and Lorraine, which indeed she did, without ever making a peace treaty. The French said: 'It's always been ours, and we'll just move into it.' The problem of German frontiers lay on the eastern side.

A considerable problem of the peace conference takes us straight back to the peace congress of 1814. What was the main problem of 1814? It was whether Poland should be resurrected. What was the predominant or a predominant problem of the peace conference of 1919 and 1920? It was not so much whether Poland should be resurrected, the Allies had agreed that that was to happen, but what territories should Poland have? Should it have solely the territory inhabited by Poles or was it entitled to go back to the earlier, say seventeenth-century, frontiers and claim vast territories which Poland had occupied? The Polish question was to give, before the conference ended, the most acute problems and bring the Allies nearest to war again.

There were other territories which were lost to Germany – a bit of territory to Belgium, a bit of territory to Denmark, but the main consideration was two-fold.

One – the Allies, the British and the French, had ended the war with a promise that Germany should be made to pay. Pay what? Pay street damages which the Germans had caused? Pay on a high grade of penalties? Or simply pay all the costs of the war, including what it had cost to England, France, America and anybody else? Actually, the Americans did not ask for the costs of the war, but the British did and the French still more, and then the Belgians took the view that they had been particularly badly treated because Germany invaded them without any excuse whatsoever and that they ought to be compensated down to the last franc.

Then, two, there was a problem which took up a lot of time and negotiation. War criminals should be punished. But what are war criminals? War criminals are leaders on the other side who have not so much caused the war as lost it. That is why war criminals get punished. They do not get punished because they started the war, they get punished because they were fools enough to lose it. In 1919 the Allies had one chief criminal, the ex-Kaiser, who had taken refuge in Holland. The Dutch refused to release him. The

Allies talked of banning Holland, occupying Holland, blockading Holland. The Dutch just said, 'We do not surrender the Kaiser.' And after two or three years of argument, they did not surrender him, but it was put in the treaty that he was a supreme war criminal. There were trials in Germany of a few war criminals that amounted to nothing.

Indemnities took up a lot of discussion. And then there was a discussion as to whether the Allies should dictate a new form of government. Fortunately, the Germans themselves had had a revolution and had established a parliamentary republic, so the actual dictation of a form of government did not arise. There was, too, a problem associated with the distribution of territory. It was not only a matter of depriving Germany of home territory – what should happen to the German colonies? The British, in particular, held the view that they should get the German colonies on a very simple principle: when Great Britain goes to war, she always gets some colonies. The British, therefore, invented the idea that the Germans were worse at ruling colonies than they were and that they, or the Dominions as they were called, should get some of the German colonies.

Most important of all were the precautions which should be taken so that Germany could not renew the war or have a second world war. And precautions were of two kinds. One, the actual size of the German army was restricted to, altogether, 100,000 men, and the armaments were restricted – no tanks, no aircraft, and so on. The other precaution that was taken was that the whole of West Germany, that is to say Germany up to the Rhine and in certain cases beyond, was put under allied occupation. The Treaty of Versailles did not speculate how long, though it did suggest it would be for fifteen or twenty-five years. Then there was something else very important from the British point of view – not only was the German navy to be surrendered (and it was surrendered so wholeheartedly that the Germans then sank it just at the time when the peace treaty was being signed), but the Germans were to have no more navy, at any rate until the peace treaty could be revised in ten or twenty years.

These were some of the things which were discussed by the

Supreme Council, and in time they got a peace treaty ready and finally they had an elaborate ceremonial at the Palace of Versailles. When the German delegates came in, they were told that they could not make any reply, though in fact one of them made a short speech, just saying more or less that the loser has to have a peace treaty imposed on him and that the Germans signed purely after protest. The most symbolic act at the peace conference was the signing of this extraordinary document. One could not call it a peace treaty; it was a treaty calculated to provoke the Germans and lead them to work for a wholesale revision of the treaty and a restoration of Germany back into the ranks of civilized nations.

At the same time President Wilson was very anxious indeed to get the League of Nations going. Indeed he made it a condition with his allies that they should draw up a charter of the League of Nations before they did anything else, and that it should be the first clause in the German peace treaty, because the German peace treaty would be the first to be signed, and therefore he could get the League of Nations in first.

The curious situation is that, although Wilson always thought highly about the treaty, he had not thought about it in practical terms and he had no draft of how it should be constituted – no constitution, no rules, no charter altogether of the League of Nations. Wilson was hopeless about this, saying, 'Well, we must . . . when can we do this?' when the British Foreign Secretary said, 'Oh, we went into this at the beginning of the war, we drew up a charter of the League of Nations and here it is.' So what, in fact, Wilson imposed on the world was a draft League of Nations which had been prepared by the British really under quite different circumstances.

It was regarded by Wilson, and by many people at the time, as the greatest step forward. The principle of the League of Nations was to bring all the powers together and to lead to international affairs being carried out not only by negotiation but through the instrumentality of the League of Nations, which would gradually make rivalry, hostility, between the independent states unnecessary and unlikely. At any rate, if one was to say what people thought at the time was the really sensational thing about the Paris Peace

Conference, they would not have said, I think, the Treaty of Versailles – that was something that was bound to happen, that you take it out on the Germans – but the League of Nations, which was to bring something quite new and quite special. The great powers directed the League of Nations. There was a League of Nations Council composed of the greater powers, and then an Assembly with all the lesser ones . . . the greater powers were, it was supposed, committed to support the League of Nations and somehow to solve the problem of enforcing the declarations of the League of Nations without armed force, though what would be done when one of the members of the League of Nations broke away was not clear at the time. The League of Nations was a promise for the future. It was not dealt with at Paris at all.

The peace conference at Paris spent more time drawing up frontiers in central and eastern Europe than in dealing with the German frontiers, which were done in a couple of days. The whole of east Europe was in a turmoil. The older states, particularly Austria-Hungary, had collapsed and great stretches of territory were disputed. Broadly speaking, the various committees drawn up tended, when they were faced with a decision to make between two powers, always to support the allied power, or one which had claimed to be the allied power. This is very true in regard to Italy. Italy had been promised South Tyrol. South Tyrol was inhabited by Germans. But because Italy had won, German-speaking Austria was given to Italy. More gravely than this, in what you might call the eastern side of Italy the territory which had been Austrian was inhabited by Yugoslavs, partly by Croats, mainly by Slovenes. But the Italians said, 'We can't allow them to go into the hands of Slovenes or Croats because that would give us an enemy on our frontier.' And a great block, most of the Slovenes of Austria, were in fact transferred to Italy and were not liberated from Italy until after the Second World War.

Hungary, as I have said, came off very badly. Whenever there was a decision to be made as to how the territories should go, it went against the Hungarians. The Hungarians lost a great deal of territory to the Czechs, they lost territory to the Romanians, territory which incidentally is still in Romanian hands. There is a curious point arising from this too. The Czechs inhabited a territory which had been entirely Austrian – or, rather, part of the Austrian empire – and if the Austrian empire had been an enemy, then the decision ought to have gone against the Czechs. But the Czechs managed to claim that they had liberated themselves and set up a territory of Czechoslovakia on their own, so the decisions always came down on their side. As a result, out of ten million inhabitants in Czechoslovakia, at least three million were German; and it was this grievance which led Hitler to move against Czechoslovakia twenty years later. It is difficult to believe that it was a grievance without any justification.

The treatment of the Hungarian minority was and is scandalous. They are not allowed to use their own language, they are compelled to use Romanian, and they are one of the aggrieved nationalities who have gone on being aggrieved right to the present day. This was the doing of the peace conference in 1919. But as soon as one looks at it, one is bound to say to oneself, 'What other policy could they have followed?' When they had to decide what should happen over certain territories, they were bound to incline to those who were, or claimed to be, allies. Curiously enough, the British were very soft on the Czechs, although the Czechs had not done any fighting on the allied side, except when Czech prisoners-of-war in Asia had turned themselves into a Czech legion and fought against the Bolsheviks. It has to be said that that was always a good recommendation in 1919, to be against the Bolsheviks.

There is a great deal more to be said about the peace conference, but the two most important things in settling the pattern of Europe were the various indemnities. Poor, reduced Austria (which was bankrupt) had to pay an indemnity; Hungary had to pay an indemnity, although the only way in which she could do it was to borrow money from either American banks or British banks (in the end, it was the British banks who paid). And there was plenty that was left over, which was to raise problems in the future. Turkey broke away from the system because the Sultan was overthrown (though the Allies continued to recognize him) and a new Turkey started in Asia Minor, led by Kemal Ataturk. This nearly caused a war in 1922. But in the end Turkey came off much better than anyone else because, by having broken with the Sultan and turned into a rebel revolutionary state, she had been able to assert herself as a great power or something like it. At any rate, the Turks did not pay any indemnity and nor did they lose any territory; rather the reverse.

The gravest problem at the peace conference which the leaders were never able to solve was what to do with Soviet Russia. Soviet Russia had made peace with Germany. Then, the moment that the Germans gave in, the Bolshevik government had simply repudiated the treaty of Brest Litovsk, and therewith had not paid any more indemnities to the Germans, or indeed to anyone else. The Bolsheviks simply declared their independence.

The Allies held a great deal against the Bolsheviks. Firstly, they had made peace. For this they ought to be punished. Secondly, when the peace came they had repudiated the peace treaty with Germany: they were no longer paying indemnities to anyone, but were trying to build up their own state. Thirdly, of course, they were Bolshevik – which was very undesirable in 1919, and one of the minor activities of the Supreme Council was to conduct a very ineffective war of intervention in which the French and the British, and to a lesser extent the Americans, all joined.

By 1920 the problem had become acute, not in terms of either direct intervention in European Russia or Asiatic Russia, but because Poland, quite without any justification, had decided to reclaim all the territory which she had possessed in the seventeenth century. Marshal Pilsudski led an army as far as Kiev, which is deep inside Russia, not a single Pole inhabiting it. Much to the dismay of everyone, the Bolsheviks hit back. The Red Army, directed by Trotsky, defeated the Poles and drove them right out of Russia, and then advanced on Warsaw. They were within sight of Warsaw, and, if they had got there, would certainly have proclaimed a Bolshevik Poland and then marched on into Germany.

Fortunately for the Poles, the Russian advance was stopped, and they were able to counter-advance in their turn and to acquire not only the territory which had been rectified by the Allies, but some which they had claimed themselves. Yet Poland was still in danger in August 1920. The French said they must intervene on the Polish side. Lloyd George spoke on the issue and was threatened with a general strike by the TUC. Fortunately, before he had to make a decision – it was quite clear he never intended to support the Poles, he took a very poor view of them and was much more in favour of the Bolsheviks – the whole affair fizzled out. There was no armed assistance from the Allies and they regarded Poland with great irritation for having caused this crisis. But the Polish crisis of 1920 was only one of many crises which would originate from the logical consequences of the Peace Treaty of 1919. And in the end it was Poland, which had nearly caused a war in 1920, which caused a war in 1939.

The Second World War

The First World War ended with peace and, apart from the Treaty of Brest Litovsk, the fighting all came to an end in November 1918.

The Second World War was much more ragged. It began to end as early as June 1940 and it went on, in Japan, until September 1945. In June 1940 France went out of the war and made an armistice with Germany. From 1940 to 1944, official France at any rate was not at war. It is true that parts of France were occupied by the Germans, but an unassuming, non-political Frenchman could have passed the years 1940 to 1944 without noticing that there was a war on at all. It was only with the return of de Gaulle and the victory of the Allies that France was drawn into the war for the last peace. But there was an actual ending of the war, too, for what was after all a very considerable country. More significant – or more preparatory, shall I say – to the ending of the war was the way in which Italy, after some difficulty, drew out of the war in 1943. In July of 1943 Mussolini was overthrown when the official state council turned against him. He was at first interned and later withdrew into northern Italy to set up the Italian Socialist Republic which did not amount to very much. There was however a new government in Italy officially appointed by the king under Marshal Badoglio and from the beginning, that is to say the end of July 1943, it began to put out feelers for a peace arrangement or armistice or short-lived peace treaty. Negotiations went on until October. Earlier in the year, in January, when President Roosevelt met Churchill in Morocco, he had brought into being a new concept, that of unconditional surrender. Roosevelt said, 'We don't want a lot of negotiations, we don't want armistice terms and so on, what we demand from the Axis Powers is unconditional surrender and we'll accept nothing less.'

The first time that this was discussed with the Italians, it went on for some six weeks, mainly with the British High Command in North Africa. The British High Command simply could not stomach the idea that there should be unconditional surrender, and that the allied commanders should be in supreme control of Italy. They negotiated the terms of unconditional surrender, so that one can say that, in a sense, Italy made a conditional surrender. It was only when the Italians had accepted the short-term conditions of this very long negotiation that they eventually accepted the longer-term conditions in the course of the autumn. But there were terms of a sort and, most importantly, Italy – official Italy, that is – withdrew from the war and the Italian government put itself under the control of the supreme allied command – at that time headed by a British general.

This was less successful than the British and Americans had hoped for. They believed that when they took over Italy they would be able to put themselves into the position of the Italian government and exercise over Italy the supreme control which previously had belonged to the Italian government itself. They allowed the negotiations to go on too long. By the time that they had agreed on unconditional surrender with Italy, the Germans had been able to bring up the German forces to supersede the Italian forces (which were now not fighting at all) and to occupy practically the whole of Italy. It was not until mid-1944 that the British and Americans reached Rome, and it was not until the very end of the war (at the beginning of 1945) that the British and American forces penetrated up into northern Italy. There were two Italies – in fact there were three Italies. There was an Italy exclusively occupied by the Allies, there was an Italy exclusively occupied by the Germans, and then there was an area in between which was technically under the control of Mussolini and the Italian Socialist Republic. That did not amount to much: he simply had to do what the Germans told him. But Italy, at any rate, became an unusual sort of combatant. The only Italians who did any fighting were not the official Italian army, which simply disarmed itself, but the Italian partisans, who increased in activity during the last year of the war. This was the most significant withdrawal from the war as a sign that the Axis defeat was beginning.

The withdrawal of France in 1940 was a recognition of German power. The withdrawal of Italy from the war in 1943 was significantly enough an indication that Italy, the second Axis power, had lost all faith in German victory and was trying to get out of the war. What it meant instead was that the Germans superseded Italian forces and had to exercise military operations in a wider field. It was not until the next year that the habit of unconditional surrenders spread. There was nothing very decisive. What characterized that year was that it was the great year of fighting. In 1944, indeed, the allied landings in France after D-Day meant that within a relatively short time France could be brought into the war, and well before the end of the war the French army was in effective action. By early 1945 some of the German generals had come to recognize that the war was lost and that the wisest course was to make an agreement of some sort with the Allies as soon as possible. The sooner the better, because they might be allowed to retain some of their authority.

In the late winter – February of 1945 – the German High Command had a series of unofficial secret negotiations through Switzerland with the allied High Command. They ran up against the difficulty all the time that the allied High Command had to insist on unconditional surrender, whereas what these generals wanted was, of course, conditional surrender in which they would be perhaps even accepted as allies.

There was another difficulty which sprang up for the first time now. Throughout the war Russia, of course, had had to follow an independent path because she was cut off from her allies by the whole of central Europe. As the Russians drew closer into Europe they began to concern themselves that they, as one of the three Great Powers, should also have a say in dealings with Italy in the West. And when they heard rumours that the secret negotiations with the Germans in Italy were afoot, they accused the Western powers of secretly negotiating with the Germans and trying to make a separate peace and then prepare to resist any further Russian advance. These Russian suspicions, which were almost entirely unjustified, made it impossible for the British to go on negotiating with the Germans for fear that the Russians would hear about it and object. Whether the Russians ever negotiated separately with the Germans and tried to deal with them is still a disputed point. It has been alleged that at some time in 1943 Molotov, the then Russian Foreign Minister, flew over to Germany and met Ribbentrop for discussions which went on for two days. This has always been denied by the Russians and it is difficult to substantiate, but at any rate the possibility was there. And one can say on the other side that much earlier in the war there had possibly been some sort of negotiations with the Germans. When Hess came to Britain in 1941 there is every indication that he thought he was going to meet groups of British people who were anxious to sit down and talk about peace with Germany. He never had his conversations, even if they were allowed. In any case, that was a long time in the past. By the spring of 1945 the Western and the Eastern allies were contemplating the certainty that negotiations with the Germans would take place. What actually happened was more complicated.

In the earlier months of 1945, not only the German command in Italy but the German command in Western Europe began to urge that there should be some attempts at approaching the Allies, particularly the Western allies, in order probably by now to make unconditional surrender, but in any case an agreement. What was in the minds of some Western commanders already was that if they could make a quick peace with Germany, then the German forces could remain mobilized and could check any Russian attempt to move further into Europe. This again is a dark subject. That there were negotiations with the German army in Italy is certain. Whether there were ever German negotiations with the Allies in northern Europe is much more doubtful, for a very simple reason – that right until the last moment Hitler continued to exercise effective supreme control. German generals talked about unconditional surrender, about negotiations with the Allies, but they ran up against Hitler's ruthless will. Nobody dared go against him. There was more than one attempt, but none of them came off. And right up until the last minute, until the beginning of May 1945, Hitler was still rigidly determined that resistance should go on to the last German.

It was only the suicide of Hitler at the end of April 1945 that opened the way for the Germans to negotiate with the Allies. And the Germans had left it rather late. If they had offered negotiations during the Normandy campaign of 1944, they might have got some response. By 1945 the Allies were clearly not only winning, but they were achieving complete success and no longer needed to think of how to eliminate the German armies. The German armies were being defeated, the Russians were on their way to Berlin, and the Allies were on their way to the Elbe line. There is no evidence at all that the Western powers contemplated doing a deal with the Germans as late as May 1945. As soon as Hitler was dead, the remaining authorities in Germany, both the generals and the successor to Hitler, so far as there was one – Hitler claimed to have appointed Admiral Dönitz his successor as Chancellor of Germany, and though Dönitz was shut away somewhere near the frontier of Denmark, in so far as there was a German government after Hitler's death, it was Dönitz's – sent Jodl, one of the Chiefs of Staff, to Paris to offer unconditional surrender.

The deal was done in a very short time, and the surrender marked for most people in the West the end of the war. Or, in so far as we contemplate the war at all now, we think of it as ending on 8 May, for 8 May was the day on which Jodl signed the agreement of unconditional surrender with Eisenhower as Supreme Commander on the Western front. The German Marshal Keitel then had to go to Moscow as well or to the Russian front in order to sign the agreement for unconditional surrender to the Russians with Zhukov, and that was not signed until a day later. This explains the curious fact that, whereas the Western powers celebrate the end of the war on 8 May, the Russians and the rest of the Eastern front celebrate the end of the war on 9 May, the day after.

The war in Europe was ended. There were confused times. For instance, by June 1945 British troops in northern Italy were contemplating having to go to war with Yugoslavia, an ally, who had insisted on occupying more than (or what the British said was more than) her share. The Yugoslavs occupied some stretches of Trieste but never managed to occupy it all and in time were persuaded to go away again. For all practical purposes the European war stopped.

The war had stopped on the Western front, it had stopped on the Eastern front, it had stopped in the Balkans. One war was still in full spate, and that was the Japanese war. Until this time, the Japanese war had been very much an American affair. The Americans had conducted the whole show and were gradually driving the Japanese back into a position of defeat. But the Japanese, although they recognized that they were going to lose the war, were determined not to surrender, or not to offer unconditional surrender. What is more, there was – and this had been a characteristic of Japanese policy all along – more than one group. There were sensible, moderate statesmen who had never liked the war against the Allies and would have been glad to get out of the war on moderate terms as early as possible. There was a hard militarist group, who had dominated Japanese policy ever since 1931, who thought in terms of military control and advance and had, of course, carried Japanese authority far down into the Pacific Ocean. The Japanese were now in retreat; but it was a retreat which had only just begun, and the militarist group were prepared to argue. They argued two things: that the longer the war went on, the more likely it was that Japan could get more tolerable terms; and, simply, that Japan ought not to offer any terms at any time but compel the Allies to destroy Japan literally before they would agree to ending the war.

By 1945 the balance was shifting somewhat from the out-and-out militarists to those who were prepared to negotiate. In June and early July the Japanese government made approaches through Russia, offering a peace of unconditional surrender on honourable terms to the Americans. The offer never reached the Americans, because Stalin, once the European war was over, was anxious that Russia should enter the Far Eastern war and acquire territory which the Russians had previously lost, after the war of 1905 and at other times. Unfortunately he had no troops in the Far East and this would take him some time. Therefore it was essential to Stalin that the war should go on, so that then he could move in and perhaps even occupy parts of Japan before the Americans were there at all.

This threw out all the Japanese calculations. They had assumed that they could use Russia, they had used Russia for a long time as a negotiating agent and had been conciliatory towards Russia, and the Russians had been conciliatory towards Japan until the war ended. But once the war ended, then Russia could turn around and simply prepare for a new war against Japan.

The Japanese could not bring themselves to make any direct offer until the last minute to the American government, and the American government was now in a great quandary. How should they complete the defeat of Japan? The navy said that they should rely on the blockade and that this would bring Japan to surrender. The army said that the American army should land in Japan and, despite the fact that there would then be enormous casualties, should go on to occupy Japan. The army preparations were not even made. It meant that the war would drift on for a long time to come. The navy argument did not demand so many casualties, but it too demanded time. Early in August came the first indications that Japan was prepared to offer unconditional surrender. The one condition that the Japanese made was that they should retain their emperor. And this, at first, was the one condition which the Americans would not accept because, quite wrongly, they blamed the emperor for the war. The emperor had been opposed to the war before it started and during it, but, despite his so-called standing, he had no real power: he had to do what the generals said.

The Americans were gloomily contemplating a war that seemed to be going on for ever when there arose, ready prepared, the atom bomb. The scientists insisted they must use it in order to justify to Congress all the money that had been spent on it. They had no idea what it would be like, they had no idea of the extent of the destruction; but there was dropped, first a bomb on Hiroshima and then a bomb on Nagasaki. Both of them caused terrible destruction and ghastly sufferings to the Japanese people. The first one left the Japanese dazed. The second led the emperor to resolve, against the generals' will, against the risk to his own life from the extremists, that, as he said, 'The war must come to an end. We must endure the unendurable.' And on 17 August he announced over the radio that he personally was accepting unconditional surrender. This was, to all practical purposes, the end of the war. Technically, however, it was not the end of the war. This is a quaint little feature to the end of the story.

The unconditional surrender had to be made to a superior high-standing American authority. There was only one American authority of the first rank in the vicinity: the Supreme Commander, General MacArthur. But General MacArthur was in the Philippines and it took him ten days to come up on a battleship to Tokyo Harbour. There, on 2 September, a Japanese statesman signed the agreement of unconditional surrender, and with that General MacArthur became, for the next five years almost, supreme ruler of Japan. The Second World War was over.

Present Chaos

There is a curious thing about the earlier great wars which I have been talking about. Each ended with a great conference. The war of 1814 ended with the Congress of Vienna. The First World War of the twentieth century ended with the Paris Peace Conference in the first six months of 1919.

The greatest of all wars so far, the Second World War, ended raggedly. People find it very difficult to define the moment and say, 'Now the Second World War is over.' Normally what we do is accept the date of 8 May 1945, when the Germans agreed to unconditional surrender. But that only affected one war, the war against Germany. If we were talking about the Italian war, we would say either in 1943, when some of Italy agreed to unconditional surrender, or, more technically, 1947, when the Allies negotiated a peace treaty. But if we were to say that we should wait till the last peace treaty, the final one which finished all wars, that would be the allied treaty with Japan in 1951. Then again, this is difficult because Russia made a different treaty with Japan after objecting to the proposals that our allies were making. And if we are to say that war ended when a state of peace was declared with Germany, then that could be either 1955 or even 1958. In 1955 the Western powers, Great Britain and the United States, recognized what we came to call the Federal State of Germany, that is to say West Germany, as a sovereign state no longer under Allied occupation. It would be possible to wait until the Russians recognized the East German state as a separate body. That would be either earlier or later.

It also becomes rather hard to get people to agree *where* the war ended. I think I am right in saying that the war has ended now. But it took at least ten years to get it tidied up.

What were the great obstacles and where were the stages of the ending of the war? In one sense, as I say, there was a dramatic ending of what was the biggest war, that is to say the war against the Allies, Great Britain, Russia, the United States, which ended with the unconditional surrender of Germany on either 8 May or, according to Russian calculations, 9 May. But there was no agreement of peace for a very long time.

In 1945, at the surrender, the greatest dispute between the Allies was the question of reparations. The Americans, being very rich, said they did not want any reparations and that therefore nor should the Allies have reparations either. The Russians said their whole country had been devastated by the Germans and the Germans must pay a great deal. Grudgingly, the Americans agreed to this in principle, but when it came to the practical application of it, they objected because, they said, 'What is happening is that we are paying the Germans to get Germany on its feet and you're taking away from Germany what we're giving.' But it was not until at least five years after 1945 that the Russians stopped demanding, and not always getting, reparations. Then again, the other great dispute among the Allies – the victors – in 1945 was not about Germany at all, it was about Poland.

This is a fascinating thing. The great dispute in 1814 between the Allies was about Poland. One of the great disputes among the Allies, England and France, in 1919 and particularly in 1920, was over Poland. The most practical dispute, which ran on throughout the meeting of the Allies at Potsdam in 1945, was about Poland, or rather about Poland's western frontier.

In 1920 Poland conquered a lot of what had previously been Russian territory. The Russians had always resented this. When they became the victors, they drove through this territory and took it back from Poland. Poland was thus deprived of territory. People said, 'We can't have that because Poland was numbered among the victors. It's particularly hard to take any territory from her because she has been so appallingly treated by Germany and has been such a gallant resister.' So the Poles were compensated by being given a great stretch of German territory, the frontier as it is now called of the Oder and the Neisse Line. This territory was not inhabited by Poles. And it seemed impossible for the Poles to take territory inhabited by Germans. There was, however, a simple solution which could be applied because a state of war existed. A great deal of the territory which Poland acquired had already been evacuated by its German inhabitants out of terror – although in the course of 1945 and 1946 seven million more Germans were driven out of their homes into western Germany. They have never gone back, and the territory has instead been inhabited by Poles mainly from the territory which Russia had taken from Poland. Now a whole generation has passed and people are beginning to forget these now old frontiers – or I wonder if they are?

This was not the only expulsion of populations that went on in 1945. Something like three million Germans were expelled from Czechoslovakia. People who had been in that territory as long as the Czechs themselves – maybe 1,000 years – out they went in 1945. And these were not the only people who were expelled from Czechoslovakia. About 300,000 Hungarians (or, to be correct, Slovaks who had been originally Hungarians) were cleared out. There were other minorities who were perhaps in the worst situation of all. Romania and Hungary had both, very unwillingly, fought on the German side. Romania had been able to jump about three months, perhaps six months, before the end of the war and be counted as an ally. Hungary, owing to the fumbling nature of the Horthy government, tried to get out of the war and failed. Therefore Romania was treated as an ally whereas Hungary was treated as an enemy. Romania as a result was given some territory in Transylvania. Half a million Hungarians lived there, and live there now, treated very badly because they are not given their national rights. All in all, it was an even worse sorting-out than had been attempted in 1918 and 1919.

This was one of the negotiations. But there were far more difficult problems. The Conference of Potsdam in July 1945 was the last of the great gatherings, though not great in terms of number of assembly. Potsdam was simply the last meeting of the so-called Great Powers: the United States, Soviet Russia, Great Britain. Later, though some of their representatives met again, the heads of state never met in grandeur as they had done in Teheran, in Yalta and in Potsdam. And the Potsdam Conference, far from leading to any conclusion, led to estrangement. One very significant thing was that when President Truman went to Potsdam, it was the first time he had ever been out of the United States. This in itself marked a very great change. One distinguishing feature of President Roosevelt was that he, in his skilful way, had wanted to be on good terms with Russia and had managed to be at the Teheran conference and at the Yalta conference. Indeed, one could go further and say that Yalta was the only meeting of the three Great Powers and therefore the only meeting of the great world powers in history which was a success, where all three wanted to work together and reach agreements.

Already at Potsdam Russia and the United States wanted to encourage conflict and to win against each other. There has never been, from that day to this, a really satisfactory meeting of the Great Powers; of their more modest representatives perhaps, but never of the great rulers again. When Truman came to Potsdam, he had with him a piece of secret knowledge. He believed that the first nuclear weapon would be used in the course of the summer, but until it was used he could not be sure it would succeed. It had never been tried out. When Truman was on the way back to America, he got the news on board ship that the nuclear bomb had been dropped over Hiroshima and he exclaimed, 'This is a great day in the history of the world!' He had no idea how great it was going to be and what troubles it was going to cause.

Why was the nuclear weapon used over Japan? Japan was seeking to make peace. She had sent her messages through Russia, which the Russian government had not passed on because they did not want to – they wanted to get their blow of war in. The American army and the American navy both offered eventual solutions, but there was something more than this. The scientists and technical advisers who had developed the nuclear bomb insisted that if it were to be tried, it must be tried on a real target, so that Congress should be satisfied with all the money that it had paid. Therefore the first bomb was dropped on Hiroshima, not to lead to the collapse of Japan, or even to lead to peace offers from Japan, because Japan was only too eager now to make peace offers. It was dropped as a demonstration to the American Congress.

Nobody knew what it was going to be like. Nobody had conceived the terrible devastation that was caused. What is more, the Japanese did not immediately respond by unconditional surrender. Indeed they tended to take the view, 'Well that's a bomb. We've lost 50,000 people and more killed at Hiroshima, but now the situation is as before.' The Americans had two bombs: one they could use at Hiroshima, and had done; the second, they said they must use, otherwise the Japanese would think that the Hiroshima bomb was the only one, whereas if they used two the Japanese would be overwhelmed. Even though the Japanese might have said after the dropping of the bomb on Nagasaki, 'All right, that's it. We'll stand these two catastrophes and continue with the war.' As it was – this is a very dramatic episode in history – the Japanese government ministers were fully clear that there must be unconditional surrender. None of them dared do it because they said, 'If any of us takes the lead and offers unconditional surrender to the Americans, we shall be massacred by nationalistic Japanese fanatics.' The emperor, who had never given a lead in policy in his life or, one might say, also in history – the emperor was a figurehead – asserted himself for the first and last time. In the middle of August 1945 he went on the air and announced unconditional surrender. But, as I said earlier, it was not until 1951 that the peace treaty with Japan was signed, simply because the Russians put forward terms to which the Allies would not agree, and eventually Japan had to make a separate treaty with Russia.

Meanwhile, the other treaties went forward, and there are great curiosities there. Italy had been, for something like three years, an enemy. One Italian government, though not a government which exercised authority over all Italy (not at any rate until the last days in 1945), had come over and was accepted somewhat grudgingly as an ally, or at any rate as a co-operator with the allied forces. The other one technically remained an enemy although it did not do anything as an enemy. When, in 1947, a peace conference was held in Paris, Italy was the first country that the Allies dealt with.

There were two territorial topics which concerned the Allies. One was whether any of South Tyrol should be restored to Austria, bearing in mind that it was inhabited by Germans or German-speaking people. It was easy enough for the Allies to decide this, since they could say, 'No, Italy should have it, because she's been an ally for a short time and the Austrians were never allies.' Much trickier was the fact that the Yugoslavs, who had been our allies throughout the war, were laying claim to Trieste. But now the Yugoslavs were taking a Communist line of their own, and as Communists they could not be given Trieste; it had to go to the former enemy, Italy, and that was the arrangement of the treaty which was finally made in 1947. There remained plenty of other treaties to make. Romania and Bulgaria made peace fairly quickly and there was nothing much one could dispute, except Transylvania. Hungary was accepted.

Austria was a difficult case. It was like Germany or, rather, it had been part of greater Germany but had managed to jump aside in time, and before the end of the war it had again become independent under Chancellor Renner (who had also made Austria an independent republic at the end of the First War in 1918). Austria was now a small independent republic. Who should garrison it? The four powers agreed that it should pass under their combined authority. Each had a zone of occupation, all four of them occupied Vienna. It was the only place where full allied co-operation continued for ten years after the war. To have a picture of Vienna under allied occupation, remember the Orson Welles film *The Third Man*. The other remarkable thing about Austria is that the Allies actually agreed in the end that she should be a neutral state. She was not allowed to join any of the alliances; she could have her own army and so on, but she was to remain totally independent of the coalitions. She was not an associate of the British and Americans, she was not an associate of the French, she was not an associate of the Russians. She was a guaranteed neutral independent state – which, you might think, set an example to a number of the other small independent states. It certainly worked in the case of Austria.

But the biggest problem, one which almost goes on to the present day – something of it is certainly still with us – was Germany. It was not for some years that the American Congress resolved that a state of war with Germany had ceased to exist. It was not until 1955 that the Americans actually recognized that Federal Germany should have its own independence. Eastern Germany was under Russian occupation and has remained to this day a separate state, completely under Russian control and accepting Russian direction more than the independent Communist states such as Czechoslovakia and Hungary and Romania do. These were not the only problems that came up. In the centre of the two conflicting states there was Berlin, which was divided into four, three of them belonging to the three parts of Germany belonging to the Western powers, one part under Russian control. And Berlin has become not gradually more united but more divided. Berlin was divided in 1960 at the great wall which still exists there. There was an alarm in 1948 when the Russians stopped land transport, road transport and rail transport, from West Germany into Berlin, to which the Allies replied, to everyone's astonishment, successfully with an air lift, which went on for something like a year. The American and British air forces carried everything into western Berlin. Western Germany maintained its independence or separation from Russian control and has retained it.

However, Europe still bears the scars of the Second World War and now seems as if it is resigned to them. There are still millions of Germans who complain at being evacuated from their home all those, nearly forty, years ago. There are hundreds of thousands of Hungarians who grieve at being expelled from their homes in Czechoslovakia. One could go on reciting the various things that have happened. But the greatest legacy we have had from the Second World War is without a doubt the development of nuclear fission and the transformation of this into nuclear weapons. This has now become the most terrifying, the greatest and most threatening danger that hangs over civilization.

However, do not worry. The Third World War will be the last.

MISCELLANEOUS REVIEWS
AND ARTICLES

Lord Derby

Edward Henry Stanley, fifteenth earl of Derby (1826–93), was a major political figure of the second half of the nineteenth century, yet one who fitted uneasily into party politics. He sat as Conservative MP for King's Lynn from 1848 until 1869, when he succeeded his father in the earldom. His father (1799–1869), three times Prime Minister, ensured he remained a Conservative during his lifetime, albeit a notably moderate one. He held office in each of his father's governments: junior office in 1852, Colonial Secretary, President of the Board of Control and then Secretary of State for India in 1858–9 and Foreign Secretary in 1866–8. He served as Foreign Secretary under Disraeli in 1868 and 1874–8, resigning over the Eastern crisis. He left the Conservative party in 1880. He served as Colonial Secretary under Gladstone in 1882–5 but broke with him over Irish Home Rule. He ended his political career as Liberal Unionist leader in the House of Lords, 1886–91.

This essay was first published under the title 'A Political Insider' as a review of J. R. Vincent (ed.), Disraeli, Derby and the Conservative Party: The Political Journals of Lord Stanley 1849–69, *Harvester Press, 1978, in the* Observer, *24 September 1978.*

The diaries of Lord Stanley, who became fifteenth Earl of Derby in 1869, are a great find and John Vincent has edited them impeccably. Stanley's father, the great Lord Derby, was three times a Conservative Prime Minister. Disraeli was Stanley's intimate friend, even though Stanley remarked, 'This man will never command public confidence.'

Stanley knew all the political secrets of the day. He was himself no enthusiastic Conservative – a Free Trader, a social reformer, an isolationist Foreign Secretary. But he was tied to the Conservative party by his father and his friend. He recorded a confused political era: the Conservatives divided after Peel's conversion to Free Trade and the so-called Liberals in an uneasy alliance of Whigs and Radicals. Here is essential material for the historians who seek to explain how a new Conservative and a new Liberal party emerged after the second Reform Act.

There is more to the diaries than the manoeuvring of politicians. In the fashion of the day Stanley was an eager statistician. He analysed the parliamentary speeches and debates. Thus in the session of 1852–3 Gladstone spoke 432 times, while 342 members of the House of Commons never spoke at all. In 1856, 315 were absent from at least 150 out of the 198 divisions, and 558 were absent from above 100. Of the hereditary peers only 81 out of the 350 took any part in public affairs. A number of them were insane. In 1849 Stanley noted: 'One peer (a ministerialist) came down too drunk to be presentable, but was paired nevertheless. Two insane peers were brought in and made to vote, the keeper of one being in attendance in the lobby.'

Stanley was interested in the incomes of members of the peerage. The Duke of Bedford had £200,000 a year and during his possession of the estate had paid off £1,100,000 of encumbrances. Lord Bute had £100,000 a year. The rental of the Knowsley estates, held by Lord Derby, had gone up from £31,881 in 1800 to £126,196 in 1860. Add the Irish rents, and the annual income was approaching £150,000. No wonder that Disraeli regarded the House of Lords as an instrument for emasculating the wealthy peers. If they had been free to enter the House of Commons, they could have carried all before them.

At the other end of the scale were peers who had lost their fortunes by incompetence and extravagance or had inherited nothing. They had to be provided for from public funds, a principal consideration when the appointment of ambassadors was being considered.

Stanley's father complained to him that 'an English Minister had more responsibility, more labour and less authority than the ruler of any people on earth'. Stanley replied that 'the only posts of power which appeared to remain were the Governor Generalship of India and the editorship of *The Times*'. Stanley was naturally on close terms with Delane. Indeed, he was on close terms with most leading politicians. He often noted Gladstone's violence in debate and recorded that 'of late G has been in an excited and irritable condition, for which nothing in the state of public business appears to account'. Many expected Gladstone to go mad. Lord Palmerston expected him to become a Roman Catholic, and Lord Aberdeen told Clarendon, 'You must keep that d—d fellow always in office, give him plenty to do; else he is sure to do mischief.' Gladstone's Liberal followers said of him, 'He must lead, there is no one who can compete with him, and yet his temper and restlessness make him entirely unfit.' Again on Gladstone:

At a country house last Sunday he passed the evening singing hymns with his wife, the Bishop of Oxford, who was also present, compelled to join in but revenging himself afterwards by telling the story.

Some of the best accounts are of men outside politics. Carlyle 'preached at some length after dinner, in the strain which with him is invariable':

The Irish had never been well governed except under Cromwell . . . They were a fine race when under control, but unfit to be their own masters . . . Railroads were a great mischief in that they encouraged people to run up and down without a motive; we had far too many of them . . . If he were to judge by speeches and newspaper writings he should think our case utterly desperate . . . There was no cause in Europe worth an Englishman's troubling himself about – not even that of Italy – one might wish to see the Pope put down, as the father of all lying, but were his opponents any better?

Thackeray told Stanley that the public had got tired of him. 'Miss Evans got £7,000 for one of her novels; *Esmond*, which he thought his best, had brought him only £1,500 for a year's hard work.'

As may be expected there is much about Queen Victoria. When Prince Albert was alive, the politicians complained that he decided everything. After his death they complained that the Queen refused to decide anything and yet was angry when others did so. There was constant anxiety, stimulated by the Queen herself, that she would go out of her mind. There was also apprehension about her friendship with John Brown, her devoted attendant and in reality the only disinterested friend she had. 'Mrs Brown' was already a common phrase.

Stanley himself is the most attractive figure in the book. He had no personal ambition. He kept clear of his father's political control by finding a parliamentary seat at King's Lynn instead of at a Derby pocket-borough in Lancashire. He spent more than half his annual income on good works. In 1857 he was chairman of the sanitary section of the Birmingham conference on social reform, 'and when he spoke there on reformatories, the audience on each occasion reached 3,500'. I also welcome his sturdy pedestrianism. When Foreign Secretary, he regularly walked home to his father's villa at Roehampton and, returning to Paddington from Windsor, walked from there to King's Cross. No official cars or carriages for Stanley.

Lord Randolph Churchill

Lord Randolph Churchill (1849–95), the third son of the seventh Duke of Marlborough, was a Conservative MP (1874–95), Secretary for India (1885–6) and briefly Chancellor of the Exchequer (1886). Married to the American, Jennie Jerome, the elder of their two sons was Winston Leonard Spencer Churchill.

This essay was first published, under the title 'Winston's father', as a review of R. F. Foster, Lord Randolph Churchill: A Political Life, *Oxford University Press, 1981, in the* Observer, *22 November 1981.*

Meteors are not uncommon in politics. There is the sudden incursion of some dazzling personality. Sparks fly in all directions – ideas, tactics, polished oratory. Observers agree that a new political planet has arrived. Abruptly the display is over. After much smoke and confusion the meteor vanishes and is soon forgotten.

Such was the brief career of Lord Randolph, the political marvel of the 1880s. There was one departure from the usual pattern. Lord Randolph was not forgotten, thanks to the biographical labours of his son Winston. That biography ranks among the classics of its school. It was also a skilled operation in which Winston, ostensibly justifying his father, really defended his own budding career. And indeed there were many parallels: the same arrogance, the same readiness to change party allegiance, and the same periods of failure. There was one profound difference: Winston learnt from his father's mistakes and by his patience ultimately reaped the highest of rewards.

R. F. Foster has told the story of Lord Randolph Churchill with more detachment than Winston's and also with more sources. The result is a fascinating picture of a political adventurer who aspired to behave 'like a character in a political novel'. Starting from a traditional Tory background, Randolph Churchill tried almost every conceivable combination. He inspired first a revolt, the Fourth Party, against the Tory leadership and reinforced this with an appeal to 'Tory Democracy', whatever that might mean. Sporadically he took soundings for an alliance with Joseph Chamberlain, a Radical also in revolt from his party. Alternatively Randolph contemplated crossing over to the Liberals and enlisting under Gladstone, perhaps in association with Chamberlain, perhaps against him.

These were also the days when the Home Rule party flourished under Parnell. Randolph first denounced Home Rule as treason and a threat to the United Kingdom. Then, switching round, he moved towards alliance with Parnell on the grounds that Home Rule was not a threat to the Union at all. These ideas came popping out of Randolph's head helter-skelter, with contradictions often running side by side.

It sounds chaotic, but there was an underlying theme. The two traditional parties, Liberal and Conservative, seemed on the point of breaking up. Both Whigs and Radicals were drifting away from Gladstone, while Disraeli had left the Conservatives not knowing what they should believe or practise. The Liberal party actually broke asunder over Home Rule. In slightly different circumstances the Conservatives might have broken over social policy if not over Ireland.

There was a more concrete reason for the political whirl. In those days everyone in the governing classes talked politics and many of them wrote down what they heard. Men talked politics in their clubs and at race meetings. They talked politics when they were shooting on the moors or enjoying the delights of Paris or Monte Carlo. What is more, they did a great deal of public talking. Politicians went around speaking at public meetings all over the country even when there was no general election in the offing, and their speeches were fully reported in the local Press and usually in the London Press as well. It may seem odd to conduct political manoeuvres and political bargaining from the public platform, but that is how it was. Randolph Churchill was the most prolific of these orators with the added interest that there was no knowing beforehand what he was going to say.

Mr Foster has made sense of this hurly-burly. He has not found consistency or even good sense but he sees the rhythm of impulse and inspiration which kept Churchill going. It is right that a politician should strive for success but he should not do it too blatantly. Randolph never made the slightest attempt to conceal his ambition. Yet, remarkably enough, most political leaders took him seriously. Indeed, most genuinely liked him and enjoyed his company. Even Balfour spoke warmly of Randolph after his death, though it was Balfour who ultimately put the dagger in Randolph's back.

To be more correct, Randolph committed political suicide. He had his moment of greatness: Chancellor of the Exchequer almost at his first bid for office. Then he threw it all away by a gesture of impatience and in the mistaken belief that he could dictate even to Lord Salisbury. We know that Salisbury and Balfour had been playing against Randolph for years, just as Gladstone played against Chamberlain, Randolph's counterpart in the Liberal party.

Mr Foster suggests a more immediate explanation for Randolph's wildness: Randolph, Mr Foster claims, knew as early as 1882 that he had contracted the syphilis which led to his death in 1895. This is a plausible conjecture. It does not alter the powerful impact that Randolph had on the political world in his fertile years. He might have been a great leader. In retrospect he appears a great nuisance. If I had anything to do with the Social Democratic party I should take a good look at the career of Lord Randolph Churchill, the politician who rose so high and left no mark.

William Morris: Marxist

William Morris (1834–96), designer, craftsman, painter, poet, author of News From Nowhere *and much else, was treasurer of the Eastern Question Association, 1876–8, and then of the National Liberal League, 1879–81, before becoming a Socialist in 1882 and joining the Democratic Federation in January 1883. He was a major figure in the revival of socialism in Britain in the 1880s.*

The essay was first published as a review of E. P. Thompson, William Morris: Romantic to Revolutionary, *Lawrence and Wishart, 1955, in the* Observer, *10 July 1955. Edward Thompson (1924–93) reissued the book in a revised edition in 1977. Then he admitted that the book would have reached a wider audience had the first edition been shorter and had he not 'intruded far too often upon the text with moralistic comments and pat political sentiments'.*

*William Morris was one of Alan Taylor's radical heroes. At the time of Queen Elizabeth II's coronation he deplored foreigners seeing so much pageantry and urged, 'We shall have more to show our visitors at the next coronation if we think less of economics and more of William Morris' (*Daily Herald, *23 May 1953). On another occasion he gave the verdict that William Morris had been 'the saint of the century' (*Observer, *8 March 1970).*

We judge the past by the standards of the Stock Exchange. We discover what men did, and praise those who come out with a credit balance. It is more difficult to find out what men were. Consider how badly Samuel Johnson comes out from a practical test. He compiled the first English dictionary; wrote wrong-headed pamphlets and short biographies of poets, now mostly forgotten; and passed his time in idle talk. All this is irrelevant to the great man that Johnson was.

William Morris is in even worse case – a Johnson who never found a Boswell. Though once called a great poet, most of his poetry is now unreadable – pedestrian, unbearably artificial, empty. He tried to restore simplicity in the domestic arts, but his work now seems arty-and-crafty to the last degree. In politics he founded a Socialist League that never won 1,000 members and wrote articles for a Socialist sheet that had only 100 or so readers. As a poet he was inferior to Rossetti; as a politician he counted for less than Hyndman – which is certainly setting our sights pretty low. A few people may still admire his tapestries; even fewer may open *News from Nowhere*. Otherwise he is forgotten.

Yet all this is nonsense. You cannot read a scrap of his journalism or hear an anecdote about him without feeling: 'Here was a great man, the greatest man of his time.' Morris has been unlucky in his biographers. From Mackail onwards, they admired his art but disliked his politics: and therefore treated Morris's socialism as a whim, a perversity, something that he himself wearied of before he died. Even Bruce Glasier, though a Socialist, wanted to show that Morris was never a Marxist, but unconsciously a sentimentalist on the side of the ILP. Bernard Shaw wanted to make it clear that there was only one great English Socialist: and his name was Shaw, not Morris. So Morris has come down to us almost as a figure of fun – a muddle-headed old fellow with a heart of gold; a warm human character, with enthusiasm and uplift but no sense. Three loud cheers therefore for Mr Thompson, who sticks to it firmly that Morris was a great man and starts from that to find out what all his greatness was about.

His book is of the greatest value and interest. It has also the most appalling defects. It is far too long. You have to be a genius to sustain a biography of 900 pages: and Mr Thompson cannot do it. He has no sense of what to leave out. He goes on down every by-way like a dog out for a walk. Take the Socialist League. Any ordinary biographer would be content with a footnote: 'After Morris left the League it fell into the hands of the Anarchists and faded into insignificance.' Not Mr Thompson: he gives us every detail of these sectarian wrangles to the last obscurity.

Then again, Mr Thompson is a rigid adherent of the Communist party; and he is forever telling us how Morris took a line that was later approved of by Lenin, Stalin, or Mr Harry Pollitt. Marxist jargon, always intolerable, becomes even more so when set against the clear English vigour of Morris's own prose. Morris hated tyranny and he hated ugliness. It is an insult to our intelligence to suggest that he would have approved the political system of the Soviet Union or even have admired the architecture of the Moscow Underground. The reader who can dig through all this will find some first-rate things. He will find, for instance, a sane, convincing discussion of the tragedy in Morris's private life – the estrangement from Janey, his wife, and her love for Rossetti. The last chapter, despite its Marxist affectations, works out fully Morris's political views and shows him for the wise man he was.

Perhaps the best proof of Morris's greatness is that he takes command of the book from Mr Thompson. Morris, with his blue tweeds, his beard, and his nautical role, would have liked the metaphor. Every scrap he wrote, every word he said, blows in a gale of freedom and common sense. Morris did not want a more efficient economic system; he wanted freedom and happiness for all. He believed in human equality and practised it. Beauty and happiness for a few were abhorrent to him; and he could not rest until they were shared by all alike. Marx had shown that capitalism was doomed; and Morris accepted the explanation. Nevertheless, 'even supposing I did not understand that there is a definite reason in economics, and that the whole system can be changed, I for one would be a rebel against it'.

His political work was futile and barren. But when he sat talking to a few Glasgow workers, one of them said afterwards: 'This is the greatest day of my life, and I can never see the like again. If one can speak of a God amongst men, we can speak of William Morris as he has been with us this day in Glasgow.' This is better than the dialectic. His last words to Bruce Glasier were: 'Ah, lad! if the workers are *really* going to march – won't we all fall in': and on his deathbed: 'I want to get mumbo-jumbo out of the world.'

Morris was more than a great rebel: he was a great man, one of the greatest England has ever known. No one who has fallen under his spell can ever be anything than a Socialist: which is far from saying that he will be a conforming member of the Labour party – or of the Communist party either.

Men of Labours

The first of these essays was first published as a review of E. J. Hobsbawm, Labouring Men, *Weidenfeld & Nicolson, 1964, in the* New Statesman, *27 November 1964. The second essay was first published as a review of E. J. Hobsbawm,* Worlds of Labour, *Weidenfeld & Nicolson, 1984, and was his last book review. Alan Taylor greatly admired the trilogy of books that Eric Hobsbawm (1917–) wrote on 'the long nineteenth century' (1789–1914):* The Age of Revolution *(1962),* The Age of Capital *(1975) and* The Age of Empire *(1987).*

Men of Labours

Eric Hobsbawm has chosen a skilful title for the historical essays which he has written over the last fifteen years. Once upon a time his book would have been called 'Problems in British Working-class History' or something of that kind. Hobsbawm's title is not only more eye-catching, it is also more revealing. The working class has become a technical term. It no longer means all those who support themselves by their labour, just as proletarians are no longer all those who have no property except their children. The workers or proletarians are those who follow the Marxist pattern and obey the Marxist rules. The worker joins a trade union, founds the Rochdale Pioneers, and is a vocal member of the SDF or the ILP. Later, all true workers are to be found in the ranks of the Communist party or, at the very least, on the extreme Labour Left. Workers, thus defined, are always a small minority of the population. What of the rest? The mob is derogatory; the masses are also now Marxist. Cobbett called them simply 'the poor'; Hobsbawm calls them, more romantically, 'labouring men'.

Though their written remains are few, this does not mean that their annals are short and simple. They are long and complicated, as Hobsbawm shows in his detailed analysis. The early essays in this book deal with the standard of living during the industrial revolution – a field as sharply contested as the ups and downs of the gentry in the seventeenth century, and to better purpose. The traditional view, expressed most tellingly by the Hammonds, was that the standard of living went down. This made sense. Somebody had to pay for the industrial revolution and, given the social conditions of the age, this was not likely to be the upper class. More recent economic historians have, however, sought to demonstrate that the standard of living went up. Some of these writers regarded capitalism as a perfect system and naturally therefore insisted that it was perfect even during the industrial revolution. They were, in the Webbs' phrase, chaplains of the pirate ship. Some, particularly Professor Ashton, were cool scholars who disliked literary generalizations and relied on statistics. Hobsbawm has challenged this approach in its own terms. He does not try to stand the statistics on their heads. He shows, I think convincingly, that they are inadequate for any firm conclusion. This does not surprise me. I once heard Charles Morazé say that no reliable history was possible before 1848 when statistics were first compiled. David Worswick tells me that the date should be pushed forward to 1941 – or was it 1957? At any rate, we are now back from figures to feelings, and these give a clear answer. The men of the time thought that they were worse off, and they should know.

Hobsbawm questions other accepted views. He disputes Halévy's theory that Methodism saved England from revolution. On the contrary, as Hobsbawm shows, Methodism, in its more enthusiastic forms, went hand in hand with political Radicalism: the two were associates, not rivals. Very rewarding also are the essays in which Hobsbawm discusses the practical instruments of labouring men. Machine-breaking was not merely blind anarchy: it was a recognized, and almost legitimate, restrictive practice which was secretly applauded by the more conservative employers. In the later essays, Hobsbawm gradually shifts his ground. Labouring men gradually fade out, the workers come into their own. What, for example, are Hyndman and Dr Marx doing in this company? But it does not matter. They too make interesting essays. The best is on the Fabians. Hobsbawm puts them firmly in their historical place: they spoke for the new professional classes, even – though he omits this – for the *rentiers*. They were a last splutter of the Victorian conscience: 'an adaptation of the British middle classes to the era of imperialism'. They had no working-class sentiment or loyalty: planners in the void who did not mind who they planned for so long as they planned for somebody: a historical curiosity, a spent force.

Perhaps it would be truer to say that they formed an accidental alliance with the aristocracy of labour, another concept which Hobsbawm explores. In the most detailed of his later essays, he puzzles over the survival of reformism and produces many ingenious explanations, from the inherited strength of British imperialism to the skilful concessions of the governing class. Probably the title of Hobsbawm's book provides an answer. The workers may be revolutionary. Labouring men are not. They riot when they are hungry; otherwise they labour. Marx recognized this. In his view, the revolution was inevitable because of increasing hunger. His revolutionary exhortations, and those of all Communists, were added more out of habit than anything else.

Tradition, as Hobsbawm observes, makes a great difference. The French had revolutionary traditions. The English had traditions of radical dissent. Hobsbawm ends with praise of the Campaign for Nuclear Disarmament, which he calls 'a major force in British politics'. The praise is a little out of date. Movements of emotional protest are short-lived. Labouring men, on the other hand, go on all the time.

Hard at work

This is a delightful book. It explores the lives and beliefs of labouring peoples, mainly European and mainly in earlier centuries. This at once provokes questions. Certainly there were clear distinctions between rich and poor through the centuries. But this is far from being synonymous with a distinction between those who were idle and those who worked. Hobsbawm sheds much light on this problem.

He asks, 'What is the Workers' Country?' The answer is confused and contradictory. Take the Welsh coal mines in the nineteenth century. 'The mass migration into the mines of South Wales, mainly from England, created a strong Welsh working class, but one which ceased to speak Welsh.' Most Welshmen now do not speak Welsh, but this does not prevent them from becoming Welsh nationalists.

In England as long ago as 1860 Thomas Wright reported that the older, radical and Chartist generation of workers combined a passionate distrust of all who were not workers with a John Bullish patriotism.

Ireland raised further problems. 'A labour movement which was both *political* and *industrial* and which united Protestant and Catholic, Orange and Green, skilled and unskilled, became impossible.' In Belgium the relations between Flemings and Walloons raised similar problems.

Another fascinating chapter discusses the relationship between man and woman in the revolutionary movement. It had never occurred to me that the symbol of revolution in its early days was entirely feminine and usually naked. In France the Commune was personified by a naked woman, a soldier's cap on her head, a sword by her side.

A curious feature is that as women became more emancipated they lost more of their symbolism and became more adequately dressed. The monster statues displayed by Soviet artists are all masculine. Presumably the Soviet doctrine is that woman's place is in the home.

One subject had not occurred to me earlier – the leading part played in politics by shoemakers. As long as the villages were the centre of political life it was the shoemaker who supplied the political leadership. The shoemaker had the great advantage of being able to conduct political discussion while he was getting on with his work. This remained an outstanding feature of political life in the villages until well on in the twentieth century. The village shoemaker and his leadership are a sad loss.

The latter part of Hobsbawm's book revolves around the problem of the Labour aristocracy viewed from various angles. Is the Labour aristocracy a coherent conception? Was it a name for the craft unions of the later nineteenth century? Now it seems that the distinction between aristocrats and humble proletarians is in the process of being eliminated.

If it vanishes altogether Hobsbawm's problem will be solved. However, there remain many problems with which Hobsbawm can provide intellectual entertainment of a superior order. A clever book by a clever man.

Edith Cavell

Edith Cavell (1865–1915), the eldest daughter of the vicar of Swardeston, Norfolk, trained as a nurse and, from 1906, worked in Belgium, training nurses.

This essay was first published as a review of A. E. Clark-Kennedy, Edith Cavell, *Faber, 1965, in the* New Statesman, *2 July 1965.*

Historical fame often derives from the wrong reasons. So it is with Edith Cavell. She is remembered for two things. She was a victim of German frightfulness, and she repudiated patriotism at the height of a patriotic war. Her famous words, 'Patriotism is not enough. I must have no hatred or bitterness against anyone', were engraved on the base of her statue by order of the first Labour Commissioner of Works. Yet both facts misinterpret the real events, as Dr Clark-Kennedy shows in his careful and scholarly book. Edith Cavell was head of a nursing establishment in Brussels when the Germans occupied Belgium. She assisted some hundreds of men, British, Belgian and French, to escape into Holland, knowing that many of them would join, or rejoin, the allied armies. This was an offence against the military law which the Germans had imposed in Belgium – correctly, according to the standards of the time. When arrested, she confessed everything, even frankly revealing her collaborators. She was given a fair, if somewhat brusque, trial by a military tribunal, and the sentence of death passed on her, though harsh, was not flagrantly unjust. The sentence was carried out hurriedly, without allowing time for any appeal – apparently because the German Military Governor resented any political interference. But, as Dr Clark-Kennedy writes, 'in no sense was Miss Cavell a martyr, unless the meaning of that word is stretched to include every soldier who gives his life for his country in wartime'.

Nor did she repudiate patriotism. The words for which she is remembered were spoken to an English clergyman just before she received her last sacrament, and they are what many people would have said at that moment. But her last words at the scaffold were 'I am glad to die for my country.' She remains an outstanding British patriot and will also be remembered as a very brave woman. Though she once said that her ambition was to be buried in Westminster Abbey, it was duty, not fame, which shaped her life. She became a nurse when nursing was developing into a serious profession, and Dr Clark-Kennedy illuminates her early career with expert knowledge. She did not work well with superiors, and for this reason welcomed the invitation to introduce modern methods of nursing in Belgium.

British stragglers appealed for her aid after the retreat from Mons, and she gave it at once. She may have believed that they were in danger of being shot if they were caught. In any case, they were her fellow-countrymen, and, if their escape also helped her country, so much the better. She helped Belgians and Frenchmen from the same mixture of humanity and patriotism. Her one anxiety was for her institution, not for herself. At the trial, she did not wear nursing uniform, though this would have impressed the German judges, so as not to compromise the school or her profession. She refused to make excuses or to plead for mercy. As one of the other women on trial said, 'it was Madame's cold haughty disdain that the Germans hated so much'. Edith Cavell made only the comment: 'I expected my sentence and believe it was just.' She had done her duty and recognized that the Germans, in their detestable way, were doing their duty also. Patriotism was not everything in Edith Cavell's life. Duty and the care for individual human beings usually counted for more. But patriotism shaped her course at the moment of crisis, and she died for her country. Dr Clark-Kennedy's book ends with Edith Cavell's death. He, too, has done his duty as a biographer. Another book could well be written on the two Cavell myths: first the myth created during the war by anti-German propaganda, and then that created by anti-war propaganda afterwards. No doubt these myths will survive even Dr Clark-Kennedy's demonstration of the true story.

Confusion on the Left

This essay was first published in a series entitled 'Once Upon a Time . . .' in Encounter, *3 March 1958. It was reprinted as 'Confusion on the Left' in John Raymond (ed.),* The Baldwin Age, *Eyre & Spottiswoode, 1960, and in A. J. P. Taylor,* Politicians, Socialism and Historians, *Hamish Hamilton, 1980.*

The general election of November 1922 opened the Baldwin era, though Bonar Law was in nominal control for the first few months. 'Tranquillity and freedom from adventures and commitments' was the cry which put the second-class brains into power. On the Left there was a different spirit. Walton Newbold, returned as a Communist at Motherwell, wired to Lenin: 'Glasgow won for Communism.' It seemed a pardonable exaggeration. In Glasgow itself the Clydesiders of the ILP won ten out of fifteen seats and scented social revolution just round the corner. David Kirkwood shouted from his railway carriage to the crowd which sped the departure of the Clydesiders to Westminster: 'When we come back, this station, this railway, will belong to the people!' The promise was to be fulfilled, though only after a longer delay than Kirkwood or the crowd foresaw. Still less did they foresee Kirkwood as a member of the House of Lords; one of his associates Minister of Defence authorizing the secret manufacture of atom bombs; and Maxton, supposed Robespierre of the group, the most loved and least effective member of the House of Commons. What did the Clydesiders achieve in practice? Only to make Ramsay MacDonald leader of the Parliamentary Labour Party by 61 votes to 56.

Ramsay MacDonald was to prove the left-wing counterpart of Baldwin, equally devoted to tranquillity and freedom from adventures and commitments. In 1922 he still seemed securely on the Left; still lunching every day at the 1917 Club; still frowned on by the respectable for his supposed pacifism during the Great War. In presence he was, in Shinwell's phrase, a prince among men. He had a ravishingly musical voice, every syllable ringing of Utopia. His ideas of social improvement were vague and undefined. In foreign affairs he saw clearly, wishing, in true left-wing fashion, to substitute conciliation and appeasement for alliances and the balance of power. He and Arthur Henderson were the principal targets for the abuse which flowed from Moscow. They were Social traitors, Social Fascists; and indeed the two men did more than any others to keep the British Labour movement free from communism – a service for which they deserve to be remembered.

The British Labour party, now the official Opposition and soon to form the first Labour government, was a strange alliance of two distinct forces. On the one hand the trade-union movement supplied the firm foundation and most of the money. Here the driving force was straight economic discontent. The post-war boom was over; large-scale unemployment had come to stay. The Red Flag flew on the Clyde, in Poplar, in South Wales. Here the King's writ did not run; and the Left supposed that they had only to capture central administration as they had already in these areas taken over local government. Policy and long-term planning seemed unnecessary. Capitalism would topple of its own defects; and the social revolution would come peacefully by a simple process of administrative change. The British Left believed as confidently as Lenin had done in 1917 that socialism could be made in twenty-four hours. Socialism was preached in moral terms; men had to be persuaded that it was right and just. The only problem was to win a majority; then socialism would follow of its own accord. The Labour movement had only to squeeze up wages and welfare until capitalism exploded, and the trick would be turned. Hence while the Left preached and argued, it did not lead. Economic conditions, not leadership, would produce the desired result.

The other side of the Labour party was the section of the individual members, organized in the constituency parties. Henderson had created this new system in 1918 – a creation which changed the face of British politics. Previously individuals could join the Labour party only through the ILP or lesser bodies like the SDF and the Fabian Society. Now these bodies were doomed as mass organizations, though the ILP went on pontificating, with declining membership, until the end of the decade. Moreover, by this device the Labour party could offer a home to Radicals who had formerly been Liberal. Home Rule and sectarian disputes over education – the two issues which had sustained the Liberal party – were dead or dying. The great emotional question for the middle-class Left was foreign policy; and here the Labour party had a less spotted record. MacDonald had opposed the war from the first hour; and the Labour party had denounced the Treaty of Versailles six weeks before it was signed. Also, though Labour would have nothing to do with the Communist party, it wished to end the boycott of Soviet Russia. The Councils of Action which had prevented war against Russia in 1920 were a proud memory; the mirage of Russian trade promised a solution for British economic difficulties; and, though most men of the Left knew little of conditions in Russia, they rejoiced at the social revolution there and believed that the dictatorship would lose its force when other countries held out the hand of friendship. Left foreign policy had a simple prescription. Germany and Russia were justly aggrieved; and the redress of their grievances would secure the peace and prosperity of the world.

The cleavage between the two sections of the Left was not absolute. Most trade-union officials – and their more active followers – had started as Socialist intellectuals of a working-class sort; some indeed were Communists, though without understanding what this implied. Many of the 'politicians' had started in the trade-union movement; and the others recognized an obligation to promote economic improvement. Rather than a cleavage, there was a division of function. The trade unions expected that an enlightened foreign policy would give economic benefits; and the politicians preached welfare in order to have a free hand for their foreign policy. They were held together by a common morality: a passionate rejection of social evils, and a conviction that these evils could be ended by the overthrow of the existing order. The Left was revolutionary in outlook, though not in method. The Baldwin era gradually forced the conclusion that it must become both or neither.

The promised land was not long delayed. Baldwin was no sooner in power than he went again to the polls on the question of Protection. Labour gained 49 extra seats; the Conservatives lost nearly a hundred; and when Parliament met, Baldwin was defeated by the combined Liberal and Labour votes. Ramsay MacDonald became Prime Minister, first being sworn of the Privy Council – the only Prime Minister to need this preliminary. It was a revolutionary symbol, but the only one. Labour's success was not due to socialism. It was the last victory of Free Trade – a respectable, and by now an antiquated, cause. In theory Labour stood for the community against private interests. In practice it defended balanced budgets, sound money, and free trade. Planning and a directed economy were preached by Amery and a few enlightened Conservatives so far as they were preached at all. The first Labour government took office with minority support. Hence it could plead exemption from any startling act of legislation. It was supposed to show that Labour was fit to govern. Oddly, no one observed that this had already been demonstrated. Henderson had been a member of the War Cabinet, and Clynes a successful Minister of Food. Nor was the Labour government remarkable as a showpiece. Most ministers became obstinate defenders of their departments, only Wheatley – a Catholic businessman from Glasgow – taking an initiative. A smug phrase cloaked this lack of thought or policy: Labour was 'in office but not in power'.

MacDonald was indifferent to the domestic record of his government. Foreign affairs were what mattered to him. He began the appeasement of Germany and opened the road to Locarno, which the Conservatives followed later to general surprise. Indeed after 1924 there was no Right foreign policy: MacDonald's spirit prevailed in regard to Germany whether he was in office or not. Russia was a different matter. MacDonald had never shared the Left enthusiasm for the Bolshevik revolution and now recognized the Soviet government as grudgingly as he could. The Left wanted a union of hearts and also a trade treaty opening the Russian market to British goods. Negotiations lagged, then jammed. Ponsonby, MacDonald's under-secretary, actually announced breakdown early in August. A group of Left MPs took up the running and imposed agreement – the first of many Left revolts against the official leadership and for once successful. MacDonald and the Left were brought back to harmony by a series of unexpected twists. The Attorney-General – ill-briefed in the niceties of Left politics – started to prosecute a Communist editor for appealing to soldiers not to act as strike-breakers; then withdrew when Labour MPs protested. The Liberal and Conservative parties were indignant or claimed to be. The government was defeated in the House of Commons; and MacDonald found himself fighting a general election as the patron of sedition.

The affair of the Zinoviev letter completed the reconciliation. It is a matter of little historical importance whether the letter was genuine or not. Labour men were unanimous that it was a fraud, manufactured by the anti-Bolshevik centre at Riga or perhaps by the Foreign Office itself. This was far from the 'fair play' which George V had desired for the Labour government. It was the gentlemen of England playing dirty as only they knew how to do. MacDonald had half imagined himself as national leader, transcending party. Now he was back on the Left, again the ostracized idealist of the war years. The Zinoviev letter lost the general election for Labour, or so it was said. But it also gave Labour a cover against accusations of failure. They had been tricked out of office, not defeated or discredited. Few bothered to analyse the government's record; and the legend soon became established that everything had been going splendidly until Campbell and Zinoviev cropped up. There was little in the way of new thought or new policy. Ernest Bevin, with the constructive spirit which he was later to show as Foreign Secretary, proposed that Labour should not again take office with a minority. His proposal was rejected; and from this decision to continuity of policy even with a majority was not a far step. The ILP, now at its last kick of life, proposed to arrive at socialism by means of the Living Wage. This was none other than our old friend the belief that capitalism could be made to burst of itself, if wage demands were pushed high enough.

Action, not thought, gave the Left its only outlet in these years. The General Strike was the most class-conscious act in British history (or, rather, the most working-class-conscious act – the upper classes never lose consciousness). Also, though no one cared about this, it was one of the few unselfish acts in anybody's history. But it did not fit into any pattern of Left development. There was no deliberate oscillation from political to industrial action, as some ingenious writers have suggested. The miners had been plodding steadily on with their struggle since Lloyd George swindled them over the Sankey commission in 1919. This struggle happened to reach its climax in 1926. It had little to do with Left or Right, but was in truth a struggle for existence. Trade unionists did not need to be Communists, syndicalists, or even Socialists, to sympathize with the miners; they only needed to sympathize, and in trade-union terms that could only take one form – the sympathetic strike. Certainly the avowed Left sympathized also and supported the strike as best they could. But what was there for a Left intellectual, or even for a trade-union official, to do? Speeches appealing for solidarity were agreeable to deliver, but pointless when the audience was solid already. Nor was there anything to organize. The General Council met only four times during the ten days of the strike; and the *British Worker* was hard-pressed for news. 'Spirit splendid; all out', became monotonous. Some intellectuals who could drive motor cars acted as couriers, carrying TUC secret instructions which contained no secrets. Many intellectuals could not drive. W. H. Auden, moving a car four miles during the ten days (from Old Marston to Oxford), was a symbol of Faith, not Works.

Things would have been different if the TUC had taken over the running of the country, but no one proposed this seriously. In fact, like most gestures of sympathy, once made it had served its purpose; and the only concern of those who had made it was to bring it to an end. The petering-out of the strike, and still more the defeat of the miners, certainly weakened the trade-union movement. It had no effect on left-wing thought. The General Strike had been an instinctive reaction, not a policy. Once over, it was forgotten except for the resentment which Baldwin gratuitously provoked by legislating against the trade unions in 1927. This was always his way: soft words, harsh acts. Even so there was a short period of tranquillity and recovery – the true 'age of Baldwin' – which lasted until 1929. No great strikes; no riots by the unemployed; no alarms of war. The Labour party, securely established as the official Opposition, waited confidently for the swing of the pendulum. They would come into office on the great British principle of Buggins's turn. The Left became frivolous: gay young things of intellectualism. Enthusiastic tourists visited Soviet Russia, not to see new factories or the triumph of the social revolution, but to admire co-educational schools, divorce by consent, and prisons allegedly without bars. Young writers found their spiritual home in Berlin and rejoiced at the moral emancipation shown by the homosexual prostitutes on the Kurfürstendamm. Hock became a left-wing drink; claret as shockingly Tory as it had been in the eighteenth century.

The general election of 1929 whispered the last enchantment of the Victorian age. Baldwin campaigned to the cry, 'Safety First'. The Labour party advocated a nebulous socialism in moral terms coined by F. D. Maurice and Ruskin. The result was perverse. Labour got fewer votes, more seats, than the Conservatives; not enough, however, to escape another run of being 'in office, but not in power'. There was a victory celebration at the Albert Hall, Fenner Brockway registering triumph with outstretched arm in a salute not yet branded as 'fascist', and Ramsay MacDonald appearing in white tie and tails to announce that he was on his way to Buckingham Palace. Thereafter: nothing. The Labour party had no programme except to be indistinguishable from its predecessor. In MacDonald's words there was to be no monkeying. Unfortunately events disregarded his instruction. In October 1929 the great economic storm began to blow. Unemployment passed two million, soared to three. The gold standard rocked. The Labour party had no remedy for this situation. Planned economy was no part of classical socialism. Marx, for instance, assumed that supply and demand, the law of the market, would continue to work under socialism; only private profit would be eliminated. Soviet Russia had been operating a market economy and a gold currency since the end of the civil war. The first Five Year Plan, launched in 1928, had not yet made an impact on western minds. The New Deal had not appeared on the horizon. Keynesian economics were still in conception. Only Fascist Italy claimed, however falsely, to have a planned economy.

The Labour government could therefore offer only the classical remedy of balanced budgets and economy cuts. A few Socialists, Lansbury in particular, wished to shelter the poor from the storm, and hang the expense. Mosley alone advocated this with unconscious Keynesianism. His policy was rejected, and he left the Labour party with some left-wing associates to form the 'New Party'. Later he took the full road to fascism, and most of his associates drifted back to Labour, bringing economic direction with them in their baggage. But in August 1931, when the crisis reached its height, the Labour government was still unshakeably orthodox in its economic thinking. Eleven members of the Cabinet agreed to reduce unemployment benefit by 10 per cent; nine refused. (Attlee, with his usual luck, was not in the Cabinet and so did not have to commit himself one way or the other.) The Labour government broke up. MacDonald went off happily, with Snowden and Thomas, to form a National government, which should save the pound – an ambition which fortunately it did not accomplish. Labour was massacred at the ensuing election, and for an obvious reason. The National government claimed to have a remedy, though it had in fact the wrong one. Labour did not even make the claim. Apart from the defence of unemployment benefit, its election campaign was fought solely on the ticket of Free Trade.

Yet, because of the way it had left office, Labour could again overlook its own faults and blame the manoeuvres or treachery of others. MacDonald, Baldwin, or George V had tricked the simple, high-minded members of the Labour party. Arthur Greenwood, wearily fighting his election campaign in Lancashire, reiterated at every stop, 'It's not fair,' as though the Socialist movement had a heaven-sent right to sunshine. After defeat the Left displayed old grievances, not new thought. The only conclusion which Laski, principal theorist of the party, drew from the affair was that the monarchy should be abolished. Yet Weimar Germany and the United States had the same economic difficulties and even dirtier politics. Still, some thought stirred as the dust subsided. John Strachey, breaking loose from Mosley, returned to socialism with the only Marxist classic written in English, *The Coming Struggle for Power*. Yet he and other new thinkers of the Left squinted oddly. Mesmerized by Russia's Five Year Plans, they ignored the renewed terror and the massacre of the kulaks with which these were accompanied. Moreover, they knew nothing of America. They closed their eyes to the New Deal and described America right up to 1939 as a 'Fascist economy'. Soviet Russia was again the Utopia of the Left, now on grounds of economic efficiency, not of moral superiority. The Workers' State had become the model of planned economy.

The Left became more markedly intellectual as the decade proceeded – or perhaps intellectuals became more markedly Left. The Oxford Union had its only Communist president, Philip Toynbee. The October Club, avowedly pro-Communist, was for some years the largest political club in Oxford. Working men tried to find instructions for their trade-union meetings in the poems of Auden and Spender. In this hubbub, the Left Book Club stood supreme. Each month it distributed two books as the 'Choice' – chosen, of course, not by the readers, but by a triumvirate of intellectual dictators, much as Lord Woolton decided later, though with more excuse, on the correct supply of calories and vitamins. Strachey, Laski and Gollancz provided a balanced intellectual diet, parcelling out near-communism, proletarian 'literature', and sheer crankiness. Of the two first 'choices', for instance, one by a biologist (still turning the old hurdy-gurdy in 1958) looked forward to the time when artificial insemination would enable a Lenin (or a Stalin?) to father every child in the Soviet Union. The Left Book Club was often regarded as a subversive organization. In reality it was a safety valve. Reading is a substitute for action, not a prelude to it; and the members of the Left Book Club worked off their rebelliousness by plodding through yet another orange-covered volume.

Economic problems predominated immediately after 1931: Free Trade, Imperial Preference, hunger marches by the unemployed. Within two years there was an unexpected change. Foreign affairs were thrust into the centre of the stage; and henceforth these were the great stamping-ground of the Left. Hitler caused much trouble, not of course for the British Left alone. Foreign affairs had been simple until he turned up. Appeasement of the aggrieved powers, Russia and Germany, would settle everything. Hence the Left had only to criticize the British government and oppose British armaments. But now? Most of the Left, though not all, agreed that appeasement of Hitler was hopeless and, besides, immoral. Resisting him was part of 'the struggle against fascism'. How was this struggle to be waged? By co-operating with the National government? Or by continuing to attack it? The Left never solved the problem. Usually they avoided it. Collective security – operating sanctions through the League of Nations – was an evasion of this kind. Once allied to fifty-two other governments (the number that would supposedly work with the League), co-operation with the National government would pass unnoticed. The question caused great dispute. Labour party conferences were rent by it; leaders expelled and readmitted; bitter words spoken. Yet it was all quite pointless. The problem had no solution. For whatever the Left decided about co-operating with the National government to resist Hitler, the National government under MacDonald and Baldwin had no intention of resisting Hitler in co-operation with the Left or anyone else.

In 1935 resistance to aggression had a trial run against Mussolini – a sort of provincial preview before the real first night. The argument was the biggest family quarrel in the history of the Left. The Stalinist fellow-travellers, centred on the Left Book Club, clamoured for national unity and 'sanctions', a euphemism for war. The Socialist League – an intellectualist successor to the dying ILP – stuck to criticism of the British government and proclaimed: 'Our enemy is here.' This was a hard judgement on poor Baldwin, who had not an enemy in the world except perhaps Lloyd George. He was, however, a skilful political operator. Just when the Left had decided that its advocacy of collective security would enable it to defeat the 'imperialist' government at a general election, Baldwin announced that he, too, was enthusiastic for the League of Nations. The Left had failed to win earlier elections by claiming that it was indistinguishable from Baldwin. He however won the election of 1935 by claiming that he was indistinguishable from the Left. Once the election was over, he put the League of Nations back on the shelf and returned to his somewhat amateurish pig-farming.

The dress rehearsal had not been a success. Not surprisingly, therefore, the Left was as much at a loss as everyone else when Hitler reoccupied the Rhineland and the real problem presented itself. Baldwin made an alliance with France, thus guaranteeing to lose a war where he had shrunk from winning one. The Left committed itself to rearmament, but not under the National government, one provision cancelling the other. What more could the Left do with Baldwin on their hands? They could not turn him out; the electorate had seen to that. It would have been equally futile to support him. Even the backing of a united House of Commons would not have convinced Baldwin that there was any better policy than twiddling his thumbs. It was, of course, this taste which endeared him to the electorate.

The Spanish Civil War brought the Left back to life, though not to effectiveness. Spain provided a concentrated meat-extract of all the emotions which the Left had experienced in previous years. Resistance to fascism; class war; unity of the Left – difficult slogans at home, but easy to use in Spain. It was possible to admire the Spanish Communists without favouring Stalin; and the Spanish Republic became a Utopia as Soviet Russia had been in the 1920s, with co-educational schools, enlightened prisons, and civil marriage. There was even a healthy anti-clericalism – a great improvement on Soviet Russia, for no one could feel anti-clerical about the Orthodox Church. The one thing that went wrong was unfortunately the one thing that mattered. The Left failed to break the official refusal to supply the Spanish Republic with arms. Left meetings demanded 'arms for Spain'. Major C. R. Attlee gave the Communist salute to the International Brigade. No arms went to Spain.

Still, the agitation over Spain was a real struggle, as deeply felt as the General Strike ten years before. There was genuine and justified emotion. The Left were asserting the great principles of freedom and democracy, however unsuccessfully. They were seeking to resist the systems of dictatorship which plunged the world into war only three years later. What were Baldwin and the so-called governing classes doing during this great crisis? They were fussing over the question whether a middle-aged man should marry a woman who had two previous husbands, both living. Much can be said against the Left. They were romantic, idealistic, unworldly, often foolish. But one thing can be said in their favour. No one on the Left cared whom Edward VIII married, whether he married, when, or how often. The age of Baldwin was over so far as the Left were concerned. Totting up the account, I make one thumping debit and two credits. Ramsay MacDonald was the debit: the Left's present to the British people. The credits were the General Strike and support for the Spanish Republic – two honourable causes of which any political movement could be proud. It is true that the Left failed to decide what it meant by socialism, or how to get there. But these are problems to which no one has found a solution.

Horthy-Culture

This essay was first published as a review of C. A. Macartney, October Fifteenth: A History of Modern Hungary 1929–1945, *Edinburgh University Press, 1956, in the* New Statesman and Nation, *6 April 1957. Carlile Aylmer Macartney (1895–1978) wrote several widely respected volumes on Hungarian history. He was a journalist and scholar, who broadcast to Hungary during the Second World War when he was a Foreign Office adviser.*

Miklós Horthy de Nagybánya (1886–1957) was a Hungarian admiral and Commander-in-Chief of the Austro-Hungarian Navy in 1917–18. He was Minister of War in the 'White' government of 1919 and, after crushing Bela Kun's Communist government in 1919, he ruled Hungary as Regent from March 1920 until October 1945, though in 1944 he was imprisoned by the Germans (after withdrawing from the alliance he had made with Germany in 1941). Count P. Teleki was Foreign Minister, 1920–21, and Prime Minister, 1939–41. M. Kállay was Prime Minister, 1942–4. Count M. Karolyi was Provisional President of Hungary after the Republic was declared on 16 November 1918 until 22 March 1919 (when the Soviet Hungarian Republic was proclaimed).

An art-editor once complained to Thurber that his women were not attractive. Thurber replied: 'They are to my men.' Professor Macartney feels much the same about the Hungary of Admiral Horthy. Others may find 900 pages and more a bit much when devoted to the details of political intrigue; and may weary at the attempt to distinguish every nicety in collaboration with Hitler. Mr

Macartney, however, is unabashed. His work is a monument of misplaced learning. He has assembled a vast collection of sources – probably greater than any man can ever do again; and he has supplemented this by a patient cross-examination of every surviving actor. We can follow the moves of Teleki and Kállay from day to day, almost from hour to hour; those of Horthy at the end from minute to minute. No other country in Europe has had its recent history reconstructed so microscopically. Nor, one should add, with more literary grace. Mr Macartney writes with an affectionate sympathy which extends even to Szálasi.

Unfortunately we cannot leave the book with this charitable verdict. It is a political tract despite its display of scholarship; neither more nor less than a defence of the Hungarian collaborators and, implicitly, a denunciation of those who condemned them. It echoes all the interminable volumes which have been devoted to a similar defence of the Vichy government in France. This, too, may be justified. Even scamps and rogues are entitled to have their record examined. But Mr Macartney is not content to stand on the record. He is constantly hinting that if only the British government had taken his advice and been more sympathetic to Horthy's regime all would now be well in central Europe. We ought to have favoured Hungarian 'revisionism' – that is, the seizure by Hungary of Czecho-slovak territory. We ought to have understood that Teleki was really on our side, despite his alliance with Germany. We should have appreciated that Kállay really wished to fight on the side of the Western Allies against the Soviet Union. This raking-over of historical 'might-have-beens' is futile and mistaken as well. In the heyday of Hitler's power no country in Europe could be saved from conquest and exploitation. Resistance and collaboration, courage and intrigue, were equally hopeless. What could be saved was honour. This alone is the justification for the Poles or de Gaulle; and it is enough. Horthy and his advisers chose a different course.

I must not conceal my own interest in this dispute. In the days when Mr Macartney was preaching collaboration with the collaborators, I saw the only hope for Hungary in a new democratic order under the leadership of Michael Karolyi. This, too, was a barren enterprise, as things turned out; but it was at least an honourable one. Michael Karolyi was the noblest man I have known. It turns my stomach to read Mr Macartney's cheap sneers at him – he is even condemned for living at one time in North Oxford – and at the fulsome praise of men who were not fit to clean his boots. Karolyi is dead; and these are dead quarrels. In ordinary times we could pass over Mr Macartney's perversity with a smile. But these are not ordinary times. Hungary has just made a great struggle for freedom; and it is lamentable that an English professor should choose this moment to publish a full-blooded defence of the Horthy regime. Of course we know that professors are irresponsible and that Mr Macartney's eccentric views are held only by himself. In Hungary these things are not so clear; and the book will be used to bolster the Communist legend that the Hungarian revolutionaries were hoping to restore the Horthy system with Western aid. Maybe free Hungary has no future. But those who hope otherwise should advise the Hungarians to remember the legacy of Michael Karolyi and to forget all about Horthy, as indeed most Hungarians have already done.

British-Made: Lord Haw-Haw

*William Joyce (1906–46) joined the British Fascisti, formed in 1923
in emulation of Mussolini, before joining other similar organizations, notably the British Union of Fascists. He went to Germany
in 1939 and broadcast on behalf of the Nazis during the Second
World War, becoming known in Britain as Lord Haw-Haw. He
was executed as a traitor on 3 January 1946.*

This essay was first published as a review of J. A. Cole, Lord
Haw-Haw – and William Joyce, *Faber, 1964, in the* New Statesman,
20 November 1964.

How much simpler life would be if the victims of injustice were
attractive characters. They are often shifty and suspicious, eager to
bite the hands of those who feed them. Yet justice exists largely for
such characters. There is no great virtue in being just to the virtuous.
The real test is to be just to the undeserving. British justice failed
this test in the case of William Joyce. He alone emerged from it
with credit. Lord Chancellor, Lord Chief Justice and Attorney-
General did not. It was a shameful story, as bad in its way as
anything which happened during the Popish Plot. Joyce found few
defenders. But he has now found a good historian. Mr Cole has
written a most balanced, sensible book, perhaps a little too sympathetic towards Joyce.

Joyce himself cannot be made attractive. He was bitter and
arrogant, a man of little ability, contemptuous of everybody else.
He was Mr Polly gone sour, a little man resenting the world and

doing his utmost to spite it. He thought in clichés and displayed a sham aggressiveness to hide his inner insecurity. Chess revealed his true nature: he could only play a defensive game. He encountered his future wife with the melodramatic question: 'Whence come ye?' Though he clearly loved and needed her, he treated her badly, working off on her his anger against the world, and it is not surprising that she twice left him. No one would ever have heard of Joyce if he had been merely a British Fascist, as contemptuous incidentally of Mosley, the 'Bleeder', as of everyone else. In August 1939 Joyce went to Germany in order to escape internment and became a broadcaster for the Germans. He was not the original Lord Haw-Haw, who was perhaps Baillie-Stewart or perhaps never existed. Joyce never made the broadcasts attributed to him: never said that the Banstead clock was slow or that German bombers would remove the tram-lines in Commercial Road. Lord Haw-Haw, in Mr Cole's words, 'was made in Britain', the manufacture of British gossip and British anxieties. Joyce's broadcasts were poor, ranting stuff, though probably no worse than their equivalents on the British Black Radio.

Joyce became the object of British hatreds for want of anything better. 'Hang William Joyce' was the Second World War substitute for 'Hang the Kaiser'. Worse was to come. Joyce, it turned out, was not a British subject and therefore incapable of committing high treason. He was born in New York; his father was a naturalized American; he himself remained an American citizen. He acquired a British passport on false pretences in order to leave England. This was the tawdry excuse for making him liable to the charge of high treason. Even with this excuse the case against him was never proved. Joyce was liable, if at all, only during the time he held his British passport – roughly the first year of the war. No satisfactory evidence was produced that he had broadcast for the Germans during that time. His German work-book showed that he had agreed to broadcast, but not that he had done so. Joyce was prosecuted by Sir Hartley Shawcross ('Hotcross Bun', as Joyce called him). He was condemned by Mr Justice Tucker, who had already described him as 'a traitor' in 1940. The Court of Appeal unanimously and the House of Lords by four to one ruled against him. He was hanged before the House of Lords had even stated their grounds for rejecting his appeal. He should have been fined two pounds for making a false statement when applying for a passport.

The Astors: Guardians
of Morality

Michael Langhorne Astor (1916–80) was a Conservative MP (Surrey, East), 1945–51, and was a member of the Arts Council (1968–71) and an executive member of the National Trust (1978–80).

This essay was first published as a review of Michael Astor, Tribal Feeling, Murray, 1963, *in the* New Statesman, 28 June 1963.

Every man, it is said, has one good book in him – the story of himself and his family. Fortunately few men put the saying into practice. Not all those who do produce a good book. They often try to write a book which is a work of art, and this is an accomplishment not easily learnt. The Hon. Michael Astor has not escaped this temptation. He often disappears in a cloud of fine writing. His anecdotes of, for instance, his remarks at election meetings are good for a laugh at the dinner table. They look tawdry in cold print. Again, life at Eton is a squeezed orange. There is nothing more to be said about it; and this was true a long time ago. Mr Astor has sought to describe a journey of self-discovery. The journey was interesting only to himself. He chose a country in which there was not enough to discover. His spiritual travails appear to be those of a man of independent means, stuck for a way of occupying his time. He would have been less eager to discover himself if he had had to earn a living. He draws a comparison at one point between his own book and *Father and Son* by Edmund Gosse. Gosse had superlative literary gifts, even though he ended as librarian to the

House of Lords. Mr Astor cannot compete with him. This book is not another *Father and Son*.

Even so, the book is one of consuming interest. Its theme is the Astor family, and no family has played a greater part in recent British history. Mr Astor's father, the second Viscount Astor, owned the *Observer*, presided over Chatham House, conducted interminable inquiries into agriculture and unemployment. His mother was the first woman to take her seat in the House of Commons. His uncle, Lord Astor of Hever, is Chief Proprietor, along with Mr John Walter, of *The Times*.

We need to go very much further back in order to understand how the Astors have come to occupy such great positions. John Jacob Astor, who founded the family, was born in 1763. He made a fortune in the American fur trade, and put his money into New York property. From that day to this, no Astor has worried about his daily bread. As New York grew rich, they grew richer with it. William Waldorf Astor, great-grandson of John Jacob, wished to be a patrician. The United States was not aristocratic enough for him. Ideally, as Mr Astor remarks, he would have liked to be a Spanish grandee. Failing this, he acquired Cliveden and Hever Castle. He bought his title (for £200,000, though Mr Astor does not say this) from Lloyd George. He entertained guests whom he did not like, and imposed upon them a rigid punctuality. Thus he maintained standards in a society where they were already crumbling. He died locked in a lavatory at Brighton.

John, the second son, followed his father's pattern, as *The Times* bears witness. The eldest son was angry at having his political career ruined by the prospect of a title. He quarrelled with his father, and became, within limits, a respectable rebel. Hence the difference between the *Observer* and *The Times*. Lady Astor added a fresh element. She came from a landed family in Virginia. She was gay, exuberant, romantic. She was also intensely arrogant and, despite her gaiety, intensely moral. She needed a faith that was stern though slightly erratic. She found it in Christian Science. Here were two currents of high morality – both self-confident, both intolerant, both powerful. Both ran strongly in the inter-war years. The Cliveden set were not solely the product of Claud Cockburn's fertile imagination. Those who gathered round Lord and Lady Astor at Cliveden were convinced that they knew what was best for Great Britain and for the world. They judged events in terms of morality, and the morality was of their own devising. They preached, rather late in the day, a moral reconciliation with Germany. The wickedness of Soviet Russia sustained their advocacy. No doubt the Cliveden set did not shape British policy. But they did much to nourish the climate of opinion in which their policy flourished. The Cliveden set were not alone in being mistaken about Germany. The error was so universal as to be almost respectable. Their fault was in believing that they knew better than others, and in using their resources to impose their view of things.

The power has proved ineffective. Where your treasure lies, there is your heart also. The treasure of the Astors was in New York. *The Times* and the *Observer* alike were maintained by American money in order to tell the English people how to behave. The New World was called in to redress the morality of the Old. English people read the moral instruction, and then slipped round to the public house, of which Lord and Lady Astor so much disapproved. The standards of an age have to grow from within. They cannot be imposed from outside, and those who try to do so make strange mistakes. Lord Northcliffe was no doubt a very wicked man, in the eyes of Christian Scientists. But he dismissed Geoffrey Dawson as editor of *The Times*. John Astor put him back. The Cliveden Astors have been more adventurous, Mr Michael Astor not the least of them. They added rebellion to respectability in a cautious way. But they too had property in New York.

Can they outdo the camel and pass through the eye of a needle? Will they rebel in earnest? Or will they settle in the end for respectability? The question has worried Mr Michael Astor all his life. He has not yet found the answer. Perhaps only an American government which confiscated all private property in New York would find the answer for him and for his family.

Harold Nicolson

Sir Harold George Nicolson (1886–1968) served in the diplomatic service, 1909–29, including being a member of the delegation to the Paris Peace Conference, 1919. Thereafter he was a notable author and an MP (National Labour for West Leicester, 1935–45).

These essays were first published as reviews of James Lees-Milne, Harold Nicolson: A Biography, *Volume 1 1886–1929 and Volume 2 1930–1968, Chatto and Windus, 1980 and 1981, in the* Observer, *16 November 1980 and 25 October 1981.*

Not so conventional

To outward appearance, Harold Nicolson was the most conventional of men. His earlier career followed the guide-lines of good taste: aristocratic background, Wellington and Balliol education, brilliant diplomatic record, aristocratic marriage, two sons. Clearly he was destined to end as an ambassador in a most distinguished post or even as Foreign Secretary.

Nothing of the kind. This volume of his biography, the first of two, ends with Nicolson's abrupt departure from the diplomatic service and his reappearance as a journalist in the service of Lord Beaverbrook, than which there could be nothing more incongruous. Yet there were qualities in Nicolson all along which hinted that he might not adhere to the conventional course of his earlier years. It is the achievement of James Lees-Milne to explain how the transformation took place.

Nicolson seemed a straightforward, though brilliant man. He was nothing of the kind. Lees-Milne says well, 'Harold was tradition-bound, but not the least convention-bound.' He led a double life in many senses. The first was his life in the world of sex. Everyone now knows the full story of Harold's marriage to Vita Sackville-West: she a passionate lesbian, he – in his own endearing phrase – 'not by nature very accurate about his sex-life'. Nicolson became more interested in male companions as he grew older. Vita remained prone to lesbian excursions. But the two developed also a deep love, divorced from physical relations – of which, it seems, they had none after conceiving their younger son.

There is little new to learn of this story from the present biography except to see it more sharply from Harold's side. Lees-Milne writes, 'It is questionable that he was ever helplessly *in love* with anyone except Vita in his whole life. It is equally questionable whether she was ever *in love* with him.' Harold told a radio audience in 1929: 'Sex lasts a short time: from three weeks only to three years', and a little later recommended that marriage should not be allowed so long as a couple were in love. On this basis Harold Nicolson created a secure and happy marriage.

I am sceptical whether a man's love life much affects his public career, though it ultimately affected Nicolson's in one way. He could not endure the long separations from Vita when he was in Tehran or even Berlin, while Vita preferred to be tending their garden at Sissinghurst. Hence the resignation from the diplomatic service in 1929 which changed the pattern of his life.

But this is not the whole story. Harold had a double life quite apart from sex. Unexpectedly to himself and to others he developed into a brilliant writer. This was shown first in his reports to the Foreign Office. Some senior members of the Foreign Office indeed found them too brilliant. Curzon delighted in them, Sir Austen Chamberlain was less impressed. Nicolson retaliated by defining Chamberlain's idea of good relations with Mussolini:

The Prefect of Venice should hand Lady Chamberlain a bouquet of rather sniffy chrysanthemums when she arrives at the station. In return, Sir A. Chamberlain should present Mussolini with a free hand in Albania.

Nicolson's comments on the Paris peace conference of 1919 have long been in print, and they still make good reading. I would not endorse Lees-Milne's judgement that the outcome of the conference was a disaster. The East European frontiers that Nicolson drew with such labour in 1919 have endured almost unchanged to the present day with the exception of Poland.

The Lausanne conference of 1922 evoked some of Nicolson's best writing, as shown in that entertaining book on *Curzon: the Last Phase*. His years in Tehran concluded with a dispatch which gave a warning against reliance on the Shah. This warning was resented by the Foreign Office. Nicolson however attributed the hostility of the office to the fact that he had seen Tyrrell, its head, hopelessly intoxicated.

Though some of Nicolson's books, including *Some People*, originated from his professional work, many of them did not. Even while still a full-time diplomat, Nicolson also developed high talents as a biographer. His touch was light, his tone slightly frivolous. At first sight he seemed a disciple of Lytton Strachey, though the Bloomsbury set including Strachey despised him. Nicolson disliked Strachey just as much and his biographies are quite different in tone.

I venture to suggest that Nicolson's biographies are more scholarly and have more lasting value than those of Strachey, who was either cynical or sentimental. Nicolson always treated his subjects with critical affection. He wrote at an astonishing speed. Take a few excerpts from the Tennyson record: on 2 May finished Chapter 2; on 6 May finished the Cambridge chapter; on 10 May finished the 1832 chapter; on 13th finished the 10 years' silence chapter; on 18th finished the chapter on Farringford.

Nicolson had the inestimable gift of being able to dictate perfectly-shaped prose or tap it out with one finger without the slightest fault or hesitation. With such a gift it is surprising that he took so long to find his true vocation. Clearly he doubted his own ability to earn a satisfactory income for himself and his family. Perhaps he hesitated to abandon altogether his conventional and outwardly successful career. Appropriately the last work he completed before leaving the diplomatic service was the life of his father, *Lord Carnock*, himself a distinguished diplomat. Harold rated this his best book, in which I think he was wrong. *George V* is the best, coming many years later. In 1929 Nicolson had finally escaped the slavery of the Foreign Office only to enter the slavery, as he thought, of Lord Beaverbook. His best and freest years were still to come.

It would be a shame to leave this book without stealing a couple of anecdotes. One from Mrs Asquith: she told George V, 'Sir, your great fault is that you don't enjoy yourself.' The King said quite simply: 'Yes, I know, but you see I don't like society; I like my wife.' Mrs Carlyle defining her marriage to Mrs Browning. 'For three weeks the pleasure of hope and for fifteen years the pleasures of imagination.'

From Embassy to Grub Street

Until 1930 Harold Nicolson was a professional diplomat who wrote elegant biographies in his spare time. In 1929 he resigned from his profession and never returned to it despite occasional twinges of regret. The principal motive for his resignation was a desire to see more of his wife, Vita Sackville-West, or so he said. Their somewhat unusual relationship has been fully chronicled in the previous volume of James Lees-Milne's biography – both were predominantly homosexual but bound together by a deep love which seems to have increased with the passing of the years.

Their relationship remained unusual. Vita now devoted herself to developing the garden at Sissinghurst. Harold joined her at weekends, advising her on the garden but not labouring in it very assiduously. During the week he lived in London, first in King's Bench Walk and later in Albany. He shared his chambers with young men friends, as sophisticated as himself. With them he hoped to capture the secret of eternal youth. He wrote of his fiftieth birthday: 'Fifty, filthy fifty.' His sixtieth birthday 'brought him only distress'.

Harold got his wish, so far as it is possible for any mortal to do so. Though his physical powers inevitably decayed he remained in spirit a fresh eager boy with adult gifts of expression and judgement.

Harold took some time in deciding what to do when he struck out on his own. He began as a journalist contributing paragraphs to the London Diary of the *Evening Standard*. This was not a success, Harold did not get on with Lord Beaverbrook. He disliked being a gossip writer. His way of escape was to join the New Party which Oswald Mosley launched when he left the Labour party. Harold edited the New Party journal, *Action*, the very thing for a romantic boy. The romance did not last. Mosley went on to Fascism. Harold broke with him and turned to occasional journalism first as a columnist for the *Spectator*, and then a radio commentator for the BBC.

He wanted more: to be a more serious writer and to enter the world of politics. He achieved both ambitions. In 1935 he was elected a Member of Parliament, for which purpose he joined that moribund party, the National Labour. He was a good, if formal, speaker, winning praise from Winston Churchill. He attacked the Hoare-Laval plan in 1935 and the Munich settlement in 1938. He admired Eden and was one of the Eden group with their cautious criticism of Chamberlain. Still, he had the honourable record of remaining seated during the lamentable display before Munich and of voting against Chamberlain in May 1940.

Once more Harold thought his opportunity had come. He saw himself in a great executive post or perhaps he might return to the Foreign Office. It was not to be. Sir Horace Wilson banned his return to the Foreign Office because of criticisms of himself in Harold's pamphlet 'Why we are at War'.

Even Churchill as Prime Minister did little for him, perhaps distrusting him as a literary playboy. At any rate, Harold had a few months as Duff Cooper's deputy at the Ministry of Information and fell out with his chief. Thereafter he became an itinerant lecturer for the British cause, for ever expounding The British Way of Life.

Harold's political career ended in 1945. He sought a peerage from the Labour government and even offered to join the Labour party if he were given one – title, Lord Cranfield. The offer was refused. Harold would have liked to represent the Combined Universities; the constituency was abolished. He contested North Croydon in the Labour interest and was defeated by 12,000 votes.

He was even defeated in an election for the Professorship of Poetry at Oxford.

After this Harold gave up. He wrote the life of George V, the best biography ever written of an English monarch and ranking high among the biographies of the twentieth century. He wrote other biographies – Benjamin Constant and Sainte-Beuve. Every week he wrote the principal book review for the *Observer*. In my opinion, and I know something of the trade, as a reviewer he has never had an equal: impeccable in his judgement, perfect in his presentation, scrupulous in presenting both the book's virtues and its faults.

There were those who slighted him, finding him aloof, as indeed he was. Edmund Wilson wrote of him: 'In spite of his travels he has only resided in one country – the British Foreign Office, approaching foreigners from a special caste.' And Lord Berners: 'He seemed reluctant to abandon the role of *enfant terrible* that, as a young man, he had played in so engaging a manner, and people began to feel that there was something really rather terrible about an *enfant terrible* who was growing middle-aged and slightly pompous.'

I never found Harold pompous: slightly precious perhaps, and I was often reminded of Lloyd George's phrase about Arthur Balfour, 'All he will leave behind in history is the scent of a pocket handkerchief.' Harold Nicolson has left far more. All his books are still as good to read as when they were new and still reveal new qualities. Whatever Harold's pose as a playboy, he ranks high among the great professional English writers of the twentieth century.

James Lees-Milne has written a biography which almost comes up to Harold Nicolson's high standards. Occasionally he overplays his hand, as when describing Harold's broadcasts to the Far East during the war he asserts that Harold had an audience of millions. This seems most unlikely, but then much of Harold's life was unlikely.

CND

The first piece, 'Campaign Report', is his account of the progress of the Campaign for Nuclear Disarmament from its foundation in 1958. It was first published in the New Statesman, *21 June 1958.*

The second piece is The Exploded Bomb, *a pamphlet issued by CND in 1959. Alan Taylor was on the executive committee of CND when the pamphlet was published. It sold for 4d (2p).*

Campaign Report

The Campaign for Nuclear Disarmament started in the columns of this journal; and its readers deserve a report how the Campaign is getting on. I offer some personal notes, based on a good deal of speaking at meetings all over the country, but with a warning that the experience of others may be different. The Campaign has succeeded in its first object. It has rallied the converted and given them confidence by showing each of them that he is not alone. Everywhere it can rely on good meetings – never less than two or three hundred, sometimes 3,000 as at Birmingham or Manchester. We must go on inspiring the converted by such means as marches and other forms of direct action. Nevertheless the predominance of the converted at meetings has its drawback. The great weapon of the Campaign, to my mind, is argument; and we cannot argue unless we have someone to argue with. The converted do not care much for argument; they want enthusiasm. I often detect restlessness in the audience when I develop the practical, even cynical argument, that we should be more secure from a military point of view without the H-bomb. The converted do not want to be secure; they do not like to be told that we should be stronger without nuclear weapons. And it is a hard task to win the waverers without losing the convinced.

My own feeling, which may well be wrong, is that our arguments are not yet finding their mark. Most people have not grasped the extent of the devastation that nuclear warfare will cause; and they cling to the contemporary faith that 'science' will somehow find both a defensive answer to destruction and a cure for radiation. We are certainly paying a bitter penalty for the general belief that there are no limits to the miracles which science can perform. In this country we have a particular disadvantage. There are far too few nuclear physicists on our platforms. This is surely a disgraceful situation. In America nuclear physicists are leading the campaign; in Germany the outstanding nuclear physicists have pledged themselves not to make the H-bomb. In Russia Peter Kapitza, now perhaps the greatest name in nuclear physics, refused from the first to have anything to do with research for destruction. He risked much and suffered much. In England most nuclear physicists do just what they are told and regard the Campaign with sceptical disapproval.

It is a gloomy thought that the pull of the Establishment here is stronger than the call of American or German patriotism or than the terror of Soviet Communism. We have biologists in plenty. As a result, people begin to agree that tests are dangerous; but are relatively unmoved by the far greater danger of nuclear war. Most of them indeed still acquiesce in the government's declared policy that it would drop H-bombs *first*, for the sake of our oil interests or even – height of absurdity – in defence of rocket-bases in Cyprus.

Our second failure is that we have not made our alternative clear or precise enough. Even when people are shaken by our account of nuclear destruction, they are inclined to answer: 'So what?' They cannot believe that there is a better way. The Campaign now stands for unilateral abandonment by this country of all nuclear weapons; but there are still traces in its policy statement of the initial attempt to include everyone from pacifists to the United Nations Association. It still talks of 'first steps' and unilateral abandonment 'if necessary';

and resolutions at meetings, when moved, often steer clear of unilateral abandonment. I thought from the beginning that this statesmanlike attitude was a mistake; and I think so more strongly now. Of course we want the Campaign to be as wide as possible; but the emphasis should be on *possible*, not on *wide*. When people ask for a solution, we ought to insist that unilateral abandonment is the only possible solution. Everyone wants to get rid of the bomb – or everyone except perhaps Duncan Sandys. We want to get rid of it in this country here and now.

Having said this, we need to go further and to show that unilateral abandonment is the best, indeed the only, method of negotiation. It is a tiny chance; but there is no other. As it is, we often give the impression of being on the defensive. We seem to admit that the country is secure now, that international negotiations are one way of getting rid of the bomb, and that we are cranks in wanting to try some other way. We need to be more insistent that the present position is one of imminent danger and that our policy offers the only way out. It is the handicap of a non-political movement that we are reluctant to offend anyone. We slip into treating those who disagree with us as men of good will; whereas good will is merely another name for inaction. We encounter another obstacle. The essence of the Campaign is that a moral challenge can be stronger than nuclear weapons. People no longer believe this. They once thought that faith could move mountains. Now they doubt whether it can move molehills.

There is a special problem here, caused by the age-distribution in the Campaign. The members of the audiences are over fifty or under twenty-five. Why this should be, I do not know. The missing generation are said to be all baby-sitting. I think rather that – having been taken for suckers in the war against Hitler – they are now resolved never to believe anything again, and regard the march to destruction with helpless resignation. At any rate the cleavage between the generations makes it difficult to strike a common note. The over-fifties remember the Peace Ballot, sanctions, and the Abyssinian war. They want the old phrases about morality and disarmament, despite the fact that these have been discredited – rightly or wrongly – by the failure to prevent the Second World

War. They are shocked by the argument that getting rid of nuclear war would enable us to spend more on conventional weapons. The under twenty-fives are exactly the opposite. My undergraduate friends at Oxford all say: 'Give us the practical arguments against the H-bomb and cut out the uplift.'

It is the same wherever students are in the audience. There is a shiver of distaste at the moral approach. Yet we must make it. The Campaign will never succeed if we are in it merely to save our own miserable skins. Mr Strachey writes: 'It is the other people's bombs, not our own, which would destroy us.' Apparently it does not worry him that we are planning to destroy millions of other people, equally innocent or perhaps – like the ten million Indians who may be poisoned by American bombs dropped in Siberia – more innocent. It worries me. Sooner or later we shall have to win the younger generation back to morality. I wonder where they learnt that it was bunkum. Was it from contemporary philosophers or from the day-to-day behaviour of statesmen? This country of ours fought two world wars mainly for high principle; and the only lesson drawn from this by the young is that might is right. It now seems unbearably priggish to say that the country which went to war for the sake of Belgium and Poland must not, in any circumstances, drop the H-bomb. But it is true.

There is another cleavage in our audiences which it is even more urgent to overcome. The Campaign is a movement of eggheads for eggheads. We get a few trade-union leaders, themselves crypto-eggheads. We get no industrial workers. Here – let me be frank about it – the Labour party has done us great harm, and done it deliberately. The party launched an anti-nuclear campaign of its own, held a few public and private meetings and issued one pamphlet. The Labour party's campaign was meant to kill us, not the bomb; and it has had an effect. Not indeed the pamphlet. Reading passages from this makes the audiences laugh so much that they often accuse me of having made them up. But the general impression of Labour's action remains, and we run against the solid loyalty that is the strongest element in the Labour movement. We are accused of being a splinter-group, though, thank heavens, we cannot be accused of being fellow-travellers. The Communists never did a better day's work than when they opposed unilateral disarmament.

The unspoken accusation against the Campaign is untrue. We are not seeking to disrupt the Labour party nor to challenge the present leadership. We are seeking to win it over. We offer it the moral leadership of the world. I understand Labour hesitations and equivocations. The Labour party backed unilateral disarmament and moral suasion in the 1930s when these turned out to be wrong; and now it shrinks from unilateral nuclear disarmament and moral suasion though they are the only hope. We must be patient with these doubts, though this is often hard in the heat of the moment on the platform. We are entitled to point out that the logic of making the H-bomb is that you must be prepared to use it. But we must never forget that ultimately we have to convert the Labour party, just as the Anti-Corn-Law League converted Sir Robert Peel. The Anti-Corn-Law League used plenty of rhetoric and emotion, but its decisive weapon was persistent argument. That is our weapon also. The H-bomb is morally wrong; and it is idiotic into the bargain. It took the Anti-Corn-Law League eight years to argue its way to victory. I doubt whether we have that long. But, whatever the time, we must go on arguing.

The Exploded Bomb

The Campaign for Nuclear Disarmament started just over two years ago. Do you remember what people said about us then? They said we should never get anywhere. We should never persuade a Great Power to give up nuclear weapons all on its own. Look at what has happened now. Unilateral nuclear disarmament is the biggest issue in politics. It is sweeping the Labour party. It is supported by some of the largest trade unions. Even the Conservative government has abandoned the 'independent deterrent', which was the central point of its so-called Defence policy.

Is this all the doing of the Campaign? Not at all. We never said that our marches and our arguments would carry the day by themselves. We said that facts would argue for us. And we have been proved right. Everything that was said by the advocates of nuclear weapons has turned out to be wrong. Everything that we said has turned out to be scientifically correct, politically wise. And yet we are the ones who are supposed to be emotional, sentimental, out of touch with reality. It has only cost us a few thousand pounds to prove ourselves right. It has cost the government and their scientific advisers hundreds of millions of pounds to prove themselves wrong. Now all they can suggest is that they should spend hundreds of millions in order to prove themselves wrong again. And the official Labour leaders are racking their brains how they can get the party to agree with the government.

The Campaign is not an emotional movement. It never was. It is not now. It certainly is a movement of morality. What is wrong with that? Is morality a dirty word which must never be used in politics? This country used to pride itself on the morality of its policy. In the last fifty years we have fought two wars for moral reasons, for the freedom of others as well for our own. Few of us would be in the Campaign if we had not been driven on originally by moral reasons. It seemed to us impossibly wicked that our country should be preparing the indiscriminate destruction of innocent millions and should be contributing its part to the destruction of all mankind. Faced with a choice between nuclear weapons and pacifism, we should choose pacifism. But we are not faced with that choice. It has always been an essential part of the Campaign to insist that nuclear weapons do not make us stronger; they make us weaker. They do not increase our security; they increase our danger. They are a provocation, not a deterrent.

If the advocates of nuclear weapons repudiate morality, we will meet them on their own terms. Let us take the case for the nuclear deterrent, and examine it as though morality had never existed in the world. The theory of the deterrent has passed through three distinct phases; and arguments which could be used in one phase cease to be valid when applied in another.

The first phase came in the years after the war. At this time the United States alone possessed nuclear weapons. It was then possible to argue that these weapons 'deterred' any attack by Soviet conventional forces. This was not a very good argument even when the facts behind it were correct. American nuclear weapons did not deter the Communists from conquering China; they did not deter the Soviet Union from consolidating its hold over eastern Europe. On the contrary, the only practical effect of the American monopoly was to 'deter' successive American governments from maintaining adequate conventional forces: and so they had to acquiesce – perhaps fortunately – in minor encroachments.

In any case, this first stage of 'deterrence' died long ago, when the Soviet Union got nuclear weapons of its own. It was inconceivable from then on that nuclear weapons could be used against the movement of conventional forces; for this would be to invite, at best, mutual destruction. The only people who failed to realize this were the British government. They went on running down their conventional forces. Only two years ago Duncan Sandys, then Minister of Defence, still asserted that we should use nuclear weapons against any Russian move with conventional forces on a massive scale. He was applauded by Harold Macmillan, who is still Prime Minister; and he was supported by the official Labour leaders, who until recently refused to declare that we should never use nuclear weapons first. This is why Duncan Sandys authorized reliance on the Blue Streak – a rocket to be launched from an open site, which could therefore be obliterated before it was fired. But this apparently did not matter; because our government was planning to fire first.

The Americans were more realistic. They recognized that nuclear weapons now cancelled each other out. There was now a supposed 'balance of deterrence', which was really a balance of terror. The West no longer dared to use its nuclear weapons; but at least the Russians would not dare to use theirs. Though nuclear weapons were no longer of any use against conventional forces, they were presented as being at any rate some security against a nuclear attack. This, too, was not a very good argument. Some Power might shake off the 'deterrent' by getting in its own blow first. This became indeed the official theory of American strategists. While they repudiated the idea of 'preventive war', launched out of the blue, they devised a variant, known as the 'pre-emptive strike'. They said: if events are moving to a crisis, if war seems imminent, then the United States should – perhaps after due warning – knock out all the Soviet bombers on the ground. So here we were: not more secure under the umbrella of the 'deterrent', but in greater danger than before – war poised over our heads whenever some American theorist chose to press the button.

But all these arguments are dead too. Mutual deterrence is as out-of-date as bows and arrows. In fact more so. Bows and arrows could still be used in appropriate circumstances; bombing aeroplanes cannot be used at all. We can still make H-bombs; the Americans can make H-bombs; the Russians can make H-bombs. Other countries can make H-bombs if they are prepared to waste countless millions in doing so. We are all up against the problem: how do you deliver them? And nobody knows the answer. For more than a generation we have taken for granted the truth of Baldwin's famous sentence: 'the bomber will always get through'. This was never as true as people thought it was. Now it is not true at all. The bomber will not get through. The Russians have shown that a single rocket can bring down an aeroplane flying at 60,000 feet. Their rockets can hit the Moon at almost exactly the time predicted; they can hit a target in the Pacific. We can go on manufacturing H-bombs; but the only way we could deliver one on Moscow would be to send it through the parcel-post. It would be foolish to claim that the rocket-screen is complete, or ever can be. An occasional bomber might slip through. But for all practical purposes the age of the bomber is over. The balance of deterrence has ceased to exist.

Now what do we do? It is pretty clear what the government are going to do. They are going to say: 'The policy we have pursued so far has been proved mistaken. Therefore let us pursue it more obstinately than ever.' We are going to pretend to have an independent deterrent, even though everyone except presumably the electorate knows that we have none. We are going to spend further millions on so-called weapons which are already obsolete or which will be obsolete before they are ready. Why should reasonably sensible men behave like this? Have they really taken leave of their senses? No. But they are afraid to tell the truth to the people. They are afraid even to tell it to themselves. They run after that will-o'-the-wisp – the independent deterrent – not because they believe they will ever find it, but because running after it gives the impression that Britain is still a Great Power. Years ago an American economist, Thorsten Veblen, laid down the theory of Conspicuous Waste, showing that rich men spent money not for pleasure, but as a form of competitive display. The independent deterrent is Conspicuous Waste, applied to the world of states. We want to prove that we are a Great Power by living beyond our means.

This is not the only course offered to us. Some of our politicians recognize that the search for an independent deterrent will ruin us, quite apart from the fact that we are unlikely to find it. But they still hanker after a deterrent of some sort. They therefore propose that we should get others to share the labour and the cost. They say: 'Let us share in nuclear knowledge, equipment, and research. They have in fact those in France and Germany.' This is a topsy-turvy idea from the practical point of view. Both France and Germany are years behind us in nuclear knowledge, equipment, and research. They have in fact nothing to pool. The Joint NATO deterrent does not mean a more effective deterrent. It simply means three provocations instead of one; offering at best the cheerful prospect that when we are wiped out, the French and the Germans will be wiped out as well. Some Labour leaders seem to be inclining to this course. Yet it is a complete reversal of the policy of a non-nuclear club, which was in theory the official policy of the Labour party. The Campaign welcomed the idea of a non-nuclear club, though we thought the Labour party was going the wrong way about it. We should certainly be glad to see even a limited number of states give up nuclear weapons. Yet we in the Campaign were condemned as disloyal to the Labour party simply because we said that the only way to get even the non-nuclear club was for us to give up our nuclear weapons first as an example. But what words can be found for Labour leaders who now propose to force nuclear weapons on the French and the Germans? How can this be squared with the non-nuclear club? Do Labour leaders intend to go round Europe with the slogan: 'Join the non-nuclear club. It will equip you with the latest nuclear weapons'? The NATO deterrent, if it ever comes into existence on paper, will be a fraud like the independent deterrent before it. It will not frighten the Russians; but it will console the fierce patriots who think that the best way to secure peace is to brandish arms which you do not possess. The NATO deterrent will be a piece of stage-furniture, designed only to impress an imaginary audience – or maybe to deceive the people of this country, as they have been deceived over nuclear weapons time and again.

We should become a non-nuclear Power, not from principle, not to give a lead to mankind, but simply from weakness. We should still say: 'We would like nuclear weapons if we could afford them, but we can't, so we have decided to do without.' This argument is the one least likely to win over the electorate. That, no doubt, is why it has been propounded by Mr Crossman – the most ingenious vote-loser of our age. What should the Campaign say to this idea of giving up nuclear weapons merely from weakness? Any reason for unilateral nuclear disarmament is better than none, and we shall be glad if this country gives up nuclear weapons even on such craven grounds. But the idea has a catch in it. Those who advocate it still 'believe' in nuclear weapons; only they want to get them on the cheap. We are to shelter under the American nuclear 'umbrella'. The Americans will provide the nuclear weapons, complete with rockets, at their sole expense. We will provide the rocket-bases, the radar-posts, all the practical set-up for nuclear war.

This means quite simply that we should abdicate as an independent country; Mr Gaitskell – who is now supporting this policy – has himself demonstrated this most forcefully. We should become an advanced-post of American nuclear power, helplessly dependent on any decisions taken by unknown men in the Pentagon. Any British influence for moderation would cease to exist. And for what should we have sacrificed our independence? In order to be more secure? No. In order to be less secure. We should become the first hostages in a nuclear war. We should not be sheltering under the American 'umbrella'; the Americans would be sheltering behind us. They could launch the nuclear 'deterrent' against Soviet Russia. Yet the Soviet answer would not fall on the United States; it would fall on British towns and British people. I have not much faith in the 'deterrent' at the best of times. But maybe a statesman is occasionally pulled up when he reflects that nuclear weapons will fall on his own country, on his own relatives, on himself. Those who propose that we should become – or remain as we are already – a gigantic aircraft-carrier for American nuclear power take away the one little bit of value which the 'deterrent' possesses. What American general will be 'deterred' by the thought that, if he presses the button, the Russians will destroy East Anglia or London in revenge? He will be safe thousands of miles away. Indeed the essence of American strategy is to hit out without being hit back. The Americans can no longer rely on geographical isolation. Therefore they accumulate so-called allies, sacrificed on the outbreak of nuclear war.

The Campaign is often accused, wrongly, of being 'pacifist'. The real pacifists are those who think that we should abdicate into the hands of America. We are to have all the disadvantages of pacifism: no arms, no independence of action. Yet we are to have none of the advantages of pacifism; we are to invite nuclear destruction more provocatively than before – our island crammed with the nuclear weapons which other countries have refused. This is really carrying devotion to the Anglo-American alliance a shade too far.

There is no escape from these dreary prospects so long as men go on thinking that nuclear weapons – ever more destructive, ever more out of control – are the only answer to other nuclear weapons. The Campaign for Nuclear Disarmament seeks to break this barren deadlock. In our view, unilateral nuclear disarmament is not the end; it is the beginning. We can think straight about the great problems of Defence and Security only when we have given up our nuclear weapons. Do that, and the way to a solution is clear. The answer is: 'defence, not deterrence'. There is no defence against all-out nuclear attack; and the deterrent, far from being a defence, is a provocation. We should be safer, more secure without nuclear weapons, particularly American nuclear weapons. But there are means of defence which increase our security against anything short of nuclear attack. We have neglected these means during our crazy obsession with the 'deterrent'. We should go back to them. It is a disgraceful thing, for example, that this country, which was the sole inventor of radar, has done nothing to develop defensive rockets; and has instead wasted its resources on H-bombs which can never be delivered. It is a disgraceful thing that, apart from nuclear weapons, this country is now more dangerously disarmed that it was at the worst time during the 1930s.

Reject all moral considerations as ruthlessly as you like. It still remains true that nuclear weapons should be at the bottom of the arms-list, not at the top. Why is Finland still independent? How can Yugoslavia ignore the Soviet complaints? Is it because these two countries are heavily equipped with nuclear weapons? On the contrary, their very lack of nuclear weapons and nuclear bases is a powerful reason why they are left alone. An even stronger reason is that they are capable of defending themselves. Invasion would be too much trouble. What the Finns and Yugoslavs have done is surely not beyond the wit of the British people.

We all know that the Russians have thousands of H-bombs and that they have fairly efficient means of delivering them – better, at any rate, than anyone else's. It is a natural reaction to feel that we should be able to hit back. But resentment is a bad teacher. First of all, we can't do it. What 'deterrence' is it that for every hundred H-bombs which hit us, we can send one back? Second, we don't want to do it. Even if we could obliterate a few Russian towns, that would not defeat Russia or win a war. Third, we can defend ourselves without nuclear weapons. Why then imitate the Russians in wickedness as they imitated the United States? Most important of all, our feeble preparations for nuclear war are themselves a provocation, not a security. When statesmen talk about the need for defence, we agree with them. But nuclear weapons are not the defence we need.

We spend much time talking about the dangers which surround us. These dangers are caused in large part by nuclear weapons themselves. Every so-called precaution against these weapons increases the danger that they will be used. The present suspicion between East and West is largely caused by nuclear weapons. The atom-bomb at Hiroshima, as we now know, was dropped in part as a warning against the Russians; and that warning ended the wartime friendship. Ever since 1945 we have scribbled up fear of the Soviet Union on the wall in order to justify nuclear weapons; and the Soviet leaders scribble up fear of us for the same reason.

What sense is there in it? What evidence is there – apart from our own fears – that the Soviet Union plans to conquer the world, still more to destroy it? The evidence cannot be found in action. The Soviet Union has not advanced the frontiers of its power an inch since 1945. Rather the contrary, the breach with Yugoslavia has compelled it to retreat. The evidence can only be found in the statements of Soviet leaders themselves. They constantly say that they expect communism to become one day world-wide. This is exactly what we say about democracy: one day we expect that to be world-wide. Of course we expect it to happen peacefully. The Communists say just the same. Why do we believe them when they say they want communism to conquer the world? and yet refuse to believe them when they say that it will happen peacefully? Is it because we want to have an excuse for keeping up the Cold War? I would not believe Soviet assurances whole-heartedly, just as I would not believe entirely the assurances of any statesman. We should take careful and accurate precautions against a Communist attack. But nuclear weapons are not precaution of this kind. They are a provocation, and indeed the one solid reason for fearing a Soviet attack at all.

Unilateral nuclear disarmament is not pacifism, not a desertion of our allies, nor treachery to the West (a strange democratic west which includes Portugal and Turkey). Abandoning nuclear weapons would make it easier for us to supply our share of ground-forces to NATO, which we are not doing at present. But it would also make NATO less necessary. Once we give up our own nuclear weapons and bring the American nuclear bases in this country to an end, we can take the lead in setting up a non-nuclear zone from the Soviet frontier to the Atlantic. Europe would then possess greater security than it has known in modern times. More than this, we should have given the proof that nuclear weapons, far from being a deterrent, are the principal cause of danger and of war. The example would not be lost on others. At the present moment, tension is again mounting in the world. That tension has been caused by mutual nuclear fear. Yet statesmen draw the moral that nuclear armament should be pushed on at a greater rate. What use are the professions, which they make at the same time, that they are theoretically in favour of disarmament? In theory everyone is in favour of disarmament. They differ only as to means. Men have tried to get disarmament by threats; they have tried to get it by negotiation; they have tried it, in the fashion of Mr Strachey, by pious wishes. All have failed. We think in the Campaign that the best chance of success is for someone to start; and we want that someone to be us. No one should be misled by the talk about negotiating bomb in hand. There is no way you can negotiate with a bomb, unless you are prepared to use it. We must never stop saying to our leaders: 'Would you use it? If not, get rid of it.'

The Campaign for Nuclear Disarmament is not a vague movement of protest and good-will. It exists to promote the safety and the moral standing of this country. Nuclear weapons are wicked. They also threaten us with destruction. We should give up, unconditionally, all nuclear weapons and all reliance on nuclear weapons, whether our own or anyone else's. This is the right road. It is the safe road. It is the way of security and the road to peace. Everything that has happened in the last two years has confirmed the policy with which we set out. We shall go on advocating this policy until it succeeds.

Looking Back at the 1950s

This essay was first published as 'Backwards to Utopia', one of several published in a feature, 'Look Back at the Fifties', in the New Statesman, *2 January 1960. The other pieces were 'The African Awakening' by Basil Davidson, 'The Jittery Fifties' by Robert Bendiner and 'The Proofs of Culture' by Nigel Calder. Kingsley Martin, in a front-page editorial entitled 'Jack's Decade' (referring to selfish self-interest embodied in the popular saying 'Pull up the ladder, Jack, I'm all right'), took a markedly different line from Alan Taylor. He dubbed it 'a Tory decade' and observed: 'Cynical, materialistic, selfish, the decade made the rich richer, the poor poorer ... Despite A. J. P. Taylor's sanguine appreciation ... it was a decade without a hero and without a message.'*

Centuries, like human beings, take half their lifetime to reach maturity. They acquire confidence and character in their fifties. Until then they squint apprehensively over their shoulder at the legacy of the past. The Great Exhibition of 1851 first announced the triumph of the Steam Age. The Hungry Forties were forgotten. Men travelled by train; wore top-hats and trousers; suffered from high-minded doubts.

In the 1950s, too, we have become contemporary, facing the problems of today instead of trying to re-create those of yesterday. No one except me agonizes over the origins of the Second World War, as everyone assiduously wrestled with the origins of the First; and I do it only as a matter of historical curiosity – not in the belief that any useful lesson can be drawn. Strategists think in terms of nuclear war when they think at all; they do not plan to resume campaigns interrupted in 1945. It is the same in the world of fashion. After the first war, fashion was in conscious revolt against the past; and the results were ugly. Fashion in the 1950s shook off the past. It was concerned to produce elegant clothes suited to modern conditions. Men have become sane; though, of course, there is still enough of the past lying around to produce insane results. It is insane, for instance, that the admirable outcome of modern production – two cars in every home – should bring city traffic to a standstill. We shall not escape to sanity until we have pulled down every building and re-made every road that existed before 1945.

The old order in international affairs has been wound up. For 300 years western Christendom dominated the world; a domination reinforced during the past 100 years by its monopoly of industrial power. This domination has now come to an end. Suez was the great symbol. The Suez expedition was pure 'throw-back' – harmless, elderly gentlemen, flexing their unused muscles in gestures of a vanished imperialism. The opposition to the Suez expedition was 'throw-back' too, recapturing the exhilaration of the pro-Boers. I found it possible to do this without any cracking of muscles; in fact, I have not enjoyed any public event so much since the General Strike.

All the same, it was not opposition which stopped the Suez aggression. It stopped of its own folly and incompetence. And the most absurd part of it was the allegation that the Egyptians would not be able to run their Canal. In fact, it has never handled so much traffic as since the Egyptians took over. Ten years ago nearly everyone was shocked at the idea that we had become a small power. Now the idea is so familiar that most people have ceased to believe that we are a power at all. This, incidentally, is the strongest popular argument against unilateral nuclear disarmament: 'If we threw away our bombs, who'd notice?'

The other great powers of the past have also gone down the drain. De Gaulle stumps around proclaiming the greatness of France. He means only that he is France and that he is a great man. In this he is right: he is the only surviving example of what is otherwise an extinct species. The French are not interested: they are concerned with great vintages, not with great powers. The Germans never cease announcing that they are no longer a great power and have no ambition to become one again. Of course, in the usual German fashion, they hope that what they are saying will turn out to be false. For once, maybe they are speaking the truth against their will. Oddly enough, in this political world, the more you give up, the more you have. The Germans are running over with prosperity because they have no domination over others; we are more prosperous than we used to be because we have parted with most of our empire; and if the French still lag behind, it is because they cling to some crumbs of theirs.

Ten years ago, it was common talk that Soviet Russia and the United States were now the two world powers, eclipsing all others, with the Americans well up in the first place. We were in for a generation of 'cold war' – the champions of two rival civilizations endlessly squaring up against each other in ring-shows all over the world. We got plenty of cold war. The conflict over Berlin was just finished. Soon there was war, medium-hot, in Korea; then one in Indo-China; later renewed tension over Berlin. Are we now back where we started? I don't think so. In Chesterton's words, 'the ice is breaking up on every side'. The sophisticated explanation for this is that the rulers of the world powers are now themselves afraid of nuclear war. So they should be if they had any sense. But there is something deeper. President Eisenhower let the cat out of the bag when he missed his place in the script while doing a television-turn here. He had to fill up with an honest gag: 'The people want peace. They mean to get it; and if the politicians don't give it to them, the politicians will be pushed aside.' Here is the writing on the wall for statesmen of powers, great and small – also, incidentally, for commentators on world affairs.

The American lead in the world has ended already. The first Sputnik was one of the three decisive events in the decade (Suez and the death of Stalin being the others). This announced the end of America's technical superiority. Henceforward she was just like any other power, except for her accumulated treasures – and they are now running down so far as the gold-reserves are concerned.

Americans no longer wish to dominate the world, if they ever did so. They are backing out of the world as hard as they can: President Eisenhower at this moment is preparing a second line from Fez to Delhi in order to be quit of Europe, and this second line will not hold for long. It was a basic doctrine of the Cold War that Russia was planning to take America's vacant place. Any square inch of the world's surface not made safe for democracy by the umbrella of atomic dollars would automatically go Communist.

No such advance was made during the 1950s. The Soviet action in Hungary was their counterpart for Suez, almost as shameful and even more foolish. The Russians are not likely to repeat it. Stalin was the last tyrant of the old school; and though Khrushchev has to carry bits of Stalin's legacy on his back, he clearly groans at the burden. Of course, there are those who cannot bear the thought that 'history' – meaning the long record of crime and folly – is coming to an end. Failing anything better, they pin their hopes, or fears, to Communist China as the next claimant to world power. They are likely to be disappointed. World conquerors are out of fashion. Sensible countries are coming into their own. After the First World War, everyone believed in the League of Nations; and it did not work. After the second war, no one believed in the United Nations; and it is working very well. We are entering Utopia backwards, constantly surprised that the future turns out so much better than we expected.

Belief is over. That was the keynote of the 1950s. Belief in national greatness and world conquest – all finished. Belief in dogmas about individual behaviour finished also. The young in the 1920s were in conscious revolt against tradition; their own beliefs and behaviour merely turned this tradition upside down. They even went to bed together conscientiously on principle. The young of the 1950s left such principles to their elders. They conducted their lives on the basis of common sense; went to bed together only when they wanted to – which turned out to be seldom; and became the sanest and healthiest generation in the history of the world. *Lucky Jim* was the symbol of a new age. He was not a rebel, as often alleged, not even an angry young man. He was the modern Everyman – more fortunate than the original and more attractive, too; no longer trailing his soul among imaginary evils, but lucky to be alive when mankind was coming to its senses.

It was Lucky Jim who marched from Aldermaston, some thousands of him. I used to worry about his gaiety. The Campaign for Nuclear Disarmament, I thought, ought to be conducted in a serious, respectable way. Now I have learnt better. Why should one be serious when faced with madmen? What can one do but laugh and play skiffle when an archbishop solemnly elaborates theological justification for the H-bomb and next proposes that adultery should be made a crime? It is a nuisance to have lunatics around, playing with fire; but it is comic too.

The sane have had a few victories during the past decade. The greatest blow struck for British freedom in my time was the coming of independent or commercial television. I daresay its programmes are not all wonderful (some are); but the principle has been established that viewers should be given what they want and not what Mr Hugh Carleton Greene or even Tom Driberg thinks is good for them. The sound-monopoly of the BBC now seems to be on the way out. This is a strong reason for looking forward to the 1960s. I cannot restrain my impatience to see the day when Broadcasting House is put up for sale.

The newspapers have been moving along the same democratic line despite an old-world adherence to principle by the Beaverbrook Press. All the rest aim increasingly at giving the consumer what he asked for. Even the *Guardian* followed this policy, somewhat belatedly, when it recognized that it had comparatively few consumers in Manchester. The recent arrival of Mr Roy Thomson into British journalism, with a strictly commercial outlook, makes it even more probable that the press will soon reflect public opinion correctly for the first time. Every successful newspaper (and weekly journal) is the proof that freedom pays, or, to put it another way, that freedom is what you pay for.

Politicians have been a good deal worried by this problem, and still are. Throughout the 1950s, political leaders, particularly in the Labour party, kept holding themselves up to public gaze in the hope that some permanent image would be impressed on their mirror-like countenances. The hope has hitherto proved vain. One of the curiosities of the decade was the insistence of politicians and moralists that this, the least selfish of any generation, was interested only in material rewards. Of course, the 1950s expected motor cars and refrigerators and television sets. But they were not interested in them. They took them for granted, part of existence as natural as eating or sleeping. In fact, the 1950s made it clear that mankind could conquer the material world as soon as it felt inclined to do so.

Or am I being too optimistic? To me it seems a wonderful decade, with all the old nonsense being shovelled underground. The best things in it, for me, were the opposition to Suez; Aldermaston; and independent television. But they are only types of a general pattern. Perhaps the marvellous summer of 1959 – best for 200 years – has twisted my judgement. Perhaps the lunatics will make a come-back in the 1960s. We have the world at our feet; and someone may be tempted to give it a kick. Such doubts suggest that I am growing old. Maybe the young will win. At any rate, if the next ten years do anything like as well as the last they will do very well indeed.

History Lesson We
Cannot Ignore

Alan Taylor, like Lord Beaverbrook, was strongly against Britain's membership of the Common Market. This essay was first published in the Mail on Sunday, *25 March 1984 (on Alan Taylor's seventy-eighth birthday).*

Now, once again, it's all our fault! Through sheer shop-keeping selfishness the British are wrecking the brave European dream.

Unless we agree to the crazy book-keeping that has one EEC member paying almost half the bills the community will collapse or Britain will be cast into outer darkness.

But would that be a cause for lamentation?

It is now twelve years since we were lured into the Common Market and I must confess I was against it even then.

Today it looks as though those of us who opposed Britain's entry into the EEC are in the process of being vindicated.

The case in favour of the Common Market, as put forward by its advocates, was quite simple: since the loss of the Empire we are out on our own economically and if we went into the big league with the other Europeans we should all be better off.

At that time only 29 per cent of our exports went to EEC countries, yet they constituted a bigger potential market than the US and the Commonwealth put together. With them we should be better off. Happy Days would be here again – if we joined.

So in 1972 Edward Heath took us into Europe with a starry vision glinting in his eyes, amid wild talk of the enormous benefits it would more or less automatically bring with its market of 300 million people.

But if this was good news, it was good news for others rather than us.

As far as I could then understand things, we paid for the privilege of being admitted to the Common Market and other countries graciously accepted what we offered them. Every year a better future was dangled before us. And every year it failed to arrive.

By the time of the referendum to decide whether Britain should stay in the Market in 1975 it had become painfully obvious that the extravagant prospects set enticingly before us in 1972 were not going to materialize.

So the pro-Marketeers switched from the carrot to the stick. If we leave the EEC, they said, the result will be mass unemployment and Britain will be cast into the economic wilderness with no markets to depend on. Now 43 per cent of our trade was with the EEC. If we left we would lose it all.

The threats worked just as the promises had done. The public voted 2 to 1 in favour of staying in.

Successive British governments remained loyal to the Common Market. They paid their dues. They set their skills to modifying the EEC's tangled economic legislation.

In fact, their most skilful and ingenious activity was to conceal from the British public the true nature of this pretentious institution.

But last week the problems and the real qualities of the Common Market became too obvious and too difficult to conceal.

Since 1973 we had paid no less than £5,000 million net into EEC coffers. And what is there to show for it? Only in one year, 1975, has Britain been a net recipient. Most years the opposite is true. In 1982, the last year for which full figures are available, our gross contribution was £2,459 million.

This meant that every man, woman and child in Britain stumped up £22 each. Apart from the Germans, and to a far lesser extent the French, every other member country drew out more than it paid in – and a country like Luxemburg drew a subsidy of £421 for each of its inhabitants.

As to trade – though we now export £26 billion worth of goods to EEC countries, they send £30 billion worth back to us. Again the Europeans get more out of this than we do.

So now the pro-Marketeers are beginning to sing a different tune.

They have given up telling us that we will benefit from the EEC with its ludicrous legislation, its unfair budget responsibilities and its bizarre agricultural policy. Instead they talk of serving a noble and idealistic cause. We shall all be happier if we remain in the Common Market together, they tell us, just as they did in 1972.

The wheel has come full circle. And still we are no better off.

The lessons of history are, in fact, that such Utopian dreams are never fulfilled.

The actual experience of mankind is that countries benefit most when they pursue their own obvious interests. Such was the old justification for free trade, and it remains sound.

So, too, does the historical truth that biggest is not always best.

What is good business sense for supermarkets is not necessarily good economics for nation states. Advocates of the Common Market cherish the illusion that nowadays any efficient unit must be of enormous size.

They fail to recognize that Great Britain was at its most successful when it rested on the ingenuity, patience and perseverance of a comparatively small entrepreneurial class, not on a mere gathering of masses.

Empires have, in the past, failed where they relied merely on their numbers. The old power of Imperial Spain foundered when it ran into a small but efficient country like Elizabethan England.

In ancient history the great empire of Persia was broken when it ran into conflict with the more efficient and smaller civilizations of Greece.

The principles of history persist. And they are as true of economic empires as they were of military ones.

You have only to look at how last week's Common Market negotiations have turned out to see that the old arguments are not working out today any better than they have in the past.

This is not to say that we should have nothing further to do with the countries of Europe. Far from it. There is still much which we and they can do in co-operation. There are still agreements which can be reached on trade, after negotiations.

But the vast projects and visions which were offered to us twenty or even ten years ago have faded away.

The Common Market has proved a dream without a reality. Up to now it has not worked. There is no reason to suppose that it will work better in the future.

The time has come to start afresh. We need not build up trade walls. We can encourage many sorts of international exchange. But the driving force of national self-interest, which operated so successfully in earlier decades, is still the system most likely to provide greatest benefits for all.

For Britain that can only mean one thing. There must come an end to this Common Market which lays down that the United Kingdom has to pay for everyone else.

Beaverbrook: The Man Who Never Stood Still

This essay was first published in the Daily Express, *25 May 1979, to mark the centenary of the birth of William Maxwell Aitken, first Baron Beaverbrook (1879–1964). Alan Taylor published his biography* Beaverbrook, *Hamish Hamilton, in 1972.*

Lord Beaverbrook was born 100 years ago today. It was our common interest in history that drew us together. I came to love him deeply and now, fifteen years after his death, still miss him every day.

Whenever anything interesting or exciting happens, I wish he were here to share the fun with me . . .

William Maxwell Aitken, first Baron Beaverbrook, was born at Maple, Ontario, on 25 May 1879. Soon afterwards, his family moved to Newcastle, New Brunswick, which he for long regarded as his birthplace.

His father was a Minister of the Church of Scotland in Canada; his mother of Ulster-Scot origin.

Beaverbrook was a man of many trades: financier, politician, writer, newspaper proprietor. He came late to the newspaper world, though it then bulked largest in his life.

The young Max Aitken began as a company promoter and was a dollar millionaire by the time he was twenty-five.

He came to Britain originally as a seller of bonds. He was lured into politics by the call of Empire and the personal appeal of Bonar Law.

Economic unity of the British Empire was the only cause in which

Beaverbrook continuously believed. He championed it when he first came to Britain in 1908. He was still championing it at the time of his death in 1964.

Beaverbrook knew little about India or Africa. The British Empire of his imagination was the white Commonwealth, held together by common origin from the British Isles.

This Empire was to be consolidated as a tariff union, with the Dominions providing the raw materials and Great Britain the industrial goods. This was a dream never fulfilled and perhaps incapable of fulfilment. Nevertheless, it commanded Beaverbrook's allegiance.

The imperial cause drew the young Max Aitken into British politics, and politics in their turn drew him into the world of newspapers. Beaverbrook did not acquire newspapers in order to make money. On the contrary, he used his money in order to acquire newspapers. As he told the Royal Commission on the Press: 'I own newspapers in order to make propaganda and for no other purpose.'

Though Beaverbrook sought to emulate Northcliffe, the two men were profoundly different. Northcliffe was a press lord first, last and all the time. Beaverbrook was a crusader, though he was not always sure what cause he wished to preach.

Empire unity, certainly. But also an exuberant optimism that faced, unshaken, the economic and international problems of the time. In economics, Beaverbrook preached expansion. Almost alone, he repudiated the deflationist policy of 1931 and announced defiantly that, having spent more money during 1931 than in any previous year of his life, he proposed to spend still more in 1932.

His newspapers also promoted personal campaigns. They promoted, first of all, Beaverbrook himself – less as a political leader than as an exciting man, which he certainly was. His editors had a standing instruction always to publish any news item about Lord Beaverbrook, good or bad.

Beaverbrook's first hero was Bonar Law, and he almost succeeded in transforming that rather shadowy figure into an inspired statesman. Most of all, he liked dynamic personalities: Lloyd George in his younger days; Churchill later on. His judgement of the two was characteristic: 'Churchill was the greater man, but George was more fun.'

Beaverbrook acquired and transformed two newspapers: the *Daily Express* and the *Evening Standard*. He created one: the *Sunday Express*. Each had a distinct character. All had one thing in common: all found readers in every class of the community and not, as other newspapers did, in the A to B or C to D groups.

All, too, had an irrepressible sense of zest and fun.

Beaverbrook exercised his control of the newspapers from afar – 'absentee ownership', as he called it. His instruments were the telephone and the dictaphone or, technically, the soundscriber.

He determined policy and dictated the news stories, great and small. His constant query to his editors was: 'What's new?' It was his conviction that something new and striking would happen every day.

Though Beaverbrook was primarily a newspaper man, there were other sides to his personality and ceaseless activity. The Empire Crusade, which he ran from 1929 to 1931, nearly drove Baldwin from the leadership of the Conservative party.

More memorable still was the part he played in the Second World War. Before the war, Beaverbrook was an Empire isolationist. He believed that Great Britain should arm powerfully and then stand aloof from the troubles of the European Continent, secure in the support of her Empire.

When, nevertheless, war came, Beaverbrook was Churchill's most steadfast adherent. Churchill did not always accept Beaverbrook's advice: he relied, nevertheless, on Beaverbrook's personal encouragement.

Beaverbrook made one imperishable contribution to British victory. As Minister of Aircraft Production he provided the fighter aircraft which won the Battle of Britain.

Lord Dowding, Chief of Fighter Command, said so emphatically: 'The country owes as much to Beaverbrook as it does to me. Without his drive behind me, I could not have carried on during the battle.'

There were other contributions. No man did more to keep Great Britain and Soviet Russia in alliance. He preached the Second Front from early days. After the war he still championed British greatness and was one of the gallant few who opposed the disastrous American loan in 1945.

Beaverbrook had another achievement less regarded by the general public: he was a great writer of contemporary history. *Politicians and the War, 1914–16* is a vital source of information and as entertaining as a novel.

In his final years Beaverbrook was embittered politically, though he had a temporary triumph in Britain's exclusion from the Common Market in 1963.

Now the Empire has perished. Beaverbrook's newspapers have changed their character in accordance with the needs of the time.

Only his works of history endure.

Malcolm Muggeridge:
Woeful Countenance

Malcolm Thomas Muggeridge (1903–90) was a journalist and television personality who delighted in shocking the middle classes during his earlier career; but he later became a notable spokesperson for Christianity. Alan Taylor and Malcolm and Kitty Muggeridge were friends from 1930, when they lived in flats in the same house in Didsbury, Manchester.

This essay was first published as a review of John Bright-Holmes (ed.), Like It Was: The Diaries of Malcolm Muggeridge, *Collins, 1981, in the* Observer, *29 March 1981.*

Malcolm Muggeridge and I belong to the same generation. Both of us grew up within sight of that Promised Land – a Socialist Utopia. Both of us were disillusioned, though in different ways and with different results. I was relieved by my loss of faith and have not sought another. Malcolm was left desolate, cynical about everything and often declaring that he had no wish to go on living.

These excerpts from his diaries are another version of Bunyan's Progress from this world to the next. But they also often recall the remark of Dr Johnson's friend Edwards, 'I have tried too in my time to be a philosopher; but, I don't know how, cheerfulness was always breaking in.' Malcolm keeps a sustained gloom for his diaries. In my recollection, now stretching back over half a century, cheerfulness was always breaking in.

Muggeridge's diaries do not attempt to repeat the continuous narrative that he provided in his autobiography some years ago. Rather they present episodes, told with some detail and then breaking off abruptly, as happens so often in life. Muggeridge has moved restlessly from one occupation to another, from one country to another and from one pattern of life to another. The one secure resting place for him was his marriage to Kitty and their love for each other. Even there, in his earlier years, he often tried to break away until Kitty quelled him with the words, 'You'd better stick to me. No one'll love you as I do.'

To my disappointment the diary as published contains nothing about Manchester where we shared a house in the early 30s. When Malcolm departed for the Soviet Utopia, I said to him, 'If Soviet Russia does not come up to your expectations, don't take it out on the Russians.' Malcolm did not heed the warning and no wonder, plunged as he was into a man-made famine which caused the death of over three million Russian peasants. Malcolm was disillusioned overnight and has retained only one fixed principle: a hatred of power-worshippers, particularly of the Communist variety. The diary entries concerning Soviet Russia are the raw material for Malcolm's masterpiece, *Winter in Moscow*. They also contain, as the book does not, hints of the new theme which has dominated much of Malcolm's life: the search for something to replace the Utopian faith he had lost.

Often he despaired: 'I here record at the age of thirty-three that I have no wish to go on living.' Often he sought refuge in work. The one thing, he declared, that interested him was writing: 'I want to be a writer, a great writer.' He rubbed the Magician's Lamp and his wish has been in one sense fulfilled. Set down the record of his journalistic career as leader-writer, foreign correspondent and book reviewer: Malcolm's output of words appears beyond numeration. But it has brought him little satisfaction. As he has gradually experienced, writing is not a way of escaping from life, only another way of experiencing it.

From Russia Malcolm went to India, which gave him many delights, especially that of watching the last days of Empire. There is one curious little touch of schoolboy romance. In March 1935 he noted that war was certain sooner or later. 'If there is war, I shall fly home at once and learn to fly. This thought made me quite happy.' When war came Malcolm did not learn to fly. Instead, after a short period as an infantry officer, he entered the Intelligence Service, which is another form of journalism – there is no escaping one's fate. The diary is blank about the war except for a brief interlude in Lisbon when Malcolm was on his way to Lourenço Marques. Maybe this is for security reasons; maybe Malcolm did not find this part of his life interesting.

The pace quickens after the war and with it the material. Malcolm was happily reunited with his family. Nevertheless, 'Although I've often been happy, I've never felt at home in the world, and know now that I never shall.' The Soviet Utopia was now reversed: 'I feel certain that Europe will be conquered by the Bolsheviks where the Nazis failed. Their triumph is coming, and is comprehensible, but still disagreeable for us and for England' (1946).

Later Malcolm was convinced that there would be a general war over Korea, but he was more cheerful at the prospect now that Montgomery would be in charge. The diary entries recounting visits to the Field Marshal are rich and rewarding, Malcolm for once appreciating a public performer of the first quality. A long visit to Churchill, though sympathetic, is less illuminating, Churchill recalling with difficulty and boredom the lines that had once inspired himself and others. Malcolm recognized a likeness to King Lear, 'imprisoned in the flesh, in old age, longing only for a renewal of the disease of life, all passion unspent'. This estimate shows Malcolm's gifts and faults at their clearest.

The diary runs on spasmodically until 1962. Malcolm became editor of *Punch*, visited China and the United States, even visited Soviet Russia where he found the people at least better fed than in 1932. He had many ostensibly happy meetings with friends. Inwardly, as he recorded in 1954, he continued 'to long for the total destruction of a society no longer entitled to exist. This longing likely to be satisfied.' Malcolm also became a success on radio and television, not to his content. 'Constant appearances on such programmes would be degrading. One would be forced to build up a synthetic, vulgar personality.'

At all such sayings I am inclined to comment 'Rubbish.' I have been a sort of Sancho Panza to Malcolm's Don Quixote for fifty years and have always experienced laughter, gaiety and good fellowship. Besides how can any man be unhappy who has such a one as Kitty as his life mate?

Commemorations

This essay was first published as a review of Isaiah Berlin, Personal Impressions, *Hogarth Press, 1980, in the* Observer, *9 November 1980. Sir Isaiah Berlin (1909–97) was an outstanding historian of ideas and one of the most respected British intellectuals of the twentieth century. Born in Riga, he was in Petrograd during both 1917 revolutions, and his family came to Britain in 1921. He was a Fellow of All Souls College and also of New College, Oxford, and the founding President of Wolfson College.*

Sir Isaiah Berlin ranks among the most notable essayists of our time. Most of his books are collections of essays and most of the essays have a double character: though they deal predominantly with ideas, they present these ideas through the medium of an individual, whether statesman, writer or friend.

The present collection has the same character, except that all the subjects were contemporaries of Berlin's and most of them his personal friends. He is himself a famous conversationalist as well as a distinguished writer. He seems to be always talking. Evidently his friends make the same impression on him. At first I thought he was exaggerating in this. On further reflection I think he is right: the impact of Isaiah Berlin is to make us talk as much as he does. He brings out the best in people and then sets it down. The essays in this book present a collection of stars and Berlin records them when they were shining most brightly.

He describes the essays in this book as 'what in the eighteenth century were called *éloges*, addresses commemorating the illustrious dead'. The subjects are praised because they merit praise and Berlin praises with discrimination. The opening essays are devoted to the two Anglo-Saxon heroes of the Second World War, Churchill and Roosevelt. Both *éloges* were written in reaction against the recrimination of the immediate post-war years. I find Berlin's reaction more convincing historically than the recrimination, especially in the case of Roosevelt. Like any good eulogist Berlin sometimes pitches his claims rather high. I echo his description of Churchill as 'the saviour of his country'. But 'the largest human being of our time'? And if Churchill was 'one of the two greatest men of action his nation has produced', who was the other? Still, Churchill merits almost any praise for what he did.

These two portraits of statesmen were drawn at a distance – Berlin knew Churchill little and Roosevelt not at all. At the other extreme are the portraits derived mainly from personal acquaintance. Many of those presented were also friends of mine and I am repeatedly astonished by the understanding with which Berlin brings them back to life. Maurice Bowra for instance was a talker whose brilliance rivalled Berlin's. He had other qualities – of scholarship, of personal affection, of courage – more difficult to set down. Berlin has recaptured them all.

On the same high level, or perhaps even higher, is the portrait of that great historian, L. B. Namier. Namier was at one and the same time an incomparable talker and a formidable bore. Berlin has got them both. Namier was my dearest friend for many years and this is a wonderful portrait of the Namier I loved. Berlin underrates him slightly as a historian. In my opinion Namier, though obsessed with the reign of George III, showed even greater mastery in his great sweeps surveying nineteenth-century Europe. Berlin has also forgotten or perhaps never knew that Namier wrote the first detached study of the origins of the Second World War when others were still writing polemics. Of course Berlin is a philosopher and I have always felt that he puts ideas (philosophy) above events (history).

Berlin and I are on common ground in his presentation of J. L. Austin, who revolutionized Oxford philosophy. I have often wondered what the revolution was about and, though Berlin does not dispel my lack of comprehension, he conveys the atmosphere of those distant contentions. I also treasure Austin's whispered remark, 'They all *talk* about determinism and *say* they believe in it. I've never met a determinist in my life, I mean a man who really did believe in it as you and I believe that men are mortal. Have you?'

Zionism has long ranked high in Berlin's ideals and among his friends. Namier was a Zionist of a special sort. Weizmann, it is clear, was Berlin's greatest hero and he here pays to Weizmann a tribute of simplicity and grandeur. As Berlin shows, Weizmann was inspired by the conviction that the Jews could attain full stature as a people only if they found a national home. Weizmann was confident that this could be established in Palestine without any conflict with the Arabs. Namier was more ruthless. When interviewing a candidate for a post at the University of Jerusalem, he asked, 'Mr Levy, can you shoot? Because if you take this post, you will have to shoot our Arab cousins. If you don't shoot them, they will shoot you.' A sad end to a noble vision.

The concluding piece is the most fascinating of all: an account, not previously published, of Berlin's meetings in 1945 and 1956 with Russian writers, particularly with Boris Pasternak and Anna Akhmatova. To recapture something of the atmosphere, I give two stories recorded by Berlin. According to the first, Stalin telephoned Pasternak and asked his opinion of his fellow-poet Osip Mandel'shtam, who was then in danger. Pasternak answered that he wished to discuss with Stalin 'cosmic turning points in the world's history'. Stalin repeated his question, Pasternak insisted that they must discuss ultimate issues about life and death, whereupon Stalin said, 'If I were Mandel'shtam's friend I should have known better how to defend him,' and put down the receiver.

In 1965 Anna Akhmatova visited Oxford and told Berlin this story. Stalin learnt of her meetings with Berlin in 1945. He exclaimed, 'So our nun now receives visits from foreign spies.' Enraged, he launched both the new wave of persecution and the Cold War. Berlin doubted whether the two of them were world historical personalities chosen by destiny to begin a cosmic conflict. But he felt that any dissent or protest would be an insult to Akhmatova's tragic image of herself as Cassandra. For once Berlin remained silent.

The Year 1906

This essay was first published in Donald Read (ed.), The Edwardian Age, *Croom Helm, 1982. It was a lecture given as 'The Year 1906' on 25 November 1981 to mark the Historical Association's seventy-fifth anniversary.*

Talking of anniversaries, it is exactly fifty years since I gave my first lecture to a branch of the Historical Association, in Preston I think. I suppose that every year since then I have done some lecturing for the Association, and secretly I am rather hoping that this lecture marks my release. But you never know what life will bring!

I remember a remark of Bernard Shaw's who told of an old lady who said that things had never been the same since Professor Tyndall gave that address at Belfast. Now I don't know what address that was, and indeed I am not at all clear who Professor Tyndall was;* but I think it applies to the year 1906, that things were never the same afterwards. It was a landmark of a year; a political landmark, promising maybe greater political changes than were to take place, but still a year which the politically knowledgeable still remember:

---

* Declan Lyons, editor of *Science & Technology*, kindly sent me an article on Professor Tyndall which appeared in the April 1981 number of that periodical. John Tyndall (1820–93) was a distinguished Irish scientist who rose to become Professor of Natural Philosophy at the Royal Institution. In 1868 he was President of the British Association, which met that year in Belfast. His Presidential Address 'stated the viewpoint of scientific naturalists with an arrogance and intellectual imperialism calculated to raise hackles . . . Tyndall succeeded in sparking perhaps the most intensive debate in the Victorian conflict of science versus religion.'

'Ah, the general election of 1906.' But it is also convenient in another way. It was the central point of that short but, I think, fascinating period of the Edwardian Age, difficult though it is to call it an age when it lasted only ten years. Yet it had a marked character and it is about this character that I want to talk first.

At the beginning of the twentieth century, the end of the reign of Queen Victoria, there was a feeling of the end of things. Great Britain was struggling through the Boer War, you can't say success-fully, but eventually to some sort of conclusion. Compared to the optimism of the mid-nineteenth century, the end of the century had been a period of decline, of depression, of decadence. Then for no particular reason, except that it was entering into a new century with a new reign, the Edwardian period, though maybe it had little justification for imagining that it was stronger and more powerful and more successful than its Victorian predecessor, found a greater exuberance. Not that the Edwardian Age, or the whole of the pre-war period, was a period of great economic recovery. If one looks at the statistics, it was a period when real wages did not go up at all. Nearly every historical book I read now remarks on this. The British economic position declined; British exports declined. The balance of trade was maintained only by the yield from invest-ments overseas. I think we overrate the influence of these statistics. Nowadays, they affect us all. We all ask, when are the unemployed going to be three million, or when will the balance of our exports be even blacker than it is now? But I don't think that in the Edwardian Age people read these statistics. In fact, I doubt whether they were obtainable. The tables of real wages for instance, which every statistician uses nowadays, were not in popular use in those days. The working man, maybe, was not getting quite the real wage in 1910 that he had done in 1901; but for many reasons he found it a more cheerful period.

One of the rules that historians should lay down for themselves is not to attach overmuch importance to the statistics which they have calculated. Statistics are enlightening sometimes as a measure, but they are dangerous as a guide to the spirit of the age. I would apply that to even later periods when obsession with financial figures became greater. So that there was, maybe, something of a contradiction. It was an exuberant age, and one might say that it had no reason to be. The change of monarch, although perhaps not very significant politically, was certainly significant psychologically. After the restraint of the late-Victorian Age Edward VII was outgoing; he carried along with him the aroma of scandal and cigars, and his was an age, I think, not only worldly but actually mercenary. Wealth had become virtue, and wealth was more rated than anything else by the Edwardians, much more than in the Victorian Age which we think so mercenary. The leading figures all aspired to be wealthy and many of them were indeed rich. Edward VII himself had his attractive side; he was more used to the weaknesses of human nature, shall we say, than Queen Victoria. He had also more experience of society, of his surroundings, than Queen Victoria had. For example, he knew the Liberal leader, Sir Henry Campbell-Bannerman, socially far better than many politicians did. Edward VII had wide experience, not much judgement. He is supposed to have been a sage adviser on foreign affairs, but if one studies his record this is by no means the case. I came across a comment of his on some papers relating to the preparations for the Anglo-French *entente* which said that Anglo-French relations should be improved, and that this could be done if the French were given a free run in Morocco. The King wrote in pencil a comment which would have been appropriate some ten years before. 'The French are very greedy. We must not let them have Morocco,' and then underlined this twice. Six months later he was approving a deal by which they got Morocco, because he was told it was the right thing to do.

I would add another final point when talking about the King. It is not uncommon for close relatives to quarrel. Indeed, it marks the intensity of family feeling. Edward VII and his nephew, the Kaiser, were often not on good terms; but I think the whole story that the estrangement between them made William II anti-British and helped to bring on the whole turn of German policy against Great Britain is a grotesque exaggeration. They quarrelled because nephews and uncles normally quarrel. They were also very often on excellent terms. Before the Kaiser turned up at Cowes, the King would remark how unfortunate it was that he was coming, but when he came they had a jolly time together; and I think it was in a spirit of rather admiring criticism that the Kaiser remarked, 'Ah, my uncle's out yachting again with his grocer,' because Edward VII was yachting with Sir Thomas Lipton. Certainly, the King gave something of a character to the period.

I think that the period was fully expressed for the first time during its middle years. I had hoped to tell you of a number of striking coincidences – of writers, artists, musicians, who were particularly expressing the Edwardian spirit during the year 1906. This approach is not very rewarding. So far as literature goes, there are two very good coincidences. One was the publication of Galsworthy's *The Man of Property*, the first volume in *The Forsyte Saga*. It was characteristic because *The Forsyte Saga* presents perfectly an Edwardian family. It was characteristic also in title. To be a man of property you need not now be a landed squire; property of any kind, even (you remember Wemmick's phrase) portable property, was important in the Edwardian Age. Now I will remind you of another masterpiece which, I think, expresses something of the Edwardian Age; and that is *The Tale of Mr Jeremy Fisher*, which was published in 1906. Mr Jeremy Fisher lived in a small cottage, but he was an active angler and his two friends, you will remember, were men of some modest distinction. Margaret Lane suggests that Sir Isaac Newton with his black-and-yellow waistcoat was a member of the Reform Club. Alderman Ptolemy Tortoise was something already characteristic of the Edwardian Age, a food fad. He brought a salad with him in a string bag. It would have been difficult to fit in Peter Rabbit, but without any doubt at all Mr Jeremy Fisher was a leading Edwardian and, what is more, must have been a member of a club himself, boring members with his stories about the size of the fish which had nearly eaten him. It would be wrong, however, to leave literature in this way. By 1906 Bernard Shaw had already written his most remarkable works until his renaissance after the Great War. In 1906 the only new Shaw play running was *The Doctor's Dilemma*, which marked a return by Shaw to the well-made play and, incidentally, was written in order to provide an attractive female part for one of the ladies whom he very inadequately pursued. But in the years around 1906 appeared the H. G. Wells masterpiece novels, *Kipps* in 1905 and *Tono Bungay* in 1909.

Move on to *Ann Veronica* (1909) and this marks, I think, the beginning of the breakdown of the Edwardian compromise of outward respectability and never mind what happens when you weren't being respectable. The *Spectator* described *Ann Veronica* as 'capable of poisoning the minds of those who read it', because when Ann Veronica is out walking with her tutor he asks her, 'What do you want?' and she answers with a terrible emphasis which had never been used by a woman before, 'You!' – poisonous, the end of the Edwardian compromise!

When I pick up a Wells novel I still feel a spirit which was so characteristically Edwardian, of exuberance and of hope. These writers and others were – I was going to say preachers, I do not mean to say in a basic religious way, but there was a widespread belief in this Edwardian decade that by offering people higher standards of enlightenment you would carry them forward. Look at Wells, a writer all his life of Utopias. Some of them were composed for purposes of entertainment, but most of them were written from the genuine conviction that if you write a plausible Utopia it will actually convince people and they will – I don't say adopt it at once – but work towards it. Nowadays people write Utopias in order to console you for the fact that life isn't going to be like that at all. Wells, Shaw to a lesser extent but even Shaw, and other writers, offered hope for the future; they expected that it would be better, and this leads me on to another aspect of the period.

It marked, for a variety of reasons and in a variety of ways, the greatest period of influence for what were then called the 'Free Churches', since the time of Cromwell. It has been claimed that in the Parliament of 1906 there were more Nonconformists than Conservatives. Certainly there were a lot of Nonconformists, more than there had ever been before or, I think, than there has ever been since. Where in the nineteenth century there had been great evangelical preachers or great ritualists, a feature of the Edwardian Age was the great Free Church preachers in Hampstead and in other parts of London, in Birmingham and elsewhere, and quite a number of them were actually elected to the House of Commons in 1906. They were elected for a particular reason, but they provided the Nonconformist spirit. One of them has become even a sort of local saint. Silvester Horne has tablets to him at Church Stretton in Shropshire simply because he had his country cottage there. But Silvester Horne, R. F. Horton and others were the last generation of Christian preachers of any kind who could fill a large church, Sunday after Sunday, with a doctrine that was, although Christian, concerned with the practical things of this life. Looking back at it, I think in some ways one might even be tempted to describe the Edwardian Age as an age of mild dissent – a mild Socialist movement, a mild trade-union movement, mild Liberalism, except of course for the aggression with which they were expressed. If I began to describe to you now the programme which Lloyd George promoted when he became President of the Board of Trade in 1906, you would hardly be perturbed by it; 'Why,' you would say, 'even Conservative governments do that nowadays.' But at the time his name aroused the most bitter indignation, hostility getting worse year by year from all Conservative civilized classes. So it wasn't by any means a gentle time. There were even refusals to pay rates. Dr Clifford, Baptist teacher and preacher, went to prison. The issues which seem to us so remote were once highly fought over.

Now I ought, I suppose, to say something about the general election of 1906, which was indeed remarkable. It was remarkable, though, not only in figures but in its character. The Liberal party was never going to gain such a great victory again, though not the greatest majority it had ever won, its greatest majority over the Conservatives. Historians, any of us who look at 1906, may be tempted to exaggerate the sensational character. The actual swing over was not very great. There was a much increased poll, but that was for a simple reason – there were a lot more candidates. And there was a transference of votes. There were sensational Liberal victories. The former Prime Minister, Balfour, was beaten in Manchester. And yet the surprising thing was the unevenness; the way in which, for instance, Joseph Chamberlain and his protectionist block held on not only to Birmingham and its area, but to other towns. It was the smaller towns, suburbia, rural areas, which had never been Liberal before and were never to be Liberal again, which went Liberal in 1906. The chief factor was alleged to be Free Trade; and incidentally, here is a point which I have not seen made before.

Farmers were in favour of Free Trade, despite the allegation that tariff reform would mean protection for farmers and despite the fact that the whole Liberal cry of 'dear food' was based on this. What people overlooked, which Chamberlain had overlooked when he proposed that foreign corn should be taxed, was that the bulk of British farmers had moved over from growing wheat to raising cattle. And they were doing this by feeding their cattle with foreign corn. So that those cattle were just as much exposed to the threat of taxation of food as were human beings, and some of the most completely agricultured districts returned the largest Free Trade majorities.

Cheap food was mentioned in all the election addresses, and it provided one of the two sensational propaganda weapons of the campaign. The first of these was the 'big loaf'. Someone who had been a candidate in 1906 told me how he had two loaves baked each morning, a big loaf – the present result of Liberal policy; and a small loaf – the predicted result of Conservative policy. And he took them around with him all day long. Politicians, incidentally, did a lot more 'going on the stump' than they attempt nowadays. Little meetings were held in little halls at any time from the early afternoon to late evening. Another visual propaganda device which this same man used related to 'Chinese slavery'. This issue was mentioned in nearly all the addresses. Chinese coolies had been drafted into South Africa to work in the mines. My informant actually managed to hire a Chinaman from Liverpool who followed him around.

The issue which created the greatest disturbance in the Conservative party, indeed almost a split between the Conservatives and the Liberal Unionists, was of course the Education Act of 1902. There are some curiosities. Old age pensions came in all right, and it was no surprise when they were started by Asquith two years later. Not a word about the wider embryonic welfare state that Lloyd George was to introduce, no word about health insurance, no word about unemployment insurance; they were invented two or three years later. Instead there was a very remarkable element which produced no echo whatsoever when Parliament met. Nobody ever raised the question, and yet the great majority of Liberal candidates had named as a prime object the nationalization of railways and canals. The question of railways was carried so far at any rate that Hilaire Belloc in one of his political novels attributed the fall of an imaginary Liberal government to the proposal to nationalize the railways in the Isle of Wight. They didn't even get as far as nationalizing these.

The Liberal candidates, and here again is a point which I had not appreciated, were mostly men with previous election runs. There had been after all a modest Liberal victory in 1892, and many a Liberal who had sat from 1892 to 1895 now came back. So that the successful Liberal party was not markedly younger than the Conservatives. The Conservatives tended to recruit from younger people because Conservative members were richer and could go into politics earlier. The characteristic Liberal Member of Parliament after 1906 was a well-to-do businessman who, having devoted the first thirty years of his adult life to making enough money, had then aspired to enter Parliament. You must remember that being an MP was rather expensive. Candidates were normally expected, though there were exceptions, to pay all election expenses. At that time this even meant paying the returning officer. It was only in 1918 that the returning officers got put down to the cost of the rate-payers. Not only did candidates have to pay the expenses of election, they had to contribute to party expenses, more or less in full. It was just like the eighteenth century. If you wanted to get into Parliament you bought your way in, only now you didn't buy the borough from a borough owner, you bought it from the election committees.

One feature of the election was that trade unions paid the expenses of their members who were running either as Liberals or as Labour candidates, and this was no new thing. Another fascinating feature – it applied at all general elections, but the impact was much greater at this one – was that voting was spread over a fortnight, or even longer. Each borough or county district decided its own election date, so that early election results could well influence those later on. This, the Conservatives said rather sulkily, explained the extent of the Liberal victory; it was unfair because the Liberals began winning at the beginning and everyone got on to the bandwagon.

The matter is of some moment to me because I attended the displays outside the *Southport Guardian* offices, which was the local newspaper, when the results were flashed on a screen which showed Liberal victories day after day. My mother was a passionate Liberal politician and loyally went to watch these. It is true that she was heavily gone with child and had to go in a bath-chair; but I can say that I witnessed the greatest Liberal triumph of all time – if from a somewhat privileged position! And this event lives vividly in my mind because I was brought up on it as a story. In 1910 I actually shook hands with the Liberal candidate at Southport: he did not get in.

Apart from the size of the Liberal majority, there were two other noteworthy party totals. One was the limited triumph of the Liberal Unionists, who held on much better than anyone else did; and the other was of course the appearance of a Labour party. This was in fact less significant than was made out later. The Labour party was no more than a transformation of the Labour Representation Committee, and it was concerned to represent Labour interests rather as the Irish group represented Irish interests. That brings me back to the list of proposals which election candidates put forward. In all the Liberal addresses that I have looked at, the question of Ireland is either only briefly mentioned or (more often) is not mentioned at all. Occasionally, improved local government for Ireland is proposed. This scant interest anticipates what followed thereafter until the 1910 elections. Ireland had almost ceased to be a topic of controversy or disturbance in British politics. It has been well said that under the regime of Augustine Birrell, the Liberal man of letters who became Irish Secretary in 1907 and remained so until 1916, Ireland was better governed and was more at peace than it had ever been since the time of Brian Boru. Incidentally, I often read that Ireland has never been united; of course it was united for hundreds of years. It was only in 1922 that it was disunited with the creation of an imaginary and catastrophic frontier which has been a great nuisance ever since. Until then Ireland was governed as a unity with all the government offices in Dublin and with a unitary policy. Ireland was coming alive, but it was coming alive in ways of culture much more than in politics. Even Patrick

Pearse, who was to put his name to the declaration of the Republic in 1916, was more concerned before the war in developing the Gaelic language; and when *The Playboy of the Western World* was put on at the Abbey Theatre in Dublin it caused far more trouble than any assertion of British authority in Ireland. The Irish Home Rulers, and there were some eighty of them in the House of Commons, included many busy journalists. One of them, T. P. O'Connor, represented Liverpool, and ran his own very successful weekly newspaper. Many of them were members of the Reform Club, some of even more august bodies. Ireland had become part of – I was going to say of England – had accepted the united constitution much more than it was to admit a few years later. It was only the accident of the electoral results of 1910 which brought the old Irish question back into politics.

The Liberal government of 1906 is said to have been one of the most remarkable governments of modern times. It certainly had a great array of distinction. It was expected that Campbell-Bannerman would be a rather ineffective Prime Minister. He lives in history by the way in which he answered Balfour when Balfour managed to scrape back into the House of Commons, not surprisingly from the City of London, by interrupting Balfour's logic-chopping with the famous phrase, 'enough of this foolery'; and it made Campbell-Bannerman's name. He was a wonderful balancer. A number of the ministers had served in Gladstone's Cabinet; some of the most distinguished were starting for the first time, and there was a remarkable range of ages. The Marquis of Ripon had been born in 10 Downing Street in 1828 when his father, Lord Goderich, was briefly Prime Minister. At the other end of the scale, one Cabinet Minister (Lloyd George) was to remain in the House of Commons until 1945, and another junior minister was to retire from 10 Downing Street in 1955 (Winston Churchill). The Liberal majority were indeed triumphant. Yet their triumphs were limited. They ended Chinese slavery, though it was 1910 before they managed to get rid of all the Chinese coolies; thanks to Campbell-Bannerman's enthusiasm, they restored full colonial self-government to what had been the two Boer republics; they passed a somewhat offensive vote of censure on Milner for the way in which he had dealt with South

Africa, but another vote of high praise of Milner was passed in the House of Lords.

As I discovered when I read the *Annual Register* for the year, the parliamentary session of 1906 was devoted chiefly to a total waste of time, dealing with two measures which were of great importance then and seem of very little importance now. One was the Education Bill, which turned on the sectarian question of why Church of England schools were receiving some assistance from the rates under the 1902 Act. It has always been a mystery to me that for religious people it is better that children should be brought up in blank ignorance than that they should be brought up by a denomination of which the person concerned does not approve. Rather than have Welsh children receive instruction in the way that the Church of Wales wanted, they seem to have favoured no instruction at all. At the same time it is extraordinary that the Lords made such a fuss about the Bill. It was a possible way of resolving the complication. The House of Lords simply rejected it because it was a Liberal measure. They also rejected – it is a mystery to me that people got disturbed about it one way or another – a Licensing Bill, which would have reduced the number of public houses. Whether this was desirable then or is desirable now is a matter of some interest, but not much. Yet it excited much more passion than topics such as the future foreign policy of the country. As a matter of fact, the brewers have continually cut down the number of public houses from that day because many of them have been unprofitable. As to the conflict over religious instruction and control, when you consider what the Church of England has done to the prayer book, it is lamentable that religious schools are allowed to go on at all! I daren't mention the Bible because it is now unreadable.

1906 is of enormous importance in the history of England not only because of the Liberal victory, though that was important enough, but because it witnessed the beginnings of profound change in British foreign policy. This was marked in two ways. In February 1906 the Cabinet went down to Portsmouth in order to see the launching of Sir John Fisher's latest marvel, HMS *Dreadnought*. The *Dreadnought* was the first all-big-gun ship. It put all existing battleships out of date. It was supposed, therefore, to increase enormously British naval security. But previously Britain had possessed some forty-three battleships, the Germans twenty-two. Now the British had one *Dreadnought,* and the Germans had none; but the possibility of the Germans catching up became much greater. From that day in February 1906 there stemmed a whole course of naval rivalry between Great Britain and Germany which first, I think, caused really intense bitterness between the two countries, reaching a climax in 1909. I do not say it actually provoked the war of 1914. Indeed, by 1914 the British had confidently and satisfactorily won the naval race at some expense, and naval relations between Great Britain and Germany were better than they had been for years. But there had never been a naval race between England and Germany before; between England and France, certainly, but as France was the old and traditional enemy, that had never caused any fresh bad feelings. It was what you expected the French to do!

Far more dangerous was an episode which was wrapped in secrecy at the time and remained controversial for years thereafter. There had been in 1905 a diplomatic dispute between France and Germany over the future of Morocco. In brief terms, France was hoping either to annex Morocco or to establish a protectorate over it. The Germans had an idea that as they had not picked up many colonies they would like a share in Morocco. Such a partition very often happened. But on this occasion there had been considerable tension. The tension had been, to put it abruptly, lessened by the proposal to have a conference at Algeciras, which incidentally represented a great landmark for another reason. This was the first occasion, apart from a conference over the Congo in 1884, when the United States had involved itself in a congress over European affairs. This was a short-lived development due to the fact that Theodore Roosevelt was ambitious to make the United States a world power; but it was a symptom of what was to come. Forty years later or thereabouts, the American landing in Morocco really restored Moroccan independence from the French. The temporary outcome, which is what I am talking about, was that the French raised an alarm that Germany was preparing to invade France. Sir Edward Grey, the new Liberal Foreign Secretary, was presented with the inquiry, 'Would Great Britain stand by France?' The question had been asked earlier in 1905, but given an evasive answer by Lord Lansdowne, Grey's Conservative predecessor. The election was in full swing, the Cabinet could not be told, or so it was alleged later, and the French Ambassador revealed that the members of the Imperial General Staff and French staff officers had already been in consultation. Ever since 1901 and 1902, from the end of the Boer War, the British authorities and staff officers had been anxious to produce a remodelled army, an army that was up to date and not one organized solely for colonial wars. It should be an army which could intervene in western Europe, a thing Great Britain had not done for nearly 100 years. In this sense the technical requirements of the general staff created, or shaped, British foreign policy. The staff officers were already wanting to have staff conversations. After all, once you have created an army which is supposed to be designed for intervention in European affairs, you must find somewhere to interfere. Ever since 1902 the general staff had been looking for somewhere to interfere; here was the God-sent answer, to interfere on the side of France. Grey said he wanted to keep his hands free to decide at the time whether England wished to assist France or not. He was told that he could not do so unless preparations had been made to aid France. If the plans had not been made, if the expeditionary force was not prepared, if all train timetables had not been laid down, then Great Britain would have to say, 'Sorry, we can't help you.' A Foreign Secretary can depend upon the army only if the army is ready. Even then, you cannot expect to use it all over the world; you have to choose one ally and one enemy. And in January 1906 Grey chose the one ally, France, and the one enemy, Germany. It is hardly too much to say that at that time Grey, quite unwittingly and from the highest of motives, determined that when there was a great war in Europe between France and Germany, Great Britain would be committed for military reasons on the French side. A curious point about it is that Campbell-Bannerman himself, the Prime Minister, was informed and agreed that it would not be suitable to mention such a topic to the Cabinet. This was, I think, because he had been Secretary of State for War in two previous Gladstone governments, and probably thought that it really wasn't very wise to tell Cabinets how incompetently the War Office was running its affairs. But in any case, the danger passed, the decision was pulled back; but the general staff accepted the instruction and from that moment on, encouraged by Haldane, the Secretary of War, the preparations for a landing in France were deliberately made.

I will finish by telling a story which perhaps illustrates changed political habits. In December 1905, Balfour, the Conservative Prime Minister, resigned in the hope of creating an embarrassing position for the Liberals. There was still considerable conflict between Liberals who had supported the Boer War and those who had not. Balfour thought that Campbell-Bannerman would have difficulty in forming a stable government. Three of the so-called Liberal Imperialists, Asquith, Grey, Haldane, had made a pact that they would only take office if Campbell-Bannerman would take the three of them and if he agreed to go to the House of Lords, because they believed that the old boy was getting past it. He could well have replied 'enough of this foolery' to this remark too. Campbell-Bannerman was well prepared and decided to offer the Exchequer to Asquith, knowing that Asquith would fall for what was virtually an offer of the succession. He knew that then the other two would have to come in. But where was Asquith at this important moment? Campbell-Bannerman had to send urgent messages for him. Asquith was spending the night at Hatfield, seat of the Marquis of Salisbury, a leading Conservative of a very reactionary kind, in the company of Balfour. Now doesn't that seem an odd thing to do? Yet that was what they did in those days. Asquith came back and took the office of Chancellor, and the whole cabal broke down. But notice the extraordinary contrast between the bitterness displayed in public, which was I think much greater than any displayed now, and the easy social relations between politicans. Hilaire Belloc has another first-rate novel called *Pongo and the Bull* (1910) in which he describes how the Prime Minister is anxious to resign and to hand over to the Leader of the Opposition, in order to get back later on. I can't remember all the complications, but it is a deal between the two front benches. It all goes astray because the Prime Minister is held up by a bull in a field, and when he ought to be delivering a denunciation of the Opposition he isn't there, and so he wins the ballot. But, quite seriously, if you want to understand Edwardian politics, and maybe if you want to understand any British politics, I think the novels of Hilaire Belloc are your best guide, particularly *A Change in the Cabinet* (1909) which describes how reshuffles are really made. As an epilogue, I give you Hilaire Belloc's judgement on the general election of 1906, in which incidentally he was himself a successful Liberal candidate:

> The accursed power which stands on Privilege
> (And goes with Women, and Champagne and Bridge)
> Broke – and Democracy resumed her reign:
> (Which goes with Bridge, and Women and Champagne).

When You Have Life
Don't Waste it

This essay was written shortly before Alan Taylor's eightieth birth-day on 25 March 1986. The birthday party in Soho took place on the evening of his birthday in 'The Gay Hussar', Soho Square. The essay was first published in the Mail on Sunday, *23 March 1986.*

Next Tuesday I shall be eighty. For years, 25 March was for me an annual marker of progress.

From kindergarten to school, school to university, university to an education in the world which is still not ended.

Now, it is a rather more sinister anniversary in what is mainly a record of decline which will obviously accelerate.

I can no longer walk from Camden Town to Fleet Street, as I used to. I shall not walk Offa's Dyke or climb a mountain again. Even books are more of a strain.

Yet, I find many of these troublesome restrictions bring their own consolations.

Like Arthur Koestler, I have Parkinson's disease and cannot perform as well as I used to.

But, unlike him, I would never bring my life to an end, and I find I have a low opinion of him for ending his. I think he was foolish.

Since I have no more religious beliefs than he did, this may seem surprising. To some extent, it surprises me.

But I find it a simple calculation. When you have life in you, why waste it? You are not going to get much more, so you had better cling to it.

If you kill yourself, you have made a decision. If you stay alive then the decision is still open. You can't just walk out and then say: 'I want to come back.'

So, I am struggling to keep going. When you get to eighty, the tendency is just one way. You are going out. But I don't propose to get impatient about it.

If there are some things I can no longer do, I am discovering others that I am exploring for the first time.

For instance, I used to walk in places as remote from London as possible. Now, I am finding smaller areas of country closer to London which are a delight.

As long as you can get out in the country, there is still something to rejoice in. Who can tell how long it will survive?

We no longer preserve good country like we used to. Everything, it seems, must have houses built on it.

But most of it is safe as far as I am concerned. It will see me out.

There are more books I want to read. I am looking forward to the third volume of a new biography of Lord Montgomery.

I was his favourite historian, he once told me. He was certainly my favourite field marshal. I think he will hold his own over the centuries.

There are records that I want to listen to again – many that I had forgotten I had.

I am surprised to find how much Mozart I have.

Not very much modern music. Mahler is a bridge I have never crossed.

I still live a cheerful life with my wife, Eva, and my family. Not a week passes without our having friends to dinner.

I can still hold my own in conversations. I am still as quick as any of my friends and usually quicker.

I cannot say, looking back, that there are things I regret not having done. If there were such things, I would have done them.

At the end of my book, *English History 1914–1945*, I wrote: 'The British Empire declined; the condition of the people improved. Few now sang "England Arise". England had risen all the same . . .'

Despite some disappointments, I still hold to much of that. There has been great progress since the war. It is not wholly a story of failure.

It is true that we now have a radical Conservative government seemingly dedicated to rolling back much of what has been achieved.

But the truth is that this government has really done very *little*. That is admirable. That is what governments ought to do.

There are some things I am glad I shall not see.

Some people are rather shocked when I say I am convinced that a nuclear war will happen. But this is not dogmatic on my part.

It is a rational conclusion which, to some extent, can be drawn from history.

It is unsafe to count on the great powers having the sense not to use the nuclear weapons they have.

As for what lies ahead for me, I see no possibility of continuing existence of any kind after death.

That comes from a deep conviction rather than anything logical. It is one I have had since I was very young and it has not changed as I approach my eightieth birthday.

It seems to me so obvious that one of these days the machine will run out and won't come to life again.

It does not depress or frighten me in the least.

But, meanwhile, there are things to look forward to.

Next week, I shall have two birthday parties, one given by my family at home and the other in Soho by my old friend, Michael Foot. They may be something of an ordeal. But also they are something to look forward to.

There are worse things than being eighty. Some people tell me that being eighty-one is one of them. I am curious to verify this.

In any case, I am on the move to somewhere which will be full of surprises.

Manchester

This essay was first published as the first in a series of essays, 'The World's Cities', in Encounter, *3 March 1957, and was reprinted in A. J. P. Taylor,* Essays in English History, *Harmondsworth, Penguin, 1976. In his introduction to the essay in the Penguin collection he wrote,*

I wrote this description of Manchester just on twenty years ago. Since then much has changed. The city is now clean and the people have brightened up also. The Midland Hotel has emerged a glossy red. Victoria Park has lost its toll gates and most of its wealthy inhabitants. The Royal Cotton Exchange has closed. A repertory company now treads the boards once crowded with cotton merchants. The John Rylands Library has been absorbed by the University. The Manchester Guardian *has moved to London and dropped 'Manchester' from its title. Though it still has a Manchester office, this is no longer housed in the historic building where C. P. Scott, W. P. Crozier and A. P. Wadsworth edited the paper. Manchester has become an agreeable provincial town. It is no longer one of the world's great cities.*

When I recall the great cities of Europe, I see myself first of all clambering in and out of a motor coach on a conducted tour. Some of them later became places to live in, to belong to, but they began as sights. Not so Manchester. There are no conducted tours, no waiting coaches in Albert Square or touting guides in Piccadilly. Yet Manchester is as distinctive in its way as Athens or Peking. It is the symbol of a civilization which was, until recently, an ambition of mankind, though now little more than a historical curiosity. Manchester is the only English city that can look London in the face, not merely as a regional capital, but as a rival version of how men should live in a community. I do not know how Piccadilly, Manchester, got its name. Maybe it was a gesture of piety, but I prefer to think of it as an act of defiance or even contempt, a joke at the expense of Piccadilly Circus. There is no satisfactory English word for what Manchester represents. If 'Burgher' were genuinely acclimatized, instead of being restricted to Carlisle and Calais, that would do. Manchester is the last and greatest of the Hanseatic towns – a civilization created by traders without assistance from monarchs or territorial aristocracy.

Manchester is, however, older and – in some ways – nicer than *das Manchestertum*. It was not represented in the unreformed Parliament and was incorporated only in 1838. Hence we think of it casually as a new town, a mushroom growth of the Industrial Revolution. This is not so. It was a historical accident that Manchester remained a private manor instead of becoming a borough. Even in the Middle Ages it was a bigger town than many places which had two representatives in Parliament, and by the eighteenth century it was already the commercial centre of Lancashire. Indeed, Manchester is older still. It had a Roman foundation, though not worth lingering on. The fragment of wall in a goods yard at the bottom of Deansgate ranks as the least interesting Roman remain in England, which is setting a high standard. The market town of pre-industrial times, however, survived almost intact until Hitler's war. The collegiate church, Cheetham's hospital, the old grammar school and the market place stood unchanged, as they had been before the steam engine was thought of. You could still recapture the Manchester of de Quincey or imagine the scene at the market cross when Prince Charlie passed through on the road to Derby. Still, this too is antiquarianism. It would be perverse to visit Manchester solely to discover what it was like before the Burghers took over.

The most revealing spot in Manchester is not the historic centre or even the Royal Exchange, but Victoria Park. This is still a private estate, with toll gates and keepers in uniform. Gothic palaces jostle each other; gardeners dust the soot from the leaves of the trees; and the ghosts of merchant princes walk in the twilight. These were the men who gave Manchester its historical character. We think of them in retrospect as Radicals, and so they were in lack of respect for traditional authority or in their ruthless destruction of whatever stood in their way. But they were far from a belief in economic equality or even in democracy, if we mean by that putting the needs of the majority first. They had succeeded by their own energy, and they supposed that the duty of society was discharged if it gave others the chance to do the same. It did not worry them that, while the rich man was in his mansion, the poor man at the gates of Victoria Park lived in a slum. The road to success lay open for those who wished to take it. Like the men of the Renaissance they exalted the individual. They lacked one Renaissance characteristic. Of all dominant classes, they were the least equipped with aesthetic taste. Perhaps Money is less beautiful than Intrigue or Wickedness – the Renaissance routes to power – or perhaps it is so beautiful in itself as to destroy the need for beauty elsewhere. At any rate, the result is the same: Manchester is irredeemably ugly. There is no spot to which you could lead a blindfold stranger and say happily: 'Now open your eyes.' Norman Douglas had a theory that English people walked with their eyes on the ground so as to avoid the excrement of dogs on the pavement. The explanation in Manchester is simpler: they avert their eyes from the ugliness of their surroundings.

The great days of Manchester certainly came at a bad time from an architectural point of view, but Manchester comes off badly even by its own standards. It has nothing to compare with St Pancras Station or Keble College. The town hall and the older part of the University are in a rigid Gothic which looks as though it had been bought by the square yard. The remarkable feature of the Midland Hotel is the colour of its brick, not its design. More recent buildings keep the same quality of grandiose tastelessness. It would of course be useless for the Central Library to challenge the pre-eminence of the new Bodleian as the most hideous library in existence, but it would win an honourable mention. Apart from being out of tune with its surroundings, it is remarkable for presenting an exact model of an iced wedding-cake on a gigantic scale. One expects members of the library committee to emerge on high at any moment and cut it into slices. There is also a striking civic building which now fills the gap between the library and the town hall. This tones down their irreconcilable contrast by being itself in a style alleged to be Dutch domestic of the seventeenth century.

The ugliness is not only on the outside of the buildings. Some of the great mansions are comfortable within, though not many; none is pleasing. This character too has been maintained to the present. The professors of the University are accommodated in bare cells with prison furniture, while their common room attains the impersonal comfort of a modern waiting-room at a Continental station. The Midland Hotel once had a Palm Court of unique Oriental style – I remember a Frenchwoman who used to escape from Manchester merely by sitting there. Now it has vanished, and the Midland has an ordinary cosmopolitan interior like the new House of Commons. The City Art Gallery has a lot of expensive pictures but few good ones: even the pre-Raphaelites seem to have lost colour. The people, too, are remarkably unattractive in appearance. When I was a lecturer at Manchester, I used to peer along the serried rows of note-takers in the hope of finding a pretty girl. The only one I ever spotted turned out to be an Italian visitor. No doubt Puritanism makes the women dress so badly. The stunted growth of men and women alike is said to be due either to their Danish ancestors who settled in the Mersey valley or to the long hours spent by more recent forebears in the cotton factories. I doubt both explanations. Men adapt themselves to their surroundings, as Americans for instance develop crinkly hair and thick lips, and the people of Manchester are anxious to show that they are devoted to the Business of life, not its Art. Manchester is also very dirty – the soot continuously dropping from home fires which are more thickly concentrated than anywhere else in the world. The climate rounds off the gloom – not remarkably rainy as is often alleged, but persistently moist which is even more depressing. There are times when it seems merely wrongheaded to call Manchester the centre of a civilization.

But it is. Manchester has everything except good looks, or had until recently. Though the Burghers have gone, their independent spirit remains. Manchester is the only place in England which escapes our characteristic vice of snobbery. Manchester cares no more for the Royal Family and the landed gentry than Venice did for the Pope and the Italian aristocracy. When patrons are wanted for a charity or a club, they are found among the few remaining rich, and these are without titles. The only exception is the Earl of Derby, who has a special position as the decorative leader of Lancashire. There are few royal statues in Manchester – only the Prince Consort in Albert Square and Queen Victoria in Piccadilly. The others are local dignitaries or Liberal statesmen. Many of the Burghers were German in origin and, having shaken off subservience to their own authorities, felt no awe of any other. They sent their sons to Rugby, not to Eton; and this produced highmindedness, not snobbery. Achievement is what matters in Manchester, not a historic name or a cultivated accent. It is an added advantage, of course, that Manchester is in Lancashire and can have its own way of speaking without anyone worrying about it. Manchester is not the best type of Lancashire accent – you have to go to Bury or Rochdale for that, but it is a great improvement on the flat talk of Liverpool.

Manchester could not have been so independent without a region behind it, though I suspect that Manchester has shaped Lancashire much more than the other way round. Of course Lancashire is quite a place – with the best country in the world to my mind, and the nicest people. Cultivated Englishmen who never go further than Stratford-on-Avon or perhaps Lichfield regard all 'the North' as one in character and scenery – hard, bleak, rugged. Yorkshiremen are hard all right – living in stone houses and sharpened by the east wind. But the Pennines are a truer frontier than the Trent or the Mersey, and Lancashire people are the very opposite from those in Yorkshire. This is the land of the south-west wind, bringing an atmosphere that is always blurred and usually gentle. The men are independent without being aggressive: tolerant, affectionate, sentimental – almost mawkish. Balzac describes Lancashire as 'the county where women die of love'. I think this very unlikely. I have always assumed, though with little first-hand experience, that Lancashire women are as brisk and businesslike in love-making as in everything else. The men provide the romantic atmosphere. It delights them to imagine that the women die of love. In reality a Lancashire woman would merely reply: 'Come on, lad. Let's get it over!'

The men of Lancashire are great tale-tellers. The last great writer in the vernacular, T. Thompson (a bookbinder from Bury), combined the sentimental and the humorous into works of high art, but I've heard many a story almost as good in a public-house corner. Northern people in every country like to think of themselves as more honest and straightforward than those further south. They may be honest in Lancashire; they are certainly not straightforward. They are one and all 'romancers'. I don't think that my father ever gave my mother a strictly accurate account of his doings in all their many years of married life, even if he had only been out of the house for half an hour. A fictitious narrative was more interesting to him and, he hoped, to her. But also he was like a man with a lisp: things were bound to come out reshaped however truthful he meant to be. In much the same way the inhabitants romanticize Manchester and themselves. Their softheartedness runs over in the most unlikely places. Harry Pollitt, former Communist leader, revealed his Manchester origin when, kidnapped by Fascists, he spent the weekend playing solo whist with his captors. Left to themselves, the people of Lancashire would have gone on believing in witches and clinging to a hazy Jacobitism as they did in the eighteenth century. It was the 'foreigners' of Manchester – Germans, Greeks, Armenians and Jews – who prodded them into zestful life; also romantic in their way, but without the easy-going Lancashire spirit.

Manchester is truly a frontier-town, as Professor Toynbee thinks every successful capital should be. It is squeezed into the south-eastern corner of Lancashire right up against the Pennines. The frontier with Yorkshire, which I have mentioned already, is the sharpest. As a boy, I always felt that the dark tunnel at Victoria Station which took me to school at York was the beginning of an alien world, and I am still surprised not to see Customs officials on the platform as they are at Salzburg. But Manchester also straddles between Lancashire and Cheshire. The Mersey is no true dividing line. South Manchester is an extension of the Cheshire Plain. The real break comes exactly down the middle of St Ann's Square. There can be no doubt as you move north from there that you are in real Lancashire country. The division is economic as well as geographical. There are no mills in Cheshire though there used to be – except some that remain in Stockport, which is a sort of Lancastrian colony. For that matter, commerce has carried the day in Manchester itself. The mills have all been pushed further north. There are engineering works and industries of every variety, but no mills. All the same, cotton still dominates the city as it did when Manchester was first called Cottonopolis. The Royal Exchange occupies the most central position in the city – a position which its appearance does nothing to deserve. The most characteristic sight in Manchester until just the other day was the great horse-drawn dray, slowly carrying bales of cotton to the warehouses. Like all traders, the merchants of Manchester have time to spare or at any rate to chaffer, and they sit for hours at a time in underground cafés playing dominoes. A thorough grounding in advanced dominoes was, I think, the only useful instruction I received from my father.

Cotton is a nice industry to spring from and to live among. The making and selling of cotton is one of the few human activities which is wholly beneficent. It never did anyone harm and it has done mankind much good. Every piece of cotton cloth is going to make someone warmer or cleaner or more comfortable. You don't have to conquer people in order to turn them into your customers, and you suffer no imperialist craving to control your own raw materials. The cotton trade conspires with the climate to make the inhabitants of Manchester a kindly people, inclined perhaps to rather simple solutions, but gentle and sensible. It is no doubt foolish to believe that cotton cloth contains the secret of human happiness, but it is at any rate less foolish than to believe it of motor-cars or machine-guns. Even the local vice of gambling in cotton futures seems somehow a less speculative proposition than running after stocks and shares, though many members of Lancashire families have discovered that this is a mistaken view. Cotton itself has turned out a chancy affair ever since the First World War, and Manchester has lost something of its special character as cotton lost its pre-eminence. But enough remains, much as we still regard Oxford as an academic town though comparatively few of its inhabitants now make a living from learned pursuits.

Manchester grew great as a centre of business, and its other distinctions have come, as it were, by accident. It would be silly to pretend anything else. If you think that buying and selling is a wicked affair in the way many people do when they are comfortably off – as Marx did once Engels was rich enough to provide for him – then Manchester will not win forgiveness by its other activities. Once admit that a civilization can be founded on commerce, and everything takes on an acceptable pattern. Manchester society wanted solid worth. The houses were well built, the women plump, the food substantial. There has never been much in the nature of public show in Manchester – no idiocy of a Lord Mayor's banquet, for instance. Private hospitality on the other hand was lavish. The great houses gave dinner-parties to twenty or thirty guests as a normal routine. I used to go to one such house where, only twenty years ago, each male guest received on arrival a card with the name of the lady whom he was to take into dinner; we went in formal procession arm-in-arm. On the other hand that detestable rigmarole of the men sitting over the port was no more than a utilitarian survival; it broke up as the flush of the lavatory died away. There was no nostalgia, as there is in gentry-circles, for the common rooms of Oxford. The women counted for as much as the men – particularly of course the woman who had a fortune of her own.

A society based on money has the great merit of freedom from class. The only difference between the very rich in Manchester and the moderately well-off, or between the moderately well-off and the skilled artisan, was in the amount they spent. All lived on the same pattern, though not on the same scale. The professors of the University and the leading figures on the *Manchester Guardian* also gave grand dinner-parties to a rather smaller company. Samuel Alexander had eight or ten to dinner every week almost until his death – among the most agreeable evenings I ever spent. The thought of Samuel Alexander makes me feel that I have been unfair to Manchester civilization – stressed too much its devotion to money and business. Alexander, too, was a representative figure – also a foreigner (in his case an Australian Jew) who could never have penetrated ordinary English society, but became fully at home in Manchester. How much at home could be seen at the Hallé Concerts on a Thursday evening, when he sat among the very rich in the front row and read the *Manchester Guardian*, with much rustling of leaves during the pieces that did not interest him. These were frequent.

The Hallé Concerts were the highest expression of Manchester civilization. Most of the audience were regular subscribers who occupied the same seats year after year. When they changed, it was to move up in the price-list – not in the social scale – until they arrived with the Burghers in the front rows. But the whole audience was a single community, with personal acquaintanceship running from the front rows to the standing room at the back. The orchestra belonged to this community also. Its members greeted their friends in the Hall, and the conductor himself gave a little bow of recognition to the more distinguished citizens. For after all, this was the one genuinely permanent orchestra in England, with the only permanent conductor. In the Free Trade Hall on a Thursday evening, I had no reason to regret my season ticket to the Vienna Philharmonic. Under Richter, the orchestra, I suspect, had been heavily Germanic, and there was still too much Brahms for my taste. But Harty gave us also the new and the unusual to an extent greater than we get now from the Third Programme of the BBC. In other ways the Hallé Concerts were agreeably old-fashioned. The society was technically 'owned' by the £100 guarantors until, in the 1930s, economic need forced a democratic revolution and admitted an inferior class – with inferior rights – of those who could only guarantee £10. The programmes gave the precise duration of each piece in the margin, and one waited eagerly to see whether the conductor would break his previous record. Patrons were also informed when carriages should be ordered, while the announcement of a Special Concert Train from Central Station consoled the less opulent.

The Free Trade Hall itself had a special claim to fame, though not from its architecture. It stood on St Peter's Fields, where the battle of Peterloo began the break-up of the old order in England. Its name announced the greatest victory against that order. Other great halls in England are called after a royal patron or some figure of traditional religion. Only the Free Trade Hall is dedicated, like the United States of America, to a proposition – one as noble and beneficent as any ever made. Richard Cobden formulated it in the words: 'As little intercourse as possible between Governments; as much intercourse as possible between the peoples of the world.' It was difficult to sit in the Free Trade Hall, and still more difficult to speak from its platform (as I once did), without recalling its political significance. The men of Manchester had brought down the nobility and gentry of England in a bloodless, but decisive, Crécy. The Free Trade Hall was the symbol of their triumph.

Manchester looked at southern England in Cobden's spirit. It cared little for what was going on 'down there'. London was not expected to provide either ideas or material direction. Manchester had its own daily newspaper of international reputation and, for that matter, its own Sunday journals of somewhat different character. It had too in the *Clarion* the best Socialist paper ever produced in this country. It had its own banks and, as well, a branch of the Bank of England. It had its own University – not a 'civic' or 'provincial' redbrick, but a rival version to Oxford and Cambridge or what a national University should be. Its founder revolted against the monopoly of the Church of England. The only conditions he insisted on were that there should be no chapel and no denominational tests, even for the professors of theology. His trustees added the condition of no discrimination between the sexes. The University followed the models in Scotland and Germany, not of the Anglican institutions further south. The example had its drawbacks. The professors reigned over a crowd of helot-lecturers. But I never knew anyone at Manchester who owed his place to good manners, high-born connections, education at an expensive public school, or the right accent, and anyone who has ever heard Great Tom sound his 101 strokes will admit that this was quite an achievement. Fifty years ago or so, when Rutherford, Tout, Alexander, and George Unwin were in their prime, Manchester University had no rival in intellectual distinction.

With all these advantages, Manchester had good reason to be self-sufficient, though not self-satisfied. Nor was it parochial except in the sense that its parish was the world. The great men of Manchester had family connections with Germany and the Near East. They shipped cotton cloth to India and China and often spent some years there as representatives of their firms. They owned mills in Russia, Austria and South America. The Ship Canal completed the picture when it made Manchester a world port. Only one part of the world was unknown to them: England south of the Trent. Why should they ever want to go there? They had a wonderful sea coast on their doorstep – Blackpool for the masses, Southport always more genteel. The Lake District was only eighty miles away; North Wales even nearer. They could slip off for an afternoon to Old Trafford or spend an agreeable summer's day in the Peak District. Every Sunday in the 1930s saw a mass exodus from London Road Station to Kinder Scout, but the struggle which won a right-of-way over Jacob's Ladder was fought as long ago as 1894. For Manchester men England ended at Buxton or at Matlock. My grandfather, I think, never went further south in his life except once on his way to France. My father had been in Egypt and India; he knew Russia and most countries in Western Europe. He spent exactly three days in London and hated them. This was not plain dislike of a city, for he worked in one. He felt that London was the enemy; it represented everything he disapproved of and which he supposed, perhaps wrongly, that Manchester had defeated.

Was my father right, or has Manchester now been defeated in its turn? What remains of the Burghers and their civilization? I went back recently after an absence of nearly twenty years and looked with full consciousness at the things I had previously taken for granted. To start with looks. Manchester is quite as ugly as people say. In fact it has got uglier. I don't much mind the nineteenth-century squalor, though it is only fit for a museum, but the recent buildings are worse. Parts of Manchester are now as bad as Queen

Street, Oxford, which has few rivals in England. What is more depressing, this is not Manchester ugliness; it is the architecture of Mr Everyman, and I begin to regret the ugliness that was peculiar to Manchester. Character is fading in other ways. My former impression of Manchester was of double-decker trams in blocks half a mile long, stationary like patient elephants. Now they are gone, and the buses make Manchester look like anywhere else. Their disappearance has one advantage. All the streets have the opulent width of a capital city.

I could produce much more in the way of nostalgia. The professional entertainer is disappearing from the public houses. There are 'concerts' on licensed premises now only once a week, and even these are few and far between. The oyster bars are being smartened up in the modern way. Jolly red-faced women no longer consume stout and oysters with uproarious laughter. Instead there is an air of elegant fatigue, and prices have gone up correspondingly. One house of the old style survives in the Shambles, where the rich food is slapped down on bare boards and no one worries about his appearance. The decline of the tripe shop is sadder still. You have to search hard now for a plate of tripe and onions in a back room, where you used to find it on every corner. Lancashire cheese, almost the county's finest possession, is now made in factories and has lost much of its flavour. Manchester never got the best of it, but I doubt whether perfect cheese can be found even in the Fylde. Yet there must still be rich eating in Manchester. The food shops in the remaining fragment of the Market Place display a richness and variety unknown in southern England. The University remains the dishonourable exception that it always was. The food in its refectory would close a factory the same afternoon if it were served in a workers' canteen.

In other ways the University is changing its character. It is much richer than it was. New buildings are going up all the time; the staff is larger and better paid. But it has given up the struggle against Oxford and Cambridge which its founder enjoined on it. Instead, it seeks to imitate them and, as an imitation, naturally slips into the second rank. The strongest feature of Manchester University originally was its close link with the local community. Most of its students used to live at home. Now it is perversely aspiring towards halls of residence, which will echo our ancient and deplorable colleges. Our enlightened educational policy also works, unexpectedly, to the detriment of the newer universities. Before the war, poverty kept many first-class students from Oxford and Cambridge, even when they won scholarships. Now the means test operates only against the professional classes, who would not send their children to Manchester in any case, and the intellectual level is going down. No one, I think, could claim for Manchester University the pre-eminence that it enjoyed fifty years ago.

Shortage of money has hit the John Rylands Library, which is probably the greatest private library in England. It is still an incomparable place to work in, with no other readers to disturb your peace. The absence of readers, by the way, is fortunate, for the architect, in the usual perverse way of his profession, forgot to provide for them. They have to be accommodated in nooks and crannies, some, one suspects, reserved for readers long dead. What the library now lacks is money to buy books, and no new benefactor is likely to present himself. Already there is a touch of the Sleeping Beauty as you mount the Gothic staircase. Some venturesome visitor of the future will find librarian, staff, books and a single reader plunged in sleep for a hundred years. By then the building may be all that is left of historic Manchester.

The streets outside have a bustle and prosperity, astonishing to one who remembers the depression twenty years ago. But it is the sort of bustle and prosperity that might be anywhere. The local speech is dying; it will have gone within a generation. 'Regionalism' means only that some radio and television programmes and the northern editions of some papers are produced in Manchester as a matter of convenience. They are no different from what is produced elsewhere. The *Manchester Guardian* itself has ceased to represent Manchester except in name. Everyone says rightly that it has never been better. It is the only newspaper produced outside London to be included in every national survey along with such lesser organs as the *Daily Express* and *The Times*. But it is now a national paper pure and simple. Fifty years ago, the City Council was reported in more detail than the House of Commons; Montague and Monkhouse wrote at great length on the local theatre; Langford at even greater on the Hallé concerts. James Bone sat alone in the London office and wrote the London Letter unaided. Now all is changed. The London office provides most of the paper. It has a political correspondent, a parliamentary correspondent, a scientific correspondent, a diplomatic correspondent and a London editor with a large staff of reporters. Only the leaders are written in Manchester, and even this is being sapped – at least two leader-writers are now stationed in London. A. P. Wadsworth often edited the paper from the London office – a thing which never happened in C. P. Scott's time. When Scott visited London to expostulate with Sir Edward Grey or Lloyd George, it was as the leader of Manchester liberalism, not as the editor of a national paper. Now the editor plays little part in local politics.

The *Manchester Guardian* now speaks for the enlightened everywhere, not for Manchester. When it went against public opinion during the Boer War, it lost circulation generally. During the recent crisis over Suez, it lost readers in Manchester and gained about twice as many from other parts of the country. I look forward to the announcement: 'Practically nobody in Manchester reads the *Guardian*.' The moment of divorce is fast approaching: sooner or later (and I would guess sooner) the *Manchester Guardian* will be printed in London. British Railways can carry no more of the London edition, and the paper, which has trebled its circulation in recent years, is missing thousands of readers only because it cannot reach them in time. When this great change comes, the citizens of Manchester will lose their last advantage, one which they have done little to deserve: they will no longer be the only ones to read a *Guardian* at breakfast with real news – new news – on the front page. They ceased to be able to read local news long ago.

The readers of the *Manchester Guardian* have no particular wish to be told what is going on in Manchester. What is more, very little is going on to tell them about. The local theatre began to decline when Miss Horniman withdrew her support during the First World War. Now it is dead except for an occasional piece being tried out before its London run – and even then Manchester is lucky if it can get in ahead of Blackpool. Nobody makes great political speeches at the Free Trade Hall. Only the Hallé concerts remain in their glory – still the best series in England, still the only genuinely permanent orchestra with its own conductor. The audience is now so large that the concerts have to be given two nights running, though only every fortnight instead of once a week. In these audiences Manchester is still alive. The circle of civilization has indeed widened. The Hallé Orchestra also gives concerts at Belle Vue on a Sunday afternoon among the popular entertainments and the animals.

There is one reservation. The members of the audience no longer think about the Special Concert Train from Central Station, but most of them are going to be carried far from Manchester by bus or car. Like the Russian soldiers in 1917, they have voted with their feet. They have voted against Manchester and run away. This withdrawal has been going on a long time. I once heard the late Sir John Clapham describe how as a boy he lived in the centre of Manchester; when the family went away for a week or so, the domestic servant was locked in the house with a supply of provisions. By the beginning of this century the wealthy had all moved to Withington and Fallowfield; soon after they reached Didsbury and Whalley Range. Now they have evacuated into Cheshire. And not only the wealthy. The City Council has cleared the slum areas of Hulme and Ancoats, and has resettled the inhabitants in Wythenshawe, ten miles off. This is part of Manchester only in name. The writing of doom became clearer still just the other day. The great store of Finnegans, which has been in Deansgate for more than a century, allowed its lease to run out and moved itself bodily to Wilmslow, far off in Cheshire. If this goes on, central Manchester will soon offer offices, warehouses and vast stretches of desolation. You can already stand in the districts cleared of slums and feel as solitary as in the Sahara; only the rows of street-lamps remind you that human beings once lived here. The destruction of German bombing has not been rebuilt. What was once the Market Place is now a vast car-park, crammed during the day, deserted at night, with dirty paper ankle-deep. The effect is like a mouth from which most of the teeth have been extracted. The Cathedral stands in refurbished isolation. It certainly has been restored – in such a polished manner that, whereas previously the Rylands Library looked like the Cathedral, now the Cathedral looks like the Rylands Library.

Manchester might keep alive without its centre. The decline of Didsbury and the other suburbs is a graver matter. The merchant princes have departed. They are playing at country life in Cheshire or trying to forget Manchester in Bournemouth and Torquay. There are no more dinner-parties, no more bustle of social occasions. Some of the great houses have become private hotels; some are the headquarters of insurance companies or trade unions – an ironical turn of the wheel. A few have been broken up into flats. For this they are highly unsuitable. The grand rooms are too big, and the fortunate flat-dwellers are those who find accommodation in the attics. Some of these mansions may have found another use. When I asked my friends what has happened to the Burgher palaces, I always received the same answer: 'Brothels.' I cannot vouch for this from experience, and suspect another touch of Lancashire romanticism. Manchester men have always liked to think that their city was great in vice as in everything else. My father told me that no decent woman could be in Oxford Street after five o'clock in the afternoon, indeed that no one could walk down it, so thick were the whores on the pavement. Oxford Street was never like that in my day. Now I doubt whether the former palaces of the Burghers are as disreputable as they are made out to be. If indeed these mansions deserve their present fame, then Manchester must be the scene of orgies such as the world has not known since the reign of Heliogabalus.

The *Manchester Guardian*

This essay was Alan Taylor's introduction to W. L. Webb (ed.),
The Bedside Guardian 25: Selections from the Guardian 1975–76,
Collins, 1976.

In his autobiography, A Personal History, Hamish Hamilton,
*1983, he recalled of his young days, 'I read the newspapers from
an early age, spreading the sheets over the floor and crawling over
them. We took the* Daily News *and the* Manchester Guardian, *the
latter rather beyond me and, as I now discover when going through
it for some historical purpose, pretty bad at that time as a purveyor
of news.' He also recalled his parents' swing to socialism by the
end of 1917. 'Socialist pamphlets had taken the place of* The Nation.
Of course the Manchester Guardian *still counted. I remember
reading its reports of the secret treaties which the Bolsheviks published and later the reports that Philips Price sent from Russia. I
was converted along with my parents.'*

*The Taylor family lived in Buxton during the First World War,
leaving after Christmas 1918. M. Philips Price was the* Manchester
Guardian's *reporter in Russia from 1914 until 1918. Later he was
a Labour MP and wrote for the* Manchester Guardian *on the
Near East. Robert Dell was a foreign correspondent specializing
in France, being expelled from Paris in May 1918, but returning in
1929. (Sir John Frederick) Neville Cardus was a reporter for the*
Manchester Guardian *from 1917, making his mark from 1919
reporting cricket (under the pseudonym 'Cricketer'). C. E. Montague was a chief leader-writer. He joined the paper in 1890 and
retired in 1923. The Lowry referred to is the painter, Laurence
Stephen Lowry (1887–1976).*

I have been reading the (*Manchester*) *Guardian* for the last sixty years. As a little boy I read it in bed before my father took it off to read in the train from Buxton to Manchester. I have a vague recollection that I tried to make sense of the second general election in 1910. He replied, 'God made the Land for the People,' a sentiment he had learnt from the *Manchester Guardian*. My first precise memory of the paper is somewhat later. One morning in bed I read the headline, AUSTRIAN ARCHDUKE ASSASSINATED. The news made little impression on me. I remember the news of the first Russian revolution in 1917, though strangely enough not of the second. I went solemnly through every clause of the Treaty of Versailles and duly accepted the judgement of the *Manchester Guardian*, now I think mistaken, that the treaty was a bad one.

In those early days I regarded the *Manchester Guardian* as a newspaper. And so of course it is. But that is not its only function and never has been. Other papers go in for sensations and exclusive stories. The *Guardian* is more concerned to explain what the stories are about. The writers in the *Guardian* are primarily concerned to write well and always have been. The unique feature of the *Guardian* is its essays. Essays on literature, essays on music, nowadays mostly essays on ordinary people. Fashions change, and the *Guardian* changes with them. No one nowadays writes two whole columns on a symphony concert as Cardus did every Friday morning on the Hallé concerts before the war. No one writes two whole columns on a play, certainly not on a new play in Manchester. There are no new plays in Manchester. As a book reviewer with more than forty years of experience, I deplore the reduced space for book reviews in the *Guardian* as much as in other papers. Once upon a time we rarely reviewed a book in less than 2,000 words. Nowadays we are lucky to be allowed 500. The long pieces are usually about the author rather than about the book, a topic we never contemplated.

The present writers in the *Guardian* have the most extraordinary friends. They do not bother much about the great political figures, as Robert Dell knew every French prime minister and Philips Price went off for a chat with Lenin when he was reporting the Bolshevik revolution. The present generation collect their wisdom from unknown sages. Some of these sages are to be found in London, some in such far away places as Cuba or Bulgaria. The effect is dramatic. Ordinary men and women have more sense and more to tell than the public figures who are always on show even when they are trying to talk freely. Life has broken in, and conventional news has been eclipsed. I suspect that some of the unknown sages are works of fiction. But of course novelists have always featured strongly on the *Guardian* from the days of C. E. Montague, in my opinion a writer with a detestably mannered style.

We are all now resigned to the fact that the *Guardian* has settled in London and become a national paper. Indeed we even welcome this, particularly if we live in London. But I regret that Manchester has been not only abandoned, but forgotten. There are sages in Lancashire as well as in Australia. Only Lowry gets a look-in here. For many years the stories of T. Thompson were the things I read first in the *Manchester Guardian*. He has had no successor. I should like more news from Barrow and perhaps less from Timbuctoo. But I suppose this would be discounted as provincial.

The present-day readers of the *Guardian* are evidently interested in education, which has, I suppose, become a middle-class substitute for a social policy. Education is expected to work miracles and it certainly does in the *Guardian*. I am also glad to see that the readers are interested in the production of plays, though less in what the plays are about. The one interest that has remained through the years is cricket, which has never been a great concern of mine. I used to think that Cardus had invented cricket and that he was allowed to write about it in the summer so that he could be induced to write about music in the winter. I am told that it was the other way about. I wonder what favourite subjects the present writers are bribed with, when they undertake something they do not want to write about at all.

I think I know the answer. The present generation likes conversation and always manages to get it. They go into a pub, a café or a beer cellar and immediately someone comes along with the wisdom of the ages. This never happens to me. If I enter a place of public refreshment in any foreign city or even in London, no one exchanges a word with me and I sit silent the whole evening, probably catching up on my reading of the *Guardian*. After all, someone has got to read it as well as write it. I have learnt much from reading the present volume. For instance, coal miners are still badly paid. Gorillas do not enjoy sex. An Italian friar has made a fortune out of the butter mountain. The Marx Memorial Library on Clerkenwell Green put on a somewhat unusual exhibition to mark the American Declaration of Independence. Wee Georgie Wood wanted to be a gossip writer. John Arlott had snow on his jacket one day at Lord's cricket ground in June. These facts are remarkable in themselves. They are even more valuable as topics for prolonged conversations in public houses. And who could claim as much for a speech by our revered Prime Minister, Jim Callaghan? I used to think that the best conversation now was on television. This volume corrects me. The best conversation is where writers or even readers of the *Guardian* are gathered together. Of such is the kingdom of good essayists.

And now I come to why I really like this volume. I am in it. Not as a writer. I am a feature, one of the unknown sages who speak with invariable wisdom. I once gave a lecture on Politics during the First World War. After it the late Lord Stansgate, who had been a Radical MP at the time, said to me, 'I had no idea it had been like that.' I feel much the same when I read Richard Gott's piece about myself. I expect some of the other sages featured share my feeling.

Liverpool

This essay was first published as a review of P. J. Waller, Democracy and Sectarianism: A Political and Social History of Liverpool 1868– 1939, *Liverpool University Press, 1981, in* London Review of Books, *18 June 1981.*

Liverpool has always been a special case in British politics. At first glance the pattern may appear much the same as anywhere else: Whig and Tory, Liberal and Conservative, with Labour intruding towards the end. The names may be the same: their significance was widely different. For instance, Unitarians provided early nineteenth-century Liverpool with its intellectual aristocracy. Somewhat later, Liverpool more than anywhere else produced that strange anomaly, the Conservative working man, who, in exchange, kept Liverpool Toryism afloat. Liverpool was also distinguished by the rule of the party boss. The Conservatives had a whole dynasty of them: Sir Arthur Forwood, Sir Archibald Salvidge and Sir Thomas White. Even Labour followed the example thus set, in the person of John Braddock, a founder member of the Communist party who lapsed into respectability. Perhaps one should include Braddock's wife Bessie in the list.

Equally special was the composition of the Liverpool electorate in its changing form. Religion, or, as Waller's title has it, sectarianism, was a more influential factor than in any other great city of the nineteenth century. Liverpool had long been distinguished by its Protestantism, partly maybe in reaction to the Roman Catholicism which was still strong in the Lancashire countryside. This factor was dwarfed by the flood of Irish immigrants that followed the Great Hunger of 1846. The Irish intrusion was not all of one kind. Liverpool had long possessed a native Orange movement. This now found Papist targets in politics as well as in creed. There were further twists. Liverpool's Anglican churches were peculiarly inclined towards Ritualism, or so it seems. This was answered by demonstrations of extreme Protestantism that outdid any seen at St George's in the East, Stepney. As a result, political life in Liverpool developed a unique complexity: the rival parties not only playing, as it were, up and down the field but across it.

Philip Waller has set out to disentangle the confusions of Liverpool politics and has done so with intense detail. Social history is treated as background to the political narrative, which in its turn becomes an analysis of each succeeding general election, with a by-election intruding here and there. Liverpool entered the age of parliamentary democracy with nine constituencies in 1868 and has occasionally had more. Philip Waller has clearly had plenty of material to work on. The task of reducing it to order has taken him ten years. Now we have a monument of research and learning.

1868 is the right place to start. With the Second Reform Act there was something like a genuine electorate to be managed – not very substantial by our standards, but greater than what had gone before. Education brought in a fresh complication. Sometimes it stimulated an alliance between Roman Catholics and Liberal Nonconformists, sometimes between Catholics and Anglicans. Whichever alliance was attempted broke down because of fundamental differences, another example of playing across the field. Joseph Chamberlain's success in managing Birmingham aroused the jealousy of Liverpool Conservatives, who determined to achieve the same management in their own city. The outcome was Tory Democracy, an attempt to capture the working-class vote. By the early 1880s, Forwood, the Conservative manager, was seeking to enlist Lord Randolph Churchill as a possible leader. Waller remarks of Tory Democracy: 'The skilled seducers of "the uneducated" were not Radicals or politically-conscious working men ... but the traditional governing class.' Lord Randolph said light-heartedly that Tory Democracy was 'principally opportunism'. Churchill could not be expected to take as much trouble over Liverpool as Chamberlain did over Birmingham. In any case, he soon lost interest in the game. Forwood moved tactfully away and explained that he himself was not a Tory Democrat but merely a democratic Tory, a revealingly subtle difference.

The greatest transformation in Liverpool politics came in 1885–6 with the Third Reform Act and Gladstone's attempt at Irish Home Rule. The Reform Act created a democratic electorate, even though only slightly more than half the adult male population had the franchise. Home Rule made Ireland the central issue in British politics, and in Liverpool made the Roman Catholics an independent force. Parnell thought he could push the Irish Roman Catholics any way he liked, and late in 1885 was on the point of running for a Liverpool constituency on a Home Rule/Conservative ticket. The manoeuvre did not work even when Parnell stood down in favour of O'Shea. The Conservatives would not vote for a Home Rule candidate: the Irish would not make an alliance with Orangemen.

Although Gladstone's Home Rule Bill was defeated early in 1886, Home Rule became a permanent issue in Liverpool politics. The Scotland division of Liverpool was the only English constituency ever to return a Home Rule candidate, T. P. O'Connor, whose hold was so strong that he went on to become Father of the British House of Commons. There were also Home Rule members of Liverpool City Council, though it is difficult to grasp what relevance their political outlook had to municipal affairs. At first glance religion brought electoral victories to the Unionists. But the gain was not all one way. Many Roman Catholics were not Home Rulers and the Unionists wished to conciliate them. This evoked indignant protests from the Orange lodges, which were more concerned to fight Catholicism than to resist Home Rule.

Ritualism provided another complication. The reason why it flourished at this time within Liverpool's Anglican churches is not clear. Maybe the missionary spirit which brought young clergymen to the impoverished districts of Liverpool tended to go with High Church practices. The violence of the extreme Protestant response increased with the years. Its leader was George Wise, a worthy successor to John Kensit and the most accomplished brawler in

Liverpool's history. The Kensitites, rather than the early Socialists, were the first to transform processions into occasions for street warfare. Wise specialized in the tactics that we know so well: Protestant processions through Roman Catholic quarters, disruption of Roman Catholic processions and, above all, accusations that the police and the City Council were in a conspiracy together to destroy the free-born Protestant Englishman's right to march through the streets. In the last decade of the nineteenth century, Wise and his followers caused more trouble in the streets than Home Rulers and Orangemen put together. The oddest feature of the movement is that Wise and a few of his associates became city councillors, though they seemed as much out of place in that role as the Home Rule councillors.

This confused situation weakened Unionist control over local politics. Liverpool never had the outstanding reputation of Birmingham in municipal affairs. Housing improvements dragged on slowly. Electric trams came towards the end of the century. The beginning of an independent Labour movement was an additional worry for the Unionists, which culminated in the dock strike of 1890. Tom Mann took over Liverpool as his special sphere of activity. Liverpool Labour, though not yet formidable, contributed further confusion to Roman Catholic and Orangeman, Unionist and Liberal. The Unionist boss, Forwood, was growing old and had been dazzled by the political lights of London, which brought him a baronetcy and membership of the Privy Council. His predestined successor, Salvidge, was already advancing his position. Until he took the lead, 'the Liverpool democracy had votes, but no leader and no cause'.

The general election of 1892 gave the Unionists a fright. The Liberals, an almost forgotten party, won a slender majority in the House of Commons and, what was more alarming, a majority on Liverpool City Council: the first Liberal administration for fifty years. But Liberal achievement was not significant; for instance, little was done to get rid of the slums – and Labour found more to criticize in the Liberal than they had done in the Unionist record. By 1895, the Liberal majority had faded, though Labour rivalry still counted for little. Robert Holt, the Liberal leader, withdrew from active politics. He was the only man to refuse a baronetcy after his appointment had been already gazetted and thus ensured that his refusal, too, had to be publicly announced. Holt also deserves a mention as the financial patron of E. D. Morel.

The Unionists won back Liverpool in the general election of 1895. More important was the fact that when Forwood died in 1898, Salvidge succeeded him as party manager. Salvidge had a sharper vision of Unionist strategy. He made the Working Men's Conservative Association the keystone of his position and Protestantism the dominant note in his recruiting appeal. This made the politics of Liverpool unique. In no other English city was Protestantism strong enough to provide the stable centre of a political party. Here was Salvidge's strength, but it did not always work to his advantage. Roman Catholics, too, had votes and many of them would support the Unionists if only denunciation of Papistry did not go along with it. What was worse, the anti-Ritualists trespassed on to Salvidge's territory. They alone, they claimed, were the true defenders of Protestantism and the Reformation. Wise opposed the building of a cathedral, 'the Bishops' church – the church of the rich'. Wise asked: 'Did ever the drones of a cathedral hive assist in ... slum work?' – the very appeal to working-class sectarianism that Salvidge was making in more moderate form. John Kensit himself appeared and led the Orangement literally into battle. In Birkenhead, he denounced 'besotted Romanists'. On the way back he was felled at the ferry by an iron file and died a few days later. The file became a sacred piece of Protestant martyrology.

Salvidge seemed to have lost control of Liverpool Unionism. He climbed back by running the Protestant cause himself. In the Tariff Reform controversy he took Joseph Chamberlain's side at first and then decided that it was a dangerous card to play in Liverpool. By falling back on Protestantism Salvidge preserved Conservative dominance almost undented in the general election of 1906. This was the line he continued to follow during the years of Liberal government. As he explained to Walter Long, 'Things do not run on the same lines in all parts of the country. A thing I have to remember is that though Liverpool politics are more complicated, they are always more alive because of religious feelings and the

Nationalist and Orange factions.' This tactic, though it preserved the Tory majority, made Liverpool a city of violence quite without parallel at that time elsewhere in England or even in Ireland. Processions were broken up. Catholic families fled from 'Protestant' streets. Priests were threatened with violence. Now and then some unfortunate man was beaten to death.

Labour had been a minor element of disorder compared to the Protestants. This situation changed with the railway and dock strikes of 1911. Liverpool was put under military occupation. A battleship and a cruiser arrived in the Mersey. Two civilians were shot dead by the troops: whether they were strikers, Protestant rioters or innocent passers-by is not recorded. Whoever they were, they established Liverpool's claim to be the last English city where citizens were killed during a trade dispute. Tom Mann was again active, seconded this time by James Larkin, in whom he saw a rival rather than an ally. Ironically, Liverpool was also the centre of a police strike immediately after the war.

The electoral situation was changed again by the extension of the franchise in 1918. As elsewhere, this meant the virtual extinction of the Liberal party. It meant also a stronger threat from Labour. Salvidge in alarm became the champion of the Lloyd George Coalition – hence his advocacy of the treaty with Ireland, which he helped to carry through the Conservative Annual Conference. Bonar Law proved a more welcome ally, unfortunately short-lived. Sectarianism was still Salvidge's main resort, with the result that Labour had to make allowances for Catholic grievances if it was going to extend its vote. The project to build a Roman Catholic cathedral revived sectarian jealousy. When Salvidge died in December 1928, Sir Thomas White took up the old weapons and used them as persistently as ever. Apart from unemployment, the political sensation of the 1930s was an incursion by Randolph Churchill, a curious echo of his grandfather's similar incursion that had started Tory Democracy all those years ago.

In a post-war epilogue, Philip Waller presents a changed city. Sectarianism has lost much of its force, though the Catholic Archbishop was stoned in Rossart Street in 1958. Churchmen and Nonconformists have co-operated over educational issues. In 1975, only 2½ per cent of Liverpudlians attended Anglican services. The docks have vanished. Liverpool's staple industries have mostly perished. Liverpool itself has disappeared, merged into that bureaucratic monstrosity, Merseyside. Waller concludes: 'Where once it was hard to define Merseyside, now it was hard to distinguish Liverpool.' His book, though heavy going, is enlivened by many penetrating strokes of wit and is a worthy tribute to the once-great city.

A Gourmet's Europe

This essay was first published in a holiday travel section of the New Statesman and Nation, *26 February 1955.*

The safest recipe for eating well is much the same as for making a collection of paintings: some taste and a great deal of money. If you buy established masters, from Giotto to Picasso, your collection will not be exciting, but it will be composed of masterpieces. Similarly, if you stick to Lapérouse or the Vert Galant in Paris, and go straight to the Chapon Fin at Bordeaux, you can still experience the elegant sophistication of old Europe. But this is cheating. The more enterprising gastronome will limit his expenditure, say, to twice what he would spend in this country, and then seek for meals that are interesting, if imperfect. His field of search is limited. Most gastronomic advice is negative – where not to go; though you may stumble on good food in unlikely places. There is one good restaurant in England (outside London). There is even Bailey's in Dublin, to contradict the view that Irish cooking is the worst in the world.

Good food, in the sense of food prepared with art and care, is confined in Europe to Western Christendom. It goes with a settled, peaceful civilization and a prosperous middle class. Russian food, pervaded by sour cream, is mainly an excuse for drinking vodka, if any were needed; and the experience of eating stewed mutton or goat in the mountains of Macedonia, though memorable, is not a gastronomic pleasure. It would be tempting to add the generalization that Protestantism produces gross rather than good meals.

Scottish cooking is an exception on the one side (though not in Scottish hotels), as Irish is on the other. Perhaps the truth is rather that northern Europe is ruined for the gastronome by the predominance of the pig. Something can be done with pigs' feet, as in north-eastern France. Otherwise the pig is superlative only when cold – ham or salami – or in sausages. The best thing in Germany is that vast porcine miscellany, the *Kalte Platte* (of which the French provide an inferior version with the strange inappropriate name of *assiette anglaise*). The gastronome who is unfortunate enough to find himself in Germany should always eat at the restaurant of the local town hall. The city fathers see to it that he gets the best that Germany can offer. More wisely, if he wishes to experience German cooking, he will stick to Alsace, which in this, as in so much else, possesses German merits without German defects. There is nowhere in the world better to eat in than Strasbourg, as the members of the Council of Europe discovered long ago. The wisest among them no doubt escape to the valleys of the Vosges, where they can also eat trout with almonds.

But of course the conscientious gastronome will spend most of his time in France, if only because of the many guidebooks which tell him where to pursue the study of his subject. Not that all French cooking is good. In fact, most of it is conventional and lifeless. By a curious chance, people hardly ever eat well either by the sea or in the mountains – the two principal holiday resorts. Only Dieppe redeems the coast of Normandy, though there is wonderful food inland. The best meal I ever ate in my life was at Vieux-Port, a little restaurant on the lower Seine which exists solely for eating: the only view is of oil-tankers passing by. Brittany is a blank land for the gastronome once he has eaten fresh sardines. Shrimps, even lobsters, soon become a bore. The same is true, in my opinion, of many regional specialities, which are eaten only as a local curiosity. Snails, pike, goat's cheese, even the *bouillabaisse* of Nice, are not things that I would eat for choice, just as home-made versions of *vieux marc* can be justified only by a prurient inquisitiveness.

Fancifulness is well on the way to ruining French eating-places. The amenities are becoming more important than the food. Many years ago, when I first tried one of the half-dozen restaurants to which Michelin gave three stars, I ate in a tin shack with no view, bare boards and cane chairs. But the food was perfect. Last summer, I found another. A beautiful situation by a lake; coloured napkins and great comfort; excellent service. But the fish and the chicken had the same cream sauce; and there was neither a green vegetable nor salad on the menu. A meal to provoke a bilious attack, not aesthetic appreciation. The only restaurants to have escaped this prettification are the station buffets, which motorists usually ignore; and it is still worth taking a train from Paris to Dijon, solely for the lunch at Dijon station.

A safe rule is that the food is best where there is the best wine. Burgundy offers classical French cooking, once you get off the main road to the south – dishes that seem to have simmered almost as long as French civilization. The country behind Bordeaux, especially on the lower Dordogne, is equally good and freer from transient motorists. Here there are not merely Romanesque churches, but the cave-paintings of prehistoric man, to remind us how much art and sophistication lie behind good food.

The essence of French cooking is patience; of Italian, haste. The poor live on spaghetti; only the rich eat well. The frying pan settles everything. Italian meals always verge on a banquet if they have any character at all. They have the luxury of a country which is still wild underneath. Italy's showplace for food is Bologna, as good in its way as Dijon. But there is something gross in the way veal, ham, and cheese are piled in alternate layers, with a fried egg on top. Venice has been ruined by the tourists. Most of the food is no better than at Blackpool. But the railway station offers the best breakfast which is to be had on the Continent of Europe.

There is not much to provoke gastronomic travel beyond Italy and France. Spain has a wonderful rice-dish, which combines chicken and oysters; otherwise Spanish food is as heavy as the wine. Austrian cooking is much admired by some, but its main courses are commonplace and the vegetables thickened with flour. Only the peasant dish *Beuschl* (made from strips of lung) is outstanding. Where Austria scores is in soups and sweets, both incomparable. Nothing in the world can challenge *Apfelstrudel*, but it must be *ausgezogener* (drawn out), not made of *Butterteig*. Otherwise make do with *Salzburger Nockerln*, a sort of cream omelette. Even wiser is to eat cakes at Demel or Gerstner. They will go some way to persuade you that old Austria understood the art of civilized living after all.

From Amateurs
to Professionals

This essay was first published as a review of John Kenyon, The
History Men, *Weidenfeld & Nicolson, 1983, in the* Observer, *27
March 1983.*

Men have been writing history in England ever since the days of
the Venerable Bede. But John Kenyon is right in starting his survey
of historians at some time in the sixteenth century. From then on
the writing has become increasingly sophisticated and the standards
of scholarship shown by the writers have become increasingly
rigid.

Even so one can argue that Kenyon has started too soon. In the
strict sense there was no profession of History until the twentieth
century. Before then even the greatest historian was an amateur,
laying down his own rules, living from his earnings as a writer.
Gibbon, for instance, among our greatest historians, never looked
at an original manuscript and no one thought any the worse of him
for it.

Kenyon's entertaining book deals with the remote days of history
when no historian was 'trained' and each one went his own way.
Historians rarely communicated with one another and each laid
down his own rules. During the seventeenth century historians were
mainly obsessed with the great constitutional issues which began
with Henry VIII and reached something like a settlement only with
the Glorious Revolution. Did William the Norman conquer England
or were the Anglo-Saxons already a free people? These were the
questions that defied an answer.

After the turmoil of the Civil War and of the subsequent Revolution, men attempted to write history nearer their own time. Clarendon after his fall wrote a Royalist history of the Civil War. John Kenyon says wisely that Clarendon's great work was as valid as the war memoirs of Lloyd George or Churchill. Bishop Burnet wrote memoirs of great historical value, memoirs which as a bishop he was too busy to complete. But though Clarendon and Burnet have much to tell us, they lack any sense of the historical past.

History as an intellectual process, involving a study of the past, began with the eighteenth century. This is because Scottish universities, unlike the English, already had professors who could approach history as an academic study. This was true above all with David Hume who wrote a history free from party ties, a work which kept its value until well into the twentieth century.

Of course Gibbon has to be fitted in somewhere even though he never touched English history and ignored the most elementary principle of the historian's profession – that the past is different from the present. Gibbon would have assumed that the Romans wore wigs if he had thought about the subject at all. Nevertheless from sheer artistry Gibbon remains the most magical of historians and the one most agreeable to read. Fortunately perhaps he left no school behind him. He set an example to his successors by giving a sharp answer to his critics in that delightful work, 'Mr Gibbon's Vindication'.

In the nineteenth century history really came into its own. Macaulay occupies the leading place. There has never been a narrative historian to compete with him, and narrative history is the most valuable type of history, or so I think. Kenyon asserts that much of Macaulay's chapter on social history is wrong. I'd sooner be wrong with Macaulay than right with any of his critics. Admiration for him is no longer common. Indeed he was a target of abuse from the first. Acton said of him, 'He remains to me one of the greatest of all writers and masters, although I think him utterly base, contemptible and odious.' What can Acton have had in mind? As for Acton himself, it is not necessary to pass any judgement on him because he failed to write history of any moment.

Carlyle has come off even worse, and Kenyon has difficulty in finding anything in his favour. When I last read Carlyle on the French Revolution I thought it the finest evocation of a great revolution ever written. Perhaps other revolutions have now superseded it. At any rate Carlyle was not a professional historian though he drew a healthy reward from some of his writings. But there were plenty of historians in the nineteenth century who combined scholarship and invective. Froude in particular attracted their vehemence. Freeman wrote in the margin of Froude's *History of England*: 'Beast!'; 'Bah!'; 'may I live to disembowel James Anthony Froude'; 'Froude is certainly the vilest beast that ever wrote a book.' However, Froude outlived Freeman and inherited Freeman's Regius chair at the age of seventy-four.

A new factor intruded into history during the later nineteenth century – the college tutors in Cambridge and especially in Oxford. These tutors, though little more than crammers, regarded the professors with extreme jealousy, the Regius Professor most of all. This jealousy reached its height early in the twentieth century when Charles Firth was made Regius Professor in Oxford. Firth was probably the most distinguished historian to become Regius Professor during the twentieth century. The college tutors imposed a boycott of him on their pupils and he was thus deprived of any audience for most of the twenty years that he held his chair. This was a most discreditable performance.

Tout was made of different metal. A follower of Bishop Stubbs, he held that the object of a History School was to train other historians – a doctrine that he preached from Manchester so successfully that he carried the day and now even history tutors have to know some history. But feuds and technical disputes are still common. The fiercest dispute of our day was started by Sir Lewis Namier, who held that all scholars except himself were lacking in scholarship. I suspect that no one can now remember what it was all about, but it certainly caused much bad blood while it lasted.

I add a footnote. In my opinion the greatest of all English historians after Macaulay was F. W. Maitland, author of *Domesday Book and Beyond*. He gets no more than a passing mention in Kenyon's book. We all have our lapses.

The Namier View of History

Sir Lewis Bernstein Namier (1888–1960) was born in Polish Russia and came to Britain in 1908. He wrote major works on eighteenth-century British history and also substantial works on nineteenth- and twentieth-century European history. He held the chair of modern history at the University of Manchester, 1931–53. He was knighted in 1952.

He was a major influence on Alan Taylor, who enjoyed his stories of Central Europe and his insights as a historian; as a young lecturer, Taylor learned to improve his style from Namier's example (among others). Alan Taylor, who had canvassed support for Namier for the Regius Chair of Modern History at Oxford University in 1947, broke with his friend and mentor in 1957 when Taylor was a leading contender to secure the post, but Namier did not support his nomination.

This essay was published before Alan Taylor broke his contact with Namier. It appeared in the Times Literary Supplement, *28 August 1953.*

Twenty-five years have passed since *The Structure of Politics* appeared; and its influence can be traced in work on periods of history remote from the eighteenth century. Yet the book remains fresh and stimulating, many of its ideas still not worked out even by the author himself. Its very title announced a revolution. The political history of modern England had been written in terms of causes and leaders. Parties had been accepted as fully fledged organizations; and public opinion, centred on national issues, had been supposed to determine the fortunes of governments. Sir Lewis Namier abandoned this traditional approach. He turned from Parliament to the constituencies, from the leaders to the followers. He asked in the initial essay: why did men go into Parliament? And his answer laid down the pattern of the new method. National issues disappeared: the party system was dissolved. We were left with the pursuit of private advantage and social prestige; the defence of sectional interests and, sometimes, a vague impulse for public service. The men of the time ceased to be historical characters, performing according to a preconceived script. They became human beings, whose motives could be understood only by someone who had read Freud and Marx as well as their own private letters.

Sir Lewis Namier inaugurated social history of a new sort. What had been agreeable anecdotes of private life became the foundation for political events. Parliamentary debates and divisions were seen as the end-process of a complicated chain, expressing what men felt, rather than themselves determining the course of history in isolation. The House of Commons was a 'microcosmos' of the political nation, not a controlled experiment detached from its surroundings. The method which Sir Lewis began has been widely followed. Indeed it has been the most formative and original influence in most of the political history written since that time. Mr McFarlane has applied the 'Namier method' to the fifteenth century; Professor Neale, with glowing success, to the age of Elizabeth I. To name but a few for later periods, Professor Aspinall has illuminated the reign of George IV; and Mr Gash carried on the process, only the other day, to the years after the first Reform Bill. We can push the claim further and say that the Nuffield surveys of the three general elections since the last war were also 'cut from Namier's cloak'. We understand the process of politics only when we know why the last individual voter cast his vote in the way he did. And for this we need to grasp the social and intellectual background of an entire generation.

This approach demands an immense accumulation of detail. The fragments have to be brought together one by one, until the final picture seems to emerge by accident, as in the construction of a jigsaw puzzle. *The Structure of Politics* itself, in spite of the high-sounding title, is simply a collection of detailed biographies: each individual seemingly unimportant, but contributing to the sum of general understanding. There was already implicit in this first book the grandiose project in which Sir Lewis Namier is still engaged: a history of Parliament, which shall provide short biographies of every known member. The attention to detail was also an attention to accuracy. Many a trivial slip of previous historians was corrected in *The Structure of Politics* – sometimes quietly, sometimes with a justified satisfaction. Here, too, a later work was implicit: the *Additions and Corrections* to the first volume of Sir John Fortescue's *Letters of George III*, the slim volume in which Sir Lewis displayed his scholarship in its purest and most deadly form. Novel ideas can often be brushed aside; but a scholar's reputation cannot survive the proof that his dates and transcriptions are wrong, and a whole generation of historians fell with the ruin of Fortescue.

But history is more than scholarship, more even than a method of research. It is above all a form of understanding; and the general reader will not put a historian in the highest rank unless he has supplied a new version and a new vision. Let us grant Sir Lewis his unrivalled mastery of detail; let us agree that great political decisions can be understood only as the sum of many petty interests; and let us read the entertaining stories of families and constituencies. But we want results. In the last resort, the work of even the greatest historian must be boiled down to ten or twenty lines in a school text-book. And we must ask: What are the twenty lines that are to be taken out? What is to go in? How does *The Structure of Politics* affect our general conception of the eighteenth century? Sir Lewis did not give his original readers much help. His outlook was clear in his own mind, and perhaps for this very reason he hardly troubled to draw attention to its novelty. In fact one is tempted to borrow a sentence which he once pronounced on another subject and to say of the eighteenth-century system: 'There would be little to say on this subject, were it not for the nonsense that has been written about it.' We have had to wait until the Romanes lecture which Sir Lewis delivered last year for a general summary: and even this was disguised as advocacy for the History of Parliament. Nevertheless the new version can be worked out by the careful reader; and perhaps after twenty-five years we can even judge how far it may command acceptance.

The older historians who wrote of the eighteenth century accepted a party system ready-made. They supposed that Whig and Tory were established at the Revolution, two parties as coherent and universal as in Gilbert's lines about the little Liberals and Conservatives of their own day. They further supposed that the personal rule of the monarch ceased with the Revolution. James II was the last king to govern. William III made some attempts to keep his initiative by playing off the two parties against each other; but with the Hanoverian succession the King was taken prisoner by the Whig oligarchy. George I knew no English; George II had no sense. Power fell into the hands of an executive committee, the Cabinet, which was made up strictly on party lines. The old version ran into difficulties here. According to the purer doctrine Walpole was the Whig leader; therefore his opponents were Tory, and a gallant attempt was made to devise a regular alternation of Whig and Tory ministries. When this proved unworkable our historians grudgingly conceded that, though of course the two-party system existed in all its rigour, the Tories never managed to obtain office between 1714 and 1760. But all this was of little moment, compared with the exciting events which followed the accession of George III.

The young King, educated as a Tory, aspired to restore the powers of the Crown as they had existed before the Revolution or even before the Great Rebellion. He threw the Whigs out of office; secured a Tory majority with the aid of vast sums from the secret service fund; and established his personal rule. Lord Bute and Lord North were the King's favourites; therefore Tories. This dastardly attempt at tyranny was foiled only when George's obstinacy and incompetence led to the loss of the American colonies. Then the two-party system, and with it British liberties, was triumphantly asserted by Charles James Fox. The younger Pitt defeated Fox by appealing to public opinion and by 'winning' a general election, in the approved modern style. But Pitt's victory was not also a success for George III. The King's Friends had disappeared; and the King had henceforth only the choice between Whigs and Tories. The two-party system was safely restored; and George III was compelled to be a constitutional king.

Little now remains of this rigmarole, which satisfied serious historians for more than a century; and most of it has been destroyed by Sir Lewis Namier. His innovations may be systematized under three heads: the Cabinet, the Crown, and the parties. A body called the Cabinet council certainly existed in the early eighteenth and even in the seventeenth century: but it was not the executive committee of later days. The Grand or Nominal Cabinet was an assembly of great dignitaries, to advise the King on matters of general policy. Its most consistent task was to consider the draft of the King's speech – a function which, as Sir Lewis has shown, it continued to perform until 1921. The Inner Cabinet or 'efficient few' was a more casual matter: at first no more than a meeting of the chief ministers to co-ordinate administrative detail. We shall probably never discover when these meetings began. But even in the early nineteenth century the Cabinet was still a committee of the King's servants, though now rather out-of-hand. Hence the survival of Cabinet minutes, not as a record of proceedings, but recommendations to the King. Decision remained with the Crown; and it would be rash to discover full 'cabinet-government' before the time of Sir Robert Peel.

This distinction between Outer and Inner, Nominal and Effective, Cabinet is now generally accepted. The consequence is startling. If the Cabinet did not govern, who did? There can only be one answer: the King. He was head of the executive, very much as the President of the United States still is; and we can now see that when the Americans drew up their constitution, they formalized British practice as they understood it. George III did not attempt to recover the powers of the Crown; they had never been lost. He had his personal likes and dislikes, much as an American President has; but these were no part of a system. George III never read *The Patriot King*; never worked with Tories; never tried to subvert the constitution. He was as much a Whig king, an adherent of the Glorious Revolution and the Protestant Succession, as those who preceded him: and the politicians whom he employed were Whigs on the pattern of Walpole or Pelham. They were also King's Friends; but there was no contradiction between the two terms. This part of Sir Lewis

Namier's doctrine has taken longer to triumph. Popular writers are still inclined to treat George III as either hero or villain; and cannot reconcile themselves to a constitutional king, playing an active part in politics. But a formidable array of scholars has shown that the composition of government depended on the King's impulse and decision until well into the nineteenth century. Professor Barnes has demonstrated this for the younger Pitt: Professor Roberts for the ministries between 1807 and 1812. Canning was made Prime Minister as a King's Friend in 1827; and even the great Reform Government of 1830 owed its origin to the choice of William IV rather than to popular enthusiasm.

If ministries were chosen by the King and depended on royal favour, what then was the role of party? Sir Lewis has gone as near as he can to answering: it had none. Yet he has shown his uneasiness at this answer by constantly promising to revise it. His first and only volume on *England in the Age of the American Revolution*, which followed *The Structure of Politics*, ended with the declaration: 'My next volume, if it is ever written, will be on the Rise of Party.' The promise has never been redeemed. Certainly there was no party organization in the middle of the eighteenth century; and party was therefore, perhaps rightly, excluded from a work that dealt with the structure of politics. But it is difficult to believe that Samuel Johnson, for example, did not know what he was talking about when he called himself a Tory. One may venture an alternative explanation for the omission. Party terms retained most meaning in ecclesiastical affairs, once the Stuart cause was finally lost; and the Church was the one sphere of politics into which Sir Lewis did not seek to penetrate.

But when we review the body of Sir Lewis Namier's work since *The Structure of Politics*, we can detect a deeper cause, and one which reflects the outlook of the intervening generation. Sir Lewis has always disliked 'intellectuals' in politics from Burke to the German Liberals of 1848. He applauds those who defend their interests, whether they be landowners, merchants or trade-union leaders; and he admires great men of action – Chatham, Bismarck, Sir Winston Churchill. A true son of his age, he can understand men who seek money or power: he can even understand a bureaucratic taste for efficiency and service. But it bewilders and irritates him that men should uphold some abstract ideal, still more that they should try to force reality to conform to it. When he analysed the motives which took men into politics in 1760, he discovered self-interest and ambition; he did not discover a zest to promote the Whig principles of liberty and security. Perhaps the zest was not there to find: but Sir Lewis was not sorry at its absence. For him party means organization – a further device in the structure of politics; and certainly we must wait long for organized party of this kind. But could men not have principles even if they lacked a programme? When the men of 1760 spoke of the Glorious Revolution, did this mean nothing except humbug? We are perilously near the suggestion that the Glorious Revolution itself meant nothing. Perhaps Sir Lewis Namier betrayed his own Toryism when he wrote off the Whiggism of the great Whigs. Or perhaps this was inherent in his method. Darwin was accused of taking mind out of the universe; and Sir Lewis has been the Darwin of political history – in more senses than one. The absence of mind from the universe is a defensible proposition, certainly a hypothesis that works. But a political structure without principles does not even work; it runs inevitably to ossification. Every modern historian of the younger generation must regard Sir Lewis as his master; and yet we must beware of the flaw. Sir Lewis has wielded every weapon except one. He has exploited Marx and Darwin and Freud; he has appreciated both tradition and revolution. He has ignored the liberal spirit. And this is not surprising. This spirit led his predecessors into many errors, from which Sir Lewis has spent his life delivering us.

Historical Wisdom

This essay was first published as a review of Marc Bloch, The Historian's Craft, *Manchester University Press, 1954 in the* New Statesman and Nation, *5 June 1954.*

Marc Bloch (1886–1944) was an outstanding historian of medieval and later rural France. In 1929 he founded with Lucien Febvre (1878–1956) the journal Annales d'histoire économique et sociale. *This was a focus for the Annales school of history, which was very influential, especially until the late 1960s. It was marked by a way of thinking, or approach to history, which included less regard for narrative and more concern for broad social, cultural and physical analysis. The* Historian's Craft *was published posthumously, Bloch, a member of the Resistance, having been captured and shot by the Nazis in June 1944.*

Though historians often write long books, they are usually inarticulate about themselves. They find it hard to explain what they are trying to do. They are embarrassed when they have to talk of the significance of their work, and cannot formulate a clear picture. They leave it to others to write 'philosophies of history' and are puzzled what these are about. The great historian Seignobos described 'what is the use of history?' as 'an idle question', and most historians would agree with him. Marc Bloch, too, would probably never have tried to answer the question, if it had not been for the last war. Cut off from his books, absorbed in the Resistance, he reflected on the meaning of his profession and its tasks. He was killed by the Germans in 1944; and his little book, unfinished and unpolished, remains as the testament of one who was a great historian as well as a great man. We should find it moving and impressive even if we knew nothing of his life. But it is doubly moving when we remember the cause of human integrity for which he died. This is a better tract against German rearmament than all the arguments of the politicians. These men killed Marc Bloch. A civilization which needs them for its defence had better perish.

What is the use of history? Marc Bloch did not find this an idle question. History conditioned his life and gave it meaning. He believed that it could give meaning to others. The use of history, he replied, is to deepen our understanding. Of course history also gives us entertainment and satisfies our curiosity – good enough reasons in themselves. But the right sort of history tells us things about human behaviour which we did not know before. Marc Bloch spent his life preaching a particular sort of history; and the reader will not appreciate this book fully unless he knows something of the long campaign which Bloch and Lucien Febvre waged against the narrow 'historizing history' – history for its own sake – which dominated French academic life. They challenged the worship of 'the fact' and the belief that the historical record was a fixed object which the historian had merely to observe. Past events, they argued, did not determine the work of the historian; rather his judgement brought out the events which were important. All study of the past involves selection. And it is the historian who does the selecting; events do not select themselves. The historian selects what seems to him significant. What determines this significance? Marc Bloch answered: 'men in society'. He was a social historian, fighting against the political exclusiveness of the time. It was, and is, common form to write, say, the history of religion in the reign of Louis XV. Marc Bloch pointed out that it would be equally sensible to write 'Diplomatic history from Newton to Einstein'. There are those who regard social history as merely 'history with the politics left out'. Bloch taught that it was rather history with everything put in – a hard doctrine, but the only one worth applying.

Only the first chapter deals with this theoretical approach. Most of the book is given over to explaining how the historian works and what it is he tries to do. This is one of the most difficult things to make clear to the outside observer. The historian's problems are supposed to be over when he discovers the written record. Really they are only beginning. Who wrote the document? What did he write it for? What sort of a document is it, and what sort of a man wrote it? The questions are endless. The good historian asks them automatically. And setting them out in order is rather like a gardener with green fingers trying to explain why the seeds he sows always come up. Bloch had green fingers, as his own works on medieval history show; and the miracle still escapes us even when he tries to reveal the secret. There could be no better introduction than this book to work on history. But in the last resort the best introduction is work itself; and it cannot be conveyed by any manual. Bloch did more than preach a doctrine. He set an example; and the fragments of it which he left here rank among the noblest inspirations which a historian could give.

History in a Changing World

This essay was first published under the title 'Sales Talk' as a review of Geoffrey Barraclough, History in a Changing World, *Oxford, Blackwell, 1956, in the* New Statesman and Nation, *17 March 1956. Geoffrey Barraclough (1908–84) was a younger contemporary of Alan Taylor at Bootham School, York, and at Oriel College, Oxford University. Alan Taylor wrote* From Sarajevo to Potsdam, Thames & Hudson, *1966, for a series that Geoffrey Barraclough edited.*

History remains the most popular choice for a general education, despite the competition of economics and Eng. Lit. Yet professional historians seem to fear that they will soon be out of a job unless they can show that their study has some immediate, practical use, like, say, nuclear physics or town-planning. 'Study history,' they cry. 'It will do you good.' And so it will, but not in the way that Snibbo does. A knowledge of history will neither cure indigestion nor produce a foolproof answer to communism. It will not even make men more sensible than they were before. Some wise men have studied history; this is a very different thing from claiming that the study of history makes men wise. Men only get from history what they put into it. Sir Charles Oman, an admirable historian, was one of the silliest Members of Parliament ever known; and all that Dr G. M. Trevelyan learnt from history was to become a supporter of the National government. Is there a single case of a historian changing his religious or political convictions as the result of his studies? Quite the contrary, the historian finds in history the confirmation of his existing prejudices. When the world changes, our interpretation of history changes with it; not the other way round.

Professor Barraclough has been explaining the 'relevance' of history for the last ten years; and he has now brought his essays together. Many of his ideas are brilliantly exciting; some, to my mind, less carefully considered. For instance he is inclined to suggest that because a thing is dead now it has been dead always. He emphasizes again and again that since 1945 Russia and America have been the only Great Powers and that the European Balance of Power has disappeared. Correct. But does it follow that we should rewrite history solely from the angle of Russian and American relations with Europe and should discard the Balance of Power as something that never existed, a mere blunder imposed upon us by Ranke? Professor Barraclough is contemptuous of those who take Bismarck's Europe seriously. We ought apparently to fix our eyes on the steppes or the prairies. But surely we are talking about two different sorts of history. What Bismarck did in 1870 was more important for the men of 1870 than what was happening in San Francisco or Odessa; though maybe (I am not even sure of this) what was happening in San Francisco or Odessa is more important for us now.

Take the obvious analogy with classical Greece. Anyone who wrote a history of the Greek city-states after their conquest by the Roman republic without mentioning Rome would obviously be wasting his time; this does not alter the fact that it would be pointless to try to bring Rome into a history of Athens in the time of Pericles. If I treat Sweden as more important than Russia or America in the seventeenth century, Professor Barraclough accuses me either of liking the Swedes or of thinking that Sweden is more important than Russia or America now. Not at all. I merely think that Sweden was more important then. Suppose the Chinese conquer Europe in fifty years' time. Would this knock the sense out of books of European history that do not mention the Chinese? It is one thing to say that our view of the past changes in the light of the present; quite another to claim that the past itself changes. Historians are rather in the position of a man walking round a cathedral. He sees at one moment Romanesque architecture, at another Perpendicular; but he cannot see Palladian, however fashionable it may be. And, what is more, the cathedral is still there, even when no one is looking at it.

It is not enough to show that some factor is 'relevant' to us; we have to show that it was 'relevant' to its own time. The present impact of Russia has reminded Professor Barraclough that historians distort the Middle Ages when they leave out the Byzantine Empire. A stimulating idea, and probably a true one. But it cannot be proved by pointing to the present influence of Russia. It can only be proved by contemporary evidence, and Professor Barraclough does not know enough about the Eastern Empire to be able to prove it. Generalizing again without a firm background, he falls into the common error of treating Russia as the heir of Byzantium. But the distinguishing mark of a civilization is its alphabet. 'Europe' is simply the geographic area which uses the Latin script; and the proof that Russia has a related, but not the same, civilization is her use of Cyrillic. Equally this divides Russia from Byzantium. The only heirs of the Eastern Empire are the Greeks; and their inheritance has been so much pillaged that there is probably not much for them to inherit. Let us study Byzantine or Russian history by all means; but let us also beware of claiming that European history cannot be understood without them. Must we really dismiss Louis XIV and Napoleon and Bismarck as 'neolithic figures' and spend all our time with Alexander the Great and Julius Caesar, on the guess that World States are the winning card? Professor Barraclough seems to think that not merely should we write history with one eye on the present, but that we should try to anticipate the future. The future has a way of turning out quite different from what we expect; and a Swiss historian who goes quietly on with the history of his canton may be the one most secure for immortality.

The reader will see that I have found exciting and provocative ideas in Professor Barraclough's book. He is very good in producing ideas about history; less good, I think, in suggesting how the past should be studied. And, in the last resort, I believe that this attempt to justify history is a great mistake. History needs no justification other than itself. Like music or poetry, it is its own justification. It satisfies a basic human need. There is no more sense in asserting that history exists in order to serve the community than there would be to claim that the community exists in order to serve history. The only thing we learn from history is that nothing is as white or as black as it is painted. Despite this, men go on painting, historians included.

The Use and Abuse of History

This essay was first published under the title 'Sagacity' as a review of Pieter Geyl, Use and Abuse of History, *Yale University Press, 1955, in the* Manchester Guardian, *6 April 1956. Pieter Geyl (1887–1966) was Reader, then Professor of Dutch History and Institutions at University College, London (1919–35), and then occupied the chair of modern history at Utrecht. He was a noted revisionist of Dutch history. In a memorial address in honour of Geyl, Alan Taylor concluded, 'If I were asked to name the historian whom I have most venerated in my lifetime, I should not hesitate for an answer. I should name: Pieter Geyl' (*Observer, *8 January 1967).*

Once men enjoyed themselves. Now we demand improvement. Cookery books tell us how to reduce our weight. Even historians hold out the promise of great moral lessons. At last a historian who is both a great scholar and a wise man knocks some sense into the affair. In true historical spirit, Professor Geyl does not dogmatize what history should do. He reviews what historians have done.

The writing of history starts as glorification of the hero; it becomes in the Renaissance a search for the illuminating example. The Enlightenment used history to demonstrate the superiority of the present over the past. Then came the German school of the nineteenth century on whom most historians rest to the present day. Ranke discovered 'historism' – the doctrine that we should study history for its own sake, seek to relive the past, and measure it in its own terms. A noble and fascinating doctrine – one that every

422

historian is bound to applaud, yet not without its dangers. When we judge the past by its own standards we tend to forget our own; and we end by judging everything by the one standard that is eternal – success. The good general is the one who wins; the good ruler he who dies in his bed and leaves a throne to his heir – never mind how many other human beings perished in the process.

Professor Geyl has kept his own standards intact. It is not enough for the historian to be honest; he must also be wise. We should study the past not for moral or immoral lessons but to appreciate the complexity of human existence. Of course even Professor Geyl has his flaws. He is perhaps just a little too Olympian; and his love for the past pulls him a little towards conservatism. He loves, for instance, the national diversity of Europe – particularly, dare one say, of Holland? He believes, perhaps rightly, that it will survive; but also, as a historian, he wants it to survive. Surely a historian can savour the riches of past ages and yet want to improve on them. We can preserve the cathedrals without preserving the slums. But essentially Professor Geyl reaches the right conclusion. He insists that history can never be more than one man's view of past events. It is 'an argument without end': and all attempts to impose a pattern on history, whether by Marx, Spengler, or Toynbee, are intellectual distortions or, to be frank, lies. Gibbon defined once for all the task of the historian. He wrote for his own amusement and that of his readers. The historian can be happy if he does no harm.

Index